The Art of Seating

The Art of Seating

200 Years of American Design

Brian J. Lang
Edited by Kelley N. Keator

With Collector's Statement by Diane DeMell Jacobsen, Ph.D.

g

The Thomas H. and Diane DeMell Jacobsen Ph.D. Foundation,
in association with D Giles Limited

This book was published by The Thomas H. and Diane DeMell Jacobsen Ph.D. Foundation in association with The Mint Museum, Charlotte, North Carolina.

Mint Museum Randolph
2730 Randolph Road
Charlotte, North Carolina 28207
www.mintmuseum.org

First published in 2022 by GILES
An imprint of D Giles Limited
66 High Street,
Lewes, BN7 1XG, UK
gilesltd.com

ISBN (hardcover): 978-1-913875-21-3

For D Giles Limited:
Copy-edited and proofread by Jodi Simpson
Designed by Ocky Murray
Produced by GILES, an imprint of D Giles Limited
Printed and bound in Europe

All measurements are in inches

Front cover (Cat. No. 44)
Back cover (Cat. No. 7)
Frontispiece (Cat. No. 6)
p. 6 (Cat. No. 35)
p. 8 (Cat. No. 14)
p. 13 (Cat. No. 46)
p. 14 (Cat. No. 15)
p. 17 (Cat. No. 37)
pp. 18–19 (Cat. No. 49)
p. 20 (Cat. No. 1)
p. 68 (Cat. No. 11)
p. 118 (Cat. No. 32)
p. 170 (Cat. No. 48)
p. 236 (Cat. No. 46)

Contents

Acknowledgments

Assembling a collection of seating furniture that represents 200 years of American design is a daunting task that could not have been accomplished without the tremendous support of numerous individuals, organizations, and institutions. Additionally, writing and publishing a catalogue of nearly 60 unique chairs, many of which required all new research, was a herculean task accomplished by dedicated staff and museum professionals as well as dealers and auction houses. I would like to express my sincere gratitude to numerous talented people who contributed their time and expertise to this catalogue.

Deborah Broder*, Dr. Marcelle Polednik*, and Ben Thompson of the Museum of Contemporary Art, Jacksonville (A Cultural Institute of the University of North Florida) were the first to recognize the importance of this collection, host the initial exhibition, produce an informative exhibition brochure, and direct us to several significant modernist chairs.

Andrew VanStyn was the knowledgeable dealer who provided substantial acquisition, upholstery, and conservation guidance, conducted research, wrote chair descriptions, and provided photography support. The result of these efforts has been incorporated in this catalogue. Michael Koryta and Douglas J. Eng shared their artistic talents in supplying the photography for a majority of the chairs in this catalogue.

Peter M. Kenny*, of the Metropolitan Museum of Art, directed us to important chairs, appropriate fabrics, and qualified restorers.

Walter Raynes provided unmatched expertise and attention to detail in conservation efforts. Although chairs are durable, they experience some hard use, which often requires restoration by a skilled conservator. Without Walter, the chairs could not have been brought back to their original splendor. A superb craftsman, he also helped when chairs were damaged on their 28-venue exhibition journey.

Chief Curator Brian J. Lang hosted the exhibit at the Columbia Museum of Art in South Carolina as well as the Arkansas Museum of Fine Arts. Brian is the principal author, and without his tireless research and consultation, the completion of the collection—as well as this catalogue—would not have been possible. He is a true expert in this field.

To the staff of the Foundation, both past and present, thank you for all you have done and for always being dedicated to this project. Kelley N. Keator, former Chief Administrative Officer for the Foundation, was with us from the beginning, even before there was a formal Foundation. She wrote exhibition labels and preliminary essays and gave tirelessly of her time. Her English major, coupled with her attention to detail, earned her the fond title of "Eagle Eyes." Kelley should be recognized for the significant role she played in the creation of this catalogue.

The Foundation staff, including Heidi Smith, Chief Administrative Officer, and Joan Oklevitch, Program Director, organized images, edited essays and bibliographies, thoroughly examined text and footnotes, and shepherded the catalogue through publication. Independent researcher Dr. David Kammerman contributed to early scholarship as well.

Dr. Jonathan Stuhlman, Senior Curator of American Art at the Mint Museum in Charlotte, North Carolina, guided us through the publication process since this was our first catalogue and he had written and published many.

Special thanks to the 28 museum venues who hosted the exhibition, *The Art of Seating: 200 Years of American Design*, organized by International Art and Artists (IA&A). Oftentimes they provided valuable insights on several of the chairs. Dr. Todd Herman and Dr. Stuhlman of the Mint Museum will host the exhibition in the future.

Many others—too numerous to individually mention—have helped over the years to make the collection (and, ultimately, this catalogue) what it is today. I am forever indebted to everyone who has contributed to this project for their guidance, support, and enthusiasm for the unique artistry of American chair design.

Diane DeMell Jacobsen, Ph.D.

Brian Lang wishes to thank Diane DeMell Jacobsen, Ph.D., for her support and patience in producing this book. Thanks also go to Kelley Keator, Heidi Smith, and Joan Oklevitch at the Foundation for their insights and editing of each essay. Lastly, he would like to thank his wife, Kristin Lang, for her unflagging patience, and his sons, Jameson, Hayden, and Joseph, for being the inspiration to persevere.

Why Chairs?
A Collector's Story

Throughout the years, and especially at the beginning, friends, family, and colleagues who knew that I was trying to build a representative collection of American art asked "Why chairs?" The puzzled looks on their faces indicated that their questions were serious, not critical.

So, why chairs? Well, chairs are universal—no matter who you are, everyone has chairs. Where you work, where you live, where you meet with friends: chairs are everywhere. We can all relate to them. Vincent van Gogh (1853–1890) appreciated the artistry of chairs and famously painted his simple, straight wooden chair set in a stark, bare room with his pipe and tobacco left casually on the woven seat (Fig. 1). Interestingly, van Gogh also painted Paul Gauguin's chair, which could not be more different from his own (Fig. 2). Gauguin's chair is curved, with comfortable armrests and a cushioned seat in a richly toned, inviting room, but has a candle and books on the cushion to represent the intellectual artist. Viewed side by side, the paintings reflect the individuality of both artists and their complex personalities, seen from van Gogh's eyes, through the unique depiction of their chairs.[1]

For me, chairs are pieces of sculpture on which we happen to sit. There are very few art objects that tell the history of American design, craftsmanship, industry, and technology as well as chairs. They reflect the tastes and aesthetics of the time, the use of new technologies, changes in social activities, and political and cultural influences. Chairs demonstrate developments in engineering, such as reducing weight to make them more portable, and in manufacturing processes to facilitate mass production. Over time, improved understanding of human anatomy and increased demand for comfort produced better ergonomic designs. In much the same way that other art forms evolved over the last 200 years, so, too, has chair design.

It's hard to say exactly when the chair was first created, but humankind has been sitting for a very long time. The oldest depiction of a chair that I have seen dates from 2800–2700 BCE, in the form of a small marble sculpture of a male harp player. He's seated on an upright chair, which—despite its age—is not unlike something you might see in today's dining rooms or kitchens (Fig. 3).[2] While chairs clearly existed earlier, the oldest documented *use* of chairs was in ancient Egypt. One such example was uncovered in Howard Carter's famous discovery of King Tut's tomb in 1922 in the Valley of the Kings, Thebes. The *Ceremonial Throne of Tutankhamun* is an ornately decorated chair covered with symbolic depictions of ancient Egypt in gold, silver, and semiprecious stones (Fig. 4). With two prominently carved lions' heads on the front and raised lions' paws serving as feet, the golden throne exudes power and regality. I was fortunate enough to see this extraordinary chair when I visited Egypt in the early 1990s. Coincidentally, the first chair I purchased was the *Egyptian Revival Side Chair* created by Pottier and Stymus (c. 1875; Cat. No. 12).

I didn't start building an American chair collection until 2003. But as I did, I kept thinking about my late

husband's comment each time I brought an "antique" chair into our home. He said, "I thought when I finally made it in life, I could have new furniture. Nothing makes it through the front door that isn't a hundred years old." For sure, he did have a good sense of humor. But at the end of his life, he wanted his legacy to be American art, so I'm hoping he would have been pleased that I built this collection after his passing, and that 45 percent of the chairs are under 100 years old.

I started seriously collecting American seating furniture almost by accident. Planning for the opening of a museum gallery and exhibition in my late husband's honor, I was looking for a pair of sculpture pedestals and was introduced to Andrew VanStyn, a recognized dealer specializing in the Aesthetic Movement. He came to my home with a notebook that included a pair of Killian Brothers period pedestals. Thumbing through, I saw that striking *Egyptian Revival Side Chair*. I was drawn to its ebonized cherry and central sphinx in profile with a rayed lunette surround, and thought, "Why not include a chair in the exhibition of paintings and sculpture?" The chair needed a replacement seat covering—the original fabric on most vintage chairs has long since worn through—so he searched the National Museum of American History,

Smithsonian Institution, and found a liseré covering like they used on their Egyptian chair to replace ours. Before the exhibition, VanStyn showed me a stunning rattan *Lady's Reception Chair* from circa 1885 (Cat. No. 15). How could I resist? I purchased it for the exhibition and invited VanStyn to the opening. Being an astute dealer, he brought with him another chair. The reaction of visitors, especially children and men, was overwhelming. They loved the chairs.

As a studious scholar, I developed an outline of chair styles that represented the story of American design. Preparing that list was a "daunting" task, much like the challenge Timothy Rub, director of the Philadelphia Museum of Art, expressed in his introduction to Alexandra Kirtley's superb book *American Furniture*. To prune 200 years of history into a relatively short list of historically noteworthy chairs required far-reaching investigation and exploration into not only the artisans and designers, but also the manufacturers, materials, provenance, and condition of each and every object. The result is comprehensive and represents a style and history that can only be described as uniquely American.[3]

Deborah Broder, then director of the Museum of Contemporary Art (MOCA) in Jacksonville, Florida,

Fig. 1 Vincent van Gogh (1853–1890), *Van Gogh's Chair*, 1888–1889, oil on canvas, 36 ⅛ x 28 ¾ in., National Gallery, London.

Fig. 2 Vincent van Gogh (1853–1890), *Gauguin's Chair*, 1888, oil on canvas, 35 ⅝ x 28 ⅝ in., Van Gogh Museum, Amsterdam.

Fig. 3 *Marble Seated Harp Player*, Cycladic, 2800–2700 BCE, marble, height with harp 11 ½ in., Metropolitan Museum of Art, New York.

visited my office in 2009 and was immediately enamored of the 28 chairs I had acquired thus far. She said that we needed to do an exhibition. Oh, my—to mount a proper exhibition tracing 200 years of American chair design, I needed more chairs! So I continued to expand the collection to fill in gaps and include modern and contemporary designs.

The exhibition, *The Art of Seating: 200 Years of American Design*, opened under the direction of curator Ben Thompson in January 2011 with 43 chairs, each having a story to tell about its own genesis and our national history. After the opening at MOCA, International Arts & Artists asked to make the show a traveling exhibition. It has since visited 28 museums across the United States and Canada, reached thousands of people, and received acclaimed reviews.

In this catalogue, we have included essays on each chair in the collection that bring light to the designers and manufacturers, and the historical, cultural, and political context in which they were created. You'll find designs by George Hunzinger, Stickley Brothers, Frank Lloyd Wright, Charles and Ray Eames, Eero Saarinen, Frank Gehry, Roy Lichtenstein, Wendell Castle, and many other American artisans, past and current. Patent drawings, artist renderings, descriptions of upholstery, woods, metals, and—later—plastics are all included to complete the story of the design and production of each chair. The catalogue is organized chronologically to highlight the dramatic changes in style, materials, trends, and technology from the pre–Civil War period to Reconstruction to the Gilded Age, postwar modernism, the Space Age, and, finally, the Digital Age.

After you read the story of each chair, my hope is that you, too, will appreciate chairs as much as I do. So, curl up in your favorite seat and enjoy 200 years of American design from the unique perspective of the chair.

Diane DeMell Jacobsen, Ph.D.

Fig. 4 *Ceremonial Throne of Tutankhamun*, Egyptian, New Kingdom, 18th Dynasty, Reign of Tutankhamun, 1327–1318 BCE, wood, gold leaf, silver, semiprecious stones, and glass paste, 40 ⅛ x 21 ¼ x 23 ⅝ in., Egyptian Museum, Cairo.

1   For more information on van Gogh's chair paintings, see "Van Gogh and Gauguin's Chairs," Van Gogh Gallery, July 29, 2012, https://blog.vangoghgallery.com/index.php/en/2012/07/29/van-gogh-and-gauguins-chairs/, and "Gauguin's Chair," Van Gogh Museum, Amsterdam, accessed January 24, 2022, https://www.vangoghmuseum.nl/en/collection/s0048V1962. For more information on Gauguin, see Ann Morrison, "Gauguin's Bid for Glory," *Smithsonian Magazine*, March 2011, https://www.smithsonianmag.com/arts-culture/gauguins-bid-for-glory-226633/.

2   See Witold Rybczynski, *Now I Sit Me Down—From Klismos to Plastic Chair: A Natural History* (New York: Farrar, Straus & Giroux, 2016), 58–59.

3   Timothy Rub, George W. Widener Director and chief executive officer of the Philadelphia Museum of Art, succinctly and accurately describes the exhaustive process of showcasing a representative collection of American furniture in his foreword to Alexandra Kirtley's book *American Furniture, 1650–1840*. In curating the collection of chairs for the DeMell Jacobsen Collection, similar steps were taken. See Timothy Rub, "Foreword," in *American Furniture, 1650–1840: Highlights from the Philadelphia Museum of Art*, by Alexandra Kirtley (New Haven, CT: Philadelphia Museum of Art in association with Yale University Press, 2020), 7.

Introduction

Chairs—inherently ubiquitous and utilitarian—are not often the subject of deep thought or scholarship. So, then, what are these objects we sit upon? Are they functional, practical pieces of furniture or sculptural works of art? Do we consider them scaled-down, human-sized architecture[1] or marvels of modern technology? Chairs are all these things—overlapping and creating their own sliding scale of form and function.

The evolution of chair design—and further, uniquely American design—provides a fascinating view into our country's rich history. As George Nelson (Cat. No. 38) noted, "Design is an activity which expresses the style, the living rhythm, of a society."[2] From aesthetic trends, experimentation in new technologies and materials, and advancements in ergonomic research, the path of social and cultural developments is forged through unique political and economic contexts. Viewed in one place—chronologically organized—such themes excitingly emerge in an exquisite collection of chairs, tracing the progression of seating furniture design in tandem with our path as a nation.

This catalogue serves as an engaging survey of two centuries of American chair history, showcasing many of the innovative and creative designers, artisans, and manufacturers who helped form our national identity. Organized in four chronological sections, our journey starts with an examination of our beginnings, inspirations, and influences, and brings us to the present: the culmination of technological advancements and forward-thinking designs. Yet—despite our progress—in each period, we find nods to our past that pay tribute to our origins while simultaneously opening new doors for future exploration.

Forging a National Identity

We begin with the *Klismos Side Chair* and *Grecian Settee* attributed to the Finlay Brothers (Cat. No. 1), drawing a clear connection to our nation's idealistic vision of democracy in the wake of its independence from monarchical rule. Subsequent objects in the collection also draw inspiration from the past in both Gothic and Rococo Revival examples (Cat. Nos. 6 and 9), while glimpses of new technologies appear in Samuel Gragg's *"Elastic" Side Chair* (Cat. No. 2), made from steam-bent wood, and Thomas E. Warren's *Centripetal Spring Arm Chair* (Cat. No. 7), made from cast iron and designed for comfort in the age of rail travel. The 1857 *House of Representatives Chamber Arm Chair* (Cat. No. 10) inextricably links American chair design with our political heritage. A Shaker-made rocking chair (Cat. No. 5) balances out the period by celebrating the spirit of American handcraftsmanship.

A Nation Rebuilds

As the nation begins the period of Reconstruction at the close of the Civil War (1861–1865), we further examine innovative advancements in furniture manufacturing, new sources of creative inspiration, and fashionable trends in home furnishings in an increasingly interconnected world. The *Egyptian*

Revival Side Chair attributed to Pottier & Stymus (Cat. No. 12) demonstrates the resurging popularity of an ancient society, while influences from even further East blend our curiosity about exotic natural materials—such as bamboo—with the resourcefulness to manufacture its style domestically, seen in Robert J. Horner's *Faux Bamboo Chair* (Cat. No. 16). Imaginative reuse of discarded materials in the *Texas Longhorn Arm Chair* (Cat No. 19) as well as the continued tradition of handmade furnishings in the *Appalachian Bent Willow Arm Chair* (Cat. No. 20) reveal the vast variety of styles and techniques that were in play at the close of the 19th century.

Dawn of a New Century

Entering the modern period of the early to mid-20th century, we again look to our roots with the *Colonial Revival Comb-Back Windsor Arm Chair* (Cat. No. 26) along with the continuation of the Arts and Crafts Movement and its emphasis on traditional craftsmanship. The close relationship between furniture design and architecture also comes to the forefront during this period. As legendary chair designer Charles Eames (Cat. Nos. 29 and 31) noted, "chairs are literally like architecture in miniature ... a chair is almost handleable on a human scale, and so you find great architects turning to chairs."[3] Two such examples that demonstrate these connections are Frank Lloyd Wright's *S. C. Johnson & Son Administration Building Chair* (Cat. No. 28) and Eero Saarinen—architect of the Gateway Arch in St. Louis—in his *"Grasshopper" Chair* (Cat. No. 32), the legs of which echo the shape of his famed arch. Eames and his wife Ray also developed the groundbreaking and iconic *LCW (Lounge Chair Wood)* design (Cat. No. 31) during this era.

A Nation Matures

From the mid-century to the present, American chair designers have continued to push the boundaries of design and manufacture. In this period, we see stools that teeter on rounded bases (Cat. No. 36) and perfectly clear acrylic chairs that disappear into a room (Cat. No. 37). The interrelationship between furniture and architecture continues with Frank Gehry's corrugated cardboard stools that are strong enough to support a Volkswagen (Cat. No. 42), while Pop Art comes to life in Roy Lichtenstein's seating sculpture *Brushstroke Chair and Ottoman* (Cat. No. 44). The demand for the lightweight, durable, and affordable furniture of the future is evident in Gehry's *SUPERLIGHT Chair* (Cat. No. 47). Yet, even as we move forward, we continue to look back: Laurie Beckerman's *Ionic Bench* (Cat. No. 48) and Robert Venturi's *Sheraton Chair* (Cat. No. 43) both translate inspiration from the classical past into sleek, modern designs.

The collection includes many more examples of chairs that define the American spirit, visualize our history, and drive us toward the future while cradling us in ergonomic comfort. Taken together, the collection emphasizes the very contradictions and differences that make us uniquely American. One chair commands center stage, while another recedes into the background. One embraces the laws of physics, yet another seemingly defies them. Handmade, one-of-a-kind chairs co-exist harmoniously beside those designed for the specific purpose of efficient mass production. Within the pages of this catalogue, through extensively researched histories, patent applications, period photographs, drawings, upholstery, and trade cards, you will find the vibrant story of American ingenuity, resourcefulness, creativity, and the legacy that persists today. Are you sitting down for this?

Joan Oklevitch

1 See Cat. No. 29. Owen Gingerich and Charles Eames, "A Conversation with Charles Eames," *American Scholar* 46, no. 3 (Summer 1977): 326–37.
2 George Nelson, "Design and Values," Philadelphia Museum College of Art Commencement Address, 1962, https://archive.org/details/philadelphiamuse00nels/.
3 Gingerich and Eames, 326–37.

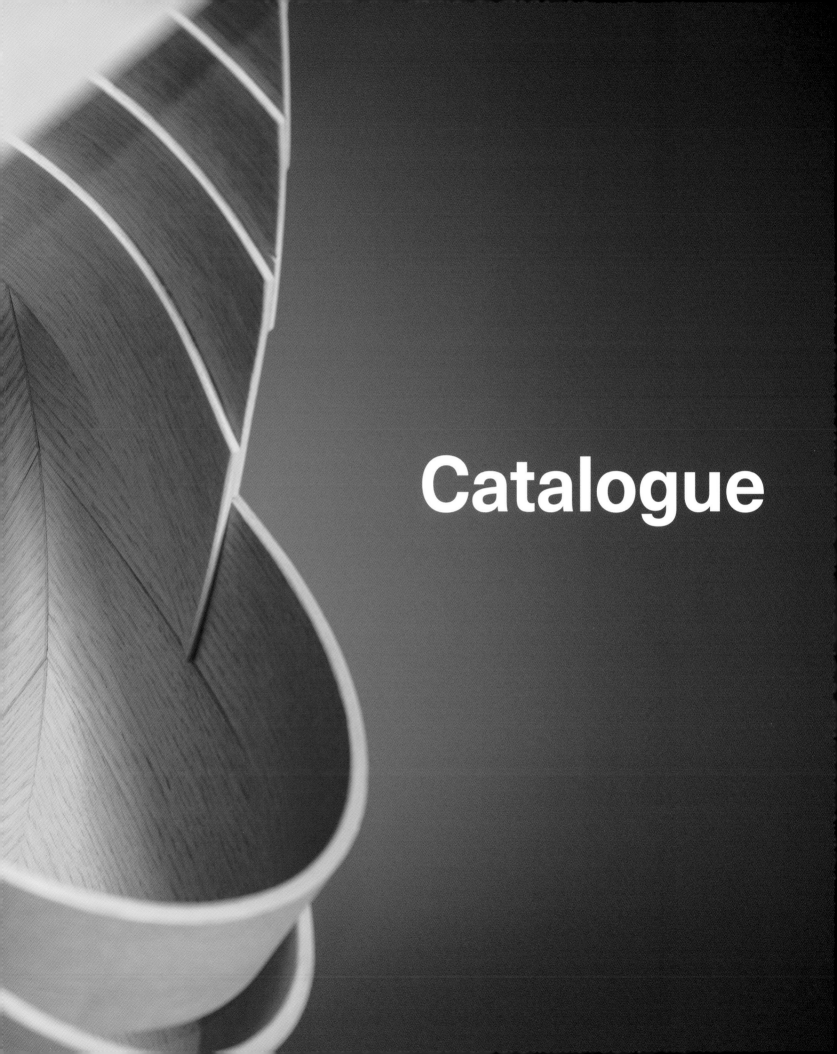

Catalogue

1

Forging a National Identity
From Neoclassicism to Rococo (1800–1865)

The Founding Fathers' inspiration for our country's guiding principles was drawn from the democratic ideals of ancient Greece and Rome and used as a model for the new nation's political system. Similarly, America's designers and artisans borrowed motifs from the classical past to reflect the moral and aesthetic values of the young republic. Pieces of furniture modeled on ancient examples were found within the most fashionable homes of Boston, New York, Philadelphia, Baltimore, and Charleston during the first quarter of the 19th century.

By the middle of the 1800s, those classical influences had given way to a number of other revival styles. Among the most popular of these was the Rococo, which was characterized by undulating lines and floral flourishes. The naturalistic motifs appearing in the decorative arts during the Rococo Revival period can also be seen as an outgrowth of the contemporaneous Picturesque Garden Movement, which promoted exploration of the outdoors and led to the creation of public parks that were used by a growing leisure class.

The profound advances in agriculture, mining, transportation, and technology at mid-century—collectively known as the Industrial Revolution—saw the establishment of textile mills and other factories across the country. The many immigrants coming to America during these years found work in these factories, helping to create mass-produced domestic goods for a rapidly expanding middle class. While American furniture manufactories remained largely influenced by the art styles of Europe for most of the first half of the 19th century, their simultaneous embrace of these advances in modern technology allowed them to create uniquely "American" forms of furniture.

Finlay Chair and Settee

1810–1827

Design and manufacture attributed to John Finlay (active c. 1799–1833) and Hugh Finlay (active c. 1800–1837; both active in Baltimore, Maryland)

Klismos Side Chair, 1810–1815
Painted maple and mixed woods, embossed wool upholstery (modern)
31 ¾ x 24 x 20 ½ in.

Grecian Settee, c. 1823–1827
Painted wood, free-hand and stenciled gilding, cane, silk upholstery (modern)
30 ½ x 76 x 25 in.

TO UNDERSTAND history is to shape the future: it is no surprise, then, that the nation's founders would embrace the democratic philosophies of ancient Greece and Rome as they established a new nation. As an embodiment of those beliefs, the furniture that harkens back to these classical styles serves as a fitting leader into our examination of 200 years of American chair design.

James Madison (1751–1836), fourth president of the United States, along with his wife Dolley Payne Todd Madison (1768–1849), commissioned a new design for the oval drawing room of the President's House (today known as the Blue Room), which was focused on social gatherings. Architect Benjamin Henry Latrobe (1764–1820) was selected by the First Lady (a moniker bestowed upon her death) to complete the redesign. In March 1809, Senator Samuel Smith (1752–1839) recommended to Latrobe the Baltimore-based firm of John and Hugh Finlay—the port city's leading craftsmen of "fancy" furniture—to execute the manufacture of the commission's seating. As a burgeoning city with growing resources and wealth in the early 19th century, Baltimore attracted numerous foreign-trained craftsmen well equipped to satisfy the desires of elite patrons for the latest fashions from abroad. The Finlay Brothers, Irish-trained ornamental painters, established themselves by 1803 and promoted their trade in furniture by 1804. The firm's 1805 advertisement in the *Federal Gazette & Baltimore Daily Advertiser* touted

their ability to provide "cane seat chairs, sofas, recess, and window seats of every description and colors, gilt, ornamented and varnished in a stile [*sic*] not equalled [*sic*] on the continent – with real Views, Fancy Landscapes, Flowers, Trophies of Music, War, Husbandry, Love, &c. &c."[1]

Latrobe saw the classical elements of the Greek Revival style as representing the ethos and integrity of the new democracy, a concept he shared with both Thomas Jefferson and James Madison. He designed "36 Cane Seat Chairs made to a Grecian Model,"[2] two sofas, and four settees for the project. Despite some delays, the Finlay Brothers delivered the Madison seating furniture by September 1809.[3] Beginning January 1, 1810, both male and female guests gathered on Wednesday evenings in the Executive Mansion (today known as the White House), relaxing and socializing on furniture that reinforced the political ideology of the nation—a perfect visual complement to the public spaces in the house of a democratically elected president.[4] The tradition of these social gatherings continued until British forces set the city and the Executive Mansion ablaze in August 1814.

Like those of Samuel Gragg (Cat. No. 2), Latrobe's designs for the Madison administration's chairs were inspired by the ancient Greek klismos form, an S-curve symbolic of grace and beauty. The curved shape of tablet backs enveloped the sitter and encouraged women, in particular, to recline gracefully. Imagery such as Jean-Baptiste-François Desoria's portrait of Constance Pipelet (Fig. 1.1) adorned in a graceful high-waisted, floor-length diaphanous dress popular in the 19th century as well as Greek women illustrated on excavated ancient pottery (Fig. 1.4) and grave stelae had surely inspired Latrobe. The seating furniture was decorated with motifs representative of the nascent republic, including laurel leaves, stars, olive branches and the Great Seal of the United States.[5] Despite the loss of these national treasures to fire, Latrobe's ink and watercolor designs for the Madison furniture suite are preserved at the Maryland Historical Society (Figs. 1.2 and 1.3).

Though already an established enterprise, the Finlay Brothers firm was revitalized by the 1809 commission. As a result of the assignment, their work

progressed from "dainty" to "sophisticated" fancy painted decorative furniture.[6] They continued with neoclassical forms featuring robust Greek patterns emblazoned on fields of contrasting colors.[7] Their creations became a coveted style in Baltimore and were often imitated by other craftsmen throughout the mid-Atlantic region, including New York and Philadelphia.

Representative of the Finlay Brothers' style following their collaboration with Latrobe, the structural form of the neoclassical *Klismos Side Chair* in the DeMell Jacobsen Collection reflects their visual vocabulary. Originally one from a set of six "Empire Egyptian Style Chairs" purchased by David Churchman Trimble (1832–1888) and Sally Scott Lloyd (1834–1913) of Wye Heights near Baltimore, generations of the family carefully preserved the chairs.[8] The painted tablet crest rail imitates a scrolled papyrus complete with rounded edges and finials denoting wooden rollers. The sweeping profile continues with the seemingly continuous curved, yet structurally joined, stiles and splayed front and rear legs. A singular bowed stay rail accentuates the clean lines of the legs, which are unencumbered by the

Fig. 1.1 Jean-Baptiste-François Desoria (1758–1832), *Portrait of Constance Pipelet*, 1797, oil on canvas, 51¼ x 39 in., Art Institute of Chicago.

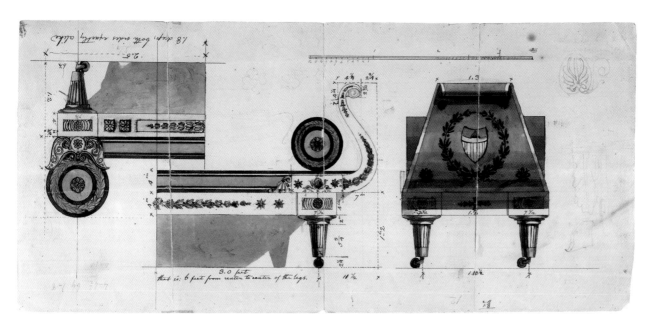

Fig. 1.2 Benjamin Henry Latrobe (1764–1820), Copyright drawings of the Madison furniture suite, 1809, Maryland Historical Society.

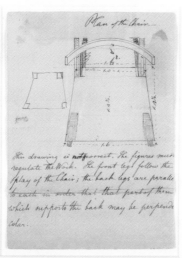

Fig. 1.3 Benjamin Henry Latrobe (1764–1820), Drawings of a chair for the President's House, 1809, watercolor, pen, and ink on paper, Maryland Historical Society.

stretchers that the earlier Madison chairs required.[9] Offering an aesthetically pleasing contrast, the red pomegranate-embossed wool fabric slip seat complements the yellow ground paint highlighted with green tints.[10] The use of a yellow pigment may have stemmed from the native abundance of iron chromate and undoubtedly appealed to local patrons.[11] A contrasting dark green paint provides a solid background for the prominent gilt-stenciled pattern drawn from Thomas Sheraton's "Ornament for a Frieze or Tablet" illustrated in *The Cabinet-Maker and Upholsterer's Drawing Book* (1802).

Influenced by the contemporaneous French Empire taste popular in Baltimore, the Finlay Brothers ornamented the

tablet with two winged Roman griffins supporting a plumed ellipsoid. Contrasting with the symbolism of democratic ideals found in earlier motifs, griffins traditionally represented divine power, a notion otherwise rejected by the new nation. The griffins' tails flank quivers holding feathers and scrolling acanthus leaves culminating in twirling flowers. Because such seating furniture was intended to be seen from all sides, decorative ornamentation continues around the scrolled tablet and along the sides of the seat rail and legs. The heart-shaped palmettes and gadrooned spindles on the stay rail and side seat rails appear to be an ornament unique to the Finlay Brothers.

In stark contrast to the delicate and sinuous forms of seating furniture in the early Federal period (1790–1810), the late Federal period (1815–1840) featured heavier and more robust forms. With its caned platform seat, cylindrical arms, and robust turned legs, the settee in the collection clearly was inspired by ancient Greek and Roman couches or beds. It is a form unique to Baltimore.[12] The overall design shows the maker's familiarity with popular pattern books of the day, specifically Thomas Hope's *Household Furniture and Interior Decoration* (1807) and Percier and Fontaine's *Recueil de decorations intérieures* (1812). The design is also strongly related to the aforementioned settees or window benches believed to have been made by the Finlay Brothers after designs by Latrobe for the Madison presidential home, the commission that set the stage for their signature work. The stenciled gilt decorative motifs on the backrest—a stylized swan-and-lyre with alternating torch and crossed arrows—and seat rails are adapted from classical and French sources and demonstrate the French taste much favored in Baltimore at the time.

Eliminating the delicate S-curved arms of the Madison designs, the Finlay Brothers flanked this settee with enlarged cylindrical upholstered bolsters.[13] The terminals are built with a capital, echinus, neck, and tapering turned ends evocative of a Doric column. The frontal ends of the side arms are decoratively painted with stylized and intertwined bellflowers in suspension, set within a gilt circle band. Instead of horizontally scrolling toward the back like a rolled parchment, as on the *Klismos Side Chair*, these ends scroll downward, highlighted by the painted leaf motif.

The robust form is enhanced by enlarged freehand and stenciled gilt ornamentation on a dark green base. Three sections combine a stylized swan-and-lyre, scrolling acanthus leaves, and three views of bellflowers. Between the sections are two motifs composed of torches with wings and crossed swords surrounded by laurel leaves. The alternating arrangements hover above a Greek-key band. Patterns on the tablet crest rail were adapted from designs in Sheraton's *Cabinet-Maker* (1802), while the front seat rail gilt and painted floral motif accented by maple leaves and bellflowers is adapted from classical and French sources. The bellflower frequently appeared on neoclassical furniture, recalling the delicate floral shape that thrived on the hillsides of ancient Greece and Rome. A modern yellow Dupioni silk fabric complements the dark green paint. The cushion, faced with a Greek-key tape continuing the theme on the back rail, covers the caned-bottom seat.

This unique Baltimore neoclassical "fancy" painted settee narrates the story of craftsmen reviving the past and establishing a new era of style and taste. Well preserved by various owners for nearly 200 years,[14] the eye-catching painted and gilded ornaments recall the genius of Latrobe, the craftsmanship of the Finlay Brothers, and their influence on the emerging American decorative taste in the early 19th century.

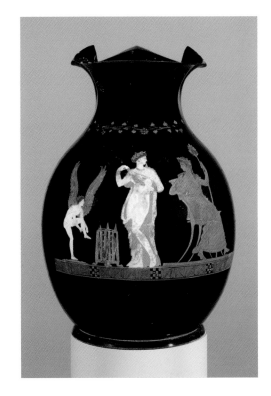

Fig. 1.4 Oinochoe (jug) depicting Pompe, the female personification of a procession, between Eros and Dionysos, seated on a klismos chair, Greek, Attic period, mid-4th century BCE, terracotta, height 9 ¼ in., Metropolitan Museum of Art, New York.

1 Quoted in William Voss Elder III, *Baltimore Painted Furniture, 1800–1840* (Baltimore: Baltimore Museum of Art, 1972), 11.
2 Alexandra Alevizatos Kirtley, "Contriving the Madisons' Drawing Room: Benjamin Henry Latrobe and the Furniture of John and Hugh Finlay," *The Magazine ANTIQUES*, December 2009, 56–63. This article provides an excellent overview of the furniture designed for the President's House during the Madison administration. Kirtley's extensive research has aided our understanding of the *Klismos Side Chair* and helped to shape this essay.
3 Gregory R. Weidman, "The Painted Furniture of John and Hugh Finlay," The Magazine Antiques, 143, no. 5, (May 1993): 744–755.
4 Kirtley, "Contriving the Madisons' Drawing Room."
5 Weidman, "The Painted Furniture of John and Hugh Finlay."
6 Weidman, "The Painted Furniture of John and Hugh Finlay."
7 Kirtley, "Contriving the Madisons' Drawing Room."
8 Two chairs from the set are in the collection of Winterthur Museum, Garden and Library (92.29.1–.2); two additional chairs sold at Sotheby's, *Important Americana*, Sale N08608, January 22–23, 2010, lots 561 and 562; a fifth chair from the set sold at Sotheby's, *Important Americana*, Sale N08950, January 25, 2013, lot 456.
9 See Kirtley, "Contriving the Madisons' Drawing Room," for an in-depth description of the Madison chairs, prior designs, and the differences between them.
10 This chair features a slip seat attached to the rear rail by two screws. The upholstery wraps over the front seat rail. During the reupholstery process, red wool fibers were located beneath a tack in a previous fabric scheme. Extensive research and conversations began with museum leaders Peter Kenny (formerly Ruth Bigelow Wriston Curator of American Decorative Arts and Administrator of the American Wing, Metropolitan Museum of Art), Nancy Britton (Sherman Fairchild Center for Objects Conservation, Metropolitan Museum of Art), Brian J. Lang (Chief Curator and Curator of Contemporary Craft, Arkansas Arts Center), Alexandra Alevizatos Kirtley (Montgomery-Garvan Associate Curator of American Decorative Arts, Philadelphia Museum of Art), Olaf Unsoeld (Furniture Conservator, Fine Wood Conservation, Ltd.), Dawn K. Krause (Curatorial Assistant, American Painting & Sculpture and Decorative Arts, Baltimore Museum of Art), Bruno Lopez (Atelier de France, Inc., Glenville, New York), and Kate Smith (Eaton Hill Textile Works). Accordingly, a red wool harateen with an embossed pomegranate was chosen based on a historical precedent in the Baltimore Museum of Art.
11 Lance Humphries, "Provenance, Patronage, and Perception: The Morris Suite of Baltimore Painted Furniture," *American Furniture* (2003), online at Chipstone Foundation, https://www.chipstone.org/images.php/671/American-Furniture-2003/Provenance,-Patronage,-and-Perception:-The-Morris-Suite-of-Baltimore-Painted-Furniture.
12 Special thanks to Alexandra Kirtley for her assistance in dating the settee in the collection.
13 Additional thanks to Andrew VanStyn for his research and expertise. His contributions helped shape this essay.
14 See Elisabeth Donaghy Garrett, "Living with Antiques, Old Richmond, the Houston guest cottage of Mr. and Mrs. Fred T. Couper Jr.," *The Magazine ANTIQUES* 112, no. 3 (September 1977), for information regarding provenance.

'Elastic' Side Chair

c. 1815

Designed and manufactured by Samuel Gragg (1772–1855; active 1808–1855, Boston, Massachusetts)

Hickory, ash, and other woods; early painted surface

34 x 18 x 24 in.

Stamped under front seat rail: S. GRAGG / BOSTON.; under back seat rail: PATENT.

2

THIS CHAIR'S elegant curves demonstrate how the Boston chairmaker Samuel Gragg reinterpreted a classical chair design from ancient Greece—the klismos chair (Cat. No. 1)—into a revolutionary and decidedly American form.[1] Responding to local consumer preferences, Gragg combined the neoclassical style of post-Revolutionary America with the rising taste for "fancy," or paint-decorated surfaces. Further, Gragg dramatically changed chair design by applying an early appreciation for ergonomics and was one of the first utilizers of the U.S. patent system.

Born in Peterborough, New Hampshire, on October 25, 1772, Gragg was presumably trained in woodworking by his father, who was a farmer and wheelwright. After spending time in upstate New York, Gragg moved to Boston, where he established a chairmaking business with his brother-in-law, William Hutchins, and began experimenting with manufacturing techniques and design. For reasons that are uncertain, Gragg and Hutchins parted ways in 1808, and Gragg relocated his workshop to the Furniture Warehouse, owned by renowned furniture maker Thomas Seymour (1771–1848).

Gragg received a patent for his "Elastic Chair" on August 31, 1808.[2] The patent document (Fig. 2.2), signed by President Thomas Jefferson and Secretary of State James Madison, provides invaluable details about the chair's methods of manufacture, types of woods used, and intended use:

> The invention of this improvement in the common parlor sitting chair consists in the application of proper pieces, or strips of oak, ash or other suitable wood, bent by being steamed, in such a manner as to form the bottom & the back of the chair. The pieces of said wood which form the back of the chair are so bent as to form the bottom of it also, and are bent as aforesaid & arranged in such a manner, that the back of the chair is completely braced, rendered very elastic, very comfortable & agreeable to the person sitting on it.[3]

At the nearby harbor, boat builders using steam to bend wood undoubtedly inspired Gragg to apply the technique to his chairs and settees in the "new, elegant, and superior style" (Fig. 2.3).[4] Similarly, Gragg was located in a fertile, creative environment at the Furniture Warehouse, where he was surrounded by numerous artisans, including cabinetmakers, turners, and ornamental painters, all of whom were producing furnishings in the newly fashionable classical style inspired by ancient Greek and Roman prototypes. Citizens up and down the Atlantic seaboard, from Baltimore in the south to Boston in the north, were decorating their houses in the prevailing taste in support of their new country's democratic ideals, which were based on those ancient republics.

These styles were transmuted to America via imported furniture as well as by patrons who traveled abroad, immigrant clientele and artisans, and the many pattern and design books being published in Britain and continental Europe. With its lithe and lyrical appearance and contoured back, Gragg's *"Elastic" Side Chair* is clearly modeled on the Grecian chair, which is first

Fig. 2.1 Detail of stamp under front seat rail.

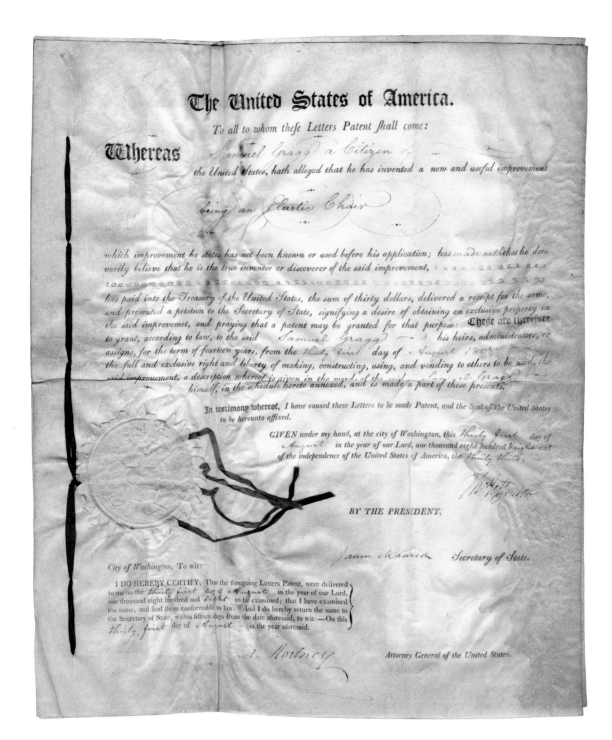

Fig. 2.2 Samuel Gragg, U.S. patent for an "Elastic Chair," issued August 31, 1808, James Madison University Library, Harrisburg, Virginia.

described in *The London Chair-Makers' and Carvers' Book of Prices for Workmanship* (1802). The Grecian chair is characterized by concave front legs and a concave back that reversed direction at the top to form a sinuous S-curve profile when viewed from crest to seat.[5] Other contemporary sources that likely influenced Gragg's design include *Recueil de décorations intérieures* by Charles Percier and Pierre-François-Léonard Fontaine (1812), Pierre de La Mésangère's *Collection de meubles et objets de goût* (1802), Thomas Hope's *Household Furniture and Interior Decoration* (1807), and George Smith's *Collection of Designs for Household Furniture and Interior Decoration* (1808).

Given his use of mixed woods in the construction of his "elastic" chairs—white or red oak, hickory, beech, maple, and ash have all been documented—Gragg contracted with an ornamental painter to unify the different elements. Many of Gragg's chairs have a polished (or japanned) painted ground, ranging from white and cream to pale yellow. Over the ground layer, the painter applied any number of neoclassical motifs, including peacock feathers, eagles, bellflowers, acanthus leaves, honeysuckle, delicate green grasses, and even goat hair. The example in the DeMell Jacobsen Collection possesses a black japanned ground with gilt piping lining the seat rails, front legs, and the center splat; gilding also highlights the goat-hoof feet, which are found on a number of Gragg chairs. "S. GRAGG / BOSTON."

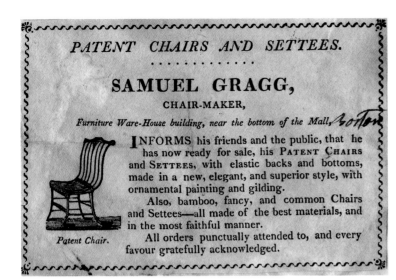

PATENT CHAIRS AND SETTEES.
. . . .
SAMUEL GRAGG,
CHAIR-MAKER,
Furniture Ware-House building, near the bottom of the Mall, Boston

INFORMS his friends and the public, that he has now ready for sale, his PATENT CHAIRS and SETTEES, with elastic backs and bottoms, made in a new, elegant, and superior style, with ornamental painting and gilding.

Also, bamboo, fancy, and common Chairs and Settees—all made of the best materials, and in the most faithful manner.

Patent Chair. All orders punctually attended to, and every favour gratefully acknowledged.

Fig. 2.3 Samuel Gragg trade card, c. 1808, James Madison University Library.

is stamped under the front seat rail (Fig. 2.1). Centered in the tablet-shaped crest rail is the monogram "DMM," for previous owner Mary May Davenport (1795–1843). A cousin of author Louisa May Alcott (1832–1888), Davenport married Joseph Henshaw Hayward (1789–1853) on October 24, 1816. Carefully preserved by subsequent generations of the Hayward family, the chair was possibly commissioned to grace the parlor or bed chamber of their home in Milton, Massachusetts.[6]

An example of American ingenuity, Gragg's progressive construction was ahead of its time. He combined available woods with a familiar slatted design, producing a lightweight chair markedly different from heavier Windsor chairs, which Gragg also produced as a popular form of the day. Lathe-turned and hand-shaped, the mechanical bent-wood process allowed for an economy of material, labor, and production time. Foreshadowing the 20th-century interest in ergonomics,[7] the curvilinear back, comprised of five continuous seat and backrest slats, absorbed and conformed to the shape of a human back by bowing both vertically and horizontally. The contoured shape also provided more comfort compared to the strictly vertical ladder-back chair.

This forward-looking, legendary form revolutionized the fabrication of chairs and highlighted the importance of the patent system to American inventors and designers represented in the DeMell Jacobsen Collection. Gragg's utilization of bent woods pre-dates the 1850s steam-bending process refined by German-Austrian cabinetmaker Michael Thonet (1796–1871).[8] Thonet's methods advanced the technology for mass production and paved the way for shaping tubular metals utilized by Warren McArthur Jr. (1885–1961), as seen in his *Lounge Chair* (Cat. No. 27). Meanwhile, Vivian Beer (b. 1977) echoed the sinuous lines of Gragg's chair while providing the illusion of bending cut steel in *Current, No. 2* (Cat. No. 46).

1   Special thanks to Alexandra Kirtley, Montgomery-Garvan Curator of American Decorative Arts, Philadelphia Museum of Art, for her contributions to this essay. Additional thanks to Andrew VanStyn for his research and expertise. His contributions also helped shape this essay.
2   For a detailed discussion of Gragg and his chairs, see Patricia E. Kane, "Samuel Gragg: His Bent-Wood Fancy Chairs," *Yale University Art Gallery Bulletin* 33, no. 2 (Autumn 1971): 26–37. See also Michael Podmaniczky, "The Incredible Elastic Chairs of Samuel Gragg," *The Magazine ANTIQUES* 163, no. 5 (May 2003): 138–45; and Michael Podmaniczky, "Samuel Gragg and the Elastic Chair," in *Boston Furniture: 1700–1990, Publications of the Colonial Society of Massachusetts* 88, ed. Brock Jobe and Gerald W. R. Ward (Boston: Colonial Society of Massachusetts, 2016), 195–207.
3   Patent for an "Elastic Chair," awarded to Samuel Gragg, August 31, 1808, Madison Memorabilia Collection, Special Collections, Carrier Library, James Madison University Library, Harrisonburg, Virginia.
4   "Patent Chairs and Settees, Samuel Gragg, Chair-Maker," trade card, c. 1808, Madison Memorabilia Collection, Special Collections, Carrier Library, James Madison University Library, Harrisonburg, Virginia.
5   Nancy Goyne Evans, "The Genesis of the Boston Rocking Chair," *The Magazine ANTIQUES* 123, no. 1 (January 1983): 246–53.
6   While Gragg advertised his chairs for use in parlors, at least one suite of furniture, comprised of 10 side and arm chairs, has a documented use in a bed chamber. A c. 1900 photograph of the "White Chamber" in The Mount, the Bristol, Rhode Island, home of the Honorable James De Wolf, shows several Gragg chairs, including his "fully elastic" model. An 1838 probate inventory taken at the time of De Wolf's death values the 10 Gragg chairs in the "White Chamber" at $1 each, while in the best bed chamber, 10 mahogany chairs with pierced splats in the Hepplewhite style were valued at $4 each. Thus, the De Wolf inventory provides documentary evidence for the use of large sets of chairs in bed chambers, as well as comparative values of painted Gragg chairs to carved mahogany examples made at approximately the same time. See Christopher P. Monkhouse and Thomas S. Michie, *American Furniture at Pendleton House* (Providence, RI: Museum of Art, Rhode Island School of Design, 1986), 184–86.
7   The term *ergonomics* was first used in 1857 by Wojciech Jastrzębowski but was not officially employed until 1950.
8   The Saint Louis Art Museum has several examples of chairs by the Austrian manufacturer Gebruder Thonet (1853–1921), founded by Michael Thonet.

'Fancy' Side Chair 3

1820–1835

Designed and manufactured by an unknown chair maker (Pennsylvania [probably Philadelphia] or New Jersey)

Painted mixed woods (probably maple, hickory, and yellow poplar), rush

32 ¾ x 17 ¾ x 20 ¼ in.

FOLLOWING THE American Revolution, Philadelphia continued as the political, cultural, and industrial center of the fledgling nation. Between 1790 and 1810, the population of the city nearly doubled, from 28,500 to 53,700, and by 1830 it had grown to nearly 80,500.[1] To provide furniture and other domestic goods to the growing populace, the city saw corollary growth in the number of cabinetmakers and chairmakers. Between 1815 and 1830, there were nearly 1,200 such workers in the city, approximately double the number that had been working between 1800 and 1815.[2]

The aspiring middle class of the early 19th century coveted modestly priced goods rather than expensively imported European ones. To satisfy the increased demand, domestic "fancy" cabinetmakers and chairmakers manufactured elaborately painted furnishings, which were cheaper than their inlaid or bronze-mounted counterparts.[3] Among those who provided painted goods were George Apple (active 1823–1831), who sold "fancy, windsor, grecian [sic], drawing room, cane seat and maple" chairs;[4] Samuel Bavies[5] (active 1825–1827), a "chair painter and ornamenter";[6] Benjamin Booth (active 1826–1840), who offered "Grecian, drawing room, and fancy chairs for sale" as well as "fancy-chair parts";[7] and Isaac H. Laycock

(active 1819–1833), who in the settlement of a debt in 1826 was forced to sell "335 fancy chairs, chair parts, an ornamenting desk, patterns, 1 workbench, and chairmaking supplies and tools";[8] among many others.

Most likely made in Philadelphia or New Jersey, the elegant simplicity of the floral-painted *"Fancy" Side Chair* perfectly illustrates this artistic creativity as evidenced by its classical form and inventive fancy-painted *trompe l'oeil* (fool the eye) ornamentation.[9] While the maker of this example is unknown, they clearly drew inspiration from the designs for a "parlor chair" that appeared in the March 1809 issue of *Ackermann's Repository of Arts*[10] (Fig. 3.1). It is also similar to an example illustrated on the billhead of Abraham McDonough, a Philadelphia "fancy and Windsor chair manufacturer, gilder, and ornamental chair painter."[11]

When viewed in profile, it is evident the chair's form is inspired by the ancient Greek klismos (Cat. No. 1). Beginning at the top, the eye gently flows downward from the tip of the outward-scrolling back stiles and continues through the outward-flaring rear sabre legs, evoking the curvature of the original Greek design. Dark-painted outlines create the illusion of a seamless line from the back stiles to the side seat rails. A trapezoidal rush

PARLOR CHAIR.

For N.º 3 of ACKERMANN'S REPOSITORY of ARTS N.º Pub. 1.ˢᵗ March 1809, 101, Strand, LONDON.

Fig. 3.1 Design for a parlor chair, from *Ackermann's Repository of Arts* (1809).

seat made of twisted and woven bulrushes (commonly known as cattails) economized the use of wood and allowed for aeration.

The anthemion motif prominently featured on the center splat is also drawn from classical antiquity (Fig. 3.2). The original painted surface is artistically rendered within the scalloped edges, allowing the *trompe l'oeil* ornament to appear as a fully carved, three-dimensional form.[12] Named after the Greek word for "flower," the anthemion was derived from the Egyptian palmette, a symbol of death and rebirth. It became

a representative motif of early American design, aligning with the aesthetic and cultural vocabulary of the ancient republics. Centered at the base of the anthemion is a stylized end view of a neoclassical bellflower, another popular motif. Above the bold splat, a ring-turned crest rail centers a tablet painted with flowers and fruit.

The classical motif continues downward through the carved and painted front stretcher (Fig. 3.3). As if a reminder to appreciate forms from all sides, the bellflower is represented from multiple

vantage points. Two attenuated side views of the flower flank a top-view central medallion, echoing the one depicted on the back splat. The floral motif continues down each face of the front legs. Bulbous in form, much like a flower's receptacle, the turned legs swell and then taper to a simple cylindrical foot. A stylized acanthus leaf, or perhaps a bellflower, emits descending dewdrops on the ovoid form, completing the allusion. Finely turned rings on the crest and seat rails, as well as the front legs, provide cohesion and symmetry in form and color.

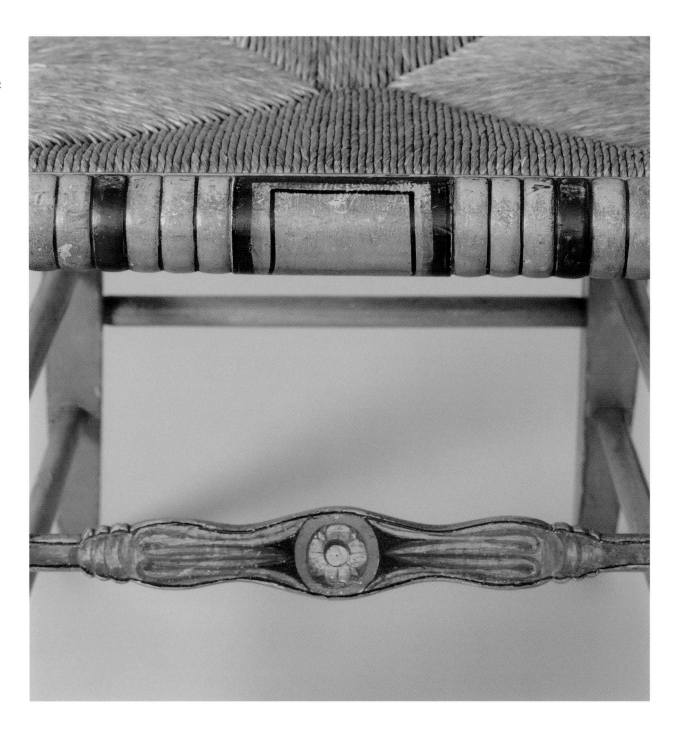

1   "Population of Philadelphia, PA: Historical Population of
    Philadelphia City for Period 1790–2014," Population.us,
    accessed February 28, 2019, https://population.us/pa/
    philadelphia/.

2   For a compendium of documented Philadelphia
    cabinet- and chairmakers, see Deborah Ducoff-Barone,
    "Philadelphia Furniture Makers, 1800–1815," *The
    Magazine* ANTIQUES 139, no. 5 (May 1991): 982–95; and
    Deborah Ducoff-Barone, "Philadelphia Furniture Makers,
    1816–1830," *The Magazine* ANTIQUES 145, no. 5 (May
    1994): 742–55.

3   For a thorough study of the origins and evolution of the
    concept of "fancy," see Sumpter T. Priddy, *American
    Fancy: Exuberance in the Arts, 1790–1840* (Milwaukee,
    WI: Chipstone Foundation, 2004).

4   Ducoff-Barone, "Philadelphia Furniture Makers,
    1816–1830," 744.

5   Also commonly spelled Bavis.

6   Ducoff-Barone, Philadelphia Furniture Makers, 1816–
    1830, 744.

7   Ducoff-Barone, 745.

8   Ducoff-Barone, 749.

9   Special thanks to Andrew VanStyn for his research and
    expertise. His contributions helped shape this essay.

10 See Pauline Agius, *Ackermann's Regency Furniture &
    Interiors* (London: Crowood Press, 1984), 41, pl. 2.

11 Ducoff-Barone, "Philadelphia Furniture Makers, 1816–
    1830," 750; for an illustration of the Abraham McDonough
    billhead, see Carl W. Drepperd, *Handbook of Antique
    Chairs* (Garden City, NY: Doubleday, 1948), 160.

12 Several similar examples are documented and possess
    a ring-turned crest rail with center tablet, ring-turned
    front seat rail, rush seat, front stretcher, and anthemion
    center splat decoration. See especially those illustrated

in David B. Warren, *Bayou Bend: American Furniture,
Paintings and Silver from the Bayou Bend Collection*
(Houston: Museum of Fine Arts, Houston, 1975), 95, fig.
178; David B. Warren et al., *American Decorative Arts
and Paintings in the Bayou Bend Collection* (Houston:
Museum of Fine Arts, Houston, and Princeton
University Press, 1998), 124, F200; and Allison Boor et
al., *Philadelphia Empire Furniture* (West Chester, PA:
Boor Management LLC, 2006), fig. 196, 338. A related
chair to these examples, but with a tablet-form crest
rail, is in the collection of Winterthur and illustrated
in Charles F. Montgomery, *American Furniture: The
Federal Period, 1788–1825* (New York: Viking Press,
1966), 456, fig. 466.

Ladder-Back Doll's Chair

4

c. 1830

Designed and manufactured by an unknown chair maker (probably Maine)

Painted wood, rush

14 ½ x 8 ¾ x 7 ⅞ in.

HANDMADE BY AN unknown New England craftsperson, perhaps located in Maine, in a rural, vernacular style, the *Ladder-Back Doll's Chair* illustrates the youthful exuberance and promise of a fledgling nation.[1] While Old World immigrants transported treasured family possessions on their passage to the New World, they also brought the long-held traditions and manufacturing skills, practiced for centuries, of their native countries. Once settled in America, they decorated their homes and reared their children according to their native customs, yet adapted them to the shared experience and mores of their new communities. Since the fundamental training of youth and modeling of social decorum began within the home, child-sized furniture mirrored adult counterparts. In particular, chairs manufactured for children—as well as those made for dolls[2]—encouraged their users to gain independence and to stretch their imagination, all the while teaching increased responsibility as they grew toward adulthood.[3]

The *Ladder-Back Doll's Chair*—much like its adult prototype—consists of four cylindrical turned posts, which taper at the feet. Between the posts, four dowels form a box-shaped stretcher, providing additional structural support and mimicking the footrest of an adult-sized chair, which encourages its user to practice proper posture. The rush seat was made from native materials—twisted and woven dried bulrushes (cattails)—often gathered in the summer. The rear stiles are joined by two arch-shaped rails, which together create the ladder back. Delicate earth-toned, hand-painted floral sprays and linear white outlines adorn the surfaces of the crest and medial rails, suggesting the artist's freedom of expression—a whimsical and uplifting embellishment to the otherwise monochromatic dark green base. Yellow or gold-painted bands on the stiles and stretchers add further embellishment and simulate bamboo turnings. Though well preserved by the owners, the crest rail and the half-rounded finials show wear, most likely from children's hands over many decades. Often multifunctional, such chairs were frequently turned over and used to support toddlers as they learned to walk.[4]

1   Special thanks to Andrew VanStyn for his research and expertise. His contributions helped shape this essay.
2   The doll pictured in the photo (property of Susan Williams Noyes) is of later manufacture and is included solely for scale. Most likely, the doll that occupied the chair would have been made of fabric or corn stalks. If owned by a well-to-do family, the luxury of a porcelain head may have been added.
3   For a discussion of child-sized furniture, see Barrymore Laurence Scherer, "Children Be Seated," *The Magazine ANTIQUES* 181, no. 6 (November/December 2014): 40–48.
4   Scherer, 40–48.

#6 Rocking Arm Chair

c. 1840

Designed and manufactured by a Shaker for a member of New Lebanon Shaker Community, New York (active 1787–1947)

Maple, reproduction cloth-tape seat

45 ¼ x 21 ¾ x 26 in.

IN STARK CONTRAST to the boldly painted exuberance of the Samuel Gragg *"Elastic" Side Chair* (Cat. No. 2) and the *Klismos Side Chair* (Cat. No. 1), the restrained simplicity of Shaker-style furniture represents a different aesthetic, one that influenced later Scandinavian and American designers—in particular, George Nakashima (Cat. No. 39)—and continues to resonate with contemporary tastes.[1] A quintessential American innovation of the 18th century, the rocking chair was purportedly first used in a domestic interior in 1787. Shaker rocking chairs were intended for elderly members to rest comfortably in, while devoting time to spiritual contemplation. The form seen in this example emerged around 1840–50 during the golden age of Shakerism in the rural New Lebanon (later Mount Lebanon) community in western New York. The community's unique vernacular style of craftsmanship is exemplified by the chair's natural finish, clean lines, and subtle curves, in harmony with the stepped pattern of the blue-and-white cloth-tape seat.

The original Shaker Church was founded in 1747 as a part of Quakerism, with beliefs of individual communication with God, the principle of the Inner Light, and a simplified lifestyle. Later, a sect diverged from Quakerism and called itself the United Society of Believers in Christ's Second Appearing. The more common name "Shakers" was acquired due to the quivering and shaking of congregation members during worship. In 1774, Mother Ann Lee (1736–1784) guided a group of eight Shakers from England to religious freedom in America and established a community in Watervliet, New York, near Albany.

Over time, 18 major and six short-term communities were established and stretched geographically from Maine to Kentucky. New Lebanon, renamed Mount Lebanon in 1861 for postal distinction, became the spiritual center for the Shaker communities and home to the Central Ministry from 1787 to 1947. While members of Shaker Society produced furniture for sale to the "outside world," this example is documented to have been made specifically for a member of the Shaker community. The chair's grace, tranquility, and durability are evidenced in its form and function, as it was inherited by successive members within the sect. The Millennial Laws of 1845 stated that "one rocking chair in a room is sufficient, except where the aged reside."[2]

Shakers believe God is both the mother and the father, influencing their belief in the equality of the sexes. The celibate "Brothers and Sisters" resided in separate quarters, "pooled goods,"[3] and worked in specialized trades. Shakers dedicated themselves to work and prayer, believing "every act of labor to be an act of worship."[4] A self-supporting agrarian community, the Shakers' principal contact with the World (as non-Believers were called) occurred when selling their products, such as chairs and furniture. They also designed and produced new inventions for the marketplace, such as flat brooms, packaged seeds, circular saws, and clothespins. Advanced technologies, such as electricity and the automobile, were welcomed because they improved efficiency, thus leaving more time for worship.

Several factors curtailed the growth of Shaker Villages. The legal termination of the children's orders adversely affected the ability to adopt members into a celibate community. Additionally, social secularization, an increase in urbanization, and the explosion of mass-produced products for retail minimized the community population. As of July 2021, Sabbathday Lake Shaker Village in New Gloucester, Maine, remains the sole active community with only two remaining members.

The Shaker religion centered on four values: humility, labor, simplicity, and purity. These beliefs were directly reflected in a typical Shaker family's domestic environment. Ornamentation was regarded as sinful pride. This fine *#6 Rocking Arm Chair* embodies the Shaker dancing prayer "Simple Gifts": "'Tis the gift to be simple, 'Tis the gift to be free."[5]

To be a Believer, as Shakers came to refer to themselves, was to promote the whole at the expense of the self. Therefore, the methods by which the outside world normally proclaimed status—typically through goods or "vain show"—were discouraged and ultimately forbidden by the Millennial Laws. The section pertaining to "Superfluities not Owned" states, in part:

> Fancy articles of any kind or articles which are superfluously finished, trimmed or ornamented, are not suitable for Believers and may not be used

or purchased; among which are the following: Viz.

[...] Writing desks may not be used by the common members; only by permission of the elders. The following articles are also deemed improper, Viz. Superfluously finished, or flowery painted clocks, bureaus or looking glasses; also superfluously painted or fancy shaped carriages, or sleighs, superfluously trimmed harness and many other articles too numerous to mention.

[...] Believers may not in any case manufacture for sale, any article or articles which are superfluously wrought and which would have a tendency to feed the pride and vanity of man, or such as would not be admissible to use among themselves, on account of their superfluity.[6]

Thus, Shakers considered their furniture to be "a three-dimensional expression of faith."[7] It was built to expose the integrity of the wood and joined with "strength and longevity"[8] in mind. Distinctive details

on Shaker chairs show evidence of the tools and hands of the craftsman from the community in which it was produced. The hand-turned tapered oval finials on this example indicate its origin in the New Lebanon Shaker Community (Fig. 5.1). Outward-scrolling handgrips were gently shaped to welcome the chair owner's tired palms after a day of manual labor, toiling at God's work. The handgrips are supported by distinctive "mushroom" posts that taper toward the top, suggesting the chair was made prior to those designed and admired by Elder Robert Wagan (1833–1883), a popular craftsman of this community during the 1860s. Slightly concave and arched for comfort, the four ladder-back slats—characteristic of Shaker rockers greater than #5 size—are pegged into the rear stiles, which also bear incised marks of the craftsman's tool to indicate their placement.

The chair rests atop short rocker blades—emblematic of the New England Puritan work ethic—with skate edges. This particular type of edge is original to the evolution of the first rocking chair in contrast

to the later longer blades used in Kentucky, where an elongated gliding rhythm was the primary purpose of a rocking chair.[9] Stained and varnished by hand, with possibly the original lacquers, the maple wood retains its strength and stability, reflecting its exceptional Shaker craftsmanship and the Shaker adage "Do your work as if you had a thousand years to live and as if you were to die tomorrow."[10]

The blue-and-white woven cloth-tape seat, which was replaced based on the original diagonal pattern, is reminiscent of the colorful handwoven wool—and later cotton—tape preferred by Shakers. Traditionally woven by Sisters through the early 19th century, tape was later made by outside fabricators and used for community chairs as well as those sold outside the sect (Fig. 5.2). Echoing the tenets of the religion, seat tape woven in patterns provided comfort, resilience, and cleanliness.

Shaker furniture is admired for its beauty, simplicity, and economy of style, which pre-dates the minimalist modernism movement on both a national and international stage.

It appealed broadly to a diverse spectrum of artists, such as precisionist painter Charles Sheeler (1883–1965). Sheeler's personal collection as well as his artwork incorporated the Shaker style. Other cultural reflections include the orchestral suite *Appalachian Spring* by Aaron Copland, debuted in 1944 for the ballet choreographed by Martha Graham with sets by Isamu Noguchi (Cat. No. 36). The musical score featured a modern rendition of the Shaker tune "Simple Gifts."

This iconic *#6 Rocking Arm Chair* epitomizes the beliefs and craftsmanship of pioneering inventors seeking freedom of religion and lifestyle. For the Shakers, "Spirituality permeates every aspect of their lives ... furniture is merely a by-product of their entire religious experience."[11]

1   Special thanks to John Keith Russell, Kenneth Hatcher, the staff at the Shaker Museums and Libraries at Mount Lebanon, Old Chatham, and New Lebanon, New York, and Sabbathday Lake, Maine, for discussions about the Shaker Society and furniture. Additional thanks to Andrew VanStyn for his research and expertise. His contributions helped shape this essay.

2   Christian Becksvoort, *The Shaker Legacy: Perspectives on an Enduring Furniture Style* (Newtown, CT: Taunton Press, 2000), 47.

3   Sabbathday Lake Shaker Village (website), accessed July 27, 2021, https://www.maineshakers.com/.

4   Becksvoort, *The Shaker Legacy*, 33.

5   *I Hear America Singing: The Shakers*, presented by Thomas Hampson, aired April 1, 2009, on PBS.

6   Michael Horsham, *The Art of the Shakers* (Secaucus, NJ: Chartwell Books, 1989), 28.

7   Becksvoort, *The Shaker Legacy*, 14.

8   Becksvoort, 14.

9   Becksvoort, 130.

10 Becksvoort, 18.

11 Becksvoort, 3.

Gothic Revival Side Chair

c. 1845–1855

Designed and manufactured by an unknown chair maker (New York, New York)

Rosewood, ash, reproduction silk-and-cotton voided velvet upholstery, brass casters

46 ½ x 19 x 20 in.

WHILE SHAKER furniture exemplifies the tenets and faith of its community, this rosewood side chair articulates the Gothic architecture of European Christian churches. Between the 12th and 16th centuries, massive churches possessing towering spires, vaulted arches, colorful stained-glass windows, light-filled naves, and buttressed supports soared toward the heavens and dotted the landscape.

By the end of the first quarter of the 18th century, the Romantic Movement arose in Western Europe. Turning against the ordered, cool rationality of classicism, the movement found inspiration in the biblical and medieval worlds, in which emotion, the unexplained, and the awe-inspiring sublime power of nature reigned supreme. Augustus Welby Northmore Pugin (1812–1852), a Catholic convert, promoted the "Gothick" style in Protestant England through his social teachings, his architectural commissions, and his influential book *Gothic Furniture in the Style of the 15th Century Designed and Etched by A.W.N. Pugin* (1835).

Elements of the Gothic Revival style began to appear in American architecture, interiors, and furniture designs by the early 19th century, as seen in Benjamin Latrobe's design of Sedgeley Park (1799–1802), built for William Crammond (1754–1843), a prominent Philadelphian, and widely credited as being the first Gothic Revival house in America. However, it was not until 1842 when Andrew Jackson Downing (1815–1852), a leading proponent of the aesthetic, and Alexander Jackson Davis (1803–1892) collaborated on their influential treatise *Cottage Residences; or A Series of Designs for Rural Cottages and Cottage-Villas, and Their Gardens and Grounds, Adapted for North America*, which introduced picturesque Gothic architecture to America.[1] That same year, Robert Conner, an English immigrant to America, published his seminal book *The Cabinet Maker's Assistant*. In it, he introduced his original designs for Gothic furniture to America with hopes it "might be of some service to such of our Cabinet friends as has not been in Europe."[2] Conner further observed, "Libraries ... are mostly furnished in oak in the Gothic style. The furniture is covered in either green morocco leather, or puce color plush."[3] Consequently, seating furniture was the most common form produced in the Gothic Revival style, especially dining side chairs and hall chairs.

The rich architectural ornamentation of Gothic cathedrals, such as pointed and ogee arches, trefoils and quatrefoils, and wheel motifs, all suitably lent themselves to Gothic Revival–style furniture, especially chair-back designs. Simulating tracery—the stonework that supported the open areas of a Gothic window—this chair back is comprised of a centered quatrefoil flanked by symmetrical trefoils surmounting three pierced, arched lancets. The tall, ogee-arched crest is ornamented by crockets and three boldly carved foliate finials, imitating church spires as they reach skyward. Tracery of cusps and foils are suspended from the lower back rail.[4]

Echoing these motifs, the front seat rail and rectangular, tapering front legs feature sunk work (concave carvings) of elongated panels, which terminate in trefoils cornered by two quatrefoils. Pendentive tracery suspended from the front seat rail enhances the design. The ash inner seat frame and finely executed carvings suggest the work of a New York firm. "The most correct Gothic furniture that we have yet seen executed in this country is by Burns and Tranque, Broadway, New York. Some excellent specimens may also be seen at Roux's," observed Downing in *The Architecture of Country Houses* (1850).[5] The dill-and-taupe reproduction silk-and-cotton voided velvet fabric depicts ivy leaves on scrolling vines, a medieval motif often used by monks when illuminating manuscripts and as border illustrations in Books of Hours, reinforcing the positive and negative spaces created by the openwork.

By the 1860s, interest in the Gothic Revival style had begun to fade from American consciousness, principally due to the onset of the Civil War and its devastating effects. In the Reconstruction years that followed, American preferences gravitated toward French and Italian sources, rather than English, and by 1870 the style had all but ceased to exist.

1   On the influence of Davis, see Edna Donnell, "A. J. Davis and the Gothic Revival," *Metropolitan Museum Studies* 5, no. 2 (September 1936): 183–233.
2   Robert Conner, *The Cabinet Maker's Assistant* (New York: Faxon & Reed, 1842), quoted in David B. Warren, "The Gothic Revival Style in America: Domestic Architecture and Decorative Arts," in *In Pointed Style: The Gothic Revival in America, 1800–1860*, by Elizabeth Feld and Stuart Feld (New York: Hirschl & Adler Galleries, 2006), 23.
3   Conner quoted in Warren, 23.
4   Special thanks to Andrew VanStyn for his research and expertise. His contributions helped shape this essay.
5   Andrew Jackson Downing, *The Architecture of Country Houses; Including Designs for Cottages, Farm-Houses, and Villas, with Remarks on Interiors, Furniture, and the Best Modes of Warming and Ventilating* (New York: D. Appleton & Company, 1850), 440.

Centripetal Spring Arm Chair

c. 1850

Design attributed to Thomas E. Warren (active 1849–1853, American Chair Company)

Manufacture attributed to the American Chair Company (active 1829–1858, Troy, New York)

Cast iron, steel, wood, sheet metal, reproduction *gauffrage* velvet upholstery, *faux bois* rosewood, metal casters

43 ½ x 28 x 32 ½ in.

BY THE MID-19TH century, American furniture design had experienced rapid changes due to advances in domestic technological and industrial capabilities, together with a marked shift away from European stylistic influences. Perhaps in no other furniture form is this better illustrated than in the highly innovative *Centripetal Spring Arm Chair* designed by Thomas E. Warren. The chair adapts state-of-the-art technology and materials first designed for use in rail travel to domestic seating furniture, while its decorative elements honor historical antecedents. An innovative design in its day, it would later prove influential in the design of the modern office chair.[1]

The unique feature of the *Centripetal Spring Arm Chair*—both technologically and aesthetically—is its revolutionary spring mechanism (Fig. 7.1), which Warren patented in America in 1849 and in Britain in 1850. The following year, the Twentieth Annual Trade Fair, held at the Franklin Institute in Philadelphia, debuted a new category, "Spring Iron Chairs." In that competition, the American Chair Company's "Centripetal Spring Chair" earned a "second premium" award and quickly garnered both national and international acclaim. Similarly, in England in 1851, Prince Albert, Queen Victoria's husband, organized "the Great Exhibition" at London's Crystal Palace—itself an architectural marvel of glass plate and cast iron—which featured a display of international industrial products. Among these were a variety of models of the "Centripetal Spring Chair"—either with or without arms or headrests—made by a number of manufacturers, all of which

furthered recognition of Warren and increased appreciation for American design in general. *The Illustrated Exhibitor*, the catalogue for the Great Exhibition, praised the "handsome piece," and provided a thorough description of its manufacture and appearance:

> The framework ... is wholly made of cast iron, the base consisting of four ornamental bracket feet, mounted on castors, and secured to a center piece, to which eight elliptical springs are attached. The springs are connected to another center piece, which sustains the seat of the chair on a vertical pin; on this the chair-seat revolves, while at the same time the springs sustaining the seat from the under-frame give to it an agreeable elasticity in every direction. The freedom with which the chair may be turned on its center, renders it very convenient to a person who may want to turn to his library-shelf or side table, as he can do so without leaving his seat. The castings are good, and the design neat and pretty; the whole reflecting much credit on the inventor and American art.[2]

The armchair in the DeMell Jacobsen Collection—like most examples of this type—possesses a cast-iron framework that consists of a novel and early use of the material, while its openwork pattern of nature-based motifs reflects contemporary Rococo and Gothic influences. Eight bow-shaped steel springs support the seat and radiate from the top of a central vertical post, which is attached to an ornate cast-iron quadruped base. These springs contract and work separately, allowing for multidirectional elasticity balanced with weight distribution,[3] while aesthetically enhancing the overall curvaceous form. Providing additional comfort, the wide rounded back, headrest, armrests, and horsehair seat are upholstered in a reproduction imported French crimson *gauffrage* velvet embossed with a leafy "Carnot" pattern, which echoes the motifs of the cast-iron frame.[4] Suspended from the seat, coordinating crimson Labrecque gimp and a Courteau tassel fringe complete the ensemble. Further enhancing the elegant appearance and reflecting period aesthetics, the sheet metal back is *faux bois* painted to simulate exotic

rosewood (Fig. 7.2), a popular wood used in Victorian parlor furniture.[5]

The movement afforded by the patented center springs was a distinct advantage for the American Chair Company, located in Troy, New York, a nexus of iron production and several rail lines. At first, the firm chiefly manufactured reclining seats for railroad cars; however, the innovation of Warren's design was quickly adapted by the company for use in one of its first productions of parlor furniture.[6] These are now widely acknowledged to be among the first designs for seating furniture to incorporate cast iron.[7] Unlike the front-to-back movement of a rocking chair, the seat on the *Centripetal Spring Arm Chair* can move vertically, tilt sideways, and revolve, allowing the sitter to move in any direction by a simple shift of his or her weight. As the *Art Journal Illustrated Catalogue* noted, "the design and fittings of these chairs are equally good and elegant, and certainly we have never tested a more easy and commodious article of household furniture" (Fig. 7.3).[8]

The casting of iron for the fabrication of furniture began in England around 1823.

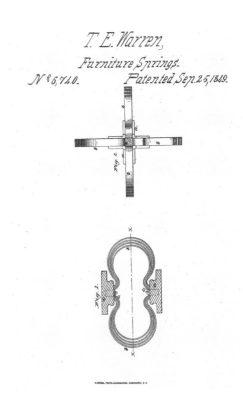

Fig. 7.1 Thomas E. Warren, "Furniture Springs," U.S. Patent No. 6,740, issued September 9, 1849, U.S. Patent Office.

Fig. 7.2 (left) Detail of *faux bois* rosewood painted back.

Fig. 7.3 (right) Entry for the *Centripetal Spring Arm Chair*, from *The Art Journal Illustrated Catalogue: The Industry of All Nations* (1851).

America has long been noted for the luxurious easiness of its chairs, which combine in themselves all the means of gratification a Sybarite could wish. The AMERICAN CHAIR COMPANY, of New York, exhibit some novelties, which even

increase the luxury and convenience of this necessary article of furniture; instead of the ordinary legs conjoined to each angle of the seat, they combine to support a stem, as in ordinary

music-stools, between which and the seat the SPRING is inserted; this we exhibit in our first cut. It will allow of the greatest weight and freest motion on all sides; the seat is also made

to revolve on its axis. The design and fittings of these chairs are equally good and elegant, and certainly we have never tested a more easy and commodious article of household furniture.

However, it was not until the 1840s that improved American coal mine production facilitated the manufacture of furniture domestically.[9] At the same time, the innovative iron T-rails for railways were developed domestically, thus ending reliance on English imports.[10] Travel by rail quickly supplanted that by stage or waterway; by 1850, the 30 states were connected by 9,021 miles of track.[11] On May 14, 1851, two weeks after the opening of the Crystal Palace Exhibition, the New York and Erie Railroad celebrated completion of the technological linkage between the Hudson River and the Great Lakes with a commemorative train ride, including passengers President Millard Fillmore (1800–1874) and Secretary of State Daniel Webster (1782–1852).[12] Warren intuitively understood the need for "an easy elastic resting position" in his 1850 Car Seat Back.[13] Passenger comfort was thus improved during jolting train rides. A decade later, the rail lines had increased to 30,626 miles of track.[14]

While government patents have protected U.S. inventions since the country's inception, the rise of "patent furniture"—created either with new materials or employing a unique process of manufacturing—increased during the 19th century. The aim of patent furniture was to enhance user comfort, facilitate movement between rooms, or convert into other forms.[15] "In America, inventive fantasy and the instinct for mechanization were the common property of the people," observed Sigfried Giedion (1888–1968), noted mid-20th-century architecture critic and historian.[16] More than a century and a half following its initial debut, Thomas Warren's design continued to inspire and contributed to a number of designs for the modern office chair.

1 Special thanks to Andrew VanStyn for his research and expertise. His contributions helped shape this essay.
2 Quoted in David A. Hanks, ed., *Innovative Furniture in America from 1800 to the Present* (New York: Horizon Press, 1981), 126.
3 Thomas E. Warren, "Furniture Springs," U.S. Patent No. 6,740, issued September 25, 1849, U.S. Patent Office. The official name of the patent is "Spring for Chairs"; however, "Furniture Springs" appears as the title in the document.
4 *Gauffrage* is a process by which a heated cylinder permanently applies a pattern to a textile. The reproduction upholstery is Edmond Petit Trianon II velvet.
5 A similar armchair in the collection of the Strong National Museum of Play, Rochester, New York (80.278), retains its original wool upholstery on its back and headrest, which guided the restoration of the DeMell Jacobsen Collection armchair. Several examples also survive with painted backs, including a pair of armchairs in the Victoria and Albert Museum with their original black (japanned) ground over which is a painted floral design and its original seat fabric and fringe; a related example with a back featuring original paint decoration is in the collection of the Brooklyn Museum (2009.27).
6 "A Rococo-Revival Painted and Gilded Cast-Iron Centripetal Armchair," Christie's, Sale 9468, lot 179, October 5, 2000, https://www.christies.com/lot/lot-1877393.
7 Hanks, *Innovative Furniture in America*, 127.
8 *The Art Journal Illustrated Catalogue: The Industry of All Nations* (London: Published for the proprietors of the Crystal Palace Exhibition by George Virtue, 1851), 152.
9 Ralph and Terry Kovel, "Cast-Iron Furniture Broke the Mold," *Florida Times-Union* (Jacksonville), February 10, 2008.
10 "First Iron Rails Historical Marker," ExplorePAhistory.com, accessed April 6, 2014, http://explorepahistory.com/hmarker.php?markerId=1-A-1A8.
11 Clifford F. Thies, *Development of the American Railroad Network During the Early 19th Century: Private versus Public Enterprise*, Independent Institute Working Paper Number 42 (Oakland, CA: Independent Institute, October 2001), http://www.independent.org/pdf/working_papers/42_development.pdf.
12 F. Daniel Larkin, "The Railroads and New York's Canals," Erie Canal Time Machine, New York State Archives, accessed March 1, 2019, https://btceriecanalcourse.weebly.com/uploads/1/4/8/4/14847764/railroads_and_new_yorks_canals_larkin.pdf.
13 For additional specifications on Thomas Warren's Car Seat Back, see Warren, "Car-Seat Back," U.S. Patent No. 7,539, issued July 30, 1850, U.S. Patent Office.
14 Stuyvesant Fish, "American Railroads," in *One Hundred Years of American Commerce, 1795–1895*, ed. Chauncey Depew (New York: D. O. Haynes & Company, 1895), 98–112.
15 See especially Jennifer Pynt and Joy Higgs, "Nineteenth-Century Patent Seating: Too Comfortable to Be Moral?" *Journal of Design History* 21, no. 3 (Autumn, 2008): 277–88.
16 Sigfried Giedion, *Mechanization Takes Command: A Contribution to Anonymous History* (New York: Oxford University Press, 1948).

Rustic Settee

c. 1855

Designed and manufactured by Janes, Beebe and Company (active 1844–1857, New York, New York)

Painted cast iron

Foundry mark on front seat rail: JANES, BEEBE & CO.

33 ¼ x 36 x 22 ½ in.

WITH PROFOUND advancements in the mining and refining of iron ore having been realized by the mid-19th century, mass-produced American cast-iron seating furniture gained in popularity as Victorian attitudes evolved within a rising middle class of consumers.[1] One of the oldest and basest metals, iron was made ornamental and a means of artistic expression through a variety of designs, which included artificial representations of nature. The cast-iron *Rustic Settee* made by Janes, Beebe and Company came to illustrate industrial progress and is a rare survival from a venerable company that rose to prominence through an important commission in the nation's capital.[2]

Rustic-style furniture is one of the earliest products of mass-produced cast-iron seating manufacture. Though rustic designs appeared in English pattern books as early as the mid-18th century, they only began to appear with some frequency in American trade catalogues between the 1840s through the 1890s, peaking during the third quarter of the century; by the 1890s rustic designs rarely appeared in American trade catalogues.[3]

A desire to invite the out-of-doors into the domestic sphere—combined with nostalgia and appreciation for pastoral panoramas—swept America at mid-century as railway expansion and industrial manufacturing tamed the wilderness. Nature, man-in-nature, and spiritual enlightenment were concepts expressed through literature, music, and the fine arts, which ultimately led to social reforms. *Kindred Spirits* (1849), the iconic painting by Hudson River School artist Asher B. Durand (1796–1886),[4] perfectly captured the cultural importance of nature and enlightenment promulgated by its subjects, artist Thomas Cole (1801–1848), founder of the so-called Hudson River School of painting, and his companion, prominent poet and editor William Cullen Bryant (1794–1878).

Bryant and landscape architect Andrew Jackson Downing promoted the need for open spaces and fresh air in New York City following the increase of industrial manufacturing and immigration. Between 1811 and 1850, the city's population had swelled from approximately 97,000 to more than 500,000.[5] In 1853, the city set aside land for Central Park and construction began four years later when the Greensward Plan by Frederick Law Olmsted (1822–1903) and Calvert Vaux (1824–1895) was submitted and accepted. In his influential publication *Villas and Cottages* (1857), Vaux illustrated a design for a bridge "in that part of the Central Park in New York which is called the Ramble" (Fig. 8.1), featuring railings constructed of cut tree limbs and similar in concept to the *Rustic Settee*.[6]

The functional, free-flowing form of the *Rustic Settee*—a rare and early example by Janes, Beebe and Company, as evidenced by the firm's name on the front seat rail (Fig. 8.3)—symbolizes an appreciation for, and domestication of, nature through its verisimilitude. Its stylized root-ball feet support slender legs that resemble tree trunks. The rear stiles bow slightly backward, placing the sitter at a gentle recline, and flank the arched back. Bent oak boughs, replete with leaves and acorns, rise to become armrests above the seat, which is comprised of evenly cut and cord-bound limbs. Below the seat, two entwined snakes writhe and unite as stretchers between the front and rear legs. Under the modern verdigris-black painted surface, the settee retains its original red-brown rust-preventive layer—possibly red lead or brown zinc[7]—as well as an early white finish layer. Structurally hard and durable, this romantic industrial imitation of natural vegetation provides an interesting contrast to the vernacular, handwrought *Appalachian Bent Willow Arm Chair* (Cat. No. 20), made nearly a half century later.

By the 1840s, an improved method of melting and molding coke-processed iron ore in sand casts replaced the blast-furnace technique, resulting in the production of a higher-quality product with a smoother surface. Newly discovered coal mines in the American East and Midwest pushed competing foundries to quickly adapt and mass-produce the aesthetically popular rustic designs. Many of these American foundries sent representatives abroad to gather inspiration and designs from their European counterparts. Janes, Beebe and Company was one such firm and specifically sent a representative to the 1851 Crystal Palace Exhibition in London to "get an insight into the manufacture of ornaments of this kind and were the first to produce and offer the work to the public."[8]

Established in 1844 by Adrian Janes (1798–1869), William Beebe (1793–1859),

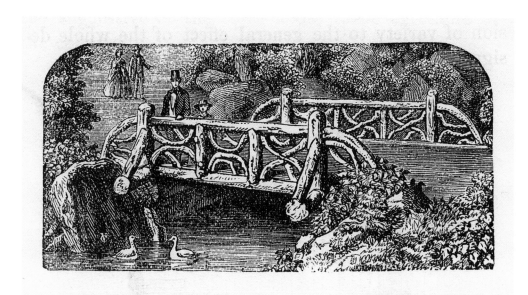

Fig. 8.1 (left) Design for a bridge in Central Park, from Calvert Vaux, *Villas and Cottages: A Series of Designs Prepared for Execution in the United States* (1857).

Fig. 8.2 (right) Cast-iron furniture designs, from Janes, Beebe and Co., *Illustrated Catalogue of Ornamental Iron Work* (1855).

and Charles Fowler, the firm opened a showroom at 356 Broadway in New York City, where it advertised itself as "[M]anufacturers of Ornamental Iron Work, Hot Air and Hot Water Furnaces, and Beebe's Kitchen Ranges" that "keep also a complete assortment of house furnishing goods, fine cutlery; silver plated spoons, forks, trays and tea sets, Japanned ware; cooking utensils and kitchen furniture."[9]

In addition to providing goods for domestic interiors, the firm offered outdoor structures and garden furniture within its inventory, as the establishment of formal pleasure gardens—both public and private—increased at mid-century. About 1852, President Millard Fillmore (1800–1874), an avid gardener, added several cast-iron settees attributed to Janes, Beebe and Company to the White House grounds.[10] The firm's *Illustrated Catalogue of Ornamental Iron Work* documents elaborate cast-iron fountains, urns, animal statuary, chairs and settees, including those purchased by Fillmore (model number 140) and one nearly identical to the *Rustic Settee* (model number 141), (Fig. 8.2). By 1871, it was reported that "the designs and patterns have been multiplied to an extent that a sample of each would make a display as attractive as an ordinary fair."[11]

Further South, in Abbeville, South Carolina, Captain Jehu Foster Marshall (1817–1862), another avid gardener, purchased a variety of cast-iron garden ornaments between 1848 and 1861 from the firm for his property, the Robertson-Hutchinson House. Among these were an elaborate three-tiered cast-iron fountain, a pair of dogs, urns, chairs, and a rustic settee nearly identical to this example. John E. Gardin, a former resident of the Robertson-Hutchinson House during the mid-1860s, recalled that the house was "set in a beautiful formal garden of the period with an imposing background of majestic red oak trees ... encompassed on three sides by a fancy picket fence with undulating lines ... extending along its entire length was a most remarkable piece of topiary work about fifteen feet high consisting of mock orange trees, trimmed to represent an arcade ... In all my travels throughout the world, not excepting the famous gardens of Versailles, have I seen anything equal to it."[12]

As the nation had grown from 16 states in 1800 to 30 states in 1850, the need to enlarge the United States Capitol building resulted in the appointment of Thomas Ustick Walter (1804–1887) as Architect of the Capitol Extension by President Fillmore in 1851. In addition to designing the new building, Walter also was tasked with designing its furnishings, which included the chairs and desks for the House of Representatives chamber in 1857 (Cat. No. 10). Janes, Beebe and Company, which grew to "be one of the largest establishments in the country,"[13] won several commissions in Washington, D.C., notably the Patent Office, General Post Office, Treasury Building, and several projects for the U.S. Capitol expansion, all of which catapulted the firm to national prominence. On January 5, 1855, firm co-founder Charles Fowler personally visited Superintendent Montgomery C. Meigs (1816–1892) to express the firm's interest in providing iron for the House ceiling.[14]

Flush from its success in providing architectural iron work throughout the U.S. Capitol and the Patent Office building—and perhaps confident in its ability to secure future government commissions—the foundry relocated in 1857 to Westchester Road, near Benson Avenue in Morrisania (now South Bronx), New York.[15] The *Morrisania and Tremont Directory* (1871) described the workshops as being "three hundred feet square, or if placed in a line would be 1,000 feet long by 50 feet wide, giving employment to a large number of hands, many of whom have been with the firm for years."[16]

Capitalizing—quite literally—on this highly visible commission, the firm advertised that in addition to its ornamental department, it was

prepared to execute orders at their foundry, corner of Reade, Centre, and Elm Streets, New York, for all descriptions of building iron work, roofs, girders, columns, lintels, sills, cornices, railings, verandahs, sky-lights, stairs, &c., and for the erection of buildings entirely of iron, for evidence of their ability in this line they refer to their work now in progress on the Capitol Extension at Washington, and at the Congressional Library Room, the Ceilings of the new Senate Chamber and

No. 140. 2 sizes.

No. 141.

No. 142.

No. 143.

No. 144.

Janes, Beebe & Co., 356 Broadway, New York.

House of Representatives, and at other work already completed on the Public Buildings at the National Capital.[17]

Consequently, the firm secured other commissions locally, nationally, and internationally. These include ornamental iron work for several bridges in Central Park, such as the Bow Bridge (1862); railings for the Brooklyn Bridge (1869/70–1883); iron frames for stained-glass windows at Trinity Episcopal Church in Abbeville, South Carolina (c. 1860). The firm also produced elaborate fountains located in Poughkeepsie, New York (Soldiers' and Sailors' Memorial Fountain, 1858); Savannah, Georgia (Forsyth Park, 1858); Abbeville, South Carolina (Robertson-Hutchinson House, 1848–1861); Madison, Indiana (Broadway Fountain Park, 1876); and Cusco, Peru (Plaza de Armas, after 1870).

Concurrent with the above projects and many others, the firm continued its principal work on the U.S. Capitol. Janes, Fowler, Kirtland and Co.—as the company was by then named—originally had been asked to provide the surface skin for the dome, which they had estimated at six cents per pound. However, seeing the possibility for additional profit, they boldly offered to fabricate the entire dome for just one penny more per pound.

The foundry's bid to construct the dome for seven cents a pound was accepted in February 1860,[18] and Abraham Lincoln was inaugurated as president under the unfinished dome in 1861. Despite the turmoil embroiling the nation during the Civil War, the temporary requisition of the Capitol as a hospital, combined with the suspension of payments, the company persevered and continued construction. "There was not a day during the Civil war when the sound of the builder's hammer was not heard at the Capitol," wrote George Cochrane Hazelton. "Even when, in May, 1861, all work was ordered to be suspended, the contractors practically continued at their own expense to put in place the 1,300,000 pounds of iron castings then upon the ground … [B]y the close of 1865 the wings and the interior of the dome were completed and Walter's work was done."[19] All told, the firm supplied slightly less than nine million pounds of iron for the dome[20] and provided cast-iron settees throughout the U.S. Capitol grounds in accordance with the plan designed by Frederick Law Olmsted.

Today, the 150-year-old United States Capitol dome stands as an architectural icon representing freedom and democracy. Similarly, this cast-iron *Rustic Settee* is a vestige of American history, culture, and technology as well as an enduring legacy of Janes, Beebe and Company.

Fig. 8.3 Detail of foundry mark on front seat rail.

1   See especially Morrison Heckscher, "Eighteenth-Century Rustic Furniture Designs," *Furniture History* 11 (1975): 59–65; for a detailed exploration of the evolution and use of Victorian-era cast-iron furniture, see Ellen Marie Snyder, "Victory Over Nature: Victorian Cast-Iron Seating Furniture," *Winterthur Portfolio* 20, no. 4 (Winter 1985): 221–42.

2   Special thanks to Andrew VanStyn for his research and expertise. His contributions helped shape this essay.

3   Snyder, "Victory Over Nature," 230.

4   Now in the collection of Crystal Bridges Museum of American Art, Bentonville, Arkansas.

5   "Parks for the New Metropolis (1811–1870)," NYC Parks, New York City Department of Parks and Recreation, accessed April 10, 2015, http://www.nycgovparks.org/about/history/timeline/new-metropolis.

6   Calvert Vaux, *Villas and Cottages: A Series of Designs Prepared for Execution in the United States* (1857; repr. New York: Harper & Brothers, 1874), 288.

7   Recent paint analysis on the cast iron door and window "dressings," or enframements, in the House and Senate wings of the U.S. Capitol, which were supplied and installed by Janes, Beebe and Company, have revealed the existence of the original brown zinc paints that were made by the New Jersey Zinc Company in Newark. The New Jersey Zinc Company was one of the first manufacturers of zinc oxide and zinc-based architectural and industrial paint in America. In addition to white, the company also made at least seven other colors of zinc paint, especially brown, for use principally as primers on metals but also for finish coats on exterior wood surfaces. In their contract to provide iron for the Congressional Library (1853), Janes, Beebe and Company was instructed "to paint the castings with two coats before shipping, to prevent rust and to lay a good foundation for the ornamental painter." See Frank S. Welsh, "Identification of 1850s Brown Zinc Paint Made with Franklinite and Zincite at the U.S. Capitol," *APT Bulletin* 39, no. 1 (2008): 17–30.

8   D. B. Frisbee and William T. Coles, *Morrisania and Tremont Directory, 1871–2* (Morrisania, NY: Times Print, 1871), xxix.

9   Frisbee and Coles, xxix.

10 Betty C. Monkman, "White House Decorative Arts in the 1850s," White House Historical Association, accessed January 3, 2022, https://www.whitehousehistory.org/white-house-decorative-arts-in-the-1850s.

11 Frisbee and Coles, *Morrisania and Tremont Directory, 1871–2*, xxix.

12 Quoted in Ann Hutchinson Waigand, "From Mexico to the U.S. Capitol: Unraveling the Mysteries of a Mid-19th-Century Garden in Abbeville, South Carolina," *Magnolia* (publication of the Southern Garden History Society) 27, no. 3 (Summer 2014): 3, https://southerngardenhistory.org/wp-content/uploads/2015/12/Magnolia_Summer2014.pdf.

13 Frisbee and Coles, *Morrisania and Tremont Directory, 1871–2*, xxviii.

14 Meigs wrote, "Mr. Fowler of the firm of Janes, Beebe and Co. was also at the office this morning. He says that they will send in a bid for the ceiling of the House of Representatives in a short time. Thinks that he could have the decorations of cast iron as sharp as I can get them made of carton pierre. I am, however, inclined to have the Senate ceiling entirely finished in iron." Quoted in Wendy Wolff, ed., *Capitol Builder: The Shorthand Journals of Montgomery C. Meigs, 1853–1859, 1861; A Project to Commemorate the United States Capitol Bicentennial, 1800–2000* (Washington, DC: U.S. Government Printing Office, 2001), 197.

15 St. Mary's Park in the South Bronx was originally named Janes Park in honor of Adrian Janes, one of the founders of Janes, Beebe and Company.

16 Frisbee and Coles, *Morrisania and Tremont Directory, 1871–2*, xxviii–xxix.

17 Janes, Kirtland & Company, *Ornamental Iron work; Fountains, Statuary, Vases, Urns, Lawn Furniture, Pedestals, Baptismal Fonts, Animals, Veranda, Summer House* (New York, 1870).

18 Margalit Fox and George Robinson, "FYI," *New York Times*, August 3, 2003.

19 George Cochrane Hazelton Jr., *The National Capitol: Its Architecture, Art and History* (New York: J. F. Taylor & Company, 1897), 60.

20 8,909,200 pounds. Fox and Robinson, "FYI."

Belter Chairs

c. 1855–1860

Designed and manufactured by John Henry Belter (1804–1863) (active 1844–1863, New York, New York)

Laminated and carved rosewood, oak, reproduction silk damask upholstery (original foundations), brass casters

Slipper Chair ("Grape Vine and Oak Leaf"),
c. 1855
43 ¾ x 18 ¼ x 20 ¼ in.

Slipper Chair, c. 1860
44 ¼ x 18 ½ x 20 in.

Side Chair ("Fountain Elms" with Foliate Foot),
c. 1855
35 ¼ x 19 ½ x 27 ¾ in.

Side Chair ("Fountain Elms" with Scroll Foot),
c. 1855
35 ¼ x 19 ½ x 27 ¾ in.

JUST AS THE USE of molded cast-iron furniture brought an idealized, tamed wilderness into the domestic sphere, boldly carved wood furnishings derived from nature were also highly esteemed by newly affluent Victorian urbanites. A penchant for naturalism in the mid-19th century—ushered in by the Romantic and Picturesque Garden Movements—stimulated the revival of several international decorative styles of the past.

One of the most desired revival styles was the Rococo Revival, which embraced the early-18th-century Parisian designs of the *Ancien Régime* of the Valois and Bourbon dynasties that had emerged in contrast to Baroque art. The word *Rococo* is a combination of the French words *rocailles* (rocks) and *coquilles* (shells), since those decorative motifs are commonly featured. Other characteristics include the serpentine C- and S-scrolls—which William Hogarth (1697–1764) referred to as "the waving line," or "line of beauty"[1]—as well as other shapes and forms derived from nature, all of which harmonize in presenting a light and airy appearance.

French influences entered the American culture when emissaries Thomas Jefferson (1743–1826) and Benjamin Franklin (1706–1790) traveled to France after the War of Independence. Later in the mid-1800s, during the French Second Empire under the reign of Emperor Napoleon III (r. 1852–1870), the Rococo style of the *Ancien Régime* reemerged and was diffused to the United States through design pattern books and emigrant French and German cabinetmakers (*ébénistes*).[2]

The concurrent rise of the Industrial Revolution in America saw the establishment of factories that created domestic goods en mass for a rapidly expanding middle class. These factories employed new technologies to produce steam-bent and laminated woods, which were often cut in fanciful patterns and embellished with rich stains and exotic veneers to heighten the visual effect. In *The Architecture of Country Houses* (1850), tastemaker Andrew Jackson Downing observed, "Modern French furniture … stands much higher in general estimation in this country than in any other. Its union of lightness, elegance, and grace renders it especially the favorite of the ladies … [The style is] known by its abundance of light, ornamental scroll-work, and foliage … and greater intimacy of detail."[3]

Nowhere are these technological innovations more evident than in the furniture produced in the New York City factory of John Henry Belter, who cleverly patented both unique machinery and methods to mass-produce his ornately carved furnishings. A trained cabinetmaker, Belter emigrated from the Württemberg area of Germany in 1833 and had become a naturalized citizen by 1839. By 1844, he had established a cabinet-making shop at 40½ Chatham Street; between 1846 and 1852 he was located at 372 Broadway. His business grew, and by 1854 J. H. Belter and Company occupied a showroom on fashionable, gas-lit Broadway and maintained a five-story factory on 76th Street near Third Avenue.[4] In contrast to his contemporary, German-Austrian Michael Thonet (1796–1871), who produced steam-bent veneered tubular wooden furniture, Belter closely guarded his wood lamination and carving production methods by exclusively hiring skilled carvers from his native Black Forest in the Alsace-Lorraine territory.

While Belter's label describes his firm as "MANUFACTURERS OF / ALL KINDS OF FINE FURNITURE,"[5] most surviving examples attributed to his factory are sofas, *méridiennes*, *étagères*, center tables, arm and side chairs, and other forms of parlor furniture; rare is the example made for the dining room, bedroom, or other domestic space.[6] Thomas Webster, a mid-19th-century writer on interior design, observed, "the style of Louis Quatorze is known … by its abundance of light ornamental scrollwork and foliage. Its elegance of form … together with its admission of every species of enrichment as carving, gilding, painting, inlaying with covering of the richest silks, velvets, and the choicest stuffs, admirably adapt it for the modern drawing room. Certainly no kind of furniture equals it in the general splendor of appearance."[7] Similarly, at New York's Crystal Palace Exhibition in 1853, Professor Benjamin Silliman Jr. noted, "we have furniture style of our own, which, though not original, bears yet the marks of our utilitarian age. It is a modification and a moderation of the style known as Louis XIV; and while it assumes the graceful motives of that style, it also reduces them to greater simplicity and moulds them into forms more consistent with comfort and constructive truth."[8]

The two *Slipper Chairs* in the DeMell Jacobsen Collection are visual *tours de force*

of the Rococo Revival aesthetic and further illustrate emerging social and fashion trends. On each, an abundance of naturalistic, intricately reticulated, carved floral and foliate ornaments embellishes the back and crest, while scrolling volutes enhance the sturdy frame. The seat back of the *Slipper Chair ("Grape Vine and Oak Leaf")*, comprised of seven layers of laminated and steam-bent rosewood, is pierced into a swirling mass of grape clusters, acorns, and both grape and oak leaves, all set within a frame of stylized grape tendrils that form the stiles. The undulating curves of the overall design draw the viewer's eye upward toward the crest rail, which contains a deeply carved floral and foliate bundle at its center. The bundle is further mirrored in the center of the front seat rail as well as on the knees of the finger-molded cabriole legs. The low seat height on a slipper chair— generally 15 inches from the floor instead of the more traditional 17 to 18 inches—made it easier for 19th-century women to put on their stockings, slipper-style shoes, and other attire, including fashionable camisoles, petticoats, laced corsets, and full-skirted dresses.[9]

Likewise, the pair of *Side Chairs ("Fountain Elms")*[10] further illustrates Belter's extensive design vocabulary. The button-tufted upholstered oval back on each is framed by carved openwork of flowers, foliage, grapes, oak boughs, and acorns suggestive of a plentiful harvest and abundance. Among the curvaceous scrolls and crested volutes are several cornucopias, themselves symbols of bounty, wealth, and prosperity. Although the two *Side Chairs ("Fountain Elms")* appear identical, the cabriole legs of each terminate in either an ornamental scroll (Fig 9.3) or foliate foot.

The Metropolitan Museum of Art period rooms demonstrate the vogue for parlors filled with suites of furniture unified by a consistent upholstery scheme. All four chairs in the DeMell Jacobsen Collection are upholstered with blue Italian silk damask matching the historical samples at the Metropolitan. Each is trimmed with blue and gold gimp. The backs of the *Side Chairs ("Fountain Elms")* possess undecorated and seamless rosewood panels, which are steam-bent into convex shapes, a Belter convention. Brass casters fitted onto the feet provided a smooth approach to a table, especially for women attired in full-bodied skirts.

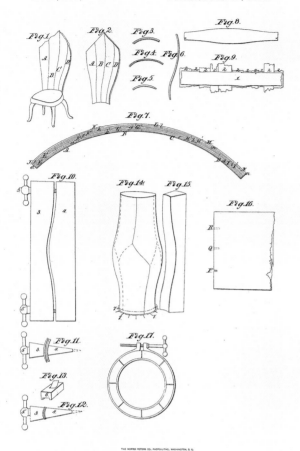

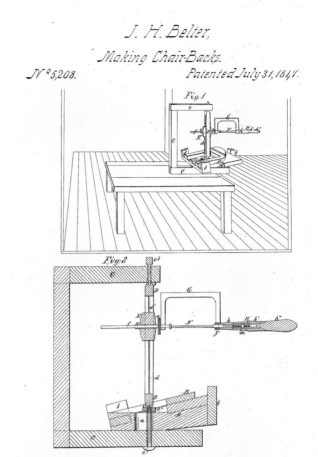

Fig. 9.1 (above left) John Henry Belter, "Improvement in the Method of Manufacturing Furniture," U.S. Patent Number 19,405, issued February 23, 1858, U.S. Patent Office.

Fig. 9.2 (above right) John Henry Belter, "Machinery for Sawing Arabesque Chairs," U.S. Patent No. 5,208, issued July 31, 1847, U.S. Patent Office.

The elaborate lacy openwork carvings belie the slim profile of the back of the chairs. Sturdy and supportive, the backs are composed using a pioneering lamination method that Belter patented in 1858 (Fig. 9.1). While laminated woods have been used since the construction of Egyptian sarcophagi and Chinese furniture of the Song Dynasty, Belter uniquely improved the method. By alternating and gluing veneers at right angles into layered staves, Belter invented "dishing pressed work,"[11]

or hollow spheres curved in height and width, that were more graceful, strong, durable, lightweight, and cost effective. Previous pressed work could only bend in one plane; however, Belter improved the strength and ability of the material to arc in multiple directions.[12] Shape-molded under the pressure of steam heat, the material was primed for detailed carving resulting in stylistic arabesques and a continuous rail and stile. One portion of pressed-work stave material, with two or more layers, could be produced in 24 hours and would provide eight chair backs.[13] Belter stressed the importance of good materials, such as rosewood for front and back veneers, with a vertically oriented grain for the front side.

Although Belter delayed sharing his pressed-work procedures, he applied for and received a patent for "Machinery for Sawing Arabesque Chairs" in 1847 (Fig. 9.2). The

multidirectional jigsaw improved the ability to manufacture the elaborate, complicated scrolling and intertwined openwork of Rococo Revival–style chair-back patterns. Having patented two other inventions for furniture manufacturing, Belter did not want his designs copied, so he allegedly destroyed the patterns and molds[14] prior to his death in 1863.[15] Family members continued the business under the name Springmeyer Brothers until 1867.

To satisfy the insatiable demand by consumers, Belter fended off competing designs produced by numerous rivals from Philadelphia, Baltimore, and Cincinnati, as well as those directly across town, including J. and J. W. Meeks and Charles Baudouine (1808–1895). Ernest Hagen, a former employee of Baudouine, recalled:[S]ome of Baudouine's most conspicuous productions were those rosewood heavy over decorated

parlour suits [*sic*] with round perforated backs generally known as 'Belter furniture' from the original inventor *John H. Belter*, 372 B'dway, who had a shop near by, and had a patent on the round backs of those chairs and sofas made of 5 layers of veneer glued up in a mould in one piece, which made a very strong and not heavy chair back only about ¼-inch thick, all the ornamental carved work glued on after the perforated part of the thin back was sawed out and prepared. Baudouine infringed on Belter's patent by making the backs out of 2 pieces with a center joint, and this way got the best of Belter, who died a very poor man."[16]

As evidenced by these four chairs, the Rococo Revival–style carvings are a sculptural manifestation and lasting vestige of 19th-century American personal economic prosperity and well-being. As the growing nation increasingly depended on urban industries linked by railways, many household incomes rose significantly,[17] and commodities such as cotton cloth, shoes, clothing, and machinery were more readily available. A bountiful land fed the Victorian table and desire for decorative items reflecting the proprietor's wealth and aspirations. Looming on the horizon, however, were conflicts between the industrial and urbanized North and the agrarian South. The issues of states' rights and slavery would create bitter debates in the newly refurbished House of Representatives, leading to civil war.

Today, examples of Belter's elaborately carved Rococo Revival–style furniture are growing increasingly rare and remain highly coveted by collectors and museums. The furniture represents both his stylistic innovations and his role in advancing technological craftsmanship, which foretold the mid-20th-century molded plywood designs of Charles and Ray Eames (Cat. No. 31).

Fig. 9.3 Detail of scroll foot.

1   William Hogarth, *The Analysis of Beauty* (London: W. Strahan, 1772), 38.

2   Special thanks to Andrew VanStyn, whose research and expertise helped shape this essay.

3   Andrew Jackson Downing, *The Architecture of Country Houses* (New York: D. Appleton & Company, 1850), 432.

4   "John Henry Belter," *History Wired: A Few of Our Favorite Things*, National Museum of American History, Smithsonian Institution, accessed April 14, 2015, https://americanhistory.si.edu/exhibitions/history-wired.

5   Quoted in Ed Polk Douglas, "Rococo Revival: John Henry Belter," in *Nineteenth Century Furniture: Innovation, Revival and Reform* (New York: Billboard Publications, 1982), 31.

6   For a thorough analysis of Belter, his production methods, and forms of furniture, see Marvin D. Schwartz, Edward J. Stanek, and Douglas K. True, *The Furniture of John Henry Belter and the Rococo Revival* (Edina, MN: Antiques and Books by Lise Bohm, 2000).

7   Thomas Webster, *Encyclopedia of Domestic Economy* (New York: Harper & Brothers, 1845), 248, quoted in Anna Tobin D'Ambrosio, *Masterpieces of American Furniture from the Munson- Williams-Proctor Institute* (Utica, NY: Munson-Williams-Proctor Institute, 1999), 73.

8   Prof. B. Silliman Jr. and C. R. Goodrich, *The World of Science, Art, and Industry Illustrated from Examples in the New-York Exhibition, 1853–1854* (New York: G. P. Putnam & Company, 1854), 185.

9   The manufacture and use of specially designed seating intended to aid and comfort women, the strength and center of the home, may have arisen from the 1848 Seneca Falls Convention for Women's Rights. While a movement for change had begun, it would not be fully realized until passage of the Nineteenth Amendment in 1920.

10 "Fountain Elms" was one of Belter's most popular patterns, though the moniker was not coined until more than a century later with the opening of the Fountain Elms period rooms at the Museum of Art, Munson-Williams-Proctor Institute. Originally owned by the Williams family, the home was named after a fountain had been erected between two elms on the front lawn in honor of the late patriarch, James Williams, in 1873. Belter furniture of this pattern was collected by the museum to furnish the parlor, hence the genesis of its name. Anna Tobin D'Ambrosio, Assistant Director and Curator of Decorative Arts, Museum of Art, Munson-Williams-Proctor Institute, email correspondence with Foundation staff, July 6 and 7, 2011.

11 John Henry Belter, "Improvement in the Method of Manufacturing Furniture," U.S. Patent No. 19,405, issued February 23, 1858, U.S. Patent Office.

12 Belter, "Improvement."

13 Belter, "Improvement."

14 Schwartz, Stanek, and True, *Furniture of John Henry Belter*, 29.

15 "The Genius of John Henry Belter," M. S. Rau Antiques, October 27, 2016, https://www.rauantiques.com/blog/the-genius-of-john-henry-belter/.

16 Elizabeth A. Ingerman, "Personal Experiences of an Old New York Cabinetmaker," *The Magazine* ANTIQUES 84, no. 5 (November 1963): 576–80.

17 "Antebellum Period Statistics," Schmoop University, last modified November 11, 2008, https://www.shmoop.com/antebellum/statistics.html.

House of Representatives Chamber Arm Chair

10

1857

Designed by Thomas Ustick Walter (1804–1887)

Manufactured by John T. Hammitt (dates not known)

Carved oak, pine, reproduction horsehair upholstery

37 ½ x 24 x 20 in.

WITH THE GROWTH of the nation from 16 states in 1800 to 30 states in 1850, the need to enlarge the United States Capitol building became ever more evident—both to functionally serve the legislature but also to stand as a visible symbol of American prosperity and the success of its democratically elected government. Following a design competition during which Congress could not come to an agreement, President Millard Fillmore (1800–1874) appointed Thomas Ustick Walter, a prominent architect from Philadelphia, as fourth Architect of the Capitol (1851–1865). Walter, like his competitors, had presented designs based on three possibilities: "making a square Capitol by building an addition on the east, placing new wings directly against the north and south walls, or attaching lateral wings to the old building via corridors. The latter, sanctioned by the Senate Committee on Public Buildings, maintained much of the original Capitol's integrity."[1] At the suggestion of Montgomery C. Meigs (1816–1892), a member of the Army Corps of Engineers and superintendent of the expansion, Walter positioned the new rectangular chambers in the center of each wing. Rising over the enlarged Capitol was a new cast-iron dome, also designed by Walter, and fabricated and installed by Janes, Beebe and Company (see Cat. No. 8).

For the new House Chamber, Walter designed a windowless room to minimize outside noise and potential distractions for the legislators. Yellow-painted walls reflected natural light introduced by a skylight, supplemented by gas fixtures. A rich, floral-patterned red carpet covered the floor. To furnish the space, Walter also designed new desks and chairs in the Renaissance Revival style (Fig. 10.3) to replace the rather simple models designed and made by Thomas Constantine and Company in 1818–19.[2]

Walter's *Design for Chairs for Halls of Congress* was approved on May 28, 1857, by his colleague and contentious rival Superintendent Meigs.[3] Robustly scaled and carved from solid oak, the chair is a veritable symbol of the strength and aspirations of the country and its elected leaders. Centering the crest rail—symbolic of placing country above self—is a federal shield bearing the stars and stripes (Fig. 10.1). Surrounding it are two motifs drawn from nature: laurel boughs, representative of victory and success, and oak boughs, symbolic of

longevity and continued growth of the republic.[4] Similarly, the five-point stars at each corner and the *guilloche* surrounding the seat frame are derived from ancient Rome and refer to its democratic system of government. Columnar legs with carved and downward-facing acanthus leaves taper to a gadrooned ring set above lobe-leafed cuffs. The chair rests atop cup-shaped casters, which facilitated legislators' movement while at their desks.

The generously proportioned chairs afforded representatives comfort as they toiled long hours in service to their country. Depending on the season, either summer or winter cushions could be placed over the seat frame. For the summer months, a caned-bottom box was placed over the seat frame to ensure members remained cool and to maintain a consistent working height at their desks.[5] Walter's original chair design shows a pleated and button-tufted system in a diamond pattern for both the back upholstery and the removeable upholstered winter seat cushion.[6] Perhaps questioning Walter's proposed upholstery schematic, Meigs consulted the chief artist of the Capitol, Constantino Brumidi (1805–1880), who specified the "cushions, not tufted, to be covered with red goat-skin morocco. The whole to be finished in the strongest and most artistic-like manner."[7]

With the furnishing designs approved in late May, there were less than six months before the House would convene in its new chamber in December 1857. To ensure completion of the commission for the 262 desks and chairs needed to furnish the enlarged House Chamber, Meigs sought proposals from two firms: Bembe and Kimbel, a New York furniture manufacturer, and Doe, Hazelton and Company of Boston. On August 12, Meigs recorded:

> I received today from Bembe and Kimbel of New York a letter with a bill for two chairs and two desks which they say have been sent for inspection. They ask a less price than that I have agreed to pay to [Doe], Hazelton and Co. of Boston for the desks of which they brought me specimens. I am surprised at the price they charge being so low. But I have not yet seen the chairs.[8]

Two days later, the Bembe and Kimbel prototype desk and chairs arrived. Meigs

Fig. 10.1
Detail of crest rail.

Fig. 10.2 E. Sachse
and Co., *The House
of Representatives,
U.S. Capitol*, 1866,
lithograph, Library of
Congress.

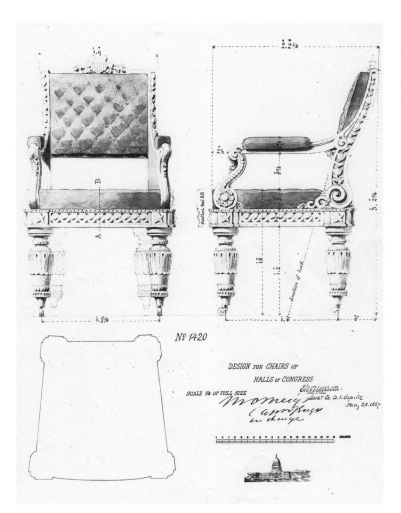

Fig. 10.3 Thomas Ustick Walter (1804–1887), *Design for Chairs for Halls of Congress*, 1857, Architect of the Capitol.

observed, "The chairs are better than the Boston chairs,[9] the desks not so good. All are cheaper."[10] The following week, Anthony Kimbel visited Meigs to discuss the prototypes and to "make a bargain for the chairs for the House of Representatives."[11] Meigs, however, was skeptical of Bembe and Kimbel's ability to meet the December deadline for the entire commission and wrote, "He will, I fear, not be able to make them in time. I shall probably give to him a small portion only of the number required."[12]

Likely through an introduction made by Walter, Meigs approached John T. Hammitt, a cabinetmaker in Philadelphia, to ensure the timely completion of the commission.[13] On August 27, 1857, Meigs "made a bargain with Mr. Hammitt of Philadelphia for one-half of the chairs for the House of Representatives at $75 each, delivered. I have telegraphed to Bembe and Kimbel of New York that they might make the other half at $70 each, not including the packing. This makes 262 chairs and the same number of desks in all for the House of Representatives

which are now engaged."[14] Despite working from the same design provided by Walter, there are noticeable differences between the chairs made by Hammitt and those by Bembe and Kimbel. The principal difference may be found by examining the running *guilloche* around the seat frame. Chairs by Hammitt feature convex, or protruding, half-rounds (bosses) within the *guilloche*, while those by Bembe and Kimbel have centers that are concave, or receding.

In early September 1857, Meigs reported that "the floor of the House of Representatives is down, except a small portion. We have begun to plaster the gallery fronts, and the painters are at work upon the iron work of these fronts and steps of the galleries, and the seats are begun. In short, the whole looks as though it would be ready long before the time required. The chairs and desks are in progress in New York, Boston and Philadelphia."[15] On November 23, 1857, Doe, Hazelton and Company delivered all the desks, one of which Meigs examined and declared to be "beautiful, well made."[16]

The House Chamber was completed by early December (Fig. 10.2), though not without its detractors. Meigs recalled that Thomas Lanier Clingman (1812–1897), a Democratic representative from North Carolina,[17] had told him "he did not like the colors yellow and red and thought that there was too much gilding and bright color in the fronts of the galleries. He did not object so much to the ceiling because that was out of sight."[18] The House Chamber was further declared to be "entirely overburdened ... by the great variety of colors ... I think it sort of [like] Joseph's coat" by Vermont Senator Jacob Collamer (1791–1865).[19] On December 16, 1857, the 35th Congress officially convened with 237 representatives and seven delegates in attendance.[20] The new House Chamber featured enhanced acoustics, ventilation systems, and an iron ceiling,[21] complete with stained-glass inserts and decorative wall paintings. *Crayon*, a mid-19th-century arts and literature journal,

Fig. 10.4 (left) Abraham Lincoln seated and holding a book, with his son Tad Thomas leaning on a table, 1865.

Fig 10.5 (right) Hiram Rhodes Revels, Republican senator from Mississippi, c. 1860–75.

described the spacious chamber as "surpassing gorgeousness ... an artistic effect unsurpassed in North America."[22] The *Washington Evening Star* noted the furniture in the chamber possessed a "peculiar pattern and ... elaborate finish; having on every possible point of its surface some curious knob, leaf, rosette, vine or other device."[23] Thomas Clingman excepting, most members of the House seemed to have been pleased by their new surroundings. Shortly into the new year, Meigs encountered "several members

of the House of Representatives ... [who] said they were getting more pleased with the Hall and that it was very comfortable," a comment that would suggest they also approved of the furnishings, though some "[h]ad some complaints still of the drafts."[24]

By 1859, Congress determined that the Walter-designed chairs were not functioning as they had initially hoped and asked for replacements to be designed. Meigs turned once again to Brumidi, who designed a series of curved benches that would radiate out from the speaker's desk. Janes, Beebe and Company of New York— makers of the dome—cast the ends for the benches in patinated bronze, while the seats were made of carved oak. The Walter chairs were removed and dispersed among Congressional offices in the Capitol or given to legislators, while a few were sold.

In 1860, Congress reversed its decision and ordered the remaining Walter chairs that could be located to be returned to the chamber until 1873, at which time all the Walter furniture was replaced by smaller desks and swivel-seat cane chairs during yet another renovation.

An iconic example of the classical aesthetic, the Walter-designed chairs have been memorialized in numerous painted and photographic portraits of elected leaders. At the initial sale dispersal in 1859, prominent Washington, D.C., photographers Mathew Brady (1822–1896) and Alexander Gardner (1821–1882) both purchased Walter chairs and used them as props in their studios.[25] In November 1863, Gardner photographed President Lincoln, stoic even as the tumult of the ongoing Civil War consumed him. Nearly two years later, in the waning days of the war, Gardner again photographed Lincoln seated in a Bembe and Kimbel example, his elbow resting on a table and his right hand clutching a book, while his son, Tad, stands opposite the table and leans on his left elbow (Fig. 10.4).

In the years and decades that followed, a veritable who's who of American elected officials also have been photographed in Walter-designed chairs, including Hiram Rhodes Revels (1827–1901), a Republican senator from Mississippi who in 1870 became the first African American to serve in Congress (Fig. 10.5); Joseph Hayne Rainey (1832–1887), a Republican representative from South Carolina who became the first African American to serve in the House and second to serve in Congress after Revels; President Ulysses S. Grant (1822–1885); President Rutherford B. Hayes (1822–1893); President James A. Garfield (1831–1881); Native American leaders; justices of the court; Union and Confederate veterans; and everyday citizens, both famous and not. Forever immortalized through these and other photographs, the chair today remains colloquially referred to as the "Brady Chair" or the "Lincoln Chair," and a Bembe and Kimbel example graces the Lincoln bedroom in the White House.[26]

1 Pamela Scott, "Temple of Liberty: Building a Capitol for a New Nation," Library of Congress, https://loc.gov/loc/lcib/9506/capitol.html, 1995, accessed May 4, 2022.

2 For a detailed study of the earlier furnishings, see Mathew A. Thurlow, "Aesthetics, Politics, and Power in Early-Nineteenth-Century Washington: Thomas Constantine & Co.'s Furniture for the United States Capitol, 1818–1819," in American Furniture: 2006, ed. Luke Beckerdite (Milwaukee, WI: Chipstone Foundation, 2006), 184–228.

3 Thomas Ustick Walter, Design for Chairs of Halls of Congress, drawing, May 28, 1857, Architect of the Capitol.

4 "Walter Chair," History, Art & Archives, United States House of Representatives, accessed April 19, 2015, https://history.house.gov/Collection/Detail/29296?ret=True.

5 For a House of Representatives chair purporting to retain its original summer seat, see the example sold at New Orleans Auction Galleries, May 22, 2016, lot 808, illustrated in the online auction catalogue, https://issuu.com/noauction/docs/untitled-1, p. 219.

6 Andrew VanStyn provided guidance on the upholstery as well as other aspects of this chair.

7 "Walter Chair."

8 Wendy Wolff, ed., Capitol Builder: The Shorthand Journals of Montgomery C. Meigs, 1853–1859, 1861; A Project to Commemorate the United States Capitol Bicentennial, 1800–2000, (Washington, DC: U.S. Government Printing Office, 2001), 520.

9 This suggests that Doe, Hazelton and Company of Boston made two chairs as prototypes; the whereabouts of these chairs are unknown, however.

10 Wolff, Capitol Builder, 520.

11 Wolff, 520.

12 Wolff, 521.

13 While a significant amount of scholarship exists about the Bembe and Kimbel firm, few details are known about Hammitt and his business. McElroy's Philadelphia Directory for 1851 lists John T. Hammitt as being a "cabinetmkr" at 10 Exchange Place. Both Ulman's Pennsylvania Business Directory and McElroy's Philadelphia Directory for 1854 similarly record him as being a "cabinetmaker" and located at the southwest corner of 2nd and Dock Streets. McElroy's Philadelphia Directory for the years 1856 and 1857—the year of the commission—does not include Hammitt's name among either cabinetmakers or chairmakers, but rather states his occupation as "pat. car seat mr.," with a business address of 111 South 3rd Street and a home address of 2nd and South Streets. The following year McElroy's Directory lists Hammitt's occupation as a "pat. car seat & deskmkr," with a new business address one block south, at 259 South 3rd Street, and a new home address across the river at 47 Stephens in Camden, New Jersey. Curiously, the McElroy Directory for 1861 no longer contains Hammitt's name, which could suggest either he relocated outside the Philadelphia area or went out of business. Unfortunately, no contemporary advertisements, or even the long-cited name of his business, Desk Manufactory Company, appear in any business directory consulted.

14 Wolff, Capitol Builder, 524.

15 Wolff, 527.

16 Wolff, 546.

17 Thomas Lanier Clingman served in the House in 1841–45 and 1847–58; he served as a U.S. senator from 1858 to 1861. During the Civil War, he refused to resign his Senate seat and was one of ten senators expelled in absentia from the Senate.

18 Wolff, Capitol Builder, 549.

19 "Historical Highlights: The Opening of the Current House Chamber, December 16, 1857," History, Art & Archives, United States House of Representatives, accessed April 20, 2015, https://history.house.gov/Historical-Highlights/1851-1900/The-opening-of-the-current-House-Chamber/.

20 "Session Dates of Congress, 30th to 39th Congresses (1847–1867)," History, Art & Archives, United States House of Representatives, accessed April 19, 2015, https://history.house.gov/Institution/Session-Dates/30-39/.

21 Wolff, Capitol Builder, 209.

22 "Historical Highlights: The Opening of the Current House Chamber, December 16, 1857."

23 "Production," History, Art & Archives, U.S. House of Representatives, accessed April 20, 2015, https://web.archive.org/web/20150604200002/http://history.house.gov/Exhibitions-and-Publications/Capitol-Furniture/Production/.

24 Wolff, Capitol Builder, 573.

25 "Fine and Decorative Arts at Auction, Cowan's Auctions, Cincinnati, Ohio," Maine Antique Digest, May 2014, 4-B.

26 Alexander Gardner, President Abraham Lincoln, full-length portrait, seated in a "Brady" chair, November 8, 1863, albumen print, Library of Congress Prints and Photographs Division, Washington, D.C., Reproduction Number LC-USZ62-8119, https://www.loc.gov/pictures/item/2009630680/.

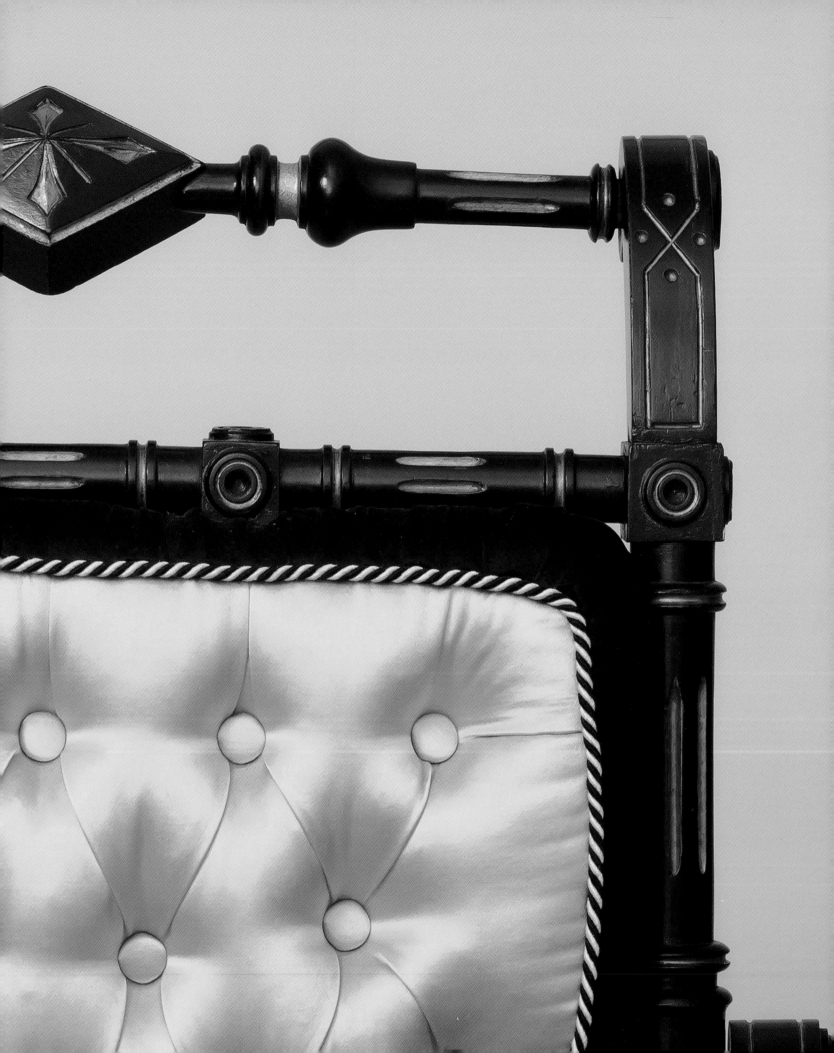

2

A Nation Rebuilds
From Ashes to the
Gilded Age (1865–1900)

The era of national growth and prosperity achieved during the first half of the 19th century was severely disrupted by the Civil War (1861–1865) and compounded by its prolonged, devastating aftereffects. The Reconstruction years following the war, however, gave rise to a second wave of industrialization, allowing for great fortunes to be amassed by a small portion of the populace who were made wealthy through banking, shipping, railroads, and the refining of steel, coal, iron, and oil. These individuals patronized full-service interior decorating and cabinetmaking firms—such as Herter Brothers and Kimbel and Cabus, among others—to finish and furnish their ostentatious "Gilded Age" homes in a number of revival styles.

The Néo-Grèc style, influenced by renewed excavations at Pompeii in 1848, saw the gradual reincorporation of classical motifs (which had been popular in America's earlier years) into furniture design. Likewise, the motifs of ancient Egypt—such as sphinxes—also experienced a revival. However, it was the exoticism of the Orient, made possible by the opening of Japan in the mid-1850s to Americans and Westerners, which had the greatest stylistic influence on European and American fine and decorative arts produced during the late 19th century.

Toward century's end, the emerging Arts and Crafts style—which celebrated handcrafted and unique pieces as opposed to mass-produced objects—began to take hold in America after having gained traction in Great Britain. The coexistence of all these styles made America fertile ground for a rich tapestry of brilliantly conceived and expertly crafted chairs.

Hunzinger Chairs

c. 1870–1876

Designed by George Jacob Hunzinger (1835–1898)

Manufactured by George Hunzinger
(active 1860–1898, New York, New York)

Side Chair with Curule Base, c. 1870
Ebonized cherry, gilding, modern silk upholstery
(original foundation)
33 x 19 x 23 in.
Impressed mark on verso of central diamond in
crest rail: HUNZINGER/N.Y./PAT.MARCH 30/1869

Side Chair, c. 1870
Mahogany, walnut, modern velvet and
woven upholstery
35 ⅛ x 21 ½ x 22 ⅝ in.
Impressed mark on left rear leg: HUNZINGER/N.Y./
PAT.MARCH 30/1869

Side Chair with Wire Seat, c. 1876
Polychromed maple, cotton-covered metal wire
31 ¾ x 19 ½ x 20 ¼ in.
Impressed mark on left rear leg: HUNZINGER/N.Y./
PAT.MARCH 30/1869; PAT.APRIL 18 1876

A SHARED FEATURE of these three chairs—specifically, a diagonal brace extending along their sides—illustrates the genius of a maverick manufacturer who transcended his time by introducing a unique modern design. In contrast to the stoic form and ceremonial ornamentation of the *House of Representatives Chamber Arm Chair* (Cat. No. 10), the designs of George Jacob Hunzinger[1] reference classical antiquity while promoting a modern aesthetic and illustrating the designer's industrial efficiency through his use of interchangeable components.[2]

Born in Tuttlingen, in the Württemberg province of Germany, Hunzinger (Fig. 11.1) hailed from a family with centuries-long ties to the cabinetmaking trade.[3] Nestled near the Swiss border, the Württemberg province was a center for the manufacture of furniture and was also home to Hunzinger's contemporaries (and later rivals), John Henry Belter (Cat. No. 9), Gustav Herter (Cat. No. 13), and Gustav's brother Christian Herter (1839–1883). Hunzinger first apprenticed under his father in Tuttlingen. In 1853 he moved to Geneva, Switzerland, where he worked briefly as a journeyman cabinetmaker. Continued economic and political troubles in the region prompted Hunzinger, like many of his fellow countrymen, to seek a better future in the United States. In 1855, at the age of 20, Hunzinger joined a wave of German craftsmen, including Belter and Herter, and immigrated to New York. Between 1840 and 1860, about 1.5 million Germans arrived in America; so many of them settled in the Lower East Side of New York City that it became known as "Kleindeutschland" (Little Germany).[4]

Little is known about Hunzinger and his cabinetmaking experience after his arrival in New York; however, his obituary states he worked with Auguste Pottier (1823–1896) for a time between 1855 and 1860.[5] Pottier himself had also worked with Gustav Herter and later with William P. Stymus, with whom he formed a long-term partnership in 1859 (Cat. No. 12). By 1860 Hunzinger had married, ventured into business for himself "in a small way in Brooklyn,"[6] and received his first patent, for an "Extension Table."[7]

In 1861, Hunzinger established a larger shop on Centre Street in Lower Manhattan. That same year he applied for and received his second patent for an improved folding and reclining chair with an attached table or writing desk.[8] With it, he laid the foundation for what would become a successful business strategy: designing and producing novel inventions that catered to diverse Victorian tastes and that appealed to consumers across economic levels. He offered his furniture in a variety of contrasting woods and finishes, including staining and gilding, as well as an extensive range of upholstery fabrics. Hunzinger produced multipurpose furniture to accommodate his clientele's insatiable desire for comfortable, lightweight, and adaptable forms, including a variety of tables, chairs, and beds.[9] Whether showcased in the firm's shop, marketed by large city merchants, or advertised in mail-order catalogues, Hunzinger's innovative designs were identified and promoted by an impressed mark that included the designer's name and patent date, attesting to both their quality and authenticity (Figs. 11.2, 11.3, and 11.4).[10] Hunzinger was so prolific and ingenious a designer and manufacturer that he secured 21 patents during the course of his career.

The DeMell Jacobsen Collection includes three chairs by Hunzinger, all of which possess his most innovative and distinctive design: the diagonal side brace (Fig. 11.5). On March 30, 1869, Hunzinger

Fig. 11.1 Unidentified artist, *Portrait of George Hunzinger*, 1880, oil on canvas, location unknown.

Fig. 11.2 (top left) Detail of impressed mark on verso of central diamond in crest rail of *Side Chair with Curule Base*.

Fig. 11.3 (bottom left) Detail of impressed mark on left rear leg of *Side Chair*.

Fig. 11.4 (right) Detail of impressed mark on left rear leg of *Side Chair with Wire Seat*.

received a patent for his "Improved Chair," seeking to remedy the looseness that "arises from pressure against the back of the chair, and from tipping the chair backward upon the hind legs."[11] In the patent application, Hunzinger described how the brace would extend diagonally along each side from the upper part of the chair to the lower part of the front legs, connected near the middle with the side of the seat or the seat frame. "By this construction," Hunzinger

continued, "the back of the chair is braced to the sides of the seat, and the front legs are similarly sustained, so that one part aids in sustaining the other under the strain to which it may be exposed."[12] The structural improvements resulted in a cantilevered seat, which continued to be an architectural and industrial design convention well into the 20th century, as evidenced in George Nakashima's *Conoid Chair* (Cat. No. 39). In the patent application, Hunzinger revealed the alignment of his artistic tastes with his efficient business strategy: "the legs and braces can all be turned in a more or less ornamental form, or the parts may be plain or carved. I prefer the turned work, as being ornamental, but not expensive."[13]

Like many 19th-century neoclassical styles based on historical precedents,

the *Side Chair with Curule Base* evokes elements of classical Greece and Rome—the term *curule* is a reference to the curved undercarriage of a Roman folding chair—reimagined in the Néo-Grèc style, which was influenced by the excursions of Napoleon Bonaparte. The ancient *sella curulis*, a stool-shaped seat supported by crossed legs, was reserved for political authorities. With its lightweight, exuberant design, the *Side Chair with Curule Base* is well suited for a domestic Victorian interior, unlike the robust forms of the *Grecian Settee* (Cat. No. 1) or the *House of Representatives Chamber Arm Chair* (Cat. No. 10). The back stiles sweep under the seat in scrolling arcs suggestive of the curule form and provide support in the absence of traditional front post legs. The precise geometric shapes—spheres,

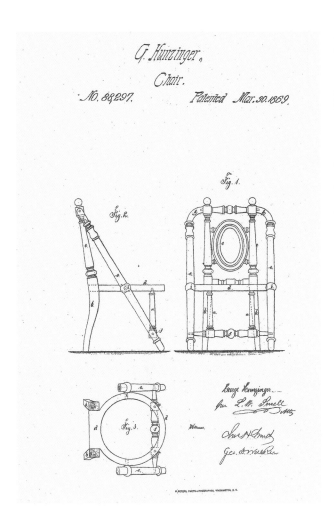

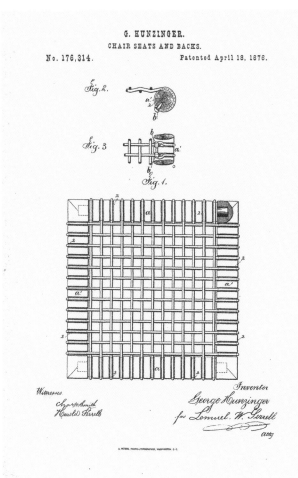

Fig. 11.5 (far left)
George Hunzinger, "Improved Chair," U.S. Patent No. 88,297, issued March 30, 1869, U.S. Patent Office.

Fig. 11.6 (left)
George Hunzinger, "Improvement in Chair Seats and Backs." U.S. Patent No. 176,314, filed January 24, 1876, issued April 18, 1876, U.S. Patent Office.

cones, squares, and diamonds—of the lathe-turned cherry elements are ebonized and highlighted with gilding in the German style (Fig. 11.7). Complementary gold-tufted silk, encased in a ruched black silk border with color-coordinated trim, covers the original foundations.[14]

Less imitative of any historical style, the *Side Chair* evokes Hunzinger's transition toward a modern aesthetic. Hunzinger incorporated exuberant ornamentations that were directly inspired by their mechanized form of production—nuts, bolts, tool posts, levers, ball handles, cone pulleys, and carriage wheels. The simple rings, bosses (raised and applied decorative disks), and geometric shapes that appear sparingly on the legs, stretchers, and back stiles also suggest their lathe-turned source. Meanwhile, an ornate crest rail, crowned with a stylized wheel or gear surrounded by ebonized bosses and acorn finials, demonstrates Hunzinger's progressive and deeply imaginative talents. Further, the mahogany

and walnut woods are strategically heightened with ebonized stain and convey Hunzinger's versatility in providing furniture for a variety of consumers.[15]

In stark contrast to both the *Side Chair with Curule Base* and the *Side Chair*, Hunzinger's third chair represented in the DeMell Jacobsen Collection, *Side Chair with Wire Seat*, is so modern in its appearance for a Victorian piece of furniture that it seems to be an anachronism. Produced around the time of the Centennial celebration, the chair's minimalist and abstract design is devoid of any clear historical precedents. The angular, lathe-turned maple frame is comprised of ring-turned rods with green-painted grooves. Enlarged knobs and bosses at the joints add geometric ornamentation, together with whimsically curved conical finials centered in the seat back (Fig. 11.8).

The innovative network of cotton-and-wool-covered copper wire for the seat bottom illustrates Hunzinger's sixth patent, for an "Improvement in Chair Seats and Backs," which he filed on January 24, 1876,

and received on April 18, 1876 (Fig. 11.6).[16] The improvement refers to Hunzinger's use of "wire in place of cane, to form an open-work seat, and to insure great strength and beauty, and to facilitate the interweaving of the wires."[17]

The first chairs to use the wire seat and back frame of the 1876 patent also featured the diagonal brace patented in 1869. A contemporary publication, *Kimball's Book of Designs: Furniture and Drapery* (1876), illustrates several examples of these chairs, including two variations of a "Dining or Library Chair," which wholesaled for $10.67 each and were available in walnut "with any color, braided wire seat and back";[18] a rocking chair was wholesaled for $8.00 and offered the same options.[19] Similarly, an advertisement from about 1879 that appeared in the *Asher & Adams Commercial Atlas* illustrates three other forms—including one with a curule base—and praised the chairs as being "as strong as they are beautiful, and as comfortable to sit in as they are graceful in appearance.

Fig. 11.7 Detail of top rail of *Side Chair with Curule Base.*

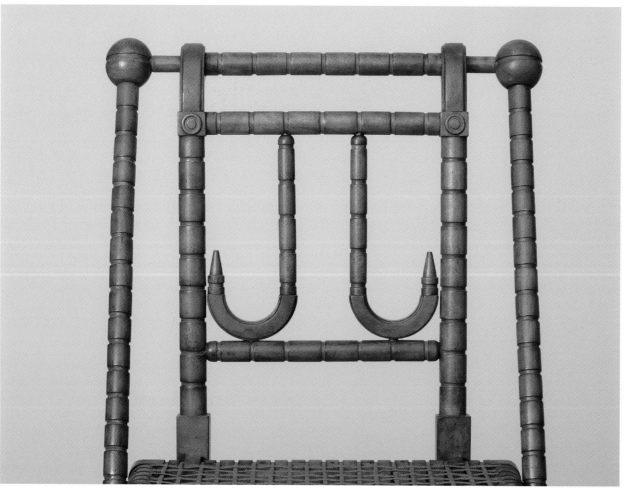

Fig. 11.8 Detail of seat back of *Side Chair with Wire Seat.*

The chairs ... with woven or webbed seats and backs present at a first glance ... an appearance nearly resembling a cane bottom chair, but, in fact, the seat and back is composed of finely tempered flat steel ribbons or springs, handsomely covered with a durable web of silk or worsted, not sewed, but woven around the steel. Nothing could be more durable, and by no other arrangement could springs more nicely adapt themselves to the forms that press against them. It is in this faculty of moulding itself to the form that the comfort of a cushion consists, no matter of what it may be composed."[20]

Through their use of innovative materials and interchangeable components, these three chairs blend traditional historical motifs with modernity and illustrate the artistic imagination, technical acumen, and marketing prowess of one of America's foremost 19th-century designers and businessmen. While not readily embraced by many of his contemporaries, who continued to produce furnishings in historic styles, Hunzinger's vanguard aesthetic undoubtedly influenced countless subsequent designers, including Warren McArthur (Cat. No. 27) and Kenneth Smythe (Cat. No. 45).

1   The marriage certificate between Hunzinger and Marie Susanne Grieb (d. 1908), dated December 25, 1859, documents the spelling of his name as "Georg Jakob Hunzinger." It is not known whether Hunzinger legally changed his name; however, his first patent, dated December 4, 1860, lists his name as "George Hunzinger." He became a United States citizen on October 16, 1865.
2   Special thanks to Andrew VanStyn for his research and expertise. His contributions helped shape this essay.
3   The most thorough examination of Hunzinger and his output is Barry R. Harwood's *The Furniture of George Hunzinger: Invention and Innovation in Nineteenth-Century America* (Brooklyn: Brooklyn Museum of Art, 1997), a publication accompanying an exhibition of the same name held at the Brooklyn Museum of Art, November 20, 1997–February 15, 1998. See also Barry R. Harwood, "The Furniture of George Jacob Hunzinger," *The Magazine ANTIQUES* 152, no. 6 (December, 1997): 832–41; Barry R. Harwood, "The Furniture of George Hunzinger: Afterthoughts on the Exhibition and Catalogue," *Studies in the Decorative Arts* 6, no. 2 (Spring–Summer 1999): 95–106; Catherine Bindman, review, "The Furniture of George Hunzinger: Invention and Innovation in Nineteenth-Century America by Barry R. Harwood," *Studies in the Decorative Arts* 6, no. 1 (Fall–Winter 1998–99): 119–22; and Milo M. Naeve, review, "The Furniture of George Hunzinger: Invention and Innovation in Nineteenth-Century America," *American Furniture* (1998): 239–42.
4   Harwood, *Furniture of George Hunzinger*, 25.
5   Harwood, 26.
6   Harwood, 27.
7   George Hunzinger, "Extension Table," U.S. Patent No. 30,823, issued December 4, 1860, U.S. Patent Office.
8   George Hunzinger, "Folding Chair," U.S. Patent No. 33,392, issued October 1, 1861, U.S. Patent Office.
9   See especially Jennifer Pynt and Joy Higgs, "Nineteenth-Century Patent Seating: Too Comfortable to be Moral?" *Journal of Design History* 21, no. 3 (Autumn, 2008): 277–88; and Clive D. Edwards, "Reclining Chairs Surveyed: Health, Comfort, and Fashion in Evolving Markets," *Studies in the Decorative Arts* 6, no. 1 (Fall–Winter 1998–99): 32–67.
10 Despite being patented, Hunzinger's designs were not immune to being copied or adapted by others. In a letter to his son, George Hunzinger wrote that William Angus, a British importer, "has immitated [*sic*] our rockers from those sent to him improving the lines and is now making new patterns"; quoted in Clive D. Edwards, "British Imports of American Furniture in the Later Nineteenth Century," *Furniture History* 31 (1995): 210–16.
11 George Hunzinger, "Improved Chair," U.S. Patent No. 88,297, issued March 30, 1869, U.S. Patent Office.
12 Hunzinger, "Improved Chair."
13 Hunzinger, "Improved Chair."
14 A chair of similar form and date that retains its original gold tufted upholstery is in the collection of the Brooklyn Museum of Art (1996.80.2) and guided the reupholstering scheme of this example.
15 A chair of identical form possessing its original velvet upholstery with decorative cord, formerly at Chadwick Villa, Newburgh, New York, and now in the collection of the Hudson River Museum of Westchester, Yonkers, New York (85.9.3), guided the reupholstering scheme.
16 Originally, steel wire rather than copper was used for the seat.
17 George Hunzinger, "Improvement in Chair Seats and Backs," U.S. Patent No. 176,314, filed January 24, 1876, issued April 18, 1876, U.S. Patent Office.
18 J. Wayland Kimball, *Kimball's Book of Designs: Furniture and Drapery* (Boston, 1876), illustrated in Harwood, *Furniture of George Hunzinger*, 92, figs. 98–99.
19 Illustrated in Harwood, 92.
20 Illustrated in Harwood, 50.

Egyptian Revival Side Chair

12

c. 1875

Design and manufacture attributed to Pottier & Stymus Manufacturing Company; later Pottier & Stymus Company (active 1859–1918, New York, New York)

Ebonized cherry, reproduction silk upholstery, brass casters

30 ¼ x 21 ½ x 22 in.

THIS EBONIZED cherry chair is fused with an unusual, complete composition of Egyptian elements. Despite a shifting perspective toward innovation and technology during the latter half of the 19th century, a sustained interest in the symbolism of historical styles and traditional craftsmanship continued. Pottier and Stymus Manufacturing Company,[1] a New York firm specializing in cabinetry and decorative interiors, revived a sentimentality for the ancient Egyptian civilization by featuring key symbols.

Europeans had been intrigued by Egypt almost immediately following Napoleon's French campaign to Egypt and Syria between 1798 and 1801. Subsequently, archaeological excavations conducted by Jean-Louis Burckhardt[2] in 1813 and Giovanni Belzoni in 1817 unearthed the ancient temples at Abu Simbel. Additional scientific research, documented in the multivolume *Description de l'Égypte* (1809–22), further promoted awareness of the area, as did Jean-François Champollion's breakthrough decipherment of hieroglyphs on the Rosetta Stone in 1822. During the latter half of the 19th century, the opening of the Suez Canal in 1869 and the performance of Verdi's opera *Aida* at the inauguration of Cairo's Khedivial (Royal) Opera House in 1871 captured global attention. For Americans, though, Egypt's participation in the 1876 Centennial Exhibition in Philadelphia brought the exoticism of the North African country directly to a domestic audience (Fig. 12.1).

Throughout the first half of the 19th century, promoters of the Egyptian style included French designers Charles Percier (1764–1838) and Pierre-François-Léonard Fontaine (1762–1853) through their *Recueil de décorations intérieures* (1812), as well as their British contemporaries Thomas Sheraton (1751–1806) and Thomas Hope (1769–1831),[3] who published *The Cabinet Dictionary* (1803) and *Household Furniture and Interior Decoration* (1807), respectively. In the early 1800s, the Egyptian Revival style was incorporated into English and American architecture but did not significantly influence furniture and interior design until the age of revivalist styles in the 1860s–70s.[4]

In the *Egyptian Revival Side Chair*, a large, low-relief, carved winged sphinx profile in the back splat offers a fascinating center of visual interest. The iconic creature, perhaps adapted from a design by Thomas Hope (Fig. 12.2), is set off by a rayed lunette, or half-moon, and tri-part lotus buds in each pendentive void.[5] All are set below a winged globe with a central star surrounded by smaller stars. Dual birds, an artistic reference to the twin Uraeus, represent the Egyptian deities Isis and her son Horus. The crest rail is composed of bound reeds or fasces—a motif representing power that originated with the Etruscans and was transported to Egypt by the Romans—and is perhaps derived from the colonnade of reeded columns in the hypostyle hall at the Temple of Luxor at Thebes (Fig. 12.3). Of the motif, British designer Thomas Sheraton stated, "reeding, amongst cabinetmakers is a mode by which they ornament table legs, bed pillars, &c. and is certainly one of the most substantial of any yet adopted. It is much preferable to fluting or cabling in point of strength; and in look much superior."[6]

Low-relief pseudo-hieroglyphic carvings adorn the rear stiles and front seat rail.

Completing the composition, the front legs are fashioned as Egyptian columns with lotus-petal capitals and terminate in metal casters (Fig. 12.4). Original upholstery foundations, including coil springs and horsehair, are covered with a modern Scalamandré striped liseré fabric.[7] A number of armchairs related to the example in the DeMell Jacobsen Collection—the first chair to enter the collection—are known and may be found in the collections of the Philadelphia Museum of Art; the High Museum of Art; the Museum of Art, Rhode Island School of Design; and one formerly in the collection of Eugene Canton.[8] Combining traditional hand-carved woods and innovative technological comfort devices, such as the steel coil springs patented in 1857,[9] the artistic designs of Pottier and Stymus were coveted by consumers of their day.

Auguste Pottier (1823–1896) emigrated from his native France to America in 1847.[10] While in France, he was apprenticed to a wood sculptor, which served him well in his later career. Once in America, he first worked for E. W. Hutchings and Son, where he trained George Hunzinger (Cat. No. 11) before forming a brief partnership with Gustav Herter (1830–1898, Cat. No. 13), who would become a future rival. In 1856, Pottier became general foreman of the Rochefort and Skarren cabinetmaking firm in New York City, where he probably met William P. Stymus, who was its upholstery foreman. Upon the death of Rochefort in 1859, Pottier joined forces with Stymus and formed the Pottier and Stymus Manufacturing Company (Fig. 12.5). Ernest Hagen (1830–1913), a cabinetmaker who

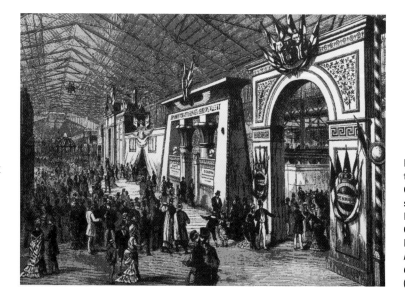

Fig. 12.1 View inside the main building of the Centennial Exhibition, showing the Spanish, Egyptian, and Danish Courts, from James D. McCabe, *The Illustrated History of the Centennial Exhibition* (1876).

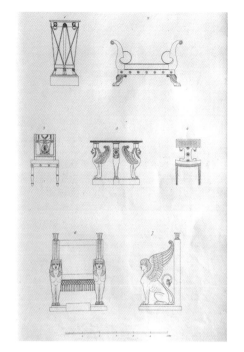

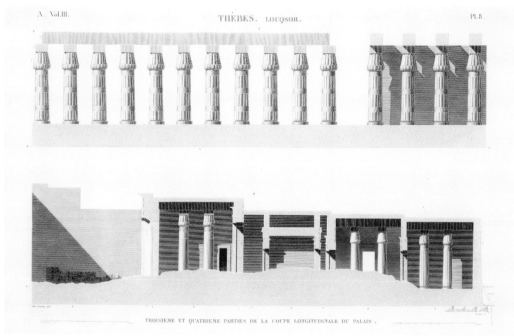

Fig. 12.2 (above left) Furniture designs, including winged sphinx, from Thomas Hope, *Household Furniture and Interior Decoration* (1807).

Fig. 12.3 (above right) Colonnade of bound reeded columns at the Temple of Luxor at Thebes, Egypt, from *Description de L'Égypte* (1809–22).

had worked in New York, recalled that the Rochefort and Skarren firm "turned out good work; and after Mr. Rochfort's [*sic*] death, his 2 foremen, Portier [*sic*] and Stymas [*sic*], continued the business."[11] The Pottier and Stymus Manufacturing Company lasted until 1888, dissolved, and reformed under new directors as a cooperative, the Pottier and Stymus Company.

In January 1884, the *New York Times* reported that the Pottier and Stymus Manufacturing Company had completed and moved into "an elegant and new structure on Fifth-Avenue" with a façade "of the most beautiful and chaste design."[12] By then, the firm had built a successful business known for its technical precision, attention to detail, and careful documentation, all of which resulted in the manufacture of top-quality furniture and designs. The new showrooms were filled with "the most sumptuous furniture and fabrics, arranged so as to present to the eye successively on each floor examples of all the different styles of art and decoration. Portions are set apart so as to show modes of furnishing rooms and suites according to all the different fashions

of epochs and ages, such as are at present imitated and reproduced."[13]

In an effort to appeal to a wide range of consumers, Pottier and Stymus produced furniture in a variety of revival styles, including modern Gothic, Renaissance, Néo-Grèc, and Egyptian.[14] For both parlor and chamber furniture, the firm used rosewood and black walnut but by far made "more mahogany furniture than of any other kind of wood."[15] While numerous extant labeled examples of their furniture certainly possess carving—usually incised lines heightened by gilding—for their more elaborate designs Moses Ingersoll, the firm's treasurer, attested that they used "brass ornaments ... almost exclusively."[16] *The Golden Book of Celebrated Manufacturers and Merchants in the United States*, published in 1875 as a report of the Centennial Exhibition in Philadelphia, noted that the firm meticulously detailed the

history of each article ... from its first entrance to the building through its various stages in the different departments ... Each piece, from the cheapest to the most expensive, is numbered in the beginning, and retains the same number till it comes forth in one of the numerous elegant productions. To the uninitiated this plan seems perfectly simple, but upon examination it develops a most ingenious combination,

particularly in view of the details of perfect fabrication, which is the prime objective of this establishment.[17]

Since Pottier and Stymus possessed a number of departments, each of which used a different technique, the numbering system "serve[d] as a complete check," and ensured "perfect order ... reigns throughout."[18] Further, the system facilitated efficiency among the woodworkers and decorators and increased quality control. As yet another measure to ensure a quality product, the firm carefully dried its stock lumber in a special brick chamber that was heated to over 120°F, which reduced the likelihood of it splitting or warping the finished furniture.[19]

Pottier and Stymus's efforts were lauded in *King's Handbook of New York City*, which proclaimed that the firm possessed a "world-wide reputation for the superior grades of furniture and wood-work which they manufacture, as well as for their artistic conceptions in interior decorations and papier-mâché work."[20] By the time the *Egyptian Revival Side Chair* was produced, the Pottier and Stymus factory operated out of a six-story building at 375 Lexington Avenue that extended about half a city block between 41st and 42nd Streets. In it, they employed more than 700 male and 50 female employees and had more than $1 million in sales.[21]

During its more than half a decade in operation, the firm received a number

of important commissions, both public and private. In 1863, they designed and furnished a suite of offices for the secretary of the Treasury in Washington, D.C. The commission elevated the firm's stature and helped promote a national identity through Renaissance Revival–style furniture replete with ornamentation representative of a Republican democracy. Following the Treasury commission, the firm designed and manufactured an eight-person table for President Andrew Johnson (1808–1875), but it was not delivered until after he left office. The table was used in the White House Cabinet Room by President Ulysses S. Grant (1822–1885) at the beginning of his first term, and the firm further supplied a sofa, eight chairs, window cornices, and an overmantel for the room. The table is perhaps the most historic piece of furniture made by the firm, having been used to sign the Peace Treaty ending the Spanish-American War in 1898.[22] Notable private commissions include such Gilded Age clients as William Rockefeller, Leland Stanford,[23] William H. Vanderbilt, Henry Lippitt,[24] Henry Morrison Flagler, Thomas Edison, John Flood, and Frederick Steinway. In addition, the firm outfitted a number of hotels in New York City, including the Fifth Avenue, the Savoy, the Plaza, and the Waldorf, as well as two in Florida, the Hotel Ponce de León in St. Augustine (now Flagler College)[25] and the Royal Poinciana Hotel in Lake Worth.[26]

1   The Pottier and Stymus Manufacturing Company operated until 1888, dissolved, and reformed under new directors as a cooperative, the Pottier and Stymus Company. For a history of the firm, see Kristin S. Herron, "The Modern Gothic Furniture of Pottier and Stymus," *The Magazine ANTIQUES* 155, no. 5 (May 1999): 762–79; and Elizabeth Chantale Varner, "Bolstering a National Identity: President Andrew Johnson's Pottier & Stymus Furniture in the United States Treasury Department, 1865" (master's thesis, Smithsonian Associates and Corcoran College of Art and Design, 2008), 12–15.

2   Johann Ludwig Burckhardt (1784–1817), also known as Jean-Louis Burckhardt, was a Swiss geographer and traveler who was the first European to encounter the ruins of Petra in Jordan while traveling through the area in 1812.

3   Not to be overlooked, the 1802 publication of *Voyage dans la Basse et la Haute Égypte* by Dominique Vivant Denon (1747–1825) was also a major influence, specifically on the designs of Thomas Hope. See David St. Leger Kelly, "The Egyptian Revival: A Reassessment of Baron Denon's Influence on Thomas Hope," *Furniture History* 40 (2004): 83–98.

4   For a study of the Egyptian influence on early-19th-century American furniture, see Donald L. Fennimore, "Egyptian Influence in Early Nineteenth-Century American Furniture," *The Magazine ANTIQUES* 137, no. 5 (May 1990): 1190–1201.

5   Many thanks to Andrew VanStyn for his efforts on this chair, including researching and writing historically accurate descriptions, locating the appropriate fabric, and overseeing the reupholstery of the seat cover.

6   Thomas Sheraton, *The Cabinet Dictionary, Containing an Explanation of All the Terms Used in the Cabinet, Chair & Upholstery Branches* (London: W. Smith, 1803), 296. Note: &c. is an 18th- and 19th-century abbreviation for "et cetera."

7   Liseré is a type of fabric constructed with a supplemental warp to create color and detail—typically stripes—on the face. The reproduction fabric is based on a documented Néo-Grèc example in the collection of the Smithsonian Institution, National Museum of American History.

8   In addition to the armchairs, at least four side chairs are known: a pair in the collection of the Museum of Fine Arts, Boston (2010.233.1–2); the DeMell Jacobsen Collection example; and a side chair formerly in the collection of Lee B. Anderson, sold at Sotheby's, January 25, 2013, Sale N08950, lot 483. See also Christopher Monkhouse and Thomas S. Michie, *American Furniture at Pendleton House* (Providence: Museum of Art, Rhode Island School of Design, 1986), 193–94.

9   For more information on steel coil springs, see Mary Bellis, "Biography of Robert Hooke," ThoughtCo, August 19, 2019, https://www.thoughtco.com/spring-coils-physics-and-workings-4075522.

10 For biographical information about Pottier, see *The National Cyclopaedia of American Biography* 6 (New York: James T. White & Company, 1896), 297.

11 Ernest Hagen, quoted in Elizabeth A. Ingerman, "Personal Experiences of an Old New York Cabinetmaker," *The Magazine ANTIQUES* 84, no. 5, (November 1963): 579–80.

12 "The Fifth-Avenue Palace of Art," *New York Times*, January 26, 1884, 5.

13 "The Fifth-Avenue Palace of Art."

14 In his journal, Ernest Hagen recalled that Pottier and Stymus "were very successful and done good work, mostly walnut which was now the dominant material. But their work was nearly all done in the 'Neo Grec' most awful gaudy style with brass gilt Spinx [Sphinx] head on the sofas and arm chairs, gilt engraved lines all over with porcailaine [porcelain] painted medallions on the backs, and brass gilt bead moldings nailed on. Other wise their work was good; but the style horrible." Quoted in Ingerman, "Personal Experiences," 579–80.

15 "Opinions of Representative Manufacturers and Dealers," *Decorator and Furnisher* 1, no. 3 (December 1882): 94–95.

16 "Opinions of Representative Manufacturers and Dealers."

17 Quoted in Herron, "The Modern Gothic Furniture of Pottier and Stymus," 765–66. Herron also discusses the various numbering schemes used by the firm, including stencil-painted, impressed, and inscribed.

18 Varner, "Bolstering a National Identity," 14.

19 Varner, 14.

20 *King's Handbook of New York City: An Outline History and Description of the American Metropolis* (Boston: Moses King, 1893), 854.

21 Varner, "Bolstering a National Identity," 13.

22 "Treasures of the White House: Cabinet Room Conference Table," White House Historical Association, accessed January 6, 2022, https://www.whitehousehistory.org/photos/treasures-of-the-white-house-cabinet-room-conference-table.

23 Diana Strazdes, "The Millionaire's Palace: Leland Stanford's Commission for Pottier & Stymus in San Francisco," *Winterthur Portfolio* 36, no. 4 (Winter, 2001): 213–43; and Diana Strazdes, "Style, Symbols, and Persuasion: Leland Stanford's Sacramento Ball of 1872," *Studies in the Decorative Arts* 15, no. 2 (Spring–Summer 2008): 65–95.

24 "The Henry Lippitt House of Providence, Rhode Island," *Winterthur Portfolio* 17, no. 4 (Winter 1982): 203–42.

25 Thomas Graham, "Henry M. Flagler's Hotel Ponce de Leon," *Journal of Decorative and Propaganda Arts* 23 (1998), 96–111; Leslee F. Keys, "Preserving the Legacy: The Hotel Ponce de León and Flagler College" (Ph.D. diss., University of Florida, 2013).

26 "Pottier & Stymus Co.," in *King's Photographic Views of New York*, (Boston: Moses King, 1895), 618.

Side Chair

13

c. 1880

Designed by Christian Herter (1839–1883)

Manufactured by Herter Brothers (active 1864–1906, New York, New York)

Ebonized cherry, gilding, silk lampas upholstery (original foundation)

34 x 17 ½ x 19 ½ in.

THIS GILDED AGE *Side Chair* incorporates a variety of artistic styles drawn from Romanesque, Anglo-Japanese, and Reform Gothic. Crafted by the nationally acclaimed firm Herter Brothers, a respected competitor of Pottier and Stymus (Cat. No. 12), the chair embodies the firm's talent for producing quality furniture and interior schemes in a variety of fashionable styles. During the late 19th century, decorative firms began providing complete interior design resources. To aid clients in purchasing beautiful objects and thematic schemes to reflect their status, firms provided a full array of services, including woodwork panels, curtains and upholstery, ornamental decorations, and either singular examples or full suites of furniture for any interior.

For their elaborate chair commissions, such as the example in the DeMell Jacobsen Collection, Herter Brothers utilized a basic rectangular frame design, which could be modified based on the client's stylistic preferences. Made of carved and ebonized cherry, heightened through gilding, the seat back features a colonnade of Moorish or Romanesque-style arches surmounted by a tablet crest carved with an elaborate Asian-inspired plant motif (Fig. 13.2). Additional details characteristic of the firm's designs include the turned cuffs above the tapered, elongated front feet. The reproduction silk lampas upholstery covers the original foundations and is based on a sample from a contemporaneous Herter sofa. Its pattern mirrors the foliage carved on the crest. Coordinating spool *passementerie* on the front seat apron accentuates the chair and illustrates a key tenet of the Aesthetic Movement: a multicultural yet fully integrated design scheme.[1]

By the mid-19th century, as the epicenter of cabinetmaking and furniture shifted from the Mid-Atlantic region to New York City, America once again benefitted from European traditions and craftsmanship brought by immigrants. The partnership of Herter Brothers (active 1864–1906), led by Gustav Herter (1830–1898) and his half-brother Christian Herter, ascended the national stage as prominent arbiters of taste.

Gustav Herter was the son of a master cabinetmaker from Württemberg, Germany, and immigrated to America at the age of 18. Like John Henry Belter (Cat. No. 9) and George Jacob Hunzinger (Cat. No. 11), Gustav settled in the Kleindeutschland (Little Germany) area of New York City, where it is believed his first employer was Tiffany and Company. That firm likely exposed him to the Aesthetic Movement's integration and embrace of diverse artistic mediums. Herter then partnered briefly with Auguste Pottier, who would become a rival, followed by a four-year venture with Erastus Bulkley. With Bulkley, Herter acquired connecting lots at 92 Mercer and 547 Broadway, near those of Tiffany

Fig.13.1 Red Room, White House, Washington, D.C., c. 1870–1900.

Fig. 13.2 Detail
of seat back.

and Company and John Henry Belter. In 1858, Gustav retained the properties for his eponymous business, filled with 100 employees who used their superb carving skills to turn its large inventory of wood into profitable furniture.[2]

Christian Herter arrived in New York in 1859. He likely followed Gustav's path by first working with Tiffany and Company. In 1864, Gustav and Christian formally combined their talents under the name Herter Brothers and opened a shop on Broadway. Under Christian's influence, the firm's designs evolved to incorporate unique patterns based on a blend of European and avant-garde sources. Following the duo's relocation to the Hoyt Building on the fashionable "Ladies' Mile" at 877 and 879 Broadway in 1869, Gustav ceded leadership the following year to Christian, who propelled the company to continued acclaim.

Reinterpreting and mixing prevalent styles such as Renaissance Revival, Néo-Grèc, and Anglo-Japanese into "a fresh and distinctly American cultural language,"[3] Christian led Herter Brothers to become one of the most successful examples of an early interior design and decoration firm setting a new standard. The consummate Renaissance man, Christian spoke German, French, and English, and was well read, intellectual, artistic, handsome, polished, elegant, and charming.[4] These qualities impressed newly affluent and influential New York clients. Christian returned from journeys to France and England in the late 1860s and early 1870s with visions of designs influenced by Eastern cultures as well as British fashion and furniture designed by E. W. Godwin (Cat. No. 17).

The firm's distinctive Anglo-Japanese-style furniture featured straight-lined ebonized woods highlighted with marquetry, along with low-relief carvings and incising heightened with gilding. French and German personnel trained in artistic marquetry empowered Herter Brothers with a coveted technique and signature style of contrasting dark and bright tones. Herter Brothers not only created furniture, they also offered advice on and production of architectural woodworking such as wall paneling and floors, curtains, decorative painting, ceiling plastering, and lighting.[5]

Herter Brothers' cosmopolitan reputation spread through personal recommendations from elite captains of industry. President Ulysses S. Grant (1822–1885) and First Lady Julia Boggs Dent Grant (1826–1902) redecorated the White House staterooms prior to the marriage of their only daughter, Nellie (1855–1922) in 1874. This chair is a variation of the Japanesque-style furnishings in the Red Room with a similar side rail composed of three centered circles and an alternative geometric scheme in the seat-back arches (Fig. 13.1).[6]

Clients from coast to coast, fortified by industrial and rail fortunes, engaged the Herter Brothers' services. Perhaps promotion by word of mouth was facilitated by the speed of the railways, telegraph, and telephone. Furniture embellished with intricate carvings and gilding, including the firm's signature Anglo-Japanese ebonized pieces, adorned urban mansions. In New York City, patrons included Cornelius Vanderbilt II, Jay Gould (c. 1882), Darius Ogden Mills (1880), J. Pierpont Morgan (1880–95), Mrs. Robert Leighton Stuart (1881), and the Eldridge Street Synagogue, for whom the firm completed an interior project. In Connecticut, the firm decorated LeGrand Lockwood's Elm Park (1868–70) and The Woodlands for Major James Goodwin, J. P. Morgan's cousin. Milton Latham's Thurlow Lodge, located in Menlo Park, California, was furnished in 1874.[7]

Christian Herter's most prominent project was the interior and exterior commission for William H. Vanderbilt (1821–1885) between 1879 and 1881. The Beaux-Arts home, encompassing the block on Fifth Avenue between 51st and 52nd streets, was constructed at the cost of approximately $1.75 million. With attention to detail, Christian Herter integrated eclectic styles and extravagant materials to reflect the social and economic status of America's self-proclaimed richest man.[8] At the grand opening party on January 17, 1882, the harmonious interiors sparkled under gaslight. The following year the power source moved to electricity, and Mrs. Cornelius Vanderbilt II (1845–1934) celebrated the Vanderbilt Ball dressed in an "Electric Light" creation by the Parisian *haute couture* fashion house Maison Worth. That same year Christian Herter sadly passed away at age 44. The Herter Brothers firm continued producing furniture and providing interior design services until 1906.

1 Special thanks to Andrew VanStyn for his research and expertise. His contributions helped shape this essay.
2 Katherine S. Howe, Alice Cooney Frelinghuysen, and Catherine Hoover Voorsanger, *Herter Brothers: Furniture and Interiors for a Gilded Age* (New York: Harry N. Abrams, 1994), 226–27.
3 Howe, Frelinghuysen, and Voorsanger, 78.
4 Howe, Frelinghuysen, and Voorsanger, 44–45.

5 Howe, Frelinghuysen, and Voorsanger, 79–80.
6 This room is identified as the Red Room in Howe, Frelinghuysen, and Voorsanger, 52; however, it is identified as "Bedroom in the President's house" in the Library of Congress Prints and Photographs Online Catalog: https://www.loc.gov/pictures/item/2017651233/.

7 Dates listed represent the time period of the patronage.
8 Alice Cooney Frelinghuysen, "Christian Herter's Decoration of the William H. Vanderbilt House in New York City," *The Magazine* ANTIQUES, 147, no. 3 (March 1995), 414–15.

Side Chair

c. 1880

Designed and manufactured by Frederick Krutina (1825–1900) (active 1862–1883, New York, New York)

Ebonized cherry, silk and velvet *gauffrage* upholstery

38 ½ x 21 x 19 ½ in.

A NEW YORK TIMES reporter observed: "The name of F. Krutina as a manufacturer of furniture is tolerably well known in this City, but people who have not previously visited his extensive ware-rooms, Nos. 96 and 98 East Houston-street, may not be aware of the class of goods in which he deals … A magnificent display of the most elegant and artistic styles of furniture, all of the newest patterns, will meet the eye of the visitor … In the style of Queen Anne, Eastlake, and Japanese, he displays suits [*sic*] of no less than 150 patterns."[1]

Certainly, when writing of the "most elegant and artistic styles of furniture," the reporter could have been referencing this exotic-looking *Side Chair*. With its tall pierced back, the chair is an American synthesis of multiple English design sources that utilize natural motifs. By the last quarter of the 19th century, the decorative arts in America were infused with a plethora of styles, which was a result of increased global trade and the diffusion of visual motifs through books, posters, and other written materials. Generally referred to as the Aesthetic Movement, the style was a reaction to the strict mores and social reform tenets of Victorian art, which drew on many design sources. Its principal influences, however, were the fluid, naturally inspired motifs of Japanese art and the rigid, geometric designs of medieval art. Few furniture manufacturers embraced the Aesthetic Movement more than Frederick Krutina.[2]

Furniture of the Aesthetic Movement often was ebonized—either painted or lacquered with a dark paint or stain—in imitation of true ebony, since that wood was expensive and difficult to carve. Cherry was much more cost efficient, easier to carve, and provided a sophisticated appearance when ebonized. On the second floor of his factory, Krutina displayed his parlor suites, which included "chairs, easy and corner chairs, of various woods and upholstered with raw silk, the new kind of tapestry, wrought in a variety of designs and colors."[3] The display also featured a "centre-table of imitation ebony," which had "a border of marqueterie work, and in its center inlaid with ivory, a copy of an antique painting."[4] Another advertisement noted, "among novelties in furniture introduced by Mr. F. Krutina … may be mentioned square-finished, ebonized, and gilt rings, made to run on ebony, mahogany, and brass curtain and portière rods … Some ebonized wood cabinet etagères, with embossed plush panels, made by the same house, are very effective for a moderate-priced article."[5]

When designing this example, Krutina may have been inspired by those of British botanist-turned-industrial-designer and preeminent Aesthetic Movement figure Dr. Christopher Dresser,[6] whose patterns reflected "the simple, flat, geometrized ornament."[7] This chair exemplifies Dresser's Anglo-Japanese style with its shallow geometric carvings. Creating a sharp contrast of positive and negative space, rectilinear grids are centered with lace-like reticulated panels. Stylized flowers, perhaps chrysanthemums, as well as leaves and other foliage provides a central, elongated back splat framed at the top and bottom by running reliefs. This motif extends to the front seat apron, which features a fourth flower centered within an arched panel. Krutina's floral patterning recalls Japanese *mon*, emblems used to identify an individual or family and often appearing on textiles or furnishings.

In contrast to the British Arts and Crafts Movement, which considered increased industrialization as a reason to look back to medieval forms of handcraftsmanship, the Aesthetic Movement embraced the machine and its ability to produce innovative forms and designs. The tremendously detailed openwork carving in this chair relied upon the innovative jig-saw technology patented by John Henry Belter in 1847 (Cat. No. 9). A pair of open trefoil-arched windows, which appear to be inspired by Moorish or Indian sources rather than Japanese, flank the reticulated back splat. Standing above and centering the crest rail, a rectangular open space mirrors the overall form and serves as either a functional headrest or a convenient handle by which to move the chair. Such devices are documented among the work of the Herter Brothers (Cat. No. 13), whose open butterfly shapes in the crest rails of their seating furniture may have influenced Krutina's design. The pleated, or ruched, yellow *gauffrage* silk velvet and gimp upholstery complement the rich black finish of the Anglo-Japanese-style chair.[8]

Born in Baden, Germany, on December 13, 1825, Frederick Krutina trained in the civil service and studied at the Lyceum in Karlsruhe. He likely acquired his skills in woodworking through

KRUTINA'S FURNITURE FACTORY, &c.
See Page 37

Fig. 14.1
"Krutina's Furniture Factory, & c.," from *Insurance Maps of the City of New York* (1877), New-York Historical Society.

his family's forestry trade. At the age of 23, he participated in the 1848 revolts, was confined to prison in Rastatt, and subsequently escaped. His flight through France ultimately led him to America by age 24.[9] By 1852–53, he was listed as a carver in New York City. From 1862 until his retirement in 1883, Krutina's furniture shop and factory occupied 96–98 East Houston Street in Kleindeutschland (Little Germany), near the German Assembly Rooms and the armory for the 96th Regiment of the New York National Guard.[10] Surrounding him were the factories of other notable furniture firms, including that of his principal competitor, M. and H. Schrenkeisen.

Krutina's showroom and factory appeared in the Perris Browne *Insurance Maps of the City of New York* (1877) and illustrate the vertical integration of marketing and manufacturing that came to dominate the New York furniture industry during the second half of the 19th century. Krutina first started his business in a six-story building on East Houston Street; as it grew, he acquired a five-story structure directly behind, which was connected via the rear courtyard and a top-floor enclosed bridge (Fig. 14.1).[11] In 1880, he opened a separate showroom specifically for the display of his cabinet

furniture at 842 Broadway, on the northeast corner at 13th Street. A newspaper account reported that "it has been stocked with handsome goods of his own manufacture in the latest style, and there will always be on exhibition numerous designs of interior decorations, comprising curtains, lambrequins, draperies, and frescoing. Mr. Krutina's old establishment at Nos. 96 and 98 East Houston-street will be continued as warerooms in connection with his factory on the same premises."[12]

Advertisements appearing in newspapers in New York City, South Carolina (*Charleston Daily News*), and Washington, D.C. (*National Republican*) touted Krutina's artistic furniture. A gracefully worded *New York Times* article encouraged "those who love elegance as well as comfort" to visit his shop and suggested "a bijou of cosiness might be created in a moment for the surprise and delight of someone" with a gift of his furniture.[13] Another promoted first-class furniture in "Queen Anne, Eastlake and other styles, with Japanese ornamentation" along with imported goods.[14] Krutina guaranteed his cabinet furniture was offered at the "lowest possible manufacturers' prices," and attested it was "manufactured on my own

premises ... under my own supervision, leaving nothing to be desired in point of that solidity and finish, for which my goods have always enjoyed a high reputation, and merited the confidence of the public for the past twenty-five years."[15]

It was undoubtedly through his reputation and marketing prowess that numerous prominent patrons within the city and across the country, especially the Midwest, sought Krutina's services. For Clover Lawn, the Bloomington, Illinois, home of David Davis (1815–1886), a U.S. Supreme Court justice and U.S. senator, Krutina supplied a Renaissance-style suite of parlor furniture (Fig. 14.2).[16] Similarly, Anna Earl Jenks Ramsey (1826–1884) of St. Paul, Minnesota, traveled to New York City in 1872 to purchase furnishings for her newly completed residence. There, she visited A. T. Stewart and Company, one of the earliest department stores, from which she purchased such a large quantity of household furnishings that they required two railroad cars to ship to St. Paul. Among them was a seven-piece suite of Krutina-made Renaissance-Revival furniture for her reception room, which consisted of a patent rocker, a large easy chair, two open-back side chairs, and two small sofas.[17] Prominently featured in a photograph taken in 1884 is the overstuffed, tufted-back easy chair upholstered in a woolen reproduction fabric in the Turkish fashion and trimmed with *passementerie* and a ruched front, like the DeMell Jacobsen Collection example (Fig. 14.3). Ramsey certainly must have been aware of the latest taste in furnishings, as a contemporary publication observed that "a parlor suit [*sic*] ... of solid walnut, plainly finished, covered with good all-wool reproduction, with upholstered seats and backs for the easy chairs, and upholstered seats for the other chairs, can be bought as low as eighty-five dollars."[18] A local newspaper acknowledged Ramsey and her decorating ability when it described the home as being furnished with "the luxury of comfort and the elegance of refinement."[19]

In addition to furnishing domestic interiors, Krutina outfitted "nearly all the large steamers plying along the Atlantic coast" during the Civil War.[20] Both before and after the war, he also furnished several hotels in Southern cities, including the Ballard House in Richmond, Virginia; the National Hotel in Norfolk, Virginia; the Kimball House in Atlanta, Georgia; and the Arlington Hotel in Washington, D.C. Of his commission for the Ballard House, Krutina proudly recounted, "When I received the $30,000 contract for the furniture for the Ballard House, it was accompanied by the request that it should be sent as soon as possible. Such were my facilities that I was able to fill the order within two weeks."[21]

Not only a successful businessman, Krutina was a philanthropist and an active member of a number of New York City organizations, especially those that related to his German heritage. He supported the Liederkranz Festival and served on the boards for several institutions and societies, including the Isabella Heimath, for the care of the indigent and aged, located at Amsterdam and 190th Street;[22] the Society of Patriots of 1848 and 1849; the German Hospital and Dispensary; the German Society of the City of New-York; and the German Up-Town Savings Bank, to name but a few. On May 22, 1883, the *New York Tribune* reported Krutina's retirement from making furniture so that he could focus on managing his real estate properties, especially those on Lexington Avenue.[23] Prior to his inventory being liquidated at auction by Daniel A. Mathews in the Madison Square Art Rooms, Krutina reflected somewhat wistfully on his experience in the furniture business:

There have been many changes in the styles and materials used in our business during my connection with the trade. In 1860 mahogany and rosewood were dropped from the list of popular woods. Walnut and cherry followed, and finally ash. Now the wheel of fashion has turned and the old woods, mahogany and rosewood, are coming into use again. The most fashionable furniture of to-day is made after the style of the Italian Renaissance. The manufacturers are introducing a high grade of carved work. Formerly the best carvers were imported from Germany and France. Now there are plenty of skillful wood-workers here, who have been trained up in the business. It costs about three times as much now to furnish a house as it cost thirty years ago. This is owing to the higher prices of the woods and labor.[24]

1   "F. Krutina," *New York Times*, December 2, 1877, 12.
2   Special thanks to Andrew VanStyn for his research and expertise. His contributions helped shape this essay.
3   "F. Krutina's Fine Furniture," *New York Times*, April 26, 1878, 8.
4   "F. Krutina's Fine Furniture."
5   *Art Amateur* 3, no. 1 (June 1880): 22.
6   In late 1876 to 1877, Dresser was the first European designer to journey to Japan, where he was received by the emperor and given extensive tours of Japanese artistic and cultural sites. A visit to New York and Philadelphia in conjunction with his voyage to Japan allowed Dresser to secure an opportunity to purchase Japanese works for Tiffany and Co., to experience the Centennial Exhibition, and to speak at the Pennsylvania Museum and School of Industrial Art. In 1882 Dresser published *Japan: Its Architecture, Art, and Art Manufactures* with descriptions and illustrations of the Japanese techniques he witnessed.
7   Katherine S. Howe, Alice Cooney Frelinghuysen, and Catherine Hoover Voorsanger, *Herter Brothers: Furniture and Interiors for a Gilded Age* (New York: Harry N. Abrams, 1994), 115.
8   The upholstery scheme is based on a variant chair, which possesses an upholstered back and retains its original Frederick Krutina paper label. The chair is in the personal collection of James Archer Abbott, Philip Franklin Wagley

Director and Curator, Evergreen Museum and Library, Johns Hopkins University.
9   "Frederick Krutina Dead," *New York Daily Tribune*, July 22, 1900, 12.
10 Howe, Frelinghuysen, and Voorsanger, *Herter Brothers*, 64.
11 Howe, Frelinghuysen, and Voorsanger, 64.
12 "City and Suburban News," *New York Times*, October 14, 1880.
13 "The Furniture Stores: F. Krutina," *New York Times*, December 24, 1874.
14 "Frederick Krutina, Manufacturer of First Class Cabinet Furniture," advertisement or announcement, September 2, 1878, Joseph Downs Collection, Winterthur Museum, Library, and Garden.
15 "Frederick Krutina, Manufacturer of First Class Cabinet Furniture."
16 Construction on Clover Lawn, designed by Alfred H. Piquenard, one of the Midwest's most prominent architects, began in May 1870 and was completed by late 1872.
17 The receipt, dated August 24, 1872, shows Ramsey paid $351 for the suite of furniture. She also purchased several lambrequins in blue fabric. For additional information regarding construction of the Alexander Ramsey House and purchase of its furnishings, see Barbara Ann Caron, "The Alexander Ramsey House: Furnishing a Victorian Home," *Minnesota History* 54, no. 5 (Spring 1995): 194–209;

Ann Frisina, "Following the Victorian Eye," *Minnesota History* 59, no. 7 (Fall 2005): 287–91; and Ann Frisina, *Krutina Furnishing Suite Tacking Edge Analysis* (St. Paul: Minnesota Historical Society, n.d.), accessed May 4, 2017, https://www.mnhs.org/preserve/conservation/reports/krutina.pdf.
18 Frank and Marion Stockton, *The Home Where It Should Be and What to Put into It* (New York: Putnam & Sons, 1872), 47, cited in Frisina, "Following the Victorian Eye," 291 n. 5.
19 *St. Paul Pioneer*, October 30, 1881, 3, cited in Barbara Ann Caron, "The Alexander Ramsey House," 200 n. 15.
20 "Retirement of Frederick Krutina," *New York Daily Tribune*, May 22, 1883.
21 "Retirement of Frederick Krutina."
22 Moses King, *King's Handbook of New York City, An Outline History and Description of the American Metropolis* (Boston: Moses King, 1893), 445.
23 Despite closing the factory at nos. 96 and 98 East Houston, Krutina apparently converted it to tenement and rear tenement housing. A *New York Times* article cited Krutina among the owners of "those deadly pests of New-York, the rear tenements." His property at no. 96 contained 59 occupants, while no. 98 contained 50. See "Disease-Breeding Homes, A List of Foul Rear Tenements in New-York City," *New York Times*, February 24, 1896.
24 "Retirement of Frederick Krutina."

Wakefield Rattan Chairs

c. 1880–1895

Designed and manufactured by the Wakefield Rattan Company (active 1855–1897, Wakefield, Massachusetts)

Lady's Reception Chair, c. 1885
Natural unpainted rattan, cane, maple, and other hardwoods
49 x 21 ¼ x 23 in.

Child's Reclining Arm Chair, c. 1880–1895
Natural unpainted rattan, mixed hardwoods, printed modern velvet upholstery (original foundation), brass
26 x 18 x 21 in.

THE MULTICULTURAL influence of styles so characteristic of the Aesthetic period encouraged imaginative and innovative uses of materials beyond conventional woods in the manufacture of furniture. Art furniture was often created from materials thought to evoke exotic Eastern sources; among these were bamboo, cane, and rattan. Woven rattan, commonly known as wicker, offered user-friendly conveniences as it was lightweight, portable, water resistant, simple to clean, and allowed for ventilation. Consistent with 21st-century decorative styles, faux bamboo and rattan furniture was considered by Victorians to be a suitable choice for exterior and interior domestic spaces, as well as the decks of passenger ships. In the late 19th century, the Wakefield Rattan Company succeeded as the foremost fabricator of artistic rattan and reed furniture, due to the imaginative innovation and acute business acumen of its founder, Cyrus Wakefield (1811–1873).[1]

The *Lady's Reception Chair* possesses an intricate and decorative design based on the popular peacock motif—which for adherents of the Aesthetic Movement was symbolic of beauty and everlasting life.[2] Using a variety of techniques—including weaving, knitting, knotting, wrapping, and curling natural rattan over a hardwood steam-bent frame—the process allows for an elegant and durable form. In *Rural Homes; or Sketches of Houses Suited to American Country Life* (1851), Gervase

Wheeler (1815–1889), a British-born architect active in New England, remarked, "the principal excellencies of [rattan] as a material for chairs, sofas, baskets, etc., etc., are its durability elasticity, and great facility of being turned and twisted into an almost endless variety of shapes; hence in chairs there is every assistance given by it in obtaining that greatest of all luxuries—an easy seat and a springy back."[3] More than a quarter century later, Clarence Cook (1828–1900), a noted art critic, observed that it "is well known, too, what a prosperity the Wakefield manufacture of rattan furniture is enjoying, and it deserves it too. Whenever the designs obey the law of the material employed, and do not try to twist or bend it out of its own natural and handsome curves, they are sure to be pleasing to look at and serviceable to use."[4]

Perfectly demonstrating the pliable qualities of this exotic material, braided reeds spiral around the back stiles—reminiscent of Solomonic columns—while double-laced loops trim the back splat. The attenuated seat back is filled with stick-and-orb diagonal fretwork and radiating scrolling fronds crested with a filigree edge of tightly linked scrolls.[5] A circular pressed-cane seat hovers above splayed legs while a demilune apron mirrors the scrolling fronds along the crest. The chair is a *tour de force* example of the hand-woven rattan technique and would have been a stunning piece of seating furniture in a domestic interior. Periodicals and decorating handbooks from the mid-1870s and later emphasized both a deliberate mixing of styles as well as informal placing of furnishings within a room. "Chairs, like after-dinner coffee-cups, seem to be selected nowadays with a view to their harlequin effect," wrote Constance Cary Harrison (1843–1920) in 1881. "Gilt wicker, flaunted with bows like a bed of poppies," she continued, "confronts the rigid dignity of a Tudor or Eastlake specimen in solid wood, while India teak and Wakefield rattan hobnob most cordially."[6]

The Wakefield Rattan Company's production line was diverse in its forms and was influenced by evolving social mores as well as other prevailing designs. To this end, the *Child's Reclining Arm Chair* represents the time-honored custom to provide child-sized seating to teach manners, good posture, and behavior, as well as to develop a child's self-identity.

Child-sized wicker furniture, much like that for adults, also had the benefit of providing good ventilation during warmer temperatures. In his *Rural Homes*, Wheeler wrote as much about a child's crib or bedstead made of rattan: "the lightness, sweetness, and coolness of the article, particularly adapted as it is to ventilation, must greatly recommend it. A very graceful use of the material is seen in the firm and delicate braid-work that is wrought upon some of the chairs and other articles."[7]

Wheeler could just as well have been referring to the *Child's Reclining Arm Chair*. Wakefield's design integrates a sturdy basket weave with ornamental scrolls terminating in bound orbs and brass-capped feet. The mixed hardwood frame provides a sturdy structure for children, while whimsical motifs add youthful playfulness. This example is well preserved with its original foundations intact. A historically correct French velvet fabric adorns the tall, boxed button-tufted back cushion.[8] With its wide arms, adjustable back (via a brass rod), and clean lines, this style of chair is often referred to as a "Morris Chair," signifying a shift in late-19th-century taste from the Aesthetic Movement to the Arts and Crafts Movement. The form is named for William Morris (1834–1896), a founder of the British Arts and Crafts Movement, who promoted the ideals of medieval craftsmanship. He is widely credited with adapting the chair design from an earlier prototype in his quest to create furnishings with a useful beauty. His designs were appreciated internationally and had a profound influence on both European and American designers.

These two examples made by the Wakefield Rattan Company demonstrate the firm's enduring success and the broad appeal of their hand-woven rattan and reed furniture. Through hard work, creative solutions, and a bit of luck, Cyrus Wakefield developed the firm with national and international connections. Born on a farm in Roxbury, New Hampshire, Wakefield moved to Boston at about age 15. There, he worked in a grocery store with a side business of selling discarded barrels and casks. Cyrus and his younger brother, Enoch, opened their own grocery store, Wakefield and Company, in 1836;[9] however, they closed the business in 1844 in favor of a new venture after Cyrus had encountered rattan on the Boston docks and realized its potential.

60

6042 A
Lady's Reception Chair

6502 A
Lady's Reception Chair
FANCY COLORED REEDS
Similar to Illustrations Shown in Front of Catalogue

Fig. 15.1 Chair designs, from *Heywood Brothers and Wakefield Company: Makers of Reed and Rattan Furniture* (1898).

of a cane-weaving mechanical loom by Wakefield's employee William Houston improved the company's status. Utilizing all parts of the product, the company produced a variety of wares including baskets, skirt hoops, matt carpets, railroad seating, and furniture. In 1855, the factory relocated to the Mill River in South Reading, Massachusetts, where it grew to become a 10-acre main campus for the Wakefield Rattan Company.

As the owner of the largest firm in South Reading, with 1,000 employees, and having gifted buildings and monuments to the area, Cyrus Wakefield was so well regarded that the town was renamed Wakefield in 1868. He was also successfully involved in importing East India spices, Boston real estate ventures, and the railroads, yet the 1873 economic panic left him bankrupt. Fortunately, less than two weeks before his death in October 1873, he secured his million-dollar rattan business by incorporating the Wakefield Rattan Company.[10] This allowed his nephew, Cyrus Wakefield II, to expand the breadth and depth of the company by purchasing the competing American Rattan Company along with their cane-splitting machine. He established factories and stores in New York City, Chicago, and San Francisco; promoted the firm's artistic rattan and reed furniture at the 1876 Centennial Exhibition; and was awarded a Gold Medal at the 1889 Paris Exposition. The company survived a fire and the death of Cyrus Wakefield II but merged with Heywood Brothers and Company in 1897 to become the internationally known wicker manufacturer Heywood Brothers and Wakefield Company (Fig. 15.1).

Shipped cargo from the East was traditionally stabilized with reams of rattan (*Calamus rotang*), a sturdy, flexible, and water-resistant Asian vine that can reach lengths of 600 feet. The stripped bark produces cane, also known as stripped rattan, while the core of the vine is known as reed. Cane was historically imported for use on chair backs and seats (see *Grecian Settee*, Cat. No. 1). Reed was shaped into popular rococo scrolls and arabesques in the late 1800s. While reed was derived from the inner plant, to which paint or stain could be applied, the outer skin of rattan was glossy and could only be varnished.

Wakefield began experimenting with cane-wrapped furniture, but also initiated the importation of split cane with the help of his brother-in-law based in China. By outsourcing the process of splitting rattan in China and transporting it in his own ships, Wakefield could sell cane for an attractive price to American furniture manufacturers. When the Second Opium War of 1856–1860 curtailed importation of rattan, Wakefield purchased the remaining supply in New York, therefore monopolizing the business. He then seized the opportunity to manufacture products by purchasing the Canal Street factory in Boston.

A competitive businessman, Wakefield sought innovative processes, properties, and employees, advancing his factories from hand to milled-water to steam power. Although rattan furniture continued to be mostly woven by hand, the invention

1   For a thorough analysis of the use of rattan in America, and the history of the Wakefield Rattan Company and its successors, see Jeremy Elwell Adamson, "The Wakefield Rattan Company," *The Magazine ANTIQUES* 142, no. 2 (August 1992): 214–21; and Jeremy Adamson, *American Wicker: Woven Furniture from 1850 to 1930*, (Washington, DC: Smithsonian Institution, Renwick Gallery, 1993).

2   The design, 6042 A, is illustrated in *Classic Wicker Furniture: The Complete 1898–1899 Illustrated Catalog* by Heywood Brothers-Wakefield Company (London: Dover Constable, 1982), 30. While the date of manufacture for the *Lady's Reception Chair* is attributed

prior to the publication of the 1898–99 Heywood-Wakefield catalogue, it is plausible the firm continued a line introduced by the Wakefield Rattan Company.

3   Gervase Wheeler, *Rural Homes; or Sketches of Houses Suited to American Country Life, with Original Plans, Designs, &c.* (New York: Charles Scribner, 1851), 199.

4   Clarence Cook, *The House Beautiful: Essays on Beds and Tables, Stools and Candlesticks* (New York: Scribner, Armstrong & Company, 1878), 60.

5   Special thanks to Andrew VanStyn for sharing his research and expertise on the history and design of this chair, which has helped to shape this essay.

6   Constance Cary Harrison, *Woman's Handiwork in Modern Homes* (New York: Charles Scribner's Sons, 1881), 190–91.

7   Wheeler, *Rural Homes*, 201.

8   Andrew VanStyn is credited with identifying the historically appropriate upholstery for this chair.

9   John Wall, "The Wakefield Rattan Industry," Wakefield Historical Commission, 1994, https://wakefieldhistory.org/2016/11/30/the-wakefield-rattan-industry/.

10 Wall.

Faux Bamboo Chair

16

c. 1885

Design attributed to Robert J. Horner (1853–1922)

Manufacture attributed to R. J. Horner and Company (active 1886–c. 1915, New York, New York)

Maple, modern cane, modern upholstery

36 ½ x 17 ¾ x 17 ½ in.

ROBERT J. HORNER and Company's *Faux Bamboo Chair* epitomizes the American preference for Eastern-style furnishings popular during the last quarter of the 19th century. Through its airy and elegant design, innovative use of material, and subtle decorative motifs, the chair also presages designs of the mid-20th century.

Bamboo has a millennia-long tradition of use as an important functional and symbolic material in several Asian cultures. An extremely strong, hollow, and rapidly growing grass, bamboo has been used as a material in architecture, the culinary arts, decorative arts, and fine arts. For the Japanese, its inherent qualities became a symbol of prosperity, fortitude, utility, and a ward against evil.[1] In China, bamboo furniture production began in the Ming Dynasty and entered Western trade markets together with faux bamboo in the 18th century.[2] Western appreciation for and awareness of Asian art and culture—especially Japanese—coincided with the opening of Japan to the West following Commodore Perry's visit in 1853, as well as the participation of China and Japan in international expositions. The Japanese-style building and artistic displays of ceramics, bronzes, and furniture from China and Japan in the 1876 Centennial Exhibition in Philadelphia significantly influenced American taste and the interior-decorating industry. Concurrently, the publications of *Art Furniture, from Designs by E. W. Godwin, F.S.A., and Others, with Hints and Suggestions on Domestic Furniture and Decorations* (1877) by Edward William Godwin (Cat. No. 17) and *The House Beautiful* (1878) by Clarence Cook further promoted the Asian aesthetic to Western consumers.[3]

Both publications contained images of bamboo-style furniture, which was thought to be more suitable for informal interiors and evoked an airy feeling of ease—a contrast to the mood induced by darker, more ornate Victorian forms. Cook called bamboo furniture "capital stuff ... to fill up the gaps in the furnishing of a country house for a summer. Even in a city house, or in city rooms, several of these bamboo articles will be found useful ... They have the merit of being strongly made and easily kept clean."[4] A decade later, the June 1887 issue of the *Decorator and Furnisher Supplement* observed the use of bamboo remained in fashion, noting that "almost every one furnishing a modern house wants a few pieces of real bamboo furniture, which by its lightness in weight and its exquisite natural finish, forms a contrast to the heavier furniture of a room, which gives delight to the artistic eye."[5] By the turn of the century, bamboo motifs were prolific in many household items, especially casual furniture for indoor spaces and garden rooms. To satisfy the seemingly insatiable demand, numerous American firms imported raw bamboo from Asia and then assembled it into furniture once stateside. Among these were Nimura and Sato in Brooklyn, New York, and James E. Wall in Boston. Meanwhile, other firms manufactured and sold imitation bamboo furniture, including Killian Brothers and C. A. Aimone and Bro. in New York City,[6] and Blake and Alden in Boston. However, none was more prominent than Robert J. Horner and Company of New York City.

Belying its delicate appearance, Horner's imitation bamboo furniture made from solid maple was more durable than furniture made from bamboo stalks. Though not labeled, the DeMell Jacobsen Collection chair is identical to a chair from a dressing suite in the collection of the Munson-Williams-Proctor Arts Institute (Fig. 16.1),[7] and both are stylistically similar to a labeled example in the collection of the High Museum of Art. The Munson-Williams-Proctor and DeMell Jacobsen Collection chairs both possess stepped brackets at opposing corners of the chair back, which are separated by a diagonally shaped back splat into which four connected circles are set. The circular forms and the diagonal splat provide delight to the "artistic eye" as it moves gracefully down the form. Perhaps a reference to the philosophy of *yin* and *yang*, the circular elements also recall *ensō*, a Zen symbol with a variety of meanings including strength and elegance.[8] A natural cane seat affords ventilation and reinforces the lightweight appearance, as do the splayed feet.[9]

Robert J. Horner began his career working for Mills and Gibb, a New York importer and retailer of lace, linens, and dry goods. His name first appeared in city directories in 1883 as a clerk for the company, and he remained with them through at least March 1886.[10] Presumably through his employment with Mills and

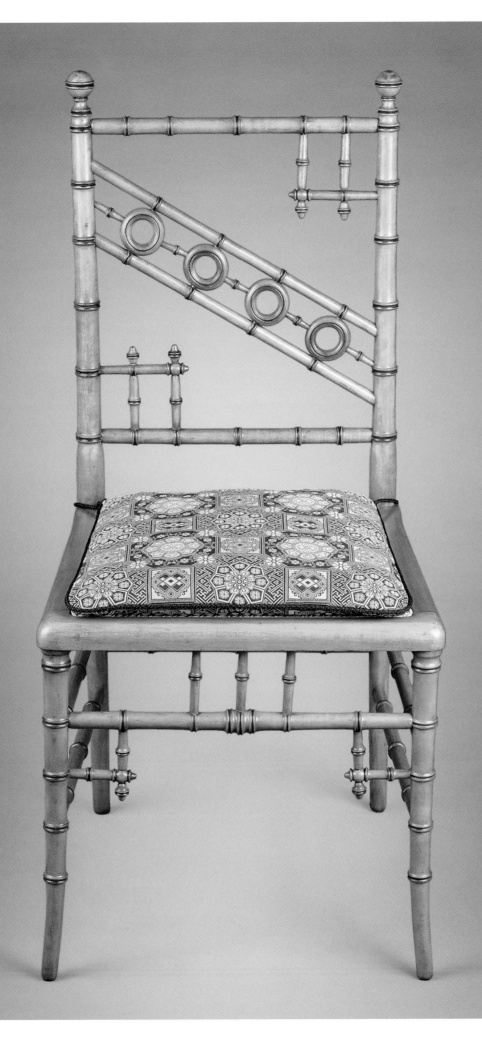

Fig. 16.1 *Dressing Table and Chair*, c. 1890, possibly manufactured by R. J. Horner and Company (active 1886–c. 1915, New York, New York), bird's-eye maple, hard maple, yellow poplar, glass (dresser), hard maple with cane seat (chair), chair: 36 ¼ × 17 ¾ × 17 ¾ in.; dressing table: 58 ½ × 42 ½ × 20 ½ in., Munson-Williams-Proctor Arts Institute, Utica, New York.

Gibb he distinguished himself in the interior-decorating and furniture industry. By November 1886, he opened his own showroom in a fashionable cast-iron-fronted seven-floor building located at 61–65 West 23rd Street. Designed by John B. Snook in the Italian Renaissance style, the building was a short walk from the "Ladies' Mile" along 6th Avenue and is still known today as the Robert J. Horner Building. From this location, Horner designed, manufactured, and marketed "the largest display of

first-class and medium quality furniture in America" that was priced "to suit the exactness of the millionaire or the artistic taste of the connoisseur."[11] By 1889, the company was valued above $100,000 and had become a leading furniture manufacturer and retailer.[12]

Like many of his competitors, Horner offered a diverse inventory in styles and prices to reach a large audience of consumers. Advertisements and articles about his company mention traditional

styles, European imports and "novelties"[13] in oak, mahogany, and walnut,[14] as well as a line of bamboo furniture, "with tables covered by huge umbrellas for garden use."[15] An 1890 advertisement promoted a "large assortment of bamboo maple furniture,"[16] manufactured on the fifth floor of Horner's massive building. There, R. J. Horner and Company craftsmen paid close attention to imitating the natural color and markings of bamboo, staining the lathe-turned maple a light color while adding a contrasting darker stain inside the evenly spaced, grooved rings.[17] The machined components were then assembled depending upon the type of furniture being fabricated. The company also mass-produced the various decorative elements—rings, balls, and finials—to facilitate production of the imitation bamboo furniture for which they were best known.

Surviving the financial panics of 1873, 1891, and 1893, Horner's company used aggressive marketing strategies in promoting their embrace of fashionable trends and novel designs. Inviting "those about to furnish or rearrange their houses," the company artfully staged room ensembles or "specimen rooms" in its large and well-lit showrooms.[18] To entice prospective purchasers to visit the showroom, the company published *Our*

American Homes and How to Furnish Them, a catalogue that could be requested by mail. An 1888 article in the *New York Times*, entitled "New Styles in Furniture: The Beautiful Assortment Offered by R. J. Horner & Company," began with a company salesman's pitch:

Talk of changes of fashion for women. They occur no more often and are no more radical than changes in furniture fashions. The manufacturer who cannot put out a new set of designs every six months in these days is behind the times. Not many years ago the same style of furniture was sold season after season. Then someone tried the experiment of novelties. It was fatal to old-fashioned ideas.[19]

Factory operations moved in 1897 from the fifth floor of the 23rd Street showroom to a dedicated facility at 126 West 25th Street; they relocated again in 1909 a few doors down to 147–149 West 25th Street. In 1904, a fire devastated the company store; however, the shop continued to operate on West 23rd Street until yet another relocation in 1912 to 36th Street, closer to Fifth Avenue. In 1914, Horner joined forces with George C. Flint and Company (Cat. No. 25) and operated under the name Flint and Horner Co. Inc. Retiring from the firm three years before his death, Robert J. Horner died at the age of 68 in 1922, having succeeded in the furniture industry, as a bank director for the Garfield National and Excelsior, and as a president of the Flower Waste and Packing Company.[20]

1   See "The Importance of Bamboo in Japan," Japanese Style, March 2, 2019, https://japanesestyle.com/the-importance-of-bamboo-in-japan/.

2   Wendy Moonan, "Antiques: Where East Meets West," *New York Times*, September 13, 2002.

3   Special thanks to Andrew VanStyn for his research and expertise. His contributions helped shape this essay.

4   Clarence Cook, *The House Beautiful: Essays on Beds and Tables, Stools and Candlesticks* (New York: Scribner, Armstrong & Company, 1878), 74–75.

5   *The Decorator and Furnisher Supplement, Devoted to the Upholstery, Carpet, Furniture and House Furnishing Trades*, in *Decorator and Furnisher* 10, no. 3 (June 1887): 91.

6   C. A. Aimone and Bro. was first located at 30 and 32 South Fifth Avenue, between Bleecker and West 3rd Streets, and later moved to 177 Prince Street. The firm advertised itself as "manufacturers of furniture in bamboo style" that made "chamber suites, chiffoniers, desks, tables, chairs, etc." See *Decorator and Furnisher* 9, no. 4 (January 1887); 20, no. 4 (July 1892); and 21, no. 1 (October 1892).

7   Two additional chairs, identical to the aforementioned examples, were sold at the Benefit Foundation Shop,

Mt. Kisco, New York, May 17, 2017, lots 29 and 299. The collection from which the chairs came was featured in Elissa Cullman, *Decorating Master Class: The Cullman & Kravis Way* (New York: Harry N. Abrams, 2008).

8   "Ensō Circle," Modern Zen, accessed June 16, 2015, https://www.modernzen.org/enso.htm.

9   See Anna Tobin D'Ambrosio, *Masterpieces of American Furniture from the Munson-Williams-Proctor Institute* (Utica, NY: Munson-Williams-Proctor Institute, 1999), 141; and Donald C. Peirce, *Art and Enterprise: American Decorative Art, 1825–1917; The Virginia Carroll Crawford Collection* (Atlanta: High Museum of Art, 1999), 230–31.

10   Horner's obituary in the *New York Times*, February 27, 1922, 13, states that "[while] a boy Mr. Horner went to work for the firm of Mills & Gibb, lace dealers, remaining with them many years and working himself up to a responsible position." A brief mention of Horner in *Decorator and Furnisher* 7, no. 4 (January 1886): 126, describes him as Mills and Gibb's "curtain expert and manager."

11   See the firm's advertisements in *Life* 12, no. 303 (October 18, 1888); no. 304 (October 25, 1888); no. 306 (November 8, 1888); no. 307 (November 15, 1888); no. 308 (November 22, 1888); and no. 310 (December 6, 1888).

12   See Peirce, *Art and Enterprise*, 231; and D'Ambrosio, *Masterpieces of American Furniture*, 140–41.

13   "Furniture in Artistic Design," *New York Times*, November 4, 1886.

14   "New Styles in Furniture: The Beautiful Assortment Offered by R. J. Horner & Co.," *New York Times*, March 29, 1888.

15   "Furniture in Artistic Design."

16   "Furniture," *New York Times*, March 9, 1890, 16.

17   Imitation bamboo furniture made by C. A. Aimone and Bro., a competitor of Horner and Company, featured "furniture made in ordinary woods imitating bamboo effects" in which "simulated joints in the wood are made at arbitrary intervals, and the ring of the joints is colored with the application of hot iron." This description could suggest that either the rings were burned, much like pyrography, by application of a heated iron rod, or they were colored with a heated stain tinted with iron. See *Decorator and Furnisher* 20, no. 4 (July 1892): 151–52.

18   *Decorator and Furnisher* 10, no. 1 (April 1887): 23–28.

19   "New Styles in Furniture."

20   Walter Grutchfield, "Flint & Horner," WalterGrutchfield.net, accessed June 17, 2015, https://www.waltergrutchfield.net/flint&horner.htm.

Slipper Chair

17

c. 1880–1895

Designed and manufactured by an unknown furniture maker (United States)

Cherry, ash, modern upholstery

29 ¾ x 18 x 19 ½ in.

DESIGNED AND manufactured by an unknown American furniture maker, this *Slipper Chair* recalls the Anglo-Japanese designs of the influential British architect, designer, interior decorator, and aesthete Edward William Godwin (1833–1886).[1] Perhaps more than any other British designer, Godwin celebrated in his art furniture the "functional, architectonic qualities of Japanese design,"[2] which "represented an honesty and abstract ornamentation."[3]

Godwin's early career focused on architecture, with designs rooted in the Gothic Revival style inspired by the works of John Ruskin (1819–1900). By 1870, however, Godwin had rebuffed the revival styles and embraced the tenets of the Art Furniture Movement, which gave rise to the subsequent Aesthetic Movement. As an aesthete, he placed an emphasis on beauty over usefulness. Focusing on design rather than craftsmanship, Godwin was not one to eschew the benefits of mass production, which led to frequent imitation of his designs by European and American manufacturers.[4]

The American maker of this chair clearly knew Godwin's style and sensitively drew from a variety of Japanese motifs and forms (Fig. 17.1). The angular frame and the rectilinear design of the chair's back suggest a familiarity with Japanese screens (*byōbu*). Its carved crest rail prominently features a stylized sunburst motif, perhaps referencing the Rising Sun Flag of the Edo period, which was later adopted as the war flag of the Imperial Japanese Army in 1870. Similarly, the incised lines on the stiles and crest rail, as well as those on the bulbous turnings, recall those used to create woodblock prints. A Japanese gold-thread obi brocade fabric in a knife-edge upholstery scheme is based on a Herter Brothers (Cat. No. 13) seat cushion in the Glessner House Museum in Chicago. Wide, woven braid tape accentuates the seat cushion top, echoing the rectilinear arrangement of the seat back. Cording binds the cushion edges, while large, ornamental tassels accentuate the front corners and integrate the color scheme. The bulbous front legs terminate in slightly bun feet, which are commonly found on several Godwin designs.

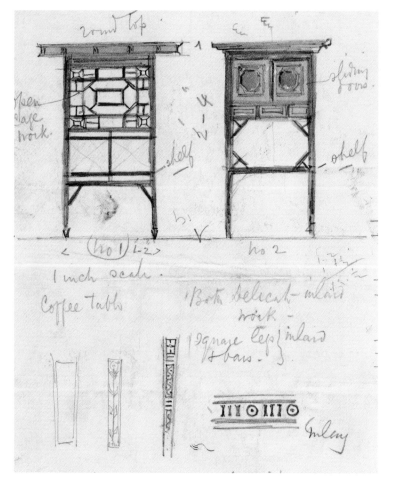

Fig. 17.1 E. W. Godwin (1833–1886), Designs for coffee tables in the Japanese style for Grey Towers, Britain, late 19th century, Victoria and Albert Museum, London.

1   For a detailed analysis of the life and artistic designs of Edward William Godwin, see Susan Weber Soros, ed., *E. W. Godwin: Aesthetic Movement Architect and Designer* (New Haven, CT: Yale University Press, 1999), and Susan Weber Soros, *The Secular Furniture of E. W. Godwin* (New Haven, CT: Yale University Press, 1999).

2   Florence De Dampierre, *Chairs: A History* (New York: Harry N. Abrams, 2006), 304.

3   De Dampierre, 305.

4   In addition to Tiffany's Associated Artists and Herter Brothers, both of New York, another firm was A. and H. Lejambre (active 1865–c. 1907) of Philadelphia. Most of the known examples of Lejambre furniture, massive and solid in appearance, are adaptations of 18th-century French forms decorated with French Renaissance details. However, several documented examples show influence and familiarity of Godwin's designs, including a table in the collection of the Museum of Fine Arts, Houston (91.1557), a table in the collection of the Saint Louis Art Museum (13.1982), and a table in the collection of the Metropolitan Museum of Art (1991.482). For additional information about the Lejambre firm, see Peter L. L. Strickland, "Furniture by the Lejambre Family of Philadelphia," *The Magazine ANTIQUES* 113, no. 3 (March 1978): 600–613, and Doreen Bolger Burke, et al., *In Pursuit of Beauty: Americans and the Aesthetic Movement* (New York: Metropolitan Museum of Art, 1986), 159, 449.

Side Chair

18

c. 1885

Design and manufacture attributed to Herts Brothers (active 1872–1908, New York, New York)

Mahogany; rosewood; inlays of copper, brass, pewter, and mother-of-pearl; brass casters; modern silk lampas upholstery

42 x 20 x 23 in.

TOGETHER WITH Herter Brothers (Cat. No. 13), George A. Schastey (1839–1894), and Associated Artists, the New York firm of Herts Brothers was one of the leading interior decorators and furniture manufacturers for Gilded Age elites. Unfortunately, few labeled examples of the Herts Brothers' furniture or photographs of their interior decorations exist, thus making firm attributions of their output difficult. Nevertheless, their furniture is characterized by a use of rich woods embellished with inlays, as can be seen on several examples of cabinets and seating furniture.[1] The mahogany and rosewood seat back of this *Side Chair* is framed by finely turned spindles, also echoed in the apron. Delicate inlay swags and floral designs composed of brass, copper, pewter, and mother-of-pearl illustrate the prevailing floral design of the Renaissance Revival style. The seat back has an elongated rectangular form framed by groupings of spindles that draw the eye toward the marquetry they surround.[2] The visual arrangement is completed by a complementary silk lampas fabric, based on an Italian Renaissance pattern, and silk gimp covering the springs and horsehair foundation.[3]

Isaac H. Herts (d. 1918) and Benjamin H. Herts (d. 1924) gained an appreciation for elegant Continental antiques and *objects d'art* from their father, Henry B. Herts, an emigrant from England. Henry established his expertise as an auctioneer and dealer of imported antiques. Expanding their market, the firm H. B. Herts and Sons also specialized in furniture made with fine woods, carvings, and finishes.

While two other brothers continued to work with their father, Isaac and Benjamin formed Herts Brothers, opening a showroom as early as 1872[4] at 806–808 Broadway and subleasing the third and fourth floors of Pierre J. Hardy's furniture factory at West 19th Street in which to produce their furniture.[5] The proximity of other furniture makers' showrooms and factories—such as George A. Schastey and Co., Alexander Roux, Herter Brothers, and George Hunzinger (Cat. No. 11)—facilitated the fertile exchange of influences and designs. Following a devastating fire in 1877, the firm opened a massive six-floor factory at 104–110 East 32nd Street, which they maintained until the firm went bankrupt in 1908. Herts Brothers regularly advertised in New York periodicals seeking

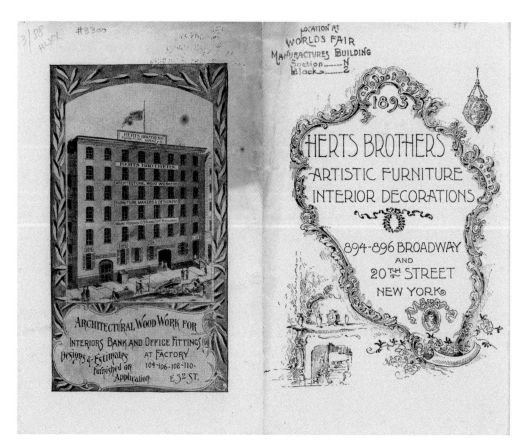

Fig. 18.1 Herts Brothers advertisement, from Herts Brothers, *Artistic Furniture, Interior Decorations* (1893).

Fig. 18.2 Herts & Co. furniture exhibit at the Centennial Exhibition in Philadelphia, 1876.

experienced "wood carvers, men only," and offering "good wages" and "steady work."[6] In 1887, Herts Brothers opened a showroom in the newly completed Goelet Building, at 894–896 Broadway (Fig. 18.1).[7] In it, they displayed their "full and varied stock of rich furniture of their own special design and manufacture" along with "choice examples of upholstery materials, textile fabrics, fine imported paper hangings, fresco painting and stained glass."[8]

Herts Brothers provided interior design and furnishings for financial offices and wealthy clientele. Commissioned projects included the New York Produce Exchange, the Columbia Bank, and the Union Square Bank; hotels such as the Knickerbocker, Hotel St. Regis, and the Woodward and Murray Hotel; numerous social clubs, including the Criterion, Progress, and Colonial; and William Astor's yacht.[9] Herts Brothers was working with the well-known architectural firm of McKim, Mead and White by 1880 to produce commissioned cabinetry for homes.

In addition to their commissions, the Herts Brothers' firm gained recognition through participation in several World's Fairs held in America. At the 1876 Centennial Exhibition in Philadelphia—the first fair held in America—Herts and Co. created a bedroom suite designed in the prevailing Renaissance Revival style (Fig. 18.2). The suite included a canopy bed flanked by side tables, a center table, a dresser with mirror, a wardrobe, a gueridon, four side chairs, an armchair with button-tufted upholstery, a button-tufted side chair with matching ottoman, a window with curtains, and a pair of oil portraits of girls. For their display in the Main Building, the firm earned both a diploma and a medal award from the Centennial Commission. However, it was the Herts Brothers' display in the Manufactures Building at the World's Columbian Exposition in Chicago in 1893 that garnered the firm great acclaim and received the premiere prize for their Louis XV–style bedroom suite. The American Renaissance style was fully realized in the temporary "White City."

The *Inland Architect and News Record* reported the display as a visual *tour de force* and noted:

> We are taken back to Versailles, and must confess that even there nothing is to be found to surpass this striking exhibit of Messrs. Herts Brothers. Certainly there is no furniture display in the foreign sections at the World's Fair that can approach it ...

No ordinary language could give more than a faint description of the beauty and harmony of this exhibit of Herts Brothers. It is at once a victory for them and a revelation to the beholder. It is a practical demonstration that henceforth our best residences and the mansions of our millionaires need not look to Europe for their furnishings.[10]

According to the aforementioned publication, the room set was completed at a cost of $25,000 and contained "two canopied bedsteads, two tables, a mantel, a wardrobe, couch, duchesse, commode and a Psyche glass, together with four chairs, a rocker and two pedestals." The furniture, ceiling, and walls were all "in exquisite harmony—rose cream, white and gold enameled." The walls were of separate panels, carved and gilded, and filled with silk fabric colored in white and gold. The ceiling contained "festoons of flowers, and a center canvas panel of oval form represents Psyche carried away to the temple of the gods." An Axminster rug, "one of the most delicate and tasteful ever designed," covered the floor. Illuminating the space were electric lights, the brackets for which were finished in ormolu. According to the review, the mantel deserved special mention and was "without question, one of the most elaborate pieces of workmanship ever put on exhibition. It is carved in the graceful, flowing style of the Louis XV period, and is flanked by panels in Vernis-Martin, representing pastoral scenes. Above the skillfully carved frame is a beautifully executed painting representing Love giving the apple at the Judgement of Paris. On each side there are elegant gilt candelabra in the design of the period. Others of a similar design are strikingly arranged about the room."[11]

In contrast to their Louis XV–style room, the Herts Brothers also provided paneling for the New York State Building at the Columbian Exposition designed by McKim, Mead and White. Designed in the Renaissance style, the building was budgeted at $77,500, while its interior and exterior furnishings were estimated to have cost more than $100,000.[12] The three-story building featured a roof with three terraces fashioned as hanging gardens. The main entrance was through an open portico guarded by two lions modeled after the Barberini sculptures. The main floor housed

reception rooms, and in the back was a topographical map of the state of New York, measuring 36 x 26 feet and viewed from a spiral stairway. The second floor housed a large banquet hall, while the third floor was reserved for the press.

As early as 1883 Frederick Krutina (Cat. No. 14) noted the Italian Renaissance style was in vogue, perhaps in the wake of the popular Grand Tour. The classical forms reemerged as a result of Americans traveling abroad and returning with a desire to emulate the European style, sometimes relocating portions of architecture to be reinstalled in their homes.

Certainly, it was within this milieu that New York's 29th governor David B. Hill (1885–1891) engaged the Herts Brothers firm in 1888 to provide furnishings for an expansion and remodeling of the Governor's Mansion in Albany. A contemporary billhead promoted the company as "manufacturers of artistic furniture in oak, walnut and ebony for parlors, dining rooms and libraries, chamber furniture in suites of walnut, ash, ebony and mahogany, hardwood work, mantels,

decorations, bedding, etc."[13] From the firm Hill procured more than $4,455 worth of furniture, "comprising such articles as sofas, armchairs in silk damask and plush, mirror, drapery, plush portieres, tapestry portieres, a mahogany extension table for $160, and a Turkish lounge, upholstered in tapestry, trimmed with fringes, $135."[14] So extravagant was the cost of the taxpayer-funded project—nearly $160,000 at the time!—that the New York Times reported it was "almost enough to pay the taxes of three or four counties that might be named. Naturally the rural taxpayer adjusts his glasses for the purpose of noting the nature and the cost of some of the luxuries in which our jolly bachelor Governor revels."[15]

An 1899 fire in the basement and first floor of the Herts Brothers factory at East 32nd Street provided yet another devastating blow to the firm, from which it never fully recovered.[16] Filing for bankruptcy in 1908, Isaac and Benjamin continued to be involved with the firm alongside Benjamin's son, Benjamin R. Herts, who became a noted playwright and interior designer of numerous Broadway theaters.

1   At least three chairs of identical form and decoration, and probably part of a set, are in the collections of the Fine Arts Museums of San Francisco (1997.31), the High Museum of Art (1981.1000.58), and the Museum of Fine Arts, St. Petersburg, Florida (2010.11). A possible fourth chair sold at Brunk Auctions, September 6–7, 2008, lot 819. A cabinet with a "Herts Brothers" stamp and possessing similar drapery motif is in the collection of the High Museum of Art (1983.201).
2   At least two other chairs with seat backs and front aprons possessing dowel arrangement are known: one was offered by Joan Bogart ("Antique Victorian Inlaid Chair," accessed April 23, 2017, https://joanbogart.com/inventoryDetails.php?productId=157); the other was documented on Prices4Antiques (accessed April 23, 2017, https://www.prices4antiques.com/item_images/medium/35/76/59-01.jpg).
3   Labeled "Tassinari & Shantal." The reupholstery of this chair was a complete reconstruction of the sprung horsehair foundation with 100 percent imported silk lampas fabric with matching Scalamandre silk gimp. The reupholstery process was also completed in line with 19th-century techniques, including hand-sewn corners and edges, the application of the show cover, and tacked gimp. Andrew VanStyn deserves special thanks for his work in locating this chair, finding the right fabric, and conducting thorough research on the chair's design

and manufacture, as well as the upholstery, all of which helped to shape this essay.
4   Katherine S. Howe, Alice Cooney Frelinghuysen, and Catherine Hoover Voorsanger, Herter Brothers: Furniture and Interiors for a Gilded Age (New York: Harry N. Abrams, 1994), 246 n. 94.
5   Gilda Acosta, "The Forgotten Brothers: The Herts Brothers and Their Contributions to the Decorative Arts in America," Devenish Group blog, September 13, 2010, https://devenishgroup.blogspot.com/2010/09/forgotten-brothers-herts-brothers-and.html.
6   New York Journal and Advertiser, September 11, 1899, 13.
7   The building was designed by McKim, Mead and White for Robert and Ogden Goelet, leaders of one of New York's social dynasties. See Christopher Gray, "Streetscapes/The 1887 Goelet Building, at 20th Street and Broadway; One Family Nurtures Another's 19th-Century Legacy," New York Times, March 19, 2000.
8   Herts Brothers brochure, New York, May 1893, courtesy The Winterthur Library: Printed Book and Periodical Collection; digital scan, Foundation curatorial files.
9   Acosta, "Forgotten Brothers."
10 "Award Presented to Herts Brothers, New York, at the World's Columbian Exposition," Inland Architect and News Record 22, no. 3 (October 1893): xviii. According to Acosta's article "Forgotten Brothers," the Herts Brothers received the "highest award in their category."

See also "High Awards at the Fair," New York Times, October 28, 1893.
11 "High Awards."
12 "New-York at the Big Fair," New York Times, July 1, 1892, 8.
13 Herts Brothers billhead, March 3, 1898. Herts Brothers, Receipt from Herts Brothers to Estate of O. Goelet, March 1898, Goelet Family Papers, Series 2: New York City real estate, 1893–1899, 33, Salve Regina University, https://digitalcommons.salve.edu/goelet-new-york/33/.
14 New York Times, February 23, 1888, quoted in Tom Miller, "The 1886 Goelet Building—Nos. 894–900 Broadway," Daytonian in Manhattan, November 3, 2012, http://daytoninmanhattan.blogspot.com/2012/11/the-1886-goelet-buildling-nos-894-900.html. For an examination of the late-19th-century interest in Oriental carpets and Turkish furniture, see Rodris Roth, "Oriental Carpet Furniture: A Furnishing Fashion in the West in the Late Nineteenth Century," Studies in the Decorative Arts 11, no. 2 (Spring–Summer 2004): 25–58. The article contains a photograph of a Herts Brothers–designed "'Den' in the Moorish Style" that originally appeared in Interior Decorator 4, no. 4 (August 1893): 202.
15 "Gov. Hill's Little Bills," New York Times, February 23, 1888, 5.
16 "Gov. Hill's Little Bills."

Texas Longhorn Arm Chair

c. 1885

Design and manufacture attributed to Wenzel Friedrich (1827–1902) (active 1880–1902, San Antonio, Texas)

Texas longhorn, ivory, oak, modern silk satin upholstery, modern silk *passementerie*, nickel-plated brass and glass casters

38 x 28 ¼ x 31 ½ in.

THE LORE OF THE American West—propelled in part by William Frederick "Buffalo Bill" Cody (1846–1917) and Annie Oakley (1860–1926), who began performing the *Wild West* show in Great Britain and Europe in 1887—particularly appealed to Europeans as an exotic novelty and a singular expression of something truly American. The popularity of horn furniture during the Victorian period of the late 19th century was reflective of both American and European consumers' obsession in furnishing their homes with goods illustrating the exotic and the wild. After more than a century of importing and reviving European décor styles, this was a unique moment of reverse consumerism, as the American style was coveted in Europe. While it is unknown who "invented" furniture made from Texas Longhorn cattle, Wenzel Friedrich, a skilled cabinetmaker from Bohemia who settled in San Antonio, certainly created unparalleled, innovative designs excelling in quality materials, "honest construction and excellent finish."[1]

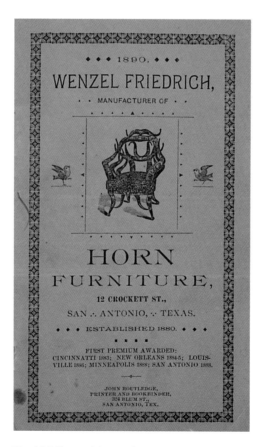

Fig. 19.1 Cover of the catalogue *Wenzel Friedrich, Manufacturer of Horn Furniture* (1890).

Many of the German furniture manufacturers represented in the DeMell Jacobsen Collection had fled the 1848 upheaval in Germany to settle in New York City, but Texas was another destination for immigrants. In 1853, eight years after Texas had entered the Union as the 28th state, Wenzel Friedrich emigrated from his native Grünthal, Bohemia. He first arrived in Indianola, Texas, a port town on the Gulf of Mexico newly created for the Adelsverein colonists, before continuing on a three-month passage via oxen train to San Antonio.[2] Formally known as the Society for the Protection of German Immigrants in Texas, the Adelsverein offered travel assistance to Germans settling in Texas between 1842 and 1853. Lured by accounts of ample land, opportunities to hunt, and a cost-efficient lifestyle, many Adelsverein colonists succeeded in establishing communities and befriending Native Americans.[3] Upon his arrival in San Antonio, Friedrich first worked as a grocer, then relied on his cabinetmaking skills. Much like Cyrus Wakefield (Cat. No. 15), who had pioneered the use of rattan, the entrepreneurial Friedrich envisioned the potential usefulness and aesthetic beauty of another commercial castoff. In 1880, Friedrich established a business constructing diverse forms of furniture made from steer horns discarded by San Antonio's slaughterhouses.

Among the earliest documented examples of American-made furniture fabricated from Texas Longhorns was a parlor sofa and chair upholstered in maroon plush made by the Tobey Furniture Company of Chicago and exhibited in 1876 at the Chicago Industrial Exposition.[4] By 1881, the Tobey Furniture Company had become "well known as manufacturers of chairs formed of cattle's horns,"[5] and in that year Charles B. Fletcher of St. Louis, Missouri, secured a patent for his "new and Improved Design for a Horn Chair."[6] Two years later, a reporter from the *Inland Architect and Builder* marveled at innovative horn furniture being displayed among the more common furnishings. "Everything is antique, or copies the antique," he wrote, "excepting those chairs with polished horn for backs, and they are as modern as the Texas cowboy and as inimitable."[7] In the fall of 1883, either the Tobey Furniture Company or a competitor exhibited an original suite of furniture, which a reporter described as "a curious set of furniture, in which the hide,

Fig. 19.2 Lang & Nau trade card, after 1882, Brooklyn Museum.

horns, forelocks and fetlocks of Hungarian steers were variously utilized ... the silken locks became fringes, the polished horns arms and legs, while the hide formed a very ornamental upholstering, with its silver-grey and black hair."[8]

The abundance of Texas Longhorn cattle—descended from a Spanish breed and English longhorn Herefords—in San Antonio began between 1860 and 1880 when American cattlemen capitalized on the thriving long-legged, tough-hoofed animals.[9] Cattlemen prospered by herding the cattle along trails to stockyards north of Texas and as far as Chicago and California. The open-range Chisholm Trail originated in San Antonio with a path toward Kansas. Operational from 1867 to 1884, the Chisholm Trail was traversed by over five million cattle.[10] The Longhorns helped stimulate the legend of the cowboy and the lure of Western ranching culture; however, technological advancements contributed to the demise of the breed. With the arrival of the railroads in Texas and the invention of barbed wire, open-range boundaries were established, discouraging long-distance cattle drives. A new controlled breeding of cattle that thrived in an enclosed area and provided superior beef products also curtailed the short saga of the Longhorn. The legendary herd was severely depleted but saved from extinction in the 1920s.

From his shop at 12 East Crockett Street, Friedrich developed a precise method of construction, which began with the careful selection of curved and unblemished horns that were purchased in pairs for about a nickel.[11] Considering the average price for a horn chair in his 1890 catalogue (Fig. 19.1) was about $60, Friedrich profited on his novel approach and innovative spirit. The entrepreneur submerged the horns in boiling water and removed the softened top layer. Sundried and buffed, the organic form glowed like polished wood. To manipulate and contour the horn, Friedrich practiced his unique system of prolonging the boiling process until the horns could be bent and shaped. The horns were then "blocked with best seasoned lumber and filled with Plaster Paris."[12] The seat frame was constructed of wood treated in a kiln. Steel tacks and wood screws securely fastened the various elements and were covered by a variety of fabrics, including silk plush, or exotic animal skins—such as Angora goat, fox, jaguar ("American tiger"), deer, and catamount (mountain lion), among others—in varying price points with coordinating *passementerie*, or decorative trim. The reproduction blue silk satin fabric, button tufting, and handmade *passementerie* on this example were selected based on a

chair of near identical form pictured on an 1882 color lithograph trade card for Lang and Nau, a Brooklyn, New York, furniture and upholstery warehouse (Fig. 19.2).[13] Once assembled, the sharp points of the Texas Longhorns were covered by either ivory spheres (as in the present example) or acorn-shaped tips "turned from horn, to protect clothing."[14] Friedrich advertised his use of "the best plated glass ball caster,"[15] which he secured from Louis Comfort Tiffany and Company in New York. The DeMell Jacobsen Collection possesses a second *Texas Longhorn Arm Chair* that has the same upholstery scheme and brass casters.

Friedrich's horn furniture was awarded gold medals at the 1883 Cincinnati Industrial Exposition, the 1884–1885 New Orleans Industrial and Cotton Centennial Exposition, and the 1886 Southern Exposition in Louisville, Kentucky.[16] His 1890 catalogue further boasted of premium awards in 1888

from competitions in both Minneapolis and San Antonio. The catalogue illustrated a sofa, ottoman, stool, flower stand, hat rack, and a variety of armchairs including an office chair, child's chair, and a lady's chair. Also included was a table fabricated with Friedrich's pioneered horn veneer process and embellished with an ivory Texas star. While Friedrich suggested specifying items with a designated catalogue number, he was willing to manufacture furniture to order. Further, he addressed his cash shipping policy in his catalogue and promised free packaging and delivery to the railway depot, where they would be shipped at an economical rate.[17] Friedrich's clientele extended nationally and internationally and included such foreign nobility as Queen Victoria (1819–1901) of Britain, Otto von Bismarck (1815–1898) and Kaiser Wilhelm I (1797–1888) of Prussia, as well as a president of France.[18]

1 Wenzel Friedrich, *Wenzel Friedrich, Manufacturer of Horn Furniture* (San Antonio: John Routledge, 1890), https://archive.org/details/wenzelfriedrichm00frie. In addition to Friedrich, there were several other manufacturers of horn furniture in San Antonio, Texas, including Charles Puppe and William Mittmann. See "Clearing Up the Confusion about Horn Chairs Made by Texas Makers Wenzel Friedrich, Charles Puppe, William Mittmann and the Appel Brothers," National Texas Longhorn Museum, accessed June 24, 2017, http://www.longhornmuseum.com/HornFurnitureWhoMadeYours.htm.

2 Richard W. St. John, *Longhorn Artist: Wenzel Friedrich* (Wichita, KS: Wichita State University Office of Research and Sponsored Programs, 1982), 5.

3 Sheena Oommen, "Hin' Nach Texas! Off to Texas!" *Cultural Crossroads: Regional and Historical Perspectives*, accessed June 24, 2015, http://www.houstonmuseumofculture.org/cr/germans.html.

4 Sharon Darling, *Chicago Furniture: Art, Craft and Industry, 1833–1983* (Chicago: Chicago Historical Society; New York: W. W. Norton & Company, 1984), 78.

5 *American Cabinet Maker* 23 (October 1, 1881): 11, quoted in Darling, *Chicago Furniture*, 78.

6 Charles B. Fletcher, "Design for a Horn Chair," U.S. Patent No. 12,490, issued September 27, 1881, U.S. Patent Office.

7 "Furniture," *Inland Architect and Builder* 1 (May 1883): 54, quoted in Darling, *Chicago Furniture*, 78.

8 "Art Notes," *Inland Architect and Builder* 2 (November 1883): 136, quoted in Darling, *Chicago Furniture*, 78.

9 J. Frank Dobie, "First Cattle in Texas and the Southwest Progenitors of the Longhorns," *Southwestern Historical Quarterly* 42, no. 3 (January 1939): 4, http://texashistory.unt.edu/ark:/67531/metapth101107/m1/4/.

10 "The History of Cattle Drives," Texas Genealogy Trails, accessed June 23, 2015, http://genealogytrails.com/tex/state/cattledrives.html#Chisholm Trail.

11 St. John, *Longhorn Artist*, 7.

12 Friedrich, *Wenzel Friedrich*, 2.

13 Many thanks to Andrew VanStyn for his tireless efforts on this chair, including writing historically accurate descriptions, locating the trade card, and conducting the reupholstery scheme for the chair.

14 Friedrich, *Wenzel Friedrich*, 20.

15 Friedrich, 20.

16 St. John, *Longhorn Artist*, 5.

17 Friedrich, *Wenzel Friedrich*, 36.

18 This could be either Marie François Sadi Carnot (1837–1894), who served as president of France between 1887 and 1894, or his predecessor, François Paul Jules Grévy (1807–1891), who was in office from 1879 to 1887. See St. John, *Longhorn Artist*, 5.

Appalachian Bent Willow Arm Chair

20

1890–1910

Designed and manufactured by an unknown chair maker (Southern Appalachia)

Willow branches, wood plank seat, hooked rug seat cushion

41 ½ x 25 ⅛ x 24 ⅞ in.

WHILE THE *RUSTIC* Settee made by Janes, Beebe and Company (Cat. No. 8) references nature through cast iron, this handmade example illustrates the pure rustic style by its manufacture from organic materials. With knowledge passed down through generations, local craftspeople created handmade furniture from abundant, naturally growing materials gathered from the local landscape. Much like the rattan furniture that was popular in the Northeast, furniture made in the South from rhododendron, mountain laurel, hickory, and willow was lightweight, could be easily cleaned, provided good ventilation, and was ideally suited for use either inside or on the porch. A photograph of President William McKinley (1843–1901), taken the summer prior to his assassination, shows him seated in a rocking chair on the porch of his home in Canton, Ohio, while behind him is a bent-willow chair (Fig. 20.1).

In the American Southeast there are approximately 12 native and several naturalized species of *Salix* (willow).[1] Sustainable resources that grow in damp soil near water sources, willow trees and shrubs mature quickly and their fallen limbs re-root rapidly. The twigs are flexible when young and green; when dry, they become hard, durable, and weather resistant. Willow-craft was first practiced by indigenous peoples, who used rawhide strips to bind the branches.[2] The techniques were later shared with European settlers, who formed the natural material with modern tools and fastened it with nails.

Inspiration for this lyrical, rustic-style chair draws upon various sources and traditions. The whimsical construction mirrors organic forms in a sophisticated, sculptural aesthetic. Thin, pliable twigs loop and coil into serpentine curves, while thicker branches provide support to the underlying sturdy frame. Though beautiful, all the elements are essential to the functionality of the chair and provide support to the structure. The continuous, sweeping line that forms the armrests, chair back, and crest rail is a timeless aesthetic, as seen in examples dating from classical antiquity, such as the klismos form (Cat. No. 1), to those by modern designers like Frank Gehry (Cat. Nos. 42 and 47) and Vivian Beer (Cat. No. 46). The natural reddish bark has been repeatedly chip-carved, exposing the sapwood and creating a visually dynamic aesthetic. The pattern likely recalls the bark of the diamond willow, which when affected by a fungus develops sculptural diamond-

Fig. 20.1 President William McKinley on the porch of his home, Canton, Ohio, summer 1901.

Fig. 20.2 *Twig Table*, 20th century, designed by Rev. Benjamin Marcus Davis (1876–1947), rustic twigs and branches, nailed and lacquered, 29 ½ x 35 x 22 in.

shaped segments with strong contrasting colors in red and white. For added comfort, and consistency with the handcrafted folk-art tradition, a cushion made from a vintage hooked rug covers the seat.[3]

Most artisans of rustic Appalachian furniture are unknown, though rustic furniture was being produced in the Southern Appalachian area as early as 1847, as evidenced by a dated chair from Valle Crucis, near Boone, North Carolina.[4] Traveling gypsies and itinerant craftsmen moved from place to place to sell their wares or traded them for goods and services. Others parked their wagons or trucks by the side of the road and offered their crafts to passing tourists. A few artisans even established businesses in areas frequented by tourists. Two well-documented makers of rustic Appalachian furniture were John Hentschel (1866–1940) and Reverend Benjamin Marcus Davis (1876–1947), both of whom operated in western North

Carolina. Born in Germany and first settling in Tennessee, Hentschel had moved by 1920 to Black Mountain, North Carolina, and later to Ridgecrest, North Carolina. While at Black Mountain, Hentschel operated a shop in which he made furniture principally from rhododendron branches. He also fabricated architectural detailing for buildings, notably the stair balustrade, front railing, and a porch swing at Pine Lodge in Black Mountain.[5] Reverend Davis was a Southern Baptist circuit preacher who traveled extensively throughout the western portion of the state. He supported his itinerant lifestyle by making furniture from the branches of mountain laurel, rhododendron, and willow, and he regularly incorporated scavenged lumber from demolished buildings (Fig. 20.2). Several of his pieces are signed and possess chip carving like that seen on the armchair in the DeMell Jacobsen Collection.[6]

Commercial promotion of Appalachian crafts began as early as 1902, when Frances

Louisa Goodrich (1856–1944) established Allanstand Cottage Industries with a mission to "revive the old industries, which were fast disappearing, and to bring interest and thrift and habits of self-help to those who, by reason of the conditions of their lives, shut in by mountains and streams, are unable to find a market for the artistic work they produce."[7] Through sales conducted onsite and by mail order, Goodrich and her artisans offered diverse inventory, including raw coverlet material, bedspreads embroidered in homespun cotton, fringe for bedspreads, hats, baskets, quilts, brooms, furniture, and even made-to-order hooked rugs. Continued growth of the business, combined with closure of the nearby roadway, prompted Goodrich to relocate the enterprise to downtown Asheville, North Carolina, in 1908 to cater to the many tourists seeking the mountain air. There, Goodrich became connected both socially and professionally to other enterprising individuals who recognized the value of handcrafted traditions. One such person was Lucy Calista Morgan (1889–1981), who in 1923 founded the Penland Weavers and Potters, a cottage industry that provided local women with looms, materials, and a means by which to market their handwoven goods. In 1929, she established the Penland School of Handicrafts, which continues in operation today and offers classes, fellowships, and residency programs for artists who work with traditional craft-based media. Vivian Beer, the maker of *Current, No. 2*, designed and fabricated the chair during her three-year residency at Penland. Through the determination and vision of women like Goodrich and Morgan, a Craft Revival

movement spread across the Southeast and helped lead to the establishment in 1931 of the Southern Mountain Handicraft Guild (today the Southern Highland Craft Guild).

Located in Asheville, the guild provided a forum for sharing and teaching traditional craft techniques and encouraged its members to create original and individual designs.[8] Its members included individual artisans and students in craft schools throughout Virginia, West Virginia, North Carolina, Tennessee, Georgia, and Kentucky, as well as Cherokee on the North Carolina reservation.[9] In 1933, the guild organized a traveling exhibition featuring artwork by its members. Circulated by the American Federation of Arts, and sponsored by

several First Ladies, including Grace Coolidge (1879–1957), Lou Henry Hoover (1874–1944), and Eleanor Roosevelt (1884–1962), the exhibition sought to "suggest to the people of our country the quantity, quality, and variety of hand work which is done in the area known as the Southern Highlands, that part of the Appalachian Range south of the Mason and Dixon Line."[10] The exhibition intended to educate people about the beautiful and useful items made in the region, including "settin' chairs,"[11] and to stimulate the economy during the Depression for the "thousands of mountain families to whom the making and marketing of these things determine largely their standard of living."[12]

1   George W. Argus, *The Genus* Salix *(Salicaceae) in the Southeastern United States, Systemic Botany Monographs*, vol. 9 (Ann Arbor, MI: American Society of Plant Taxonomists, 1986), 1.
2   Lois Gibson, "Notes on Willow Furniture: Treasure Hunting: Willow Furniture," *Los Angeles Times*, August 28, 1988.
3   Many thanks to Andrew VanStyn for his tireless efforts on this chair, including writing historically accurate descriptions, locating the appropriate hooked rug, and having the cushion made for the chair.
4   Lynne Poirier-Wilson, "Rustic Furniture of the Southern Appalachians," in *Rustic Garden Furniture and Accessories: Making Chairs, Planters, Birdhouses, Gates and More*, by Daniel Mack and Thomas Stender (New York: Lark Books, 2007), 102.
5   Sybil H. Argintar, *Town of Black Mountain, Buncombe County, North Carolina: Architectural Survey* (Asheville, NC: Southeastern Preservation Services, 2007), 13, 53, https://digital.ncdcr.gov/digital/collection/p16062coll47/id/1448/.
6   See *Twig Table*, signed "B. M. Davis," sold at Cowan's Auctions, April 12, 2014, lot 883 (Fig. 20.2); and a similar table, attributed to Davis, sold at Brunk Auctions, January 15, 2016, lot 77.

7   *Allanstand Cottage Industries* (New York: Woman's Board of Home Missions of the Presbyterian Church in the USA, c. 1901), 7.
8   *A Catalogue of Mountain Handicrafts by the Members of the Southern Highland Handicraft Guild* (Washington, DC: American Federation of Arts, 1933), 3, https://wcudigitalcollection.contentdm.oclc.org/digital/collection/p4008coll2/id/1133.
9   *Catalogue of Mountain Handicrafts*, 5, 11.
10 *Catalogue of Mountain Handicrafts*, 3.
11 *Catalogue of Mountain Handicrafts*, 7.
12 *Catalogue of Mountain Handicrafts*, 3.

'McKinley' Arm Chair

c. 1894–1896

Designed by David Wolcott Kendall (1851–1910)

Manufactured by the Phoenix Furniture Company (active 1872–1919, Grand Rapids, Michigan)

Stained oak, cane (modern)

34 ¼ x 29 ½ x 23 ¾ in.

Stenciled on inside of front apron: 443.

ALTHOUGH PRESIDENT McKinley's porch at his personal residence in Canton, Ohio, was furnished with bent-willow chairs (see Cat. No. 20), the McKinley White House contained an example of this progressively designed armchair, thus giving rise to its name. Designed by David Wolcott Kendall and made from stained oak with a cane seat, the chair is infused with elements of the Prairie School, which influenced architecture and decorative arts during the late 19th century and into the early 20th century. In addition, the chair marks a regional shift in furniture manufacturing, from the Mid-Atlantic and New England to the Midwest, specifically Grand Rapids, Michigan.

The Prairie School is a unique American adaptation of the British Arts and Crafts Movement promoted by John Ruskin (1819–1900) and William Morris (1834–1896). Established to counter industrialist manufacturing, the Arts and Crafts Movement revived the medieval practice of handicrafts, advocated for a clean and safe working environment, and encouraged support for individual craftsmen through the establishment of guilds. Embracing these concepts, but translating them to a local vernacular, the Prairie School promoted an American aesthetic inspired by the Midwest landscape. Referencing the broad flatness and horizon of the plains through its linearity and restrained use of ornamentation, the style rose to prominence following the 1893 World's Columbian Exposition in Chicago through the architecture and designs of Frank Lloyd Wright (1867–1959, Cat. No. 28), who became its principal proponent.

Between the years following the 1876 Centennial Exhibition and the 1893 World's Columbian Exposition, Grand Rapids had become known as "The Furniture City." Development of the furniture industry in the Midwest had mirrored a national westward growth, which was greatly facilitated by improved transportation systems via waterways and rail. These systems, too, helped move natural resources, such as felled logs, to market, which increased operational efficiency and reduced production costs, thus making the finished goods affordable to a growing middle class. In 1872, William A. Berkey (1823–1902) established the Phoenix Furniture Company using residual assets from the cabinetmaking firm Atkins and Soule as well as $200,000 in new capital.[1] As the company continued to flourish, Berkey constructed a new factory in town (Fig. 21.1) and opened a New York showroom in 1876 at 175–177 Canal Street. There, he advertised the company as "wholesale manufacturers of furniture of all kinds for the trade," with "wardrobe folding beds a specialty."[2]

Grand Rapids furniture companies recruited many of their talented designers from international interior design firms or furniture manufacturers. English-born Tom Handley (1874–1926) apprenticed in a London shop before moving first to New York City, where he worked for the prominent firm of W. & J. Sloane, and then to Grand Rapids, where he found work as a designer for the Luce Furniture Company. The John Widdicomb Company lured Stanley Green, who had apprenticed at the English firm Waring and Gillow. William Millington (1880–1962), who had trained at the Royal College of Arts in London, also worked at Waring and Gillow and at Sloane before going to work at Phoenix Furniture Company in 1917. The American designer David Wolcott Kendall (Fig. 21.2) followed a similar path.

A native of Rochester, New York, the talented Kendall exemplified the qualities of his Mayflower ancestors, a heritage he held in esteem. A "student, designer, artist, musician, woodcarver, traveler and inventor," he was also described as "at once a dreamer, an idealist, and a practical businessman."[3] He learned cabinetmaking from his father and apprenticed with the furniture manufacturer Bromley, Hunn and Smith. Kendall proved industrious and driven as he "studied drawing and painting, mechanical drawing, architecture, sculpture, and modeling."[4]

From Rochester, Kendall moved west and worked with several furniture companies, including the innovative Wooten Desk Company of Indianapolis, Indiana, and as a draftsman in a Chicago architectural firm. In 1879, Kendall joined the Phoenix Furniture Company at the invitation of John T. Strahan, who was superintendent and designer of the firm. Kendall worked for the company from 1879 to 1883 and took a hiatus to work for a competitor, Berkey and Gay Furniture Company, between 1883 and 1886. Later that year, he moved to Detroit, where he founded Kendall, Beardsley and Dey, which manufactured furniture for libraries. In 1888, Kendall returned to the Phoenix Furniture Company in the capacity of chief designer.

While believing in the importance of hand-carved wood, Kendall valued the "efficiency of American factories" and improved the Phoenix workrooms into "as convenient, clean, light and pleasant shops as there are in the city."[5] Kendall helped reform and elevate not only the Phoenix Furniture Company, but also the manufacturing practices in Grand Rapids and beyond. For his contributions, Kendall has been dubbed the "dean of furniture designers of the world."[6]

Throughout the 19th century, American furniture principally had been made from mahogany, walnut, and rosewood. Oak was thought to be too common a wood, lacking the dark rich color and smooth grain characteristic of the more expensive woods. Because of the increasing scarcity of walnut and the prohibitive expense of mahogany, however, furniture manufacturers in Grand Rapids and elsewhere turned to oak, which could be found in abundance in forests throughout Indiana, Ohio, and Michigan. In addition, the use of domestic woods in the manufacture of American furniture was thought to be a patriotic act. Gustav Stickley (1858–1942, Cat. No. 23), leader of the American Arts and Crafts Movement, observed as much in an editorial, "Pro Patria," that appeared in the first issue of his influential publication *The Craftsman*:

When in the decade of 1870–1880, Oriental art began to receive wide-spread attention in France, and became a favorite topic of conversation in fashionable salons, there were many connoisseurs who denied its claims to consideration. Then it was that M. Thiers, the President of the French Republic, summed up in a single pithy sentence the reasons for the narrow prejudice which refused currency to ideas other than those consecrated by long familiarity.

He declared: "One should not go to Japan with the Parthenon in one's mind."

A similar prejudice has established itself in this country regarding the use of mahogany in the finer pieces of household furnishings. The preference for this wood, founded partially upon its beauty, received a very strong impetus from the connection of the wood and of certain famous cabinet makers with our colonial history, which of late has been so thoroughly treated by American authors, and so thoroughly by our

Fig. 21.1 (above) Phoenix Furniture Company factory, Grand Rapids, Michigan, 1905–1920.

Fig. 21.2 (left) David Wolcott Kendall with his dog, date unknown.

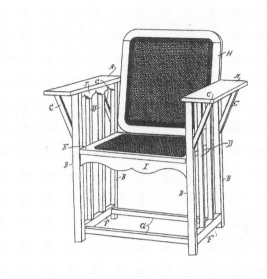

DESIGN.

D. W. KENDALL.
CHAIR.

No. 27,597.

Patented Aug. 31, 1897.

Witnesses.

Fireman Lathrop

DO. Coumin

Inventor.

David W. Kendall

By Gilley + Allgier

Attorneys

Fig. 21.3 (above) *Six-Sided Plant Stand or Side Table*, model number 496, with a Moorish stencilled design applied in a malachite and canary yellow finish, c. 1896, designed by David Wolcott Kendall (1851–1910), manufactured by Phoenix Furniture Company (active 1872–1919, Grand Rapids, Michigan), oak, 24 x 28 x 24 in., Grand Rapids Public Museum.

Fig. 21.4 (right) David Wolcott Kendall, "Design for a Chair," U.S. Patent No. 27,597, filed July 24, 1897, issued August 31, 1897, U.S. Patent Office.

patriotic clubs. Consequently, our native products have been neglected and their possibilities overlooked. But it is true that oak, ash, and elm, properly treated, possess attractions that yield to those of no other woods. The undulations of their grain, the soft, unobtrusive tones which they assume through skillful polish, the color-play which runs over their smooth surface are qualities which to be appreciated need only to be fairly observed. The intelligent craftsman in our country is now raising our northern woods to a place beside that occupied by the long-admired mahogany.[7]

At Phoenix, Kendall initially found the use of oak provided results that were "not satisfactory. The wood was unattractive

in color, lacked character and was hard to handle."[8] Kendall sought a remedy and developed several brightly colored finishes—canary yellow, copper red, malachite (green), and "Flemish" (black)—that either completely masked the oak grain or was applied in exotic patterns, such as that seen on a *Six-Sided Plant Stand or Side Table* (Fig. 21.3). Buoyed by the results, Kendall established a chemistry lab in the basement of the Phoenix factory in which he further experimented with stains and fumed finishes that enhanced, rather than covered, the natural grain of the various woods used by the firm.[9] Among them were "Cremona," a honey-color finish made to imitate the appearance of 17th- and 18th-century violins made in Cremona, Italy; a darkened, or "antique" oak; the "Sixteenth Century,"

a stain that mimicked wear patterns on old furniture; a "malachite," or green stain, which was to be his most imitated; and a "Byzantine" finish that was designed to imitate a Byzantine mosaic and included "small pieces of variegated, irregular shapes inlaid in a pattern and the surface is also irregular."[10] Another that would prove popular was a dark gray-black stain, called "Belgian." Of the finish, Kendall recalled:

We have just put out a new finish called the "Belgian." We got it up with the idea that there was a demand for dark furniture, something darker than antique oak or brown oak, and which would take the place of dark mahogany or black walnut. We have made no effort to push it, but the better class of buyers seem to

Fig. 21.5 Detail of stencil on inside of front apron.

have taken hold of it and it has been a go from the very start. It is suitable for bedrooms, libraries and halls.[11]

This Belgian finish is found on the DeMell Jacobsen Collection *"McKinley" Arm Chair*, which is assuredly Kendall's most famous and forward-thinking design and a stark contrast to the many revival styles he had designed up to that point.[12] Introduced by the Phoenix Furniture Company between 1894 and 1896, the design came in several variants, including the present example, a rocker, a settee, and a Morris chair, which had the ability to recline and possessed pierced wood panels under the arms rather than square spindles.[13] The *Michigan Tradesman* described it as being "designed on simple lines, spacious and comfortable," which "had a great sale and is said to be the basis for the modern arts and crafts furniture."[14] Later, the design became known as the "McKinley" chair, after a prototype had been given to the president for use in his office at the White House. The chair proved an instant success and was copied by several furniture manufacturers across the country, including Joseph McHugh and Company of New York; J. S. Ford, Johnson and Company of Chicago; and the Paine Furniture Company of Boston, which possibly had viewed a Kendall example at the first *American Arts and Crafts Exhibition*, held at Copley Hall in April 1897. To protect his intellectual property, Kendall secured a patent for his chair design in August 1897 (Fig. 21.4).[15]

Elements of the Prairie School style are evident in the chair's plain lines and unadorned surface. Rigid square spindles support a wide-bodied seat and "broad oblong" cantilevered armrests.[16] The simple geometry of the frame, completely joined by dowels, is physically and aesthetically enhanced with pointed Moorish- or Gothic-inspired arches between the spindles and an ornamental scrolling "girth" below the seat rail secured to the seat bottom by screws.[17] This example is marked "443." on the inside of the front apron (Fig. 21.5). These decorative elements reflect both the exotic revival tastes of the prevailing Aesthetic Movement as well as Kendall's many travels through Asia, Mexico and Central America, Europe, and the Middle East. A caned seat and back that reclined for comfort provided ventilation as well as a posture conducive to relaxing or reading. The Paine Furniture Company offered their own version of the chair in their summer 1897 catalogue, priced at $10 and available in mahogany, natural birch, or oak, and finished in dark green or "Belgian" stain. The firm touted their "reading chair":

A new design this year, and one which is attracting a great deal of attention. The cane seat and back are cool and comfortable for summer use, and the very broad arm-rests give almost the additional advantage of a side table. They are wide enough to hold books, magazines, smoking utensils, a tray or any other small articles. The chair is rigidly framed.[18]

Propelled by both its presidential notoriety and its progressive design, the chair remained in vogue for at least the first two decades of the 20th century. Contemporary photographs document examples in diverse interiors, including a "spartan Pennsylvania farm house, an elaborate mansion, in the Trellis Room of the Colony Club (New York), decorated in 1906 by the famed interior decorator Elsie de Wolfe, and in the Baker House (Wilmette, Illinois) designed by Frank Lloyd Wright in 1909."[19] Though Kendall long had championed the production of revival styles, his innovative practices led to a progressive study of ergonomics. For one of his designs, he reportedly "secured the curves for one of his chairs by having people sit down in a snowbank then drawing the curves that their bodies formed."[20] Such experimental approaches to design were uncommon at the time and undoubtedly inspired a new generation of Michigan designers, including Eero Saarinen (1910–1961, Cat. Nos. 29 and 32) and Charles (1907–1978) and Ray (1912–1988) Eames (Cat. No. 31).

1   For a thorough examination of Grand Rapids and its furniture industry, see Christian G. Carron, *Grand Rapids Furniture: The Story of America's Furniture City* (Grand Rapids, MI: Public Museum of Grand Rapids, 1998).
2   *Decorator and Furnisher* 10, no. 1 (April 1887): 25.
3   "David Wolcott Kendall," in *History of Kendall School of Design* (Grand Rapids, MI: Kendall School of Design, 1978).
4   Jane Perkins Claney and Robert Edwards, "Progressive Design in Grand Rapids," *Tiller* 2, no. 1 (September–October 1983): 36.
5   Claney and Edwards, 35.
6   *Trade* 17, no. 8, (February 23, 1910): 6.
7   Gustav Stickley, "Pro Patria," *Craftsman* 1, no. 1 (October 1890): iv.
8   "Death of Grand Rapids' Greatest Furniture Designer," *Michigan Tradesman*, February 23, 1910, 10.
9   Special thanks to Andrew VanStyn for sharing his research and expertise on the history and design of this chair, which has helped to shape this essay.
10 Claney and Edwards, "Progressive Design in Grand Rapids," 44.
11 "Modern Finishes," February 1890, 4, cited in Claney and Edwards, 55 n. 35.
12 The chair in the DeMell Jacobsen Collection also features green tones, so it is possible that Kendall layered finishes, applying the Belgian first and then applying a malachite finish to give the chair its green appearance.
13 Claney and Edwards, 48, 54–55 n. 34.
14 "Death of Grand Rapids' Greatest Furniture Designer."
15 David W. Kendall, "Design for a Chair," U.S. Patent No. 27,597, filed July 24, 1897, issued August 31, 1897, U.S. Patent Office.
16 Kendall.
17 Kendall.
18 Claney and Edwards, "Progressive Design in Grand Rapids," 48.
19 Claney and Edwards, 50.
20 Claney and Edwards, 51.

3

Dawn of a New Century
From Modest to Modern (1900–1950)

The Arts and Crafts Movement that swept America and Great Britain in the late 19th and early 20th centuries was not a rejection of the use of all machinery in the making of furniture, but rather one that emphasized individually crafted objects made in studios or small workshops. Movement leaders Frank Lloyd Wright and Gustav Stickley advocated for the creation of a distinctive American style that drew upon these ideas and that similarly integrated furnishings, architecture, handicrafts, and principles of harmonious living. Stickley promoted the idea that well-designed furnishings could help "make life better and truer by its perfect simplicity."

Yet life during the early 20th century did not remain perfectly simple for Americans. Within a relatively short timeframe, significant inventions—the airplane (1903), Hollywood movies (1910s), and the commercial radio broadcast (1920s)—would forever transform how Americans lived their daily lives.

In the years following World War I (1914–1918), what we now recognize as modern design was realized in the International Style, which relied on machines to produce furniture made from tubular metal. However, restrictions on the use of metals in the years preceding and during World War II (1939–1945) led American manufacturers to experiment with innovative materials—plastics, fiberglass, and wood laminates—in home and office furnishings, resulting in yet another exciting and innovative period of design. By the mid-20th century, American firms such as Herman Miller, Knoll, and others took full advantage of mass production and these new technologies, allowing them to create quality furnishings at ever-more-affordable prices.

Hall Chair

22

1900

Designed and manufactured by Charles Rohlfs
(1853–1936) (active 1886–1928/9, Buffalo,
New York)

Stained oak, red enamel

56 ½ x 19 x 15 in.

Impressed on rear seat rail: "Sign of the Saw"
brand [R within a bow saw] / 1900

WHILE STYLISTICALLY quite different, this chair by Charles Rohlfs and the example by David Wolcott Kendall (Cat. No. 21) share something in common: both have connections to President William McKinley and the dawn of the 20th century.[1] At the age of 43, Rohlfs had participated in several public debates in support of McKinley's presidential campaign. In 1897, the year of McKinley's inauguration, Rohlfs's exuberant, airy, and fancifully designed furniture made its public debut, providing a stark contrast to the robust, rectilinear forms of the prevailing Arts and Crafts Movement.

Born in Brooklyn, New York, Rohlfs excelled at a variety of talents, ranging from stage acting to designing patterns for stoves. He became best known, however, for his innovative furniture, which he principally produced in the two decades between 1887 and 1907. Rohlfs's exuberantly sculpted, stained, and carved oak furnishings emerged concomitantly with those of the Arts and Crafts and Art Nouveau Movements, yet they perhaps share a closer affinity to the naturalistic designs of Prairie School architects Louis Sullivan (1856–1924) and George Grant Elmslie (1869–1952). Though thoroughly utilitarian, Rohlfs's designs for chairs and other forms of furniture are also closely aligned to the Ruskinian philosophy of "art for art's sake" of the preceding Aesthetic Movement. Rohlfs rejected contemporary artistic styles and conventions and boldly proclaimed that his designs "are like those of no other period nor people. They are mine and into their execution I put all my heart and force and that is why they appeal."[2]

Likely introduced to the furniture trade by his father, a piano cabinetmaker, Rohlfs studied drafting and design at Cooper Union, and found employment as a pattern maker in local iron foundries following his schooling. In 1887, Rohlfs and his wife, noted author Anna Katharine Green (1846–1935), moved from New York City to Buffalo, New York, due to Rohlfs's employment with the Sherman S. Jewett Company, a maker of cast-iron stoves. There, the couple settled into their first home on Linwood Avenue, for which both Rohlfs and Green—harbingers of the mid-20th-century husband-and-wife designers Charles and Ray Eames (Cat. No. 31)—collaborated on the design and manufacture of several pieces of furniture. For Green's home office or study, the color

of which was described as "old gold," Rohlfs designed and made a pedestal table, as well as a settee fashioned of polished oak with cushions "of peacock blue plush, those at the back being held up by knobbed pins in the loops. The pieces of the settee are fastened by round head brass screws, no gluing being used."[3] The settee's carved ornamentation, featuring fancy scrollwork, was undoubtedly designed by Green.[4]

Following the couple's European tour in 1890, which surely exposed Rohlfs to prevailing stylistic conventions, the couple returned to America, dividing their time between New York City and Buffalo. In 1896 they relocated permanently to Buffalo, where Rohlfs established his first workshop in the attic of their home at 10 Orton Place. Two years later Rohlfs leased a larger attic workspace, located at 451 Washington Street. In it could be found numerous types of "lumber, benches, lathes, tools of all kinds, paints, drawings, photographs, and furniture at every stage of development, from the first vague conception ... to the finished product."[5] By 1900, Rohlfs's designs had garnered acclaim. In their January 1900 issue, the *House Beautiful* reviewed an exhibition of his furniture at the Marshall Field and Company department store in Chicago. The reviewer described the furniture as being "all of oak, stained black, brown, and dark green, and not too smooth or shiny. The pegs joining it are unevenly cut and are much in evidence. It is needless to add that it is unique, and it has the rare quality of fitting in anywhere; for while it is roughly executed, it has originality and a certain distinction."[6]

The *Hall Chair* in the DeMell Jacobsen Collection is very similar to one illustrated in the *House Beautiful* review and another published in the *Puritan* in August 1900. All feature wide plank seats and attenuated backs. This example possesses a rich dark brown surface, which Rohlfs achieved by fuming the wood with ammonia. His use of red enamel heightens the surfaces of the carved elements and those of the various rose-head plugs, which conceal the screws that join the component pieces to each other (Fig. 22.1). The slender back features seven vertical floriform spindles (Fig. 22.2), which surmount a vasiform element, while the adjacent attenuated stiles terminate in robustly carved finials. Centering the crest rail and the front seat rails are circular

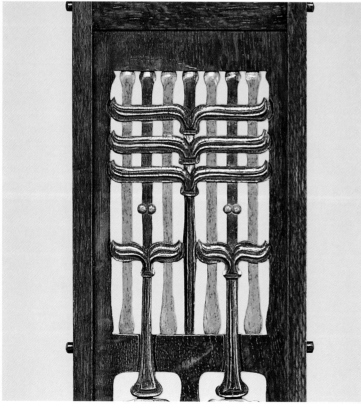

Figs 22.1, 22.2 and 22.3 Detail views of the rose-head plugs, signature, seat back, and feet.

cutouts reminiscent of those designed by the Scottish designer Charles Rennie Mackintosh (1868–1928). The *Hall Chair* is dated 1900—the same year the artist exhibited at Marshall Field and Company and participated in the *Arts and Crafts Exhibition* held at the National Arts Club in New York City. Interestingly, while Rohlfs had been making furniture professionally for more than a decade prior to 1900, he does not appear to have dated any pieces up to that point, which suggests he may have wished to document the arrival of the new century by dating his works (Fig. 22.1).[7]

In contrast to the designs of his Arts and Crafts contemporaries Gustav Stickley (Cat. No. 23) and Charles Limbert (Cat. No. 24) and those of mid-century designer George Nakashima (Cat. No. 39), for whom the grain of the wood was the sole form of decoration, Rohlfs felt compelled to "embellish" the wood by carving into it, "to evidence my profound regard for a beautiful thing in nature" (Fig. 22.3).[8] In his article entitled "The Grain of Wood," Rohlfs stated that to enjoy wood in either the rough or finished state, one must "go a step or two into the world of fancy and imagination."[9] When he observed a wood grain, Rohlfs envisioned rising smoke, storms, waves, blowing breezes, and even Santa Claus, on whose head sat a snow man! Though far removed from direct imitation, Rohlfs stated, "I owe to the natural lines in the wood the inspiration for many an effective design," and he encouraged people to "look for the beauties that nature has painted in the striking undulations shown in the grain of woods, and especially in the ash and oak."[10]

Although Rohlfs distanced himself from what he perceived as the commercial, mass-produced aspects of the Arts and Crafts Movement, and Gustav Stickley, leader of the movement, reciprocated by publicly ignoring Rohlfs, both men exhibited at many of the same venues and worked in close-knit artistic communities approximately 150 miles from each other. In 1901, Rohlfs showed several pieces of furniture in the Buffalo Pan-American Exposition, and the following year he may well have been the only American furniture maker to have participated in the First International Exposition of Modern Decorative Arts in Turin, Italy. After the exhibition in Turin, Rohlfs was elected to the Royal Society of Arts in London, and by 1903 he had become an active member in the council of the Buffalo Society of Artists.[11] In 1904, the Charles Rohlfs Workshop participated in the exhibition at the Louisiana Purchase Exposition in St. Louis. By 1907, however, interest in Rohlfs-designed furniture waned, prompting him to focus instead on local politics, social reforms, and making assorted furnishings for his family home, then located at 156 Park Street.

Today, many examples comparable to the *Hall Chair* in the DeMell Jacobsen Collection, though lacking red enamel, may be found in numerous private and public collections, including those of the Metropolitan Museum of Art, the Art Institute of Chicago, and the Saint Louis Art Museum, among others.

1   For a thorough examination of the life and artistic output of Charles Rohlfs, see especially Michael L. James, *Drama in Design: The Life and Craft of Charles Rohlfs* (Buffalo, NY: Burchfield Art Center, Buffalo State College, 1994), and Joseph Cunningham, *The Artistic Furniture of Charles Rohlfs* (New York: American Decorative Art 1900 Foundation, 2008).

2   Lola J. Diffin, "Artistic Designing of House Furniture," *Buffalo Courier*, April 22, 1900.

3   *Decorator and Furnisher* 12, no. 3 (June 1888): 78.

4   For a discussion of Green's influence, see Cunningham, *Artistic Furniture*, 34–38, and Joseph Cunningham, "Anna Katharine Green and Charles Rohlfs: Artistic Collaborators," *The Magazine ANTIQUES* 174, no. 6 (December 2008): 70–75.

5   Charlotte Moffitt, "The Rohlfs Furniture," *House Beautiful* 7, no. 2 (January 1900): 82.

6   Moffitt, 84–85.

7   Cunningham, *Artistic Furniture*, 71.

8   Charles Rohlfs, "My Adventures in Wood-Carving," *Buffalo Arts Journal*, October 1925, 21–22.

9   Charles Rohlfs, "The Grain of Wood," *House Beautiful* 9, no. 3 (February 1901): 147–48.

10   Rohlfs, 147–48.

11   "Gleanings from American Art Centers," *Brush and Pencil* 11, no. 4 (January 1903), 315.

Oxbow Arm Chair

23

c. 1903

Design attributed to David Robertson Smith
(active 1902–1915)

Manufacture attributed to Stickley Brothers
Company (active 1891–1954, Grand Rapids,
Michigan)

Oak, leather upholstery (original),
hand-wrought copper

32 ¾ x 23 x 22 in.

THE TURN OF THE 20th century brought with it considerable change and reform. Queen Victoria died in January 1901, marking the end of the Victorian age. In September of the same year, President McKinley was assassinated in Buffalo, New York, while visiting the Pan-American Exposition. Following McKinley's death, Theodore "Teddy" Roosevelt (1858–1919) led the country through his "Square Deal," a progressive policy initiative guided by a judicious conservation of natural resources, control of corporations, and consumer protections. Transportation was revolutionized with the Wright Brothers' first successful airplane flight in 1903, as well as the introduction of Henry Ford's Model T automobile in 1908.

Amidst these changes, some were advocating for a simpler way of living. The American Arts and Crafts style is most closely associated with Gustav Stickley (1858–1942), who in October 1901 began publishing *The Craftsman* to promote his philosophy through his architectural designs and interior furnishings. In the inaugural issue, Stickley made an "Argument for Simplicity in Household Furnishings":

> In all that concerns household furnishings and decoration, present tendencies are

toward a simplicity unknown in the past. The form of any object is made to express the structural idea directly, frankly, often almost with baldness. The materials employed are chosen no longer solely for their intrinsic value, but with a great consideration for their potential beauty. The qualities thus apprehended are traced to their source and then carefully developed by the skill of the craftsman.[1]

This was a philosophy shared by the five Stickley brothers, all of whom cooperated and competed in an array of furniture companies. In 1891, two of Gustav's younger brothers, Albert (1863–1928) and John George (1871–1921), relocated to Grand Rapids, Michigan, where they established the Stickley Brothers Company. In the years between 1890 and 1910, as the Arts and Crafts Movement reached its height in popularity, Grand Rapids' population had increased from 60,000 to over 112,000. Fifty-four furniture companies employed over 7,000 people, mostly of Dutch heritage,[2] and the industry's net capital reached $13,322,000 by 1910.[3]

By 1900, Stickley Brothers Company had a secure presence in the Grand Rapids furniture market, with Albert as president

Fig. 23.1 The Chinese display showing horseshoe-back chairs, Liberal Arts Building, Louisiana Purchase Exposition, St. Louis, 1904.

Fig. 23.2 (above left) *Armchair*, c. 1901, designed by David Robertson Smith (active 1902–1915) or Arthur E. Teal (1881–1927), manufactured by the Stickley Brothers Company (active 1891–1954, Grand Rapids, Michigan), with inlay by Timothy A. Conti, oak with fruitwood inlay, 36 x 25 x 17 ½ in., Fine Arts Museums of San Francisco.

Fig. 23.3 (above right) A Chinese horseshoe-back chair on a swivel base exhibited at the Louisiana Purchase Exposition, St. Louis, 1904.

and John George excelling in marketing as vice president. Although John George later departed for a new endeavor in New York with another brother, Leopold (1869–1957), Albert continued to lead the Stickley Brothers Company until his passing in 1928. Well regarded in the industry, he was elected president of the Grand Rapids Furniture Association in both 1904 and 1905.

As was the case with his siblings, Albert was an artist and a progressive businessman who advocated for the creation of a distinctive American style, one

which integrated furnishings, architecture, handicrafts, and principles of harmonious living. Albert, like his brother Gustav, traveled to England in 1896 to search for inspirations to incorporate in his own designs of Arts and Crafts furniture. The following year, Albert opened a Stickley Brothers Company factory and showroom in London (active 1897–1902) to reach British consumers. It was also in London that Albert encountered David Robertson Smith. Born in Aberdeen, Scotland, Smith had studied art at Aberdeen College and later at the Royal College of Art in London. While at the Royal College he worked as a freelance artist for a variety of London firms, including Stickley's. Accepting Albert's invitation in 1902, Smith relocated to Grand Rapids, where he helped launch new designs for the firm's "Quaint" line, an English term referring to furniture of Arts and Crafts design. Some Quaint forms were modeled after Gustav's furniture, while others show inspiration by British designers such as Mackay Hugh Baillie Scott (1865–

1945), Charles Robert Ashbee (1863–1942), C. F. A. Voysey (1857–1941), and Liberty and Company.

Smith's talent for illustration, interior design, and work in copper undoubtedly elevated the company's profile. In the introduction to the 1902 Stickley Brothers Company catalogue, Smith insisted historical styles no longer suited modern times and the new "distinctive style ... should be in keeping with the quiet dress of the period, neither profuse in rich ornamentation, nor yet blatant in the vigor of its plain simplicity."[4] While adhering to Gustav's belief that furniture should focus on "utility and simplicity," Albert Stickley and Smith introduced two styles within the Quaint brand: a plain, unadorned, and restrained Mission style and the "Bewdley" line, which sought "to relieve the severity of the too many straight lines of the simple Mission furniture" by incorporating subdued ornamentation through inlay, simple carving and metalwork.[5]

By January 1903, Grand Rapids had thoroughly embraced the marketability of the Arts and Crafts style known as "Mission." That month's cover of the *Grand Rapids Furniture Record* bore the headline "Fashions in Furniture" and illustrated a pair of Spanish monks seated on Grand Rapids Furniture Company chairs within a Southwest-style adobe interior. An article in the issue, entitled "Mission and Kindred Styles," made the following prediction:

If, as is claimed, the popularity of the simple modes of furniture and decoration are a reaction from the surfeit of elaborateness that has preceded them, it must be admitted that we have gone nearly to the extreme. It is undeniable, that the people of today desire their furniture plain, the popularity of the Colonial and the so-called Mission effects furnishing abundant evidence of this taste. The severely simple yet graceful and utilitarian appearing Mission may be a fad, as some critics affect to believe, yet it is certain to leave impress on the furniture styles of the future.[6]

The Mission-style *Oxbow Arm Chair* in the DeMell Jacobsen Collection illustrates the intentions put forth in the 1902 catalogue for furniture that featured "curves on the top rails" and supportive slats that decoratively relieve "the basic rectilinear scheme."[7] Balancing on three tapered legs that extend from crest rail to floor, the chair's structure is made rigid by a T-shaped stretcher. A single back splat divides the curved crest rail, which is composed of four pieces and terminates in upturned hand rests. The conforming original green leather upholstery is secured to the seat by 29 oversized hand-hammered copper tacks. The chair is a sharp contrast to a similarly shaped example from the Bewdley line, which possesses a center splat with elaborate floral inlay (Fig. 23.2). The curved shape of the arms on both chairs, however, recalls the general profile of the U-shaped harness of an oxen yoke, and it is perhaps tempting to note a slight similarity to the barrel-shaped seats designed by another Scotsman, Charles Rennie Mackintosh (1868–1928), whose iconic chairs graced the interior of the Willow Tearooms (see Cat. No. 24, Fig. 24.3), which opened in October 1903. Perhaps a more likely source of inspiration, though, is the "horseshoe back" chairs (*quanyi*)[8] of the Ming Dynasty.

The 1904 Louisiana Purchase Exposition in St. Louis was the first world's fair in which the Chinese government participated. Their exhibits contained a wide variety of traditional decorative arts, including traditional-style horseshoe-back chairs (Fig. 23.1), as well as a thoroughly contemporary example set atop a swivel base for use in the office (Fig. 23.3). The Stickley Brothers Company also exhibited at the exposition and received a Grand Prize for their submission, which was shown in group 38, "Office and Household Furniture."[9] A review of the installation by J. Taylor, a visitor to the fair from Glasgow, Scotland, which appeared in the *Grand Rapids Furniture Record*, praised the firm's display as being "one of the most artistic examples of a composite decorative scheme in the whole exposition … you can trace the idea of the designer and follow out the unity of the scheme. And this is one of the points that makes the contemplation of examples of the new art so interesting and instructive."[10]

The Arts and Crafts Movement celebrated the production of individually crafted objects made in studios or small workshops, although the use of machinery in the making of goods was not completely rejected. Albert Stickley admitted that "no machine can turn out as nicely finished an article as can the human hand,"[11] but he realized handmade works would be too expensive for the growing American middle class. Therefore, he embraced automation while simultaneously addressing "the reality of industrialization by attempting to find ways to improve the worker's lot within a factory context."[12] This is one of the most important and striking differences between the American Arts and Crafts Movement and that of its British counterpart. Albert Stickley—like David Wolcott Kendall and Frank Lloyd Wright, one of the founding members of the Chicago Arts and Crafts Society—believed the machine could be useful both in the development of a particularly American brand of Arts and Crafts and, more importantly, in the birth of a new American style.

1   Gustav Stickley, "An Argument for Simplicity in Household Furnishings," *Craftsman* 1, no. 1 (October, 1901): iii.
2   See Robert P. Swierenga, "The Western Michigan Dutch" (paper presented at the Holland Genealogical Society, Holland, MI, December 11, 2004), http://www.swierenga.com/hgspap1204.html.
3   Michael E. Clark and Jill Thomas-Clark, *The Stickley Brothers: The Quest for an American Voice* (Salt Lake City: Gibbs Smith, 2002), 12.
4   Quoted in Clark and Thomas-Clark, 93.
5   Clark and Thomas-Clark, 93.

6   Quoted in Christian B. Carron, *Grand Rapids Furniture: The Story of America's Furniture City* (Grand Rapids, MI: Public Museum of Grand Rapids, 1998), 60.
7   Clark and Thomas-Clark, *Stickley Brothers*, 94.
8   The Chinese name for this type of chair is literally translated as "chair with a circular back" or "circle chair." During the Song Dynasty (960–1279) this form was known as *kaolaoyang*, which refers to a large round basket made from split bamboo. The English name for this form, however, refers to the overall shape of the back and arm rests, which resemble a horseshoe.

9   David Robertson Smith also won a "special gold medal" for his work on the Stickley Brothers' exhibit at this exposition. See Don Marek and Richard Weiderman, *The 1912 Quaint Furniture Catalog*, ed. Peter A. Copeland and Janet H. Copeland (Parchment, MI: Parchment Press, 1993), vi.
10 Quoted in Clark and Thomas-Clark, *Stickley Brothers*, 99.
11 Quoted in Clark and Thomas-Clark, 105.
12 Wendy Kaplan and Eileen Boris, *"The Art That Is Life": The Arts & Crafts Movement in America, 1875–1920* (Boston: Little, Brown and Company, 1987), 223.

Plank-Back Hall Chair

24

1905

Design attributed to Charles P. Limbert
(1854–1923)

Manufacture attributed to Charles P. Limbert
Company (active 1894–1905, Grand Rapids,
Michigan; 1906–1944, Holland, Michigan)

Fumed white oak, leather (modern), brass

42 x 15 ½ x 18 in.

THE CHARLES P. LIMBERT Company produced Arts and Crafts–style furniture in Grand Rapids and nearby Holland, Michigan, combining the artistic skills of local craftspeople with a variety of international influences, as evidenced by this *Plank-Back Hall Chair*. Among Limbert's most unique and desired examples are those that possess contoured cutouts in a number of shapes, including trapezoids, trefoils, spades, hearts, and, as in the present example, squares. These cutouts demonstrate that Limbert was familiar with and influenced by diverse sources, including Scottish, Austrian, and American Prairie School architects and designers.

Born in Linesville, Pennsylvania, Charles Limbert moved with his family to Akron, Ohio, where he followed in the footsteps of his father, Levi H. Limbert, as a furniture dealer and salesman. Early in his career, Charles worked for the Monk and Roberts furniture company in Connersville, Indiana, and later for the John A. Colby Company of Chicago. During a sales trip, he became acquainted with Philip J. Klingman; in 1889 Limbert moved to Grand Rapids, where he formed a partnership with Klingman. There, they rented a spacious building and leased areas to different manufacturers, thus creating one of the first furniture marts.[1] Between 1890 and 1892 the pair manufactured their own line of chairs. The partnership dissolved and in 1894 Limbert opened his own company. In addition to offering his own styles, Limbert continued until 1905 as a sales agent for six different manufacturers throughout Illinois, Michigan, and Indiana, including the Old Hickory Chair Company.

The Charles P. Limbert Company's "most creative years of production"[2] began with their introduction of the "Dutch Arts and Crafts" furniture line in 1902. The use of "Dutch" in the name of the line may have reflected a combination of Limbert's scholarly interests, a calculated business plan, and shrewd marketing.[3] Intrigued by the synthesis of Spanish and Dutch historical influences on Arts and Crafts Mission furniture in vogue at the time, Limbert traveled to the Netherlands, where he spent "most of his time in the Dutch museums and in the various manufacturing towns, to study Dutch furniture and the latest designs in that particular style."[4] Since more than 40 percent of the Grand Rapids population was of Dutch heritage in 1900,[5] he also found the local talent advantageous.

Limbert embraced the philosophical ideals of the Arts and Crafts Movement; however, he worked hard to differentiate his company's work from competitors, such as the Stickley Brothers (Cat. No. 23) and the Phoenix Furniture Company (Cat. No. 21), by promoting old-world artistry and craftsmanship. His firm's 1903 catalogue featured a logo of a Middle Ages–era craftsman at a workbench.[6] Inside the publication, Limbert promoted handiwork, historical precedent, and attention to detail through line drawings, rather than the photograph reproductions employed by his competitors. The catalogue showcased "undeniably plain, severely simple, yet graceful and practical" items "harmonious in proportion and sound in construction," to create "comfortable" Arts and Crafts furniture.[7] Subsequent Limbert Company catalogues would include photographs of the furniture in addition to illustrations of the complete production process from forest to freight.

Limbert sought to use the best materials possible, such as naturally dried white oak that was chemically and artistically treated to draw out the essential characteristics of the wood grain, as evidenced in this fumed-oak example. Goatskins imported from South America, Asia, Russia, and Turkey were tanned in-house to become "Spanish Morocco" leather. The firm advertised its leather as being "superior to all others for the purpose," as it was sourced from wild goats with their "strength of grain and fiber ... recognized in all parts of the world as making the finest, most serviceable and best

wearing leather."[8] Like his competitors— Stickley Brothers and the Phoenix Furniture Company—Limbert's furniture was made in a factory by workers using a variety of power tools, planers, glue machines, and other machinery.[9] The simple, straight-cut lines of Limbert furniture were highly suited to machine production, though it required "a substantial amount of handiwork," especially "in making the hardware and in joining and finishing the pieces."[10]

Between 1902 and 1905, Limbert came to employ over 200 men, whom he referred to as "a guild of cabinetmakers."[11] He cared deeply about the working conditions in his factory and grew increasingly concerned that, as a growing urban industrial center, Grand Rapids was "full of the sorts of social maladies that came between workers and their work."[12] Indeed, a core tenet of the Arts and Crafts Movement purported that the Industrial Revolution had created urban centers that hampered artistry and the life

Fig. 24.1 Side view.

of the individual. Consequently, in 1905 Limbert relocated his factory to Holland, Michigan, a town 25 miles southwest of Grand Rapids with a population of 12,000. In a company catalogue of the period, Limbert explained:

As the work extended and became greater in importance, the influence of a busy manufacturing city became more and more uncongenial for these artistic craftsmen who were inspired to put their best efforts into every piece which was to bear the Limbert Trade Mark, so an environment more conducive to artistic effort and a higher quality of craftsmanship was sought and eventually discovered in the little town of Holland, Michigan.[13]

There, Limbert's craftsmen were surrounded by "attractive summer cottages and quaint houses with fertile gardens," with easy access to Chicago and other cities by water, railroad, and electric rail.[14] With its rich Dutch heritage, it was considered a place where craftsmen could "live in the proper environment and love their work, use their heads, hearts and hands, and impart an individuality and superiority to every piece."[15]

Between 1904 and 1910, Limbert's furniture achieved "greater sophistication"[16] through the influence of modernist movements in Glasgow and Vienna[17] in Europe and the Prairie School in Chicago. It was during this time that the *Plank-Back Hall Chair* was produced, with a rectilinear form similar to both a small table in the collection of the High Museum of Art and a window

Fig. 24.2 The main hall at Hill House, Helensburgh, Scotland, designed by Charles Rennie Mackintosh, 1903–1904.

bench in the collection of the Minneapolis Institute of Art. The fumed quarter-sawn oak from which the chair is made achieves its sculptural quality through geometric and symmetrical forms. The back panel is slightly angled for comfort and a well-worn area at its juncture with the seat attests to the chair's frequent use over the years (Fig. 24.1). The square cutouts, mirrored by the shape of the seat and conforming leather pad surrounded by brass tacks, are its sole decorative elements. Limbert's distinctive square cutouts possess similarities to a number of furniture designed by Charles Rennie Mackintosh (1868–1928),

Fig. 24.3 The Room de Luxe, Willow Tearooms, Glasgow, Scotland, 1903.

1   Many thanks to Andrew VanStyn for his efforts on this chair that helped to shape this essay, including researching the history and writing descriptions.

2   Charles P. Limbert & Company, *Limbert Arts and Crafts Furniture: The Complete 1903 Catalog* (1903; repr. Mineola, NY: Dover Publications, 1992), vi.

3   Wendy Kaplan, *"The Art That Is Life": The Arts & Crafts Movement in America, 1875–1920* (Boston: Little, Brown & Company, 1987), 165.

4   Charles P. Limbert & Company, *Limbert Arts and Crafts Furniture*, vi.

5   Robert P. Swierenga, "The Western Michigan Dutch" (paper presented at the Holland Genealogical Society, Holland, MI, December 11, 2004), https://www.swierenga.com/hgspap1204.html.

6   Charles P. Limbert & Company, *Limbert Arts and Crafts Furniture*, vi.

7   Charles P. Limbert & Company, cover, xi.

8   Charles P. Limbert Company, *Limbert's Holland Dutch Arts and Crafts Furniture, Booklet No. 114* (Holland, MI: Charles P. Limbert Company, n.d.), 22.

9   Kaplan, *"The Art That Is Life,"* 231.

10 Charles P. Limbert & Company, *Limbert Arts and Crafts Furniture*, vi.

11 Kaplan, *"The Art That Is Life,"* 231.

12 Christian B. Carron, *Grand Rapids Furniture: The Story of America's Furniture City* (Grand Rapids: Public Museum of Grand Rapids, 1998), 61.

13 Quoted in Carron, 61.

14 Charles P. Limbert Company, *Limbert's Holland Dutch Arts and Crafts Furniture*, 12–13.

15 Kaplan, *"The Art That Is Life,"* 167.

16 Charles P. Limbert & Company, *Limbert Arts and Crafts Furniture*, vi.

17 The man who designed Limbert's most sophisticated pieces may have been Austrian-trained William J. Gohlke. According to Don Marek's exhibition catalogue *Arts and Crafts Design: The Grand Rapids Contribution* (Grand Rapids, MI: Grand Rapids Art Museum, 2007), Gohlke designed for the company at least between 1909 and 1914, and became a vice president in 1921. He was likely familiar with the Vienna Secessionist Movement, and its influence can be clearly seen in Limbert's Arts and Crafts designs. See Carron, *Grand Rapids Furniture*, 178–79.

18 See "Charles P. Limbert," 1910 Craftsman, September 12, 2013. https://www.1910craftsman.com/2013/09/12/charles-p-limbert/, accessed May 4, 2022.

19 Grand Rapids Herald, July 11, 1923, 1.

including those for the main hall of Hill House, the home of Walter W. Blackie in Helensburgh, Scotland (1903–1904, Fig. 24.2), as well as the Room de Luxe in the Willow Tearooms (1903, Fig. 24.3). With their symmetrical and repetitive placement, the cutouts also bear close resemblance to the iconic Sitzmaschine or "Sitting Machine" designed by Austrian Josef Hoffmann (1870–1956) in 1905, and those of Koloman Moser (1868–1918), with whom Hoffmann co-founded the Wiener Werkstätte.

Limbert was the victim of a stroke in 1921, and his failing health prompted him to sell his company shares the following year.

By 1923 he had died, leaving his estate to his sister. His obituary in the Grand Rapids Herald stated:[18]

Of a retiring disposition, Mr. Limbert was in the public eye but little and found his pleasure in quiet pursuits. He was known as an exceptional fancier of flowering plants of which he collected many beautiful specimens from this and other countries. One of the delights, too, of his later years was the development of fancy breeds of poultry and his chicken pens always held some of the finest strains in the country.[19]

Side Chair

25

c. 1910

Attributed to George C. Flint & Company
(active 1868–1914/15, New York, New York)

Mahogany, modern silk upholstery

37 x 17 ¾ x 18 ½ in.

ART NOUVEAU (French for "New Art") emerged from the Arts and Crafts Movement in Europe during the last quarter of the 19th century. Like the Arts and Crafts Movement, this new artistic style eschewed industrialism by emphasizing an aesthetic drawn from natural motifs. Japanese woodblock prints, with their flat perspective, bold colors, and organic forms, were also highly influential. Sinuous curves and lively whiplashing lines evoking natural tendrils contrasted with the austere rectilinear and geometric forms of the Arts and Crafts Movement.

Louis Majorelle (1859–1926), the prominent French artist known for his stylistic furniture, was a leading proponent of the style. In 1904, his furniture earned the Grand Prize at the Louisiana Purchase Exposition in St. Louis, the same fair at which the designs of David Robertson Smith, designer for the Stickley Brothers Furniture Company (Cat. No. 23) of Grand Rapids, Michigan, earned accolades. In New York, Louis Comfort Tiffany (1848–1933) embraced the style in his "Favrile" range of lamps constructed with his patented iridescent glass. Similarly, architects Louis Sullivan (1856–1924) and Frank Lloyd Wright (Cat. No. 28) incorporated stylistic elements into their buildings in Chicago and throughout the Midwest. Nevertheless, the style was never as fully embraced in the United States as it was in Europe. Consequently, American-made Art Nouveau furniture is exceedingly rare.

Attributed to George C. Flint and Company of New York, this side chair represents the full flowering of the Art Nouveau aesthetic in America. The arched crest rail and carved stiles create a framework echoing stylistic graphic designs with linear borders. Four curved stems with carved openwork flowers in the clematis pattern create a gracefully flared fan-shape back splat (Fig. 25.2). Shallow curvilinear carvings decorate the mahogany surfaces of the back frame, serpentine seat rail, and outwardly splayed legs (Fig. 25.3). The brocade fabric patterned with trailing vines, supple stems, colorful flowers, and scrolling petals is surrounded by a scalloped gimp.[1]

The design and carving of the chair closely resembles both a labeled cabinet in the collection of the Metropolitan Museum of Art and an armchair in the collection of the Columbia Museum of Art (Fig. 25.1), with all three examples perhaps belonging to the same dining suite.[2] In 1893, a Flint advertisement observed: "Furnishings of the dining room show, perhaps, more improvement than almost any others, particularly in china closets, which are made for side walls and corners in varying shapes and have heavy glass fronts, either curved or straight. Closets for cut glass are made with shelves of heavy plate glass and mirrors at the back ... There is a rage this season for inclosed [sic] bric-a-brac cabinets with heavy plate glass shelves, and these are found in gold and mahogany."[3] Described as "a rare example of American furniture in the sophisticated Continental art nouveau style,"[4] the cabinet closely resembles the furniture designs of Louis Majorelle made between 1900 and 1905, with the Flint label on the back supporting a date of circa 1910. Flint's establishment of a Paris outpost in 1880 undoubtedly exposed his designers to the emerging Art Nouveau movement and specifically to the designs of Majorelle. By the end of the 1880s, Flint proudly proclaimed that his company "has designers both at home and abroad that are constantly making new and striking plans for the manufactory to work on."[5]

Born in Boston, George C. Flint moved to New York City, where he spent most of his 84 years in the furniture and cabinetry business. In 1868, Flint first appeared in New York City directories as a successor to the furniture firm of Henry Brunner. By 1876, Flint's showroom occupied a prime location at 104–108 West 14th Street, prominently situated along "Furniture Row" or "Homemaker's Heaven" and near Sixth Avenue and the popular "Ladies' Mile." The "young and enterprising firm" of George C. Flint and Company advertised that they "make their own goods, they sell them at greatly reduced prices, and warrant them to be as represented."[6] They offered furniture "in all the most desirable styles," including Queen Anne, Eastlake, and that featuring "Japanese forms of ornamentation to American and European models."[7] In 1880, the company received a commission to furnish the entrance hall and stairway millwork in the Seventh Regiment Armory on Park Avenue, joining its rivals—Herter Brothers (Cat. No. 13), Pottier and Stymus Manufacturing Company (Cat. No. 12), and Tiffany's Associated Artists—in decorating the many rooms inside the cavernous facility.

Fig. 25.1 *Armchair*, c. 1900–1915, designed and manufactured by George C. Flint and Company (active 1868–1914/15, New York, New York), mahogany, fabric (replaced), Columbia Museum of Art, Columbia, South Carolina.

Familiar with the "specimen rooms" of Robert J. Horner (Cat. No. 16), Flint used the six floors of his "immense establishment" on 14th Street to showcase suites of furniture in a variety of fabrics and finishes. His factory on West 19th Street was prepared to modify designs to meet "a purchaser's artistic suggestions," which could be "carried into effect with exactitude and without delay."[8] Flint's company was lauded as being a "resort at which the intending purchaser can fill his order, whether modest or ambitious"[9] and offered full-service modern remodeling and furniture delivery.

Flint clearly fared well financially during the 1893 depression, for in August 1894 the company opened a new eight-story building with a limestone façade, designed by Henry Janeway Hardenbergh (1847–1918), at 43–47 West 23rd Street, in which they displayed large suites of furniture in a

variety of styles. The new location led to an immediate improvement in their sales, as the company reported in the *New York Times*: "Whatever the cause, our sales have shown a remarkable improvement. We are doing fully 40 per cent more business than we did last year. Our removal may have something to do with this. In fact, it is safe to say it has, but the generally healthier business tone is, no doubt, a factor."[10] The aftereffects of

a devastating fire in November 1906 at the factory and warehouse,[11] combined with the declining health of the company's principal owner, Montgomery B. Cowperthwaite,[12] may have prompted the firm's merger in 1914 with its competitor Robert J. Horner to become Flint and Horner Co. Inc. The newly formed company then relocated to 20–26 West 36th Street until 1925, and then to 47th Street in May 1926.

Figs. 25.2 & 25.3
Details of crest rail, back splat and leg.

1   Special thanks to Andrew VanStyn for his assistance in reupholstering this chair with appropriate fabric.
2   *Curio Cabinet*, c. 1910, George C. Flint and Company, mahogany, glass, Metropolitan Museum of Art, New York, Purchase, Anonymous Gift, 1968, 68.132.
3   "Furniture in Novel Styles," *New York Times*, April 19, 1893, 5.
4   Berry B. Tracy, Marilynn Johnson, Marvin D. Schwartz, and Suzanne Boorsch, *Nineteenth-Century America: Furniture and Other Decorative Arts* (New York: Metropolitan Museum of Art, 1970), 273.
5   "Rich and Unique Designs," *New York Times*, October 3, 1889, 5. Flint is also known to have personally traveled to Europe. The *New York Times* reported in 1894 that "Mr. Flint, who is now in Europe, will make further purchases

of rare and beautiful articles before he returns." See "Art in Furniture Display. Excellent Appointment of the New Store of the George C. Flint Company," *New York Times*, August 22, 1894, 8.
6   "Holiday Goods. Where and What to Buy," *New York Times*, December 21, 1876, 7.
7   "George C. Flint & Co.," *New York Times*, December 3, 1877, 5.
8   "Fashion's Whims Obeyed," *New York Times*, April 11, 1888.
9   "Fashion's Whims Obeyed."
10 "Pulse of Trade Quickened," *New York Times*, September 10, 1894, 9.
11 Tom Miller, "The 1886 Robert J. Horner Building—61–65 West 23rd Street," *Daytonian in Manhattan* (blog),

December 9, 2010, https://daytoninmanhattan.blogspot.com/2010/12/1886-robert-j-horner-building-61-65.html.
12 "$2,000,000 Estate to Family. Will of Montgomery B. Cowperthwaite Filed in White Plains," *New York Times*, July 3, 1915, 7. According to the article, "Mr. Cowperthwaite was the principal owner of the George C. Flint Furniture Company and he also owned the controlling interest in the three Cowperthwaite stores ... To Mrs. Mabel C. Eilbeck, a daughter of Garden City, L.I., are given all the shares of the Flint company on the condition that she assume all of the firm's liabilities and pay another daughter, Mrs. Louise Lawrence of Manhattan, $3,000 annually."

Colonial Revival Comb-Back Windsor Arm Chair

26

c. 1930

Designed and manufactured by Virginia Craftsmen, Incorporated (active 1927–present, Harrisonburg, Virginia, and Hinton, Virginia)

Maple, oak, Southern yellow pine

46 x 27 ¾ x 25 in.

Stamped on underside of seat: 7129 / IRGINIA / CRAFTSMEN / REPRODUCTION [centered over large V]

WHEN THE FIRST Continental Congress met in 1774 at Carpenter's Hall in Philadelphia, a comb-back Windsor armchair served as the "speaker's chair,"[1] while other delegates sat in sack-back Windsor chairs. When the comb-back design was revived by Virginia Craftsmen, Inc., in the late 1920s, it was promoted as a seat "plainly for the 'head of the family.'"[2] This chair symbolizes an important decorative style from a crucial time in the nation's history as well as a continuing interest to celebrate and preserve the early American spirit.

The modern Windsor chair has its origins in the early 18th century near the town of Windsor, England.[3] The comb-back design, so named because the crest rail above the slim spindles resembled a lady's decorative hair piece, was one of the first types of Windsor chairs to be produced. Transported to the New World, Colonial craftsmen began making Windsor chairs in Philadelphia around 1730, giving rise to the name "Philadelphia Chairs."[4] In contrast to their British counterparts, American craftsmen replaced the central splat with slender spindles and added a continuous arm, which strengthened the chair and altered its appearance. During the last quarter of the 18th century, the Windsor chair was the most common form of seating furniture in America, used both indoors and out-of-doors, such as those that graced the piazza at George Washington's Mount Vernon.

The Colonial Revival style is one of the more enduring of the revival styles, one that celebrates and retains the essence of 18th-century America through its architecture and decorative arts. Appropriately beginning with celebrations surrounding the country's 100th anniversary during the Centennial Exhibition in 1876, the Colonial Revival style flourished during the first quarter of the 20th century concurrent with other revival styles, most notably the Arts and Crafts Movement. Although rather different in style from the "Mission" furniture of the Arts and Crafts Movement, the furniture of the Colonial Revival period shared many of its core tenets: strength, durability, and timelessness.[5]

In the years following World War I, the nation sought to rebuild its collective

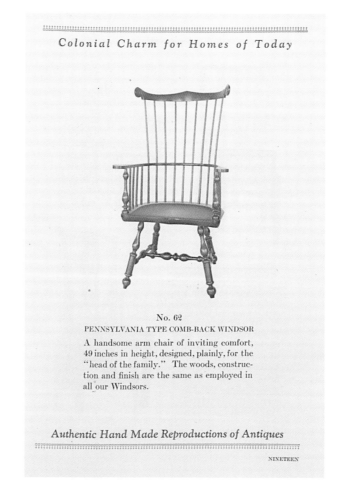

Colonial Charm for Homes of Today

No. 62
PENNSYLVANIA TYPE COMB-BACK WINDSOR

A handsome arm chair of inviting comfort, 49 inches in height, designed, plainly, for the "head of the family." The woods, construction and finish are the same as employed in all our Windsors.

Authentic Hand Made Reproductions of Antiques

NINETEEN

Fig. 26.1 Advertisement for *Pennsylvania Type Comb-Back Windsor*, from Virginia Craftsmen, Inc., company catalogue, *Colonial Charm for Homes of Today* (c. 1930s).

Fig. 26.2 Detail of stamp on underside of seat.

psyche and industry by looking to its Colonial past. Two important institutions began focusing on the nation's heritage and continue to celebrate it today: the American Wing of the Metropolitan Museum of Art (1924) and Colonial Williamsburg (1926). In addition, celebrations commemorating the bicentennial of George Washington's birthday in 1932 further propelled interest in the Colonial Revival style. There was perhaps no greater proponent of the style, however, than Wallace Nutting (1861–1941), a minister, photographer, artist, author, and scholar. Through his hand-

colored photographs, or "Nuttings," of the New England and mid-Atlantic countryside, Nutting romanticized the era, and in the process founded a furniture industry centered in Framingham, Massachusetts, that manufactured reproductions based on Colonial antecedents. He authored several books on Colonial furniture, including *A Windsor Handbook* (1917), one of the first specialized texts on the subject; *Furniture of the Pilgrim Century* (1921); and his three-volume magnum opus *Furniture Treasury* (1928–1933).[6] A consummate businessman and self-promoter, Nutting proclaimed, "All persons of taste and discernment will be glad that at last someone has had the courage to undertake the redemption of the Windsor chair."[7]

Within this era of renewed interest in the Colonial decorative arts, Walter Zirkle Sr. founded Virginia Craftsmen, Inc., in 1927 in Harrisonburg, Virginia. A circa 1930s company catalogue, titled *Colonial Charm for Homes of Today*, promoted the enduring "taste and livableness" of furniture from the "Golden Age of American craftsmanship"[8] as well as the ease and cost-effectiveness of collecting reproduction furnishings (Fig. 26.2). Adhering to traditional Colonial practices, the firm advertised its "craftsmen work as though the jazz age and the modern cult of speed had never been heard of."[9] The firm had its main showroom at the Craft House in rural downtown Harrisonburg, but it also promoted its designs to an urban clientele through satellite showrooms in

New York City, first at 427 Park Avenue and later at 59 East 52nd Street, in which it displayed and sold "fine reproductions of Georgian and early American furniture" spread throughout the building's four floors.[10] In addition to providing furniture for countless domestic interiors, the firm supplied accurate reproductions for such historic sites as Monticello, Colonial Williamsburg, and the Rotunda at the University of Virginia.

The company described its "Pennsylvania Type Comb-Back Windsor" as "a handsome arm chair of inviting comfort,"[11] and it appeared in the catalogue as model No. 62 (Fig. 26.1). The woods, construction, and finish used in its manufacture are the same as the firm's other Windsor chairs, with turnings and arms made from maple, a seat of Southern yellow pine, and spindles of either white oak or hickory. The chairs were offered either unfinished or finished in "Stained Walnut," "Stained Mahogany," or "Stained Maple,"[12] as found on the example

in the DeMell Jacobsen Collection. Splayed legs with barrel turnings are connected by an H-shaped stretcher to support the generously proportioned dished seat. The rear legs are slightly shorter than the front, which allows for a modest rake and added comfort. A continuous arm rail, which terminates in flat, curvaceous handholds, is punctured by nine evenly spaced spindles secured in holes drilled in the seat and is supported by similarly turned arm posts. The high back is capped with a steam-bent crest rail that ends in delicately carved scrolling ears. While historically many Windsor chairs were painted, this chair celebrates the natural color and grain of the wood.

1   Carl G. Karsch, "A Treasure in Plain Sight," Carpenters' Hall, accessed January 5, 2022, https://www.carpentershall.org/chairs-of-the-first-congress-info.
2   Virginia Craftsmen, Inc., *Colonial Charm for Houses of Today* (Harrisonburg, VA: Virginia Craftsmen, n.d. [c. 1930s]), 19.
3   See especially Nancy Goyne Evans, *American Windsor Chairs* (New York: Hudson Hills, 1996); and Nancy Goyne Evans, *American Windsor Furniture: Specialized Forms* (New York: Hudson Hills, 1997).
4   "Furniture Glossary: Windsor Chairs/Settees," Buffalo Architecture and History, accessed August 12, 2015, http://www.buffaloah.com/f/glos/chairs/windsor/windindex.html.
5   Special thanks to Andrew VanStyn for sharing his research and expertise on the history and design of this chair. His contributions have helped shape this essay.
6   For a thorough study of Wallace Nutting and his influence on the Colonial Revival, see Thomas Andrew Denenberg, *Wallace Nutting and the Invention of Old America* (New Haven, CT: Yale University Press, 2003). See also William L. Dulaney, "Wallace Nutting: Collector and Entrepreneur," *Winterthur Portfolio* 13 (1979): 47–60; Joyce P. Berendson, "Wallace Nutting, An American Tastemaker: The Pictures and Beyond," *Winterthur Portfolio* 18, no. 2 (Summer–Autumn 1983): 187–212; and Marianne Berger Woods, "Viewing Colonial America Though the Lens of Wallace Nutting," *American Art* 8, no. 2 (Spring 1994): 66–86.
7   Wallace Nutting, *Wallace Nutting Windsors: Correct Windsor Furniture* (Saugus Center, MA: Wallace Nutting, Inc., 1918), 1.
8   Virginia Craftsmen, Inc., *Colonial Charm*, 3.
9   Virginia Craftsmen, Inc., 3.
10 "Furniture Dealers Lease," *New York Times*, December 14, 1932, 40; and "Furniture Firms Rent New Quarters," *New York Times*, December 15, 1932, 38.
11 Virginia Craftsmen, Inc., *Colonial Charm*, 19.
12 Virginia Craftsmen, Inc., 19.

Lounge Chair

27

c. 1935

Designed by Warren E. McArthur Jr. (1885–1961)

Manufactured by the Warren McArthur Corporation (active 1932–1948, Rome, New York, and Bantam, Connecticut)

Anodized aluminum, rubber, upholstery (modern)

31 ¾ x 22 x 31 in.

WHILE SEPARATED in age by only a few years, the stark differences in the materials and overall appearance of the *Colonial Revival Comb-Back Windsor Arm Chair* (Cat. No. 26) and the *Lounge Chair* illustrate a quantum leap in the progression of American chair design. Just when the Colonial Revival style reached its apogee in 1924, Warren McArthur Jr. was creating tubular metal furniture.

His *Lounge Chair*, designed circa 1935, exemplifies a fusion between the prevailing Art Deco style along with the newly arrived International Style; McArthur's fascination with automobiles is also incorporated in the implied motion of this example. In it, he utilized a dynamic system of tubular brushed-aluminum pieces connected and strengthened by inner steel rods and joinery rings. The streamlined metallic curves are echoed in the half-round, Kapok-filled upholstery.[1] A snow-white French synthetic stretch weave trimmed with black piping completes the sleek aesthetic. Rubber guards, or "donuts," protect the floor rails from abrasion and prevent the chair from sliding.[2]

Warren McArthur Jr. was raised in an affluent family, one that embraced modern inventions. His father, Warren McArthur Sr. (1855–1924), dubbed the "Pioneer Salesman of Tubular Lanterns," was successful in his trade and later moved to Chicago when he became the branch manager and exclusive sales agent for the New York-based firm of R. E. Dietz Company.[3] The McArthurs were among the first in the city to own a car and privately commissioned Frank Lloyd Wright (1867–1959, Cat. No. 28)—then an aspiring architect in the firm of Adler and Sullivan—to build their home on the south side of Chicago in 1892.

Like his distant relative Benjamin Franklin,[4] McArthur was a consummate inventor. After receiving a degree in mechanical engineering from Cornell in 1908, McArthur joined his father as a sales manager and designer for the C. T. Ham Company and the R. E. Dietz Lantern Company. In 1912, he patented a design for the "Short-Globe" Tubular Lantern, which was sold by the Dietz Company and marketed as the Dietz "D-Lite."[5] Buoyed by this early commercial success, combined with financial support from his father, McArthur moved to Phoenix, Arizona, in 1914. There, in partnership with his brother, Charles, he opened the city's first Dodge automobile dealership—which would later grow to include 14 showrooms—founded its first radio station (KFAD), established the Arizona Club, and started the Arizona Museum.[6]

The automobile business provided a fertile environment for McArthur's innovations. Mindful of life in the Southwest, McArthur invented a radiator adaptor to prevent overheating in the hot, arid climate. Other inventions included the "Electroscoot," a predecessor to the golf cart, and the "Wonderbus," a recreational vehicle mounted atop a Dodge truck chassis.[7] The vehicle had a private driver and cook and could accommodate four travelers as they traversed the Southwestern highway system and explored its National Parks. The 1913 introduction of the Ford factory's assembly belts revolutionized industrial mass production and would become a key component in the production of McArthur's future designs.

In 1924, McArthur's father commissioned a Phoenix vacation home, which was designed by his brother, Albert Chase McArthur (1881–1951), a draftsman for Frank Lloyd Wright, and for which Warren McArthur designed the furniture using tubular metal. His designs for the home predate Marcel Breuer's (1902–1981) iconic *Wassily Chair* and position McArthur as a pioneer in the use of the material.[8] Several years later, McArthur also designed furniture made from steel and copper tubing for Arizona's Biltmore Hotel,[9] which was also drafted by Albert and for which Wright served as a consultant. The hotel opened in February 1929 and the stock market crashed the following October, resulting in the Great

Depression. The McArthurs lost control of the hotel to another investor, which resulted in all three brothers relocating to Los Angeles. There, Warren McArthur Jr. embarked on a new venture in which he produced fashionable chairs and tables made from hollow aluminum tubes.

The use of aluminum began in the late 19th century following the manufacture and electroplating process of tubular steel, which had propelled the bicycle and aviation industries. Aluminum, a silver-like metal abundant in the Earth's crust and processed from refined bauxite ore, soon became a focus of manufacturing. In 1888 the Pittsburgh Reduction Company (later renamed the Aluminum Company of America, or Alcoa) was founded in Pittsburgh, Pennsylvania, and became one of the largest producers of aluminum. With the 1923 introduction of the anodizing process, the lightweight, flexible, and corrosion-resistant aluminum alloys were favored for interior and exterior furniture production. Aluminum, along with chrome and stainless steel, were modern materials that enhanced the streamlined, geometric, and gracefully curvaceous forms of the Art Deco style. By 1933, the Aluminum Company of France sponsored the Concours International du Meilleur Siege en Aluminium, which attracted 209 designs for aluminum chairs. In the 1930s, Art Deco–style buildings, such as the Chrysler Building, Empire State Building, and Sunset Tower, were erected across the country from New York City to Hollywood.

In the motion picture capital, which thrived despite the Depression, McArthur's artistic aluminum furniture appealed to those living a fashionable lifestyle. Described as "an industrial designer with the soul of an artist,"[10] McArthur created glamorous Art Deco furniture featuring curved lines, distinctive joinery, and colorful upholstery. His iconic furniture adorned the Warner Brothers' Western Theatre, later renamed the Wiltern Theatre, and the Ambassador Hotel, where the Cocoanut Grove club was frequented by countless film stars. Hollywood directors, producers, and movie stars like Marlene Dietrich, Clark Gable, and Fredric March all decorated their homes with McArthur designs.

In Los Angeles, McArthur continued to improve his designs, modifying his materials and joinery methods. Having initially

Fig. 27.1 Warren McArthur Jr., "Furniture," U.S. Patent No. 1,932,794, filed June 16, 1930, issued October 31, 1933, U.S. Patent Office.

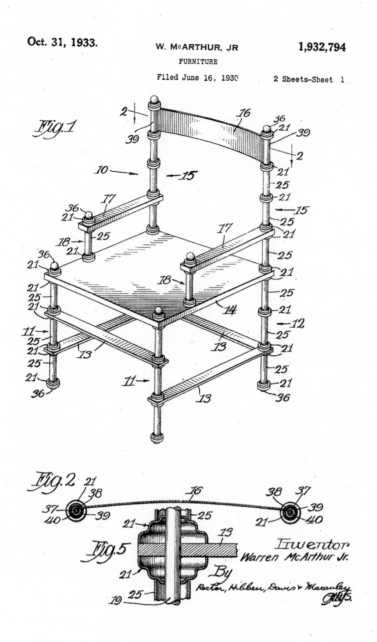

experimented with copper and stainless steel, McArthur came to the realization that anodized aluminum was the best metal for his furniture.[11] In a patent first submitted in June 1930 for Warren McArthur Furniture, Ltd.,[12] McArthur promoted the goals of his designs to ensure comfort and a "maximum strength with a minimum of weight, while also permitting the attainment of a desirable attractiveness in appearance."[13] McArthur

proposed a design for a chair (Fig. 27.1) "composed of a rod, tubular pieces and washers alternately strung on said rod."[14]

After a few years of success in Los Angeles, financial problems precipitated a move east. In 1933, McArthur established the Warren McArthur Corporation with a factory in Rome, New York, and a fashionable showroom at 1 Park Avenue in New York City.[15] McArthur reissued his

earlier patent in 1934 and added methods to strengthen curved tubular elements such as aluminum. An early Rome production, the circa 1935 *Lounge Chair*, reflects McArthur's curvaceous Art Deco style with influences of the emerging International Style.

The year prior to McArthur's arrival in New York, the Museum of Modern Art mounted *Modern Architecture: International Exhibition* with a catalogue entitled *The*

International Style. The exhibition introduced America to the Modernist architecture and design developed by Charles-Édouard Jeanneret (1887–1965), commonly known as Le Corbusier, and other members of the Bauhaus, the school of art, craft, and design located in the Weimar Republic of Germany.

Mass-produced seating furniture was machine-made with tubular metal. Marcel Breuer designed his revolutionary model B3 *Club Chair*, later known as the *Wassily Chair*, in 1925, fabricated with tubular steel inspired by the Adler bicycle. In 1927, Ludwig Mies van der Rohe developed the nickel-plated tubular steel *MR10* chair supported by large sweeping curves.

The Bauhaus chairs were expensive to manufacture due to the laborious custom welding and materials, and thus were mainly purchased by wealthy clientele until the late 1930s.[16] McArthur's seating furniture likewise reflected a minimalist machine-age aesthetic; however, the involved labor of production was too costly for the average consumer. Although manufacturing had significantly advanced in the United States, the McArthur factory continued to assemble the chairs by hand.

The Warren McArthur Corporation published a catalogue around 1936 with images similar to the *Lounge Chair* in the DeMell Jacobsen Collection, as well as a number of related designs. A more severely

angled armchair was promoted as being suitable for "a place in the Sun—For the gossiping, restful, refreshing hour at the end of a day of business, golf, or boot and saddle. Generous deep cushions, hammock swung and delightfully conforming to the contours of the body."[17] Made from interchangeable parts, McArthur's tubular metal furniture resulted in "an infinite variety of styles, applicable to any need, in business or in the home."[18]

Also furthering the number of available styles was McArthur's innovative use of the anodic process. Patented by DuPont and licensed by McArthur, the process

transforms the surface to an enduring untarnishable coat. It is next in hardness to the diamond, yet it possesses that velvety soft, smooth feel of satin silver. It will not smudge, tarnish nor show finger marks. It never needs polishing and will not develop the high shine common to ordinary metal surfaces. It is so highly resistant to corrosion that it is most satisfactorily used on shipboard and shore in any climate.[19]

Through the process, the metal was infused with a mineral dye, which prevented chipping or cracking.[20] The circa 1936 catalogue boasted "nearly 600 designs in anodic aluminum furniture," in

a diverse palette of colors that included bronze, red, yellow, orange, gold, blue, green, and ebony.[21]

In the economically depressed era bolstered by President Roosevelt's New Deal and Works Progress Administration programs, McArthur persevered and found his niche for modern, comfortable furniture. When aluminum resources were restricted for private consumption due to World War II, McArthur's factory contracted with the Navy and Air Force to produce numerous aircraft seat designs. Furniture commissions were also secured for the Union Pacific Railroad, the Chrysler Corporation headquarters, and a Marshall Field and Company beauty salon in Chicago.[22] McArthur's furniture was suitable for ships such as the SS *Milwaukee Clipper*. Beginning in 1948, the company produced aluminum furniture under the name Mayfair Industries, Inc., until Warren McArthur's death in December 1961.[23]

Another McArthur project important to this collection was the development of a prototype for Frank Lloyd Wright's S. C. Johnson Administration Building (see Cat. No. 28). In 1936, McArthur produced a tubular aluminum three-legged armchair with leather upholstery (see Fig. 28.3), desk, and table based on designs by the architect. The expense of the materials and production were prohibitive to the project, thus tubular steel was chosen.

1   The Kapok tree is indigenous to Mexico and South America. Its silk-like fibers are often substituted for down in pillows.
2   Special thanks to Andrew VanStyn for his research on this chair and his guidance on the upholstery.
3   *A Leaf from the Past: Dietz Then and Now* (New York: R. E. Dietz Company, 1914), 135–36.
4   "Warren McArthur," Irwin Weiner Interiors, December 26, 2007, https://www.irwinweiner.com/designers-we-love/2007/12/26/warren-mcarthur.html.
5   The Dietz "D-Lite" was the most expensive hand model sold by Dietz and was in production only between 1913 and 1919. See "R. E. Dietz Compendium," W. T. Kirkman Lanterns, accessed November 17, 2021, https://lanternnet.com/wp-content/uploads/R.E.-Dietz-Lantern-Model-Compendium-The-Source-for-Oil-Lamps-and-Hurricane-Lanterns.pdf. Another version of this short-globe lantern was sold by the C. T. Ham Company under the name Ham "NuStyle." Both of these early short-globe barn lanterns were the first full-size lanterns with the burner cone attached to the globe plate, starting the changeover to rising cone burners in 1913–14. See

BobbyB, reply to "C. T. Ham 'HamLight' NU Style cold blast," Highway/Street Kerosene Traffic Lanterns forum, December 20, 2009, https://members3.boardhost.com/trafficgard/msg/1261354818.html.
6   See Avis Berman, "McArthur Returns," *Art & Antiques* 20, no. 10 (November 1997): 72–77; and Wendy Moonan, "Antiques; Rediscovered: Early Master of Metal," *New York Times*, August 27, 1999, E36.
7   See Warren McArthur Jr. and David H. Hoober, "'Camping Deluxe': A Tour Through Arizona in 1924," *Journal of Arizona History* 21, no. 2 (Summer 1980): 171–88; and Edward Lebow, "Designing Men," *Phoenix New Times* (Arizona), December 2, 1999.
8   Moonan, "Antiques; Rediscovered."
9   Lebow, "Designing Men."
10 Moonan, "Antiques; Rediscovered."
11 "Modern Solutions," in "Shaping the Modern: American Decorative Arts at the Institute of Chicago, 1917–65," *Art Institute of Chicago Museum Studies* 27, no. 2 (2001), 51.
12 The Warren McArthur Furniture Corporation was chartered on December 3, 1930, in Dover, Delaware. See *New York Times*, December 4, 1930, 48.

13 Warren McArthur Jr., "Furniture," U.S. Patent No. 1,932,794, filed June 16, 1930, issued October 31, 1933, U.S. Patent Office.
14 McArthur.
15 In 1937, the corporation purchased the former Bantam Ball Bearing Company plant in Bantam, Connecticut. The building contained more than 40,000 square feet of floor space, which the new owners remodeled, "adding new loading platforms and making general improvements. They expect to be operating there at the beginning of the year." See *New York Times*, December 14, 1937, 47.
16 Judith Miller, *Chairs* (London: Conran, 2009), 155.
17 "Style No. 1000-A," *Warren McArthur Corporation Catalogue* (New York, c. 1936), 58.
18 "Style No. 1000-A," 1.
19 "Style No. 1000-A," 1.
20 "Style No. 1000-A," 1.
21 "Style No. 1000-A," 1.
22 "Modern Solutions," 51.
23 "Warren McArthur, Design Engineer, 76," *New York Times*, December 18, 1961.

S. C. Johnson and Son Administration Building Chair

28

1936–1939

Designed by Frank Lloyd Wright (1867–1959)

Manufactured by the Metal Office Furniture Company, later Steelcase Incorporated (active 1912–present, Grand Rapids, Michigan)

Enameled steel, cast aluminum, loop pile upholstery (original), brass

35 x 18 x 20 ½ in.

ENVISION THIS chair in a large open office setting filled with the sounds of typewriters clicking and telephones ringing. It was designed to complement the revolutionary interior of the Great Workroom in the Administration Building of the S. C. Johnson and Son, Inc. (later known as S. C. Johnson Wax, and subsequently S. C. Johnson, A Family Company) headquarters in Racine, Wisconsin. The chair illustrates the fluid, integrated environment designed by famed architect Frank Lloyd Wright, the needs of an American company emerging from the Great Depression, the advent of modern office architecture, and the customized furniture these new spaces demanded.[1] The evolution of this curvaceous four-legged chair from Warren McArthur's (Cat. No. 27) three-legged leather-upholstered prototype tells a story of innovation, persistence, and adaptability.

The chair's design echoes the harmonious themes of unity and nature in the Great Workroom. Although aluminum was initially used in the prototype, tubular steel was ultimately chosen to frame the furniture owing to its cheaper cost, durability, and contemporary panache. Streamlined in its aesthetic and perhaps evoking the automobile age,[2] the tubular metal—painted a Cherokee Red—echoed the curves of the walls and mirrored the shape of the Pyrex glass tubes used to light the dramatic interior. Symbolizing a circle of unity, the seat and back echo the shape of the lily-pad capitals on the columns. A comfortable and durable textured loop-pile fabric was chosen to cover the circular

seat cushions and double-sided backs. To break up the monochromatic appearance of the Great Workroom, Wright specified four upholstery colors: red for the credit department, blue for the branch house records department, green for the billing department, and beige for the sales promotion department. The seat backs could fully pivot, which allowed them to better support the user's back as well as enable them to be flipped as the upholstery became worn. Variations of the chair include those with three legs (Fig. 28.3), armrests, or interchangeable feet in the forms of rolling ball bearings or stationary brass sabots (as seen on this example), as well as a large four-legged lounge chair, which Wright called an "officer's chair." Designed for versatility, longevity, comfort, and aesthetics, the chairs continue to be an integral and essential component of the design, function, and corporate ethos of S. C. Johnson and Son, Inc.[3]

Born June 8, 1867, in Richland Center, Wisconsin, Frank Lincoln Wight (Fig. 28.1) was encouraged by his mother, Anna Lloyd Jones (1838–1923), with "boundless faith that he would succeed"[4] as an architect. To nurture and realize that destiny, she hung framed prints of cathedrals in his childhood bedroom and gave him building blocks with which to play. When his parents divorced in 1884, Wright lived with his maternal extended family, the Lloyd-Jones clan of Hillside, Wisconsin, and changed his middle name to Lloyd in their honor. From them, he learned to love and respect nature; when Wright envisioned a design for the Johnson Wax building, he desired to create a place where one would "feel as though he were among pine trees breathing fresh air and sunlight."[5]

By 1936, Frank Lloyd Wright was 69 years old and his architectural visions, such as the successful Prairie School style of the early 1900s, were no longer in vogue. His jobs tended to be costlier than their initial estimates, and his personal life was full of scandal and tragedy. Having built over 100 projects in the first decade of the 20th century, throughout the subsequent 20 years the number dwindled to just 50 projects. Despite his famous overbearing and demanding attitude, his excitement about concepts charmed his clients.

While involved with three residential projects at the time, the opportunity for

Wright to collaborate in a commercial project with S. C. Johnson and Son launched the second phase of his career with a distinctive new style. In the spring of 1936, having survived the Great Depression, the S. C. Johnson Wax Company, a wax and paint manufacturer, found the need to add space for their administrative functions. Herbert F. Johnson Jr. (also known as "Hibbert," "Hib," or "H.F.," 1899–1978), grandson of founder Samuel C. Johnson (1833–1919) and then president of the company, envisioned "a beautiful, pure, and completely American image for his company. Above all, he wanted [the new building] to be a place where his employees would be happy to work."[6] Johnson "wanted to build the best office building in the world, and the only way to do that was to get the greatest architect in the world."[7] Johnson's and Wright's visions aligned. Wright admired the company's philosophy and considered it "a model for the humane economy."[8] Similarly, Herbert was a good fit as a patron for Wright: "[Johnson] was imaginative and willing to take risks. He also had a vision of the possibilities that architecture could offer and had faith that Wright could realize them."[9] On July 23, 1936, Wright was offered the position of architect for the new administrative building and what would become its now iconic feature: the Great Workroom.

Fig. 28.1 Frank Lloyd Wright, c. 1926.

published by *Architectural Forum* in January 1938 show both three- and four-legged models. Another plan for a four-legged stationary armchair for the president's office was dated April 17, 1939. Although Wright insisted the tripod chair, with one front leg and two rear legs, would free the sitter's feet and enforce good posture, it created challenges. The chairs were known to tip over—even when the occupant was Wright himself! Over time, the company modified the three-legged chairs into four-legged models in Wright-sanctioned plans.[17]

Two companies vied for the furniture contract: the Warren McArthur Corporation and the Metal Office Furniture Company (renamed Steelcase Incorporated in 1954). The Metal Office Furniture Company won the commission in June 1938, though several manufacturers participated in the actual manufacturing process. Stow-Davis provided the wooden arms and other wood elements, the American Seating Company made the frames, the Chase Furniture Company supplied the fabric covers, and the Metal Office Furniture Company produced the sheet metalwork and assembled all the components into the finished furniture.[18]

On Friday, April 21, 1939, employees toured the building, an event followed by a weekend-long public open house. The New York World's Fair opened the same weekend, and *Life* magazine reported: "[The] World's Fair, sprawling its gigantic mass of freak and futuristic buildings, is undeniably a great show. But future historians may well decide that a truer glimpse of the shape of things to come was given last week by a single structure, built strictly for business, which opened in a drab section of Racine, Wis."[19] Frank Lloyd Wright, approaching his 72nd birthday, had revitalized his career and simultaneously introduced a design of the future. The maestro of American organic architecture, Wright went on to realize a number of significant residential and commercial commissions including the Price Tower (Bartlesville, Oklahoma) and the Guggenheim Museum (New York, New York).

For the project, Wright built upon a philosophy he had utilized in his design for the Larkin Building (1903–1904) in Buffalo, New York. Following its completion, in 1908 Wright professed his hope to ultimately create "a building, together with its equipment, appurtenances and environment, an entity which shall constitute a complete work of art."[10] He found just the opportunity in the Johnson Wax commission. For the Great Workroom, he envisioned an open-space concept with aesthetically pleasing designs to simultaneously enhance and uplift the administrative experience with reminders of the company's beliefs in the family spirit, cooperation, and efficiency. Wright described it best in his October 11, 1936, document, "The New Building for S.C. Johnson & Son, Inc.":

This office building for the S. C. Johnson Wax Company—memorializing the pioneering of a grandfather and a father— is simply and sincerely an interpretation of modern business conditions, and of business too, itself designed to be as inspiring to live and work in as any cathedral ever was to worship in.[11]

In this vanguard architecture, Wright infused the International Style with organic forms along with technical, scientific, and structural innovations. The 128 x 228-foot windowless Great Workroom[12] (Fig. 28.2) is a solid brick construction lit by skylights through Pyrex glass tubes.[13] Tree-like, or dendriform, columns, specially designed, engineered, and tested by Wright, support the ceiling. The columns represent Wright's statement that "form does not follow function. Rather form and function are one."[14] White-painted and sand-textured, the 25-foot-tall "trunks" seem to emerge from the floor, "growing" from their nine-inch-diameter bases to the 18½-foot "canopy" above. One visitor said that the room has "the effect on the observer ... as being like swimming in a large pool with water-lily pads floating above."[15]

Despite an extended completion date and rising costs, the architect persisted in seeking permission to design the furniture. Wright felt "it is quite impossible to consider the building as one thing and its furnishings another."[16] When the company directors finally relented, Wright designed the chairs and desks as a seamless expression of the technological innovations in his streamlined and organic stylistic interior. Wright applied for a patent for a chair design on December 20, 1937, which was granted in February 1938 (Fig. 28.4). Multiple designs for the chairs were drafted. Elevations and plans submitted November 1937 and

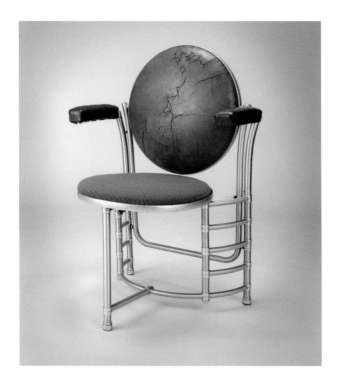

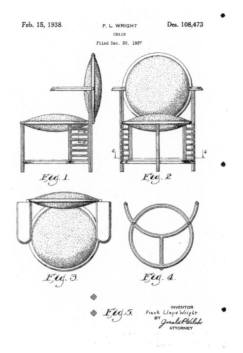

Feb. 15, 1938.   F. L. WRIGHT   Des. 108,473
CHAIR
Filed Dec. 20, 1937

Fig. 1.   Fig. 2.

Fig. 3.   Fig. 4.

Fig. 5.   INVENTOR
Frank Lloyd Wright
BY
Gerald P. Welsh
ATTORNEY

Fig. 28.3 (far left) Armchair prototype for the S. C. Johnson & Son Company Administration Building, Racine, Wisconsin. Designed by Frank Lloyd Wright; manufactured by Warren McArthur Corporation. The Wolfsonian, The Mitchell Wolfson, Jr. Collection, 83.11.8.

Fig. 28.4 (left) Frank Lloyd Wright, "Design for a Chair," U.S. Design Patent No. 108,473, filed December 20, 1937, issued February 15, 1938, U.S. Patent Office.

More than 80 years later, the building continues to inspire and awe both employees and visitors alike. Reflecting upon the effect of the building and the adjacent Research Tower (a vertical cantilevered building designed by Wright that opened in 1950) on its employees, Samuel Curtis Johnson Jr. (1928–2004), great-grandson of the company's founder, acknowledged: "We became a different company the day the building opened. We achieved international attention because that building represented and symbolized the quality of everything we did in terms of products, people, the working environment within the building, the community relations, and—most important—our ability to recruit creative people.[20]

British architect, critic, and historian Kenneth Frampton has suggested the building is the greatest 20th-century U.S. architectural project and possibly "the most profound work of art that America has ever produced."[21] In 1976, the Administration Building and the adjacent Research Tower were designated National Historic Landmarks.

1   See James M. Dennis and Lu B. Wenneker, "Ornamentation and the Organic Architecture of Frank Lloyd Wright," *Art Journal* 25, no. 1 (Autumn, 1965): 2–14; for a thorough study of the S. C. Johnson commission, see Jonathan Lipman, *Frank Lloyd Wright and the Johnson Wax Buildings* (New York: Rizzoli, 1986).

2   Coincidentally, both Wright and his patron, Herbert F. Johnson Jr., owned Lincoln-Zephyr automobiles, now considered to be one of the most streamlined cars ever designed. Of the Johnson building commission, Wright recalled in his autobiography: "It was high time to give our hungry American public something truly 'streamlined,' so swift, sure of itself, and clean for its purpose ... that *anybody* could see the virtue of this thing called Modern." Frank Lloyd Wright, *An Autobiography* (New York: Duell, Sloan & Pearce, 1943), 471.

3   See Kent F. Spreckelmeyer, "Places for a Work Ethic: An Appraisal of American Workplace Design and Research," *Journal of Architectural and Planning Research* 12, no. 2 (Summer, 1995): 104–20; see also "Furnishing the Administration Building," in Lipman, *Frank Lloyd Wright*, 85–91. Special thanks to Andrew VanStyn for his research on this chair, its design, and history.

4   *American Lives*, "Frank Lloyd Wright: Parts 1 and 2," directed by Ken Burns and Lynn Novick, season 1, episodes 5 and 6, aired November 10, 1998.

5   Lipman, *Frank Lloyd Wright*, 51.

6   Lipman, 1. Referred to as "S. C. Johnson, A Family Company" since 1998, and rebranded as "S. C. Johnson, A Family Company at Work for a Better World" in 2018, the company has long been hailed for offering innovative employee benefits, such as paid vacations, profit sharing, and pension plans. See "Timeline: SC Johnson's Corporate Identity Throughout the Years," S. C. Johnson & Son Inc., accessed November 17, 2021, https://www.scjohnson.com/en/about-us/who-we-are.

7   "Frank Lloyd Wright and H.F. Johnson, Jr.: A Legendary Partnership for American Architecture," S. C. Johnson & Son Inc., accessed November 17, 2021, https://www.scjohnson.com/en/about-us/the-johnson-family/hf-johnson-jr/frank-lloyd-wright-and-hf-johnson-jr-a-legendary-partnership-for-american-architecture.

8   Lipman, *Frank Lloyd Wright*, 13.

9   Lipman, 13.

10 "Modern Solutions," in "Shaping the Modern: American Decorative Arts at the Art Institute of Chicago, 1917–65," *Art Institute of Chicago Museum Studies* 27, no. 2 (2001): 55.

11 Lipman, *Frank Lloyd Wright*, 182 (Appendix 2: "The New Building for S.C. Johnson & Son, Inc.").

12 David A. Hanks, *The Decorative Designs of Frank Lloyd Wright* (New York: E. P. Dutton, 1979), 148.

13 Lipman, *Frank Lloyd Wright*, 68. Wright worked with Corning scientists to modify their patented Pyrex tubes, for which he was awarded several patents. The glass tubing is echoed in the tubular metal furniture frames. See also Joseph M. Siry, "Frank Lloyd Wright's Innovative Approach to Environmental Control in his Buildings for the S. C. Johnson Company," *Construction History* 28, no. 1 (2013): 141–64.

14 Lipman, *Frank Lloyd Wright*, 59.

15 Alexander O. Boulton, *Frank Lloyd Wright: Architect, An Illustrated Biography* (New York: Rizzoli International Publications, 1933), 95.

16 Lipman, *Frank Lloyd Wright*, 85.

17 Lipman, 91.

18 Lipman, 91.

19 Lipman, 93.

20 Lipman, 173.

21 Kenneth Frampton, "The Johnson Wax Buildings and the Angel of History," in Lipman, xii.

Crow Island School Chair

29

1939

Designed by Charles Ormond Eames Jr. (1907–1978)
and Eero Saarinen (1910–1961)

Manufactured by the Design Workshop of the
Illinois Craft Project

Molded ash plywood, birch

26 x 14 x 12 ½ in.

Branded manufacturer's mark on underside:
WPA / illinois / craft / project / [illegible]

JUST AS FRANK Lloyd Wright (Cat. No. 28)
sought to create a unified and integrated
environment for workers of S. C. Johnson
and Son, Inc., so too did Charles Eames and
Eero Saarinen for children attending the
progressive Crow Island School in Winnetka,
Illinois. This example was paired with a desk
for the youngest pupils.

As America continued to emerge from
the aftereffects of the Great Depression,
education was thought to be central
in propelling the country forward—
economically, socially, and politically.
Carleton Wolsey Washburne (1889–1968),
superintendent of the Winnetka Public
Schools, a proponent of the Progressive
Education Movement, and a student of
education reformer John Dewey (1859–
1952), envisioned a school that would serve
as a model for the nation. "This is to be our
dream school," Washburne said. "For years
we have been thinking about it. We want it to
be the most functional and beautiful school
in the world. We want it to crystalize in
architecture the best educational practices
we can evolve."[1]

Washburne secured a commission
for the construction of the Crow Island
School in 1938 and chose architects Eliel
Saarinen (1873–1950) and his son, Eero, to
collaborate with Lawrence Bradford Perkins
(1907–1997) of the local firm Perkins,
Wheeler, and Will (now Perkins and Will
Corporation).[2] A swampy area near a natural
bird refuge named Crow Island was selected
for the school's location. Two local Works
Progress Administration (WPA) dig projects
for the Chicago and North Western Railroad

in Winnetka and the Skokie Lagoons Project
provided fill for the foundation.[3] The WPA,
renamed the Work Projects Administration
in 1939, had been created by President
Franklin D. Roosevelt (1882–1945) in
1935 to fund public works projects and
infrastructure improvements to create jobs
and provide economic relief following the
Great Depression.

The bucolic natural setting of Crow
Island offered an ideal child-friendly
environment. Designed in the International
Style, the school's architecture embodied
modern pedagogical philosophy and
fostered an atmosphere of intrinsic
motivation, collaborative projects, and
experiential learning (Fig. 29.1). "The
International style in architecture is
especially adapted to school buildings
because functional planning, the
fundamental principle of the new
architecture, is exactly what schools need
to develop sympathy with modern trends
in scientific education,"[4] proclaimed Philip
Johnson, curator of the *Modern Architecture:
International Exhibition* at the Museum of
Modern Art (1932). Opened in September
1940 with an enrollment of about 300
children, the Crow Island School embodied
Washburne's vision and "was hailed as a
prototype for the modern American school
and became one of the most influential
school buildings in the nation."[5]

Each self-contained L-shaped classroom
provided "secure, nurturing, and stimulating
qualities,"[6] with acoustically engineered low

ceilings, natural light, and interior fittings—
blackboards, light switches, doorknobs,
display cases, and lavatory fixtures—set
at child-appropriate heights. To echo the
child-centered modern educational settings,
Eero Saarinen and Eames, together with
Lawrence Perkins, designed graduated
and flexible seating arrangements to
accommodate the physical growth of a
child. A free-standing chair was produced
in three sizes, to be paired with a free-
standing square-top table; this example
represents the smallest size (Fig. 29.2).
Children graduated to chairs with attached
desks supported by a single pedestal base,
a design that presages Eero Saarinen's *Tulip
Chair* (1955). For large assemblies in the
auditorium, molded plywood benches were
constructed in various sizes. When asked
what role the movable furniture played in
advancing intellectual freedom, Perkins
recalled, "Good God! The movable furniture
ensured the difference; the individual
patterns in seating would find their way ...
This is the core of what really happened at
Crow Island. It was the rejection of the rigid
conventional classroom."[7]

It was through Perkins and his prior
relationship with Eliel Saarinen that the
Saarinens and Eames, then based at the
Cranbrook Educational Community in
Bloomfield Hills, Michigan, became involved
in the Crow Island School project. Following
his second-place finish for the design of
the Tribune Tower (1922) in Chicago, Eliel
Saarinen emigrated from Finland in 1923,

Fig. 29.1 Crow Island
School, Winnetka,
Illinois, November 25,
1940.

briefly staying with the Perkins family before settling in Ann Arbor, Michigan, where he served as a visiting professor of architecture at the University of Michigan. During his period as a visiting professor, the Detroit newspaper tycoon and philanthropist George Gough Booth (1864–1949) invited Eliel to teach at Cranbrook and design its master campus plan. Booth and Saarinen shared an appreciation of the ideals of the earlier Arts and Crafts Movement and envisioned a campus that contained a progressive assemblage of schools in the fine and decorative arts akin to the Bauhaus. Eliel was elevated to president of the Cranbrook Academy of Art in 1932. Acclaimed as the "cradle of American modernism,"[8] Cranbrook Academy served as the center of arts education and became a crucible of mid-century design.

Cranbrook proved a fertile ground for his son Eero's life and artistic development, as well. In 1929, he left the campus to study sculpture at the Paris Académie de la Grande Chaumière before attending the Yale University School of Architecture. Returning to teach at Cranbrook in 1936, Eero worked with his father on several architectural projects, with Crow Island School being among the earliest. While at Cranbrook, Eero

forged friendships with several important mid-century modern designers represented in the DeMell Jacobsen Collection: Charles Eames; Ray (Bernice Alexandra) Eames, née Kaiser (1912–1988, Cat. No. 31); Florence Knoll, née Schust (1917–2019); and Harry Bertoia (1915–1978, Cat. No. 35). Eero's wife, Lily Swann Saarinen (1912–1995), created decorative glazed tiles for the school's exterior brick walls and designed brightly printed curtains for the classroom windows.

Born in St. Louis, Charles Eames attended architectural classes at Washington University. After two years of studies, he founded a firm with Charles M. Gray in 1930. Offered a fellowship at the Cranbrook Academy of Art in 1938, he later led its industrial design department, where he designed home and office furniture. For Eames, furniture—and especially chairs—were of great interest given their manageable scale. "The chairs are literally like architecture in miniature," Eames once said. "For an architect who has difficulty controlling a building because of the contractor and the various forces brought to bear on anything that costs money, a chair is almost handleable on a human scale, and so you find great architects turning to chairs: Frank Lloyd Wright, Mies van

der Rohe, Le Corbusier, Alvar Aalto, Eero Saarinen—any number of them doing it, because this is architecture you can get your hands on."[9]

For the Crow Island School commission, Eames and Eero Saarinen were tasked by Eliel Saarinen to design and fabricate low-cost furniture that met the aspirational vision of the school. As a sculptor, Eero Saarinen had admired the plywood designs of fellow Finnish furniture designer Alvar Aalto (1898–1976). For the project, Saarinen and Eames experimented with laminated veneers of thin wood, known as plywood, building upon the mid-19th-century techniques of John Henry Belter (Cat. No. 9). Since the introduction of Belter's patented process, technical production methods to adhere laminated veneers, mold, and mass-produce plywood had dramatically improved during World War I through advancements in aircraft design and manufacture.

The seat and back of the ash plywood furniture were molded in a single directional continuous curve.[10] Sturdy, thick birch legs are vertical in the front, angled at the back, and secured by an H-type stretcher; a similar H-shaped stretcher supports the seat. In their mandate to identify an economical manufacturer, the team contracted with the Chicago-based Illinois Craft Project of the WPA (also referred to as the Design Workshop of the Illinois Art Project)[11] to manufacture the chairs, as indicated by the branded mark on the underside (Fig. 29.3). John Walley (1910–1974), director of the Design Workshop, described the program's mission "to restore, maintain and develop new skills in unemployed craftsmen through the production of useful equipment and environments for tax supported institutions in the municipal, county, state [or] federal governments and any combination of the four."[12] Materials and services were provided by sponsors, in this case the Winnetka School District, while the WPA funded the labor and tools.[13]

Walley arranged for a privately funded consulting position for former Bauhaus student Hin Bredendieck (1904–1995), who had taught at Chicago's New Bauhaus. Bredendieck had experience in multidirectional plywood curvatures and may have shared Design Workshop productions with Saarinen and Eames, expanding their knowledge.[14] While the H-type stretcher was also employed in their 1940 chairs designed for the Kleinhans Music Hall in Buffalo, New York, the curved plywood chair was a harbinger of later designs by Saarinen and Eames.

The Crow Island School chair led to their collaborative designs for a "new type of chair" constructed for the Organic Designs in Home Furnishings competition organized by the Museum of Modern Art.[15] The entry included two armchairs and a side chair, as well as graphic designs for which Ray Kaiser contributed her artistic talents. The team's living-room furniture featured sculptural and complex curved molded plywood with metal legs and earned two top awards in the nine judged categories.[16] Eliot Noyes, director of the museum's department of industrial design, stated in the press release prior to the exhibition opening on September 24, 1941, "In an ordinary chair there are a seat and a back which support the body at two or three points ... The principle in these chairs by Saarinen and Eames is that of continuous contact and support, with a thin rubber pad for softness at all points."[17]

Since projected production costs of the award-winning designs were prohibitive for mass production and the U.S. involvement in World War II began less than a month after the close of the exhibition, Saarinen and Eames went back to the drawing board. The war would shape their subsequent materials, techniques, and designs. They would each contribute to the war effort and then collaborate on postwar projects, while also independently building a reputation as leaders of modern aesthetic designs. However, their overall spirit of integrated, organic design and inventive furniture had its genesis at Crow Island and forged the innovative aesthetic of both designers for the remainder of their careers.

1   Juliet Kinchin, Aidan O'Connor, Tanya Harrod, and Medea Hoch, *Century of the Child: Growing by Design, 1900–2000* (New York: Museum of Modern Art, 2012), 107.

2   For information about the role of Perkins, Wheeler, and Will on the Crow Island School, see Lawrence Bradford Perkins, "Oral History of Lawrence Bradford Perkins, Interviewed by Betty J. Blum," Chicago Architects Oral History Project, Ernest R. Graham Study Center for Architectural Drawings, Department of Architecture (Chicago: Art Institute of Chicago, 1986).

3   National Register of Historic Places Registration Form for Crow Island School, United States Department of the Interior, National Park Service, prepared July 15, 1989, approved September 19, 1989, https://focus.nps.gov/pdfhost/docs/NHLS/Text/89001730.pdf.

4   Kinchin et al., *Century of the Child*, 105.

5   Blair Kamin, "Lawrence B. Perkins, Architectural Pioneer," *Chicago Tribune*, December 4, 1997.

6   Kinchin et al., *Century of the Child*, 107.

7   Perkins, "Oral History of Lawrence Bradford Perkins," 64.

8   "History of Cranbrook Academy of Art," Cranbrook Academy of Art, accessed September 1, 2015, https://cranbrookart.edu/about/history/.

9   Owen Gingerich, "A Conversation with Charles Eames," *American Scholar* 46, no. 3 (Summer 1977): 326–37.

10 Lloyd C. Engelbrecht, "Wood, Plywood and Veneer, Cranbrook, the New Bauhaus and the W.P.A.: The Origins of the Eames Chair of 1946," 1987, https://scholar.uc.edu/downloads/j96021434.

11 Engelbrecht. Because several hundred chairs and desks were needed, the Milwaukee Art Project also helped to manufacture the furnishings.

12 Engelbrecht.

13 Engelbrecht.

14 Engelbrecht. See also Sharon Darling, *Chicago Furniture: Art, Craft & Industry, 1833–1983* (Chicago: Chicago Historical Society and W. W. Norton, 1984), 286–91.

15 "Museum of Modern Art to Present Entirely New Type of Chair in Exhibition of Organic Design Opening September 24," press release, Museum of Modern Art, 1941, https://www.moma.org/momaorg/shared/pdfs/docs/press_archives/733/releases/MOMA_1941_0070_1941-09-19_41919-69.pdf?2010.

16 Engelbrecht, "Wood, Plywood and Veneer."

17 "Museum of Modern Art to Present Entirely New Type of Chair."

designed 1944[1]

Designed and manufactured by the Electrical Machine and Equipment Company (Emeco; active 1944–present, Hanover, Pennsylvania)

Brushed and anodized aluminum

34 ½ x 16 x 18 ½ in.

Labeled on verso of seat: Emeco (See Fig. 30.2)

LIGHTWEIGHT YET virtually indestructible, this streamlined chair remarkably weighs only seven pounds. Commonly referred to as the *Navy Chair*, the Emeco *Model 1006* (pronounced "ten-oh-six") was just one of thousands of products designed in support of the war effort during World War II. So timeless is its design, the chair continues to be produced by the Electrical Machine and Equipment Company (Emeco) in Hanover, Pennsylvania. The chair embodies the company's principles of "quality, excellence, trust, honesty, and lasting value,"[2] and illustrates their corporate mission of environmental sustainability. Further, it is a testament to American ingenuity and resilience, as well as the nation's ambitions and anticipation of the future.

Wilton Carlyle Dinges (1916–1974) founded Emeco in 1944, harnessing the skill of local German steelworkers and craftsmen. An engineer and "master tool and die maker,"[3] Dinges also appreciated fine art sculpture, especially the bronzes of Auguste Rodin (1840–1917). Dinges considered the *1006 Navy Chair* "a handcrafted piece of art,"[4] much like those of the celebrated French sculptor whose work he collected and subsequently donated to the Baltimore Museum of Art.[5]

Emeco's first commission was to fabricate seating furniture for U.S. Navy submarines. The contract required a chair that would be able to endure torpedo blasts as well as withstand "water, salt air, and sailors."[6] The specifications further required it be lightweight, fireproof, and last a lifetime. Emeco determined the properties of aluminum—also used in the aircraft-seat designs of Warren McArthur Jr. (Cat. No. 27)—would be the ideal material to satisfy the contractual stipulations. As Emeco did not have in-house designers, Dinges collaborated with those from the Aluminum Corporation of America (Alcoa) to develop what is the now iconic chair. In a bold display of his faith in its design, and to demonstrate the chair's durability, Dinges threw an example out an eighth-floor window of a Chicago hotel in the presence of government officials. The chair survived undamaged, except for a few scratches, and the firm received the contract.[7] Another testament to the chair's strength is illustrated in a company advertisement in which five wrestlers are supported by two Emeco armchairs (Fig. 30.1).

Made from 80 percent recycled aluminum, the *1006 Navy Chair* is durable and rust resistant. Every chair is the result of a two-week, 77-step process, which has remained unchanged since 1944.[8] Beginning with sheets of soft aluminum, machines cut and fold the metal into hollow tubes and a saddle seat.[9] Dozens of craftspeople then assemble, weld, grind, and hand finish the chair's 12 component elements to create a seamless appearance. The crest rail and stiles of the chair back are formed by one continuous piece shaped like an inverted letter U. The back is comprised of three slats, joined by an arched mid-rail, and rests atop the saddle seat, which is supported by four legs, separated by a double stretcher. Once assembled, the chair is submerged in a 960°F salt bath, then into cold water, and next into an acid bath, before it is baked in an oven for eight hours.[10] Lastly, the chairs are anodized through an electrolytic process, which produces a material that approaches the hardness of diamonds and is "3 times stronger than steel."[11] So durable is the chair, it comes with a lifetime warranty.

The government continued to keep Emeco afloat through purchases of the *1006 Navy Chair* until the 1970s. For almost a quarter century, nearly all U.S. Navy ships and submarines were outfitted with the chairs. Among them was the USS *Nautilus*, the first nuclear submarine, which made a pioneering voyage under the arctic icecap from the Pacific to the Atlantic in 1958, as well as hundreds of lesser-known vessels. Following the end of the Cold War, together with the continued downsizing of the military, demand for the chairs lessened, nearly driving the company to bankruptcy by the late 1970s.

In 1979, Jay Buchbinder, then-president of a restaurant interior design and manufacturing firm, acquired Emeco. He gradually revived the company using his business contacts and innovative marketing. In 1998, Buchbinder sold Emeco to his son, Gregg Buchbinder, who further diversified the client base and introduced new products. Following a serendipitous encounter at a trade show with Philippe Starck (b. 1949)—who had long admired the *1006 Navy Chair*—Emeco began a collaboration with the designer, which resulted in new collections such as Heritage, Emeco Stool, and Broom. In

Test load per chair:
1700 lbs.!

Only 2 aluminum lightweights can take on 5 heavyweights!

2004, architect Frank Gehry (b. 1929, Cat. No. 42) and Emeco debuted another new design, the *Superlight* (Cat. No. 47), a 21st-century update of the classic *1006 Navy Chair*. Collaborations with others followed, including Norman Foster, Konstantin Grcic, Jasper Morrison, Nendo, Jean Nouvel, Christophe Pillet, Ettore Sottsass, Adrian van Hooydonk, and Michael Young.

Like earlier American companies owned by such enterprising spirits as Cyrus Wakefield (Cat. No. 15) and Wenzel Friedrich (Cat. No. 19), Emeco values the repurposing of materials. Since its founding, Emeco has primarily used recycled aluminum in its products, which are fashioned from 40 percent post-industrial waste and 40 percent post-consumer waste. Aluminum is such a successfully recycled material that approximately 75 percent of what has been manufactured since 1888 is still in circulation today.[12] In yet another demonstration of its commitment to sustainability, Emeco debuted a reinterpreted design of the *1006 Navy Chair* in 2010 at the Salone del Mobile in Milan. Made from 111 post-consumer recycled PET plastic Coca-Cola bottles, the chair is appropriately named the *111 Navy Chair*, and was originally offered in six colors: Red, Snow, Flint, Grass, Persimmon, and Charcoal.[13]

Today, the *1006 Navy Chair* has transcended its "wartime workhorse" function to become a ubiquitous icon.[14] The chair has been featured in fashion boutiques such as Armani, appeared in glossy advertisements for Verizon, and has been used in set designs for numerous films and television shows, including *The Matrix*, *Mr. and Mrs. Smith*, *Law & Order*, and *CSI*, among others.[15] Owing to the chair's timeless industrial design and its environmental sustainability, Google Inc. furnished portions of its London offices with both aluminum and plastic versions. Now no longer reliant on the military as its single largest client, Emeco praises the continued dedication of their talented craftspeople as they work collectively to "keep making things that last."[16]

1 Special thanks to Emeco for the generous donation of the 1006 Navy Chair to The Thomas H. and Diane DeMell Jacobsen Ph.D. Foundation.

2 See Emeco catalogue, undated, https://pdf.archiexpo.com/pdf/emeco/emeco-navy-1752/4170-198631-_4.html. Accessed June 6, 2022.

3 "Dinges Wilton Carlyle," Design Addict, accessed September 3, 2015, https://designaddict.com/designer/wilton-carlyle-dinges/.

4 "1006 Navy Collection: Navy® Chair," Emeco, accessed September 2, 2015, https://www.emeco.net/products/emeco-1006-navy-chair-brushed-us-navy.

5 Collection search: Gifts of Wilton C. Dinges, Baltimore Museum of Art, accessed February 18, 2018, https://collection.artbma.org/search/dinges.

6 "1006 Navy Collection: Navy® Chair."

7 EmecoChairs, "Emeco Navy Chair on Design DNA," May 2, 2011, video, https://www.youtube.com/watch?v=6fgyG4wsUhl.

8 Eames Demetrios, grandson of designer Charles Eames (Cat. Nos. 29 and 31), produced a video documenting the manufacturing process. See Emeco, "77 Steps," May 21, 2012, video, https://vimeo.com/42591587.

9 According to factory lore, the seat was modeled to fit the derrière of famed actress Betty Grable (1916–1973).

10 Mo Rocca, "Exploring the History of an Iconic Chair," *CBS Sunday Morning*, January 6, 2014, video, https://www.cbsnews.com/video/exploring-the-history-of-an-iconic-chair/.

11 "77 Steps," Emeco, accessed November 23, 2021, https://www.emeco.net/about/the-factory/77-steps.

12 "1006 Navy Collection: Navy® Chair."

13 Linda Tischler, "Coke + Emeco: Get Hitched, Spawn Chair," *Fast Company*, April 9, 2010, https://www.fastcompany.com/1613151/coke-emeco-get-hitched-spawn-chairs. A seventh color—Beach—was later introduced.

14 Linda Hales, "A Craft is Saved as U.S. Navy Chair Becomes a Design Icon: Ode to a Wartime Workhorse," *New York Times*, August 22, 2000.

15 Linda Hales, "Not Exactly a Stand-Up Move," *Washington Post*, July 9, 2005.

16 "1006 Navy Collection: Navy® Chair."

Fig. 30.1 (left) Early advertisement illustrating the combined strength of two armchair variants of the *1006 Navy Chair*, 1950.

Fig. 30.2 (above) Detail of label on verso of seat.

LCW

31

(Lounge Chair Wood or Low Chair Wood)

designed 1945;
this example executed 1946–1948

Designed by Charles Ormond Eames Jr. (1907–1978) and Bernice Alexandra ("Ray") Kaiser Eames (1912–1988)

Manufactured by the Evans Products Company for the Herman Miller Furniture Company (active 1923–present, Zeeland, Michigan)

Molded birch plywood

26 x 22 x 24 in.

Labeled on underside of seat: Manufactured by / EVANS PRODUCTS COMPANY / MOLDED PLYWOOD DIVISION / herman miller / furniture company / SOLE DISTRIBUTOR / Designed by / CHARLES EAMES

DESIGNED BY husband-and-wife team Charles and Ray Eames, the *LCW* was hailed by *Time* magazine in 1999 as "The Best Design of the 20th Century."[1] The chair was made from thin, molded, resin-bonded birch plywood, utilizing new techniques to create complex curvatures and realize the designers' objective to create an ergonomic, comfortable, lightweight, and aesthetically pleasing chair that could be economically mass produced.[2]

Manufactured by the Evans Products Company and distributed by the Herman Miller Furniture Company, the design of the *LCW* coincided with a growing American interest in modernism, promoted through a variety of media—both in print and on television—and numerous design exhibitions organized by the Museum of Modern Art. Commonly referred to as "the potato chip chair," the chair's aesthetics appear almost zoomorphic: the organic shape of the backrest (head), the seat (thorax), and the splat (spine) rest atop quadruped legs, while its rubber shock mounts cushion the components like cartilage. The *LCW* and its variants remain in production today and are widely regarded as an iconic representation of the mid-century modernist style.

Charles Eames and Bernice Alexandra ("Ray") Kaiser met while students at the Cranbrook Academy of Art.[3] Born in St. Louis, Charles first studied architecture at Washington University in St. Louis and later traveled to Europe, where he was exposed to its rich architectural history and the emerging International Style. He returned to America and opened his own architecture firm, and later joined the faculty of the Cranbrook Academy of Art at the invitation of Eliel Saarinen.

Ray Kaiser was born in Sacramento, California, and after graduating high school moved with her mother to New York City, where she studied painting with Hans Hofmann (1880–1966) at the Art Students League and became a founding member of American Abstract Artists. Following the death of her mother, Ray enrolled at the Cranbrook Academy of Art, where she met Charles, who at the time served as the head of the department of industrial design. In June 1941, Charles and Ray exchanged wedding rings, made by fellow Cranbrook friend Harry Bertoia (Cat. No. 35).[4] The following month, the newlyweds moved to Los Angeles, where they began a life that

would be fulfilled through their collaborations on innovative furniture designs, architecture, and film. There, Charles took a day job at the MGM movie studio working on set designs, while Ray worked as a graphic designer at *Arts & Architecture* magazine, a publication for which she would ultimately design 24 covers between 1942 and 1944.[5] Charles also worked at the magazine as both a contributing writer and an editorial associate.

While Charles had begun designing furniture with Eero Saarinen at Cranbrook, it was through his collaboration with Ray that he "produced some of the most visually interesting and technologically adventurous furniture of the mid-twentieth century."[6] In their spare bedroom they installed the "Kazam! Machine," a makeshift press they had constructed "out of scrap wood and a bicycle pump," so they could continue their experiments with shaping plywood.[7] The couple expanded upon Charles's single-directional curve design employed in his earlier *Crow Island School Chair* (Cat. No. 29), which evolved into the more complex curve designs he made in collaboration with Saarinen and submitted to the 1941 *Organic Design in Home Furnishings* exhibition at the Museum of Modern Art. Since the multiple-award-winning designs were not commercially viable due to a combination of their expense and America's entry into World War II, the Eameses persistently explored and later developed pioneering "new techniques for laminating and bending plywood shells into compound curves."[8]

In 1942 the couple established the Plyformed Wood Company to research and fabricate their plywood products. Their research earned a commission from the U.S. Navy "to develop plywood splints, stretchers, and glider shells molded under heat and pressure."[9] Leg and arm splints were developed, as well as a body litter. The leg splints were reportedly modeled on Charles's own leg, and in 1942 the Navy ordered 5,000 units.[10] The refined process of bonding wood veneers with resin glue and molding the plywood under heat and pressure resulted in the issuance of a patent. The molded material was referred to by its "adopted name," Plyformed.[11] In 1943 the Evans Products Company[12] of Detroit, Michigan, assumed the Eameses' company and renamed it the Molded Plywood Division.[13] Charles Eames served

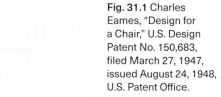

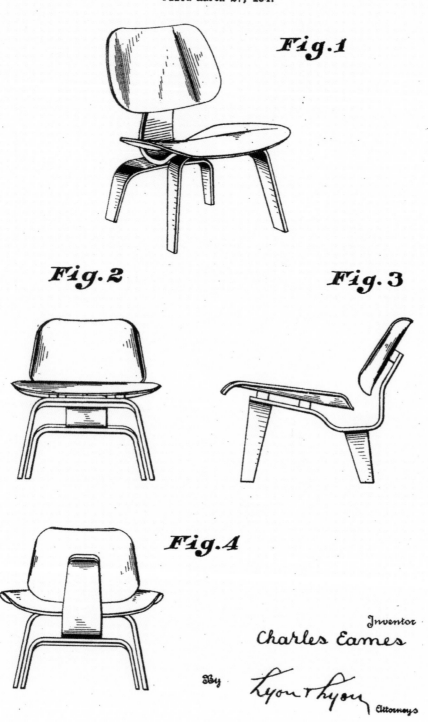

Aug. 24, 1948.

C. EAMES

Des. 150,683

CHAIR

Filed March 27, 1947

Fig.1

Fig.2

Fig.3

Fig.4

Inventor

Charles Eames

By

Lyon & Lyon

Attorneys

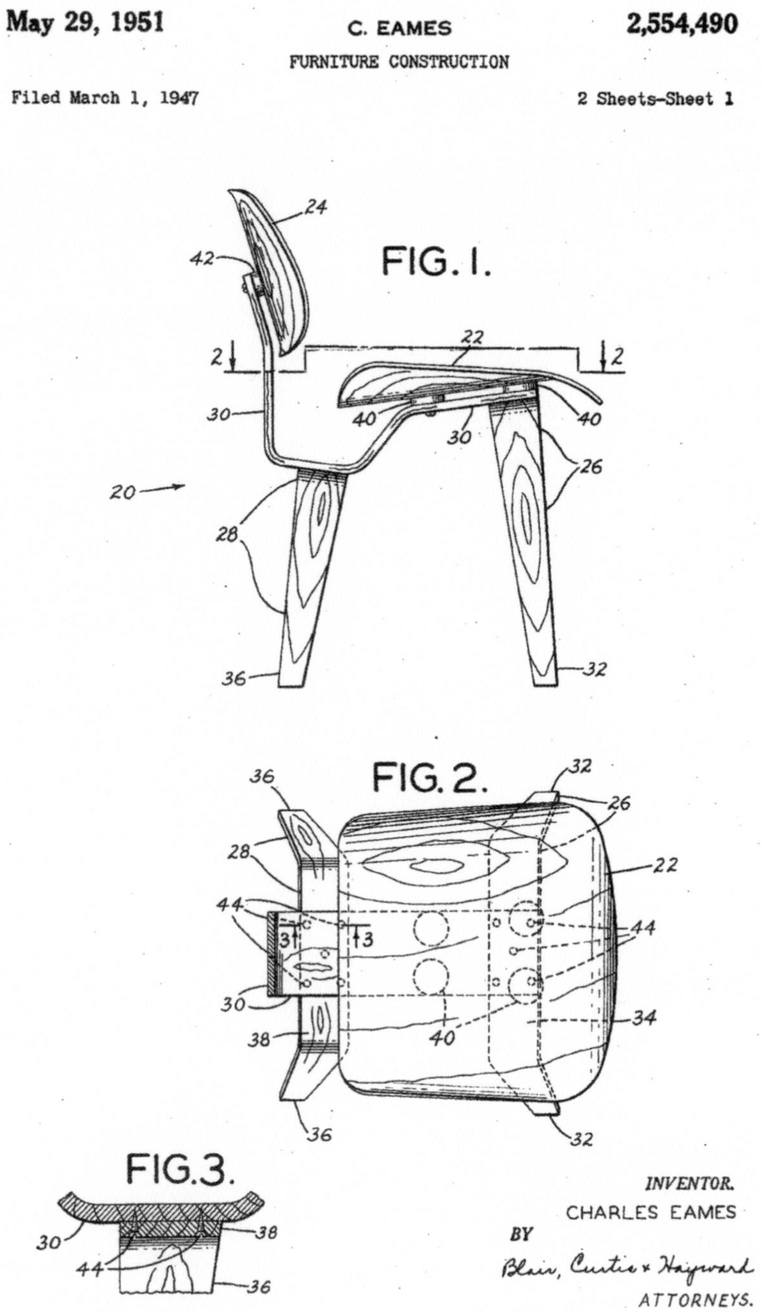

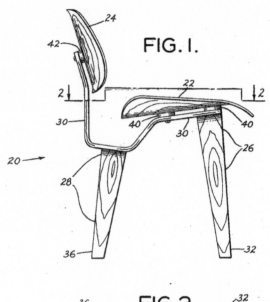

May 29, 1951   C. EAMES   2,554,490

FURNITURE CONSTRUCTION

Filed March 1, 1947   2 Sheets-Sheet 1

FIG. I.

FIG. 2.

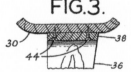

FIG.3.

INVENTOR.
CHARLES EAMES
BY
Blair, Curtis & Hayward
ATTORNEYS.

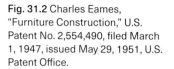

Fig. 31.2 Charles Eames, "Furniture Construction," U.S. Patent No. 2,554,490, filed March 1, 1947, issued May 29, 1951, U.S. Patent Office.

economic mass production of domestic furniture. Attempts to bend a single sheet into complex curves revealed weaknesses in the material despite their trial efforts to relieve the pressure with cutouts. By creating individual sections for the seat, back, legs, and spine, a line of biomorphic modern-style plywood furniture ultimately was born.

The Evans Products Company manufactured the chair prototypes, which debuted at the Barclay Hotel in New York City in December 1945. Three months later, the Museum of Modern Art opened *New Furniture Designed by Charles Eames* and hailed his seating furniture as "the greatest innovation in chair design since Marcel Breuer startled the furniture world with his metal chair and Alvar Aalto introduced the technique of laminated wood furniture."[16] The *New York Times* reported that much of the seating furniture, which was suitable for both interior and exterior, was "small-scaled for small rooms, light in weight, easy to keep clean and, judging by a special demonstration in which a chair is tossed about in a revolving barrel and pounded by metal hammers, it is apparently indestructible."[17] Eliot Noyes, director of industrial design at the Museum of Modern Art, praised Eames's molded plywood designs as "a compound of aesthetic brilliance and technical inventiveness."[18]

The publicity drew the attention of George Nelson (1908–1986, Cat. No. 38), then newly hired as the first design director at the Herman Miller Furniture Company.[19] Nelson negotiated a deal with Eames to allow for the continued production of the chair by Evans Products Company at a factory in Michigan, while Herman Miller would market and distribute the product from their headquarters in nearby Zeeland, Michigan, and through their showrooms in Chicago, New York, and Los Angeles.[20] The Eames team began working with Herman Miller in 1946, and they transferred production rights for the *LCW* chair to the

as director of research and development and continued to work from his office in Venice, California; he later encouraged Harry Bertoia to leave Cranbrook Academy and join the design team.

During World War II, the Allied forces developed significant advances in the use of plywood in aircraft. The Eames team designed and produced airplane components during the war, including

fuselages, stabilizer tails, and seats for pilots.[14] The pilot seat informed their subsequent applications to postwar furniture designs, specifically in seating furniture with form-fitting comfort, affordability, and an economical use of materials. In their experiments, Charles and Ray Eames pushed the "limits of the material," determined to find "the honest use of molded plywood"[15] and to resolve a technique for

Fig. 31.3 Detail of label on underside of seat.

company in 1949; manufacturing of the *LCW* and other models began at the Herman Miller factory in Zeeland that year.

In 1947 Charles applied for a chair design patent as an assignor to Evans Products Company (Fig. 31.1) and a furniture construction patent as an assignor to the Herman Miller Furniture Company (Fig. 31.2).[21] The latter described the "novel assembly of supporting parts for contour-conforming, individually mounted back and seat panels," achieving greater ergonomics and superior comfort for a sitter's seat and back.[22] The ergonomic success of this chair lies in the attention to the spine and shock mounts. Paramount to the design was the shape of the "resilient spine" with a "degree of yieldability" and properly positioned connectors.[23] Rubber mounts—components used in automobile and airplane engines—were bonded to the spine element under the seat and behind the back rest to absorb shock and redistribute pressure. Thus, the Eameses created "one of the first examples of a responsive back rest in the history of

furniture."[24] The spine supports a natural reclining position created by the varying height of the front and rear legs. Under the seat of this chair is a label listing the designer, manufacturer, and distributor (Fig. 31.3). A unique arrangement of screws in a 5-2-5 formation used by the Evans Products Company is also present.

The chair design provided "the first mass-produced seats" using the new method of "bending three-dimensional plywood ... for peacetime application."[25] The chairs set a new standard in the United States "for using a minimal amount of materials to achieve forms of maximum utility, lightness, and sculptural effect."[26] The standardized parts could be easily assembled or disassembled for shipping. Additionally, the elements could be used in the production of endless variations of the chair's design and resulted in such models as the *Dining Chair Wood (DCW)* and versions with a metal base and lumbar support—*Lounge Chair Metal (LCM)* and *Dining Chair Metal (DCM)*.

The *LCW* swiftly became one of the most visible and popular design products of the postwar era. Its high visibility was perhaps related to the concurrent rise of another

product of mass appeal: the television set. From 1942 to 1947, the number of privately owned television sets jumped from 7,000 to 44,000, with a hiatus of production during the war. The year 1946 saw the beginning of regular network broadcasts, including the creation of ABC, formerly a part of NBC. Lay's, a manufacturer of potato chips, was the first snack food company to buy television commercial time.

By 1956 it was estimated that "nearly one million Eames chairs are currently in use in American homes, giving him a record no other living designer approaches."[27] The designs had achieved almost instant recognition and the name Eames had "become almost a household word," as reported by Arlene Francis on an episode of NBC's *Home show*.[28] Introducing the team's newest design, a *Lounge Chair* and *Ottoman* (models 670 and 671), the show opened with an *LCM* spinning magically in the air like a mobile by Alexander Calder (1898–1976). An enthusiastic Francis narrated, "This chair is a familiar one to you. But ten years ago, when it was designed by Charles Eames it was a revolutionary new chair and I must say it caused quite a flurry."[29] Standing on stage accompanied by a veritable retrospective of the Eameses' work, Charles explained, "The molded plywood chairs are a result of working with a mass-production technique and in a way letting the mass-production technique show through in the result."[30]

Coincident with the appeal of the *LCW* and rising use of television was the postwar housing boom and the development of suburbs. Commonly known as the G.I. Bill, the Servicemen's Readjustment Act was signed by President Roosevelt in June 1944. As the editor of *Arts & Architecture* magazine, John Entenza (1905–1984) encouraged architects to create a new modern American home that was aesthetically pleasing, practical, affordable, and functional. In these "Case Study Houses," architects were encouraged to incorporate technologically advanced materials and mass-production methods to promote modernism with the "simplicity of form, integration of indoor and outdoor living spaces, and the avoidance of reference to historical styles."[31] The concept was embraced in Los Angeles, where "nearly 370,000 people would visit the houses in the first three years of the program."[32] Charles and Ray Eames designed two Case Study Houses, and their Case Study House No. 8—later known as the Eames House—served as the couple's home from 1949 until their deaths and was later designated a National Historic Landmark in 2006.[33]

Charles and Ray Eames perceptively "recognized the need" in design for affordable furniture with multiple functions.[34] As they continued to experiment with molded plywood, fiberglass, and aluminum, they also expanded their repertoire into the fields of graphic art, toys, exhibitions, books, and film, such as *The Powers of Ten*, a short documentary film produced in 1977. Although Charles and Ray did not have children together, their legacy continues through the efforts of the Eames Foundation and Eames Office, headed by Lucia Eames (Charles's daughter with his first wife, Catherine Woermann) and her children.

1   "Eames Molded Plywood Chairs," Herman Miller, accessed March 11, 2018, https://www.hermanmiller.com/products/seating/side-chairs/eames-molded-plywood-chairs/product-details/.
2   Special thanks to Andrew VanStyn for his research and expertise. His contributions helped shape this essay.
3   For a thorough examination of the couple, see Pat Kirkham, *Charles and Ray Eames: Designers of the Twentieth Century* (Cambridge, MA: MIT Press, 1995).
4   Scott Sendra, "Cranbrook Art Museum Presents *Bent, Cast, and Forged: The Jewelry of Harry Bertoia*," press release, Cranbrook Art Museum, February 10, 2015, https://cranbrookartmuseum.org/2015/02/11/cranbrook-art-museum-presents-bent-cast-and-forged-the-jewelry-of-harry-bertoia/.
5   "Eames Molded Plywood Chairs."
6   Donald Albrecht, "Design Is a Method of Action," in *The Work of Charles and Ray Eames: A Legacy of Invention* (New York: Harry N. Abrams, 1997), 23. See also Pat Kirkham, "Introducing Ray Eames (1912–1988)," *Furniture History* 26 (1990): 132–41.
7   Judith Miller, *Chairs* (London: Conran Octopus, 2009), 201.
8   Barbara Haskell, *The American Century: Art & Culture, 1900–1950* (New York: Whitney Museum of American Art in association with W. W. Norton, 1999), 292.
9   "Eames Molded Plywood Chairs." See also Jason Weems, "War Furniture: Charles and Ray Eames Design for the Wounded Body," *Boom: A Journal of California* 2, no. 1 (Spring 2012): 46–48.
10 Allison Meier, "How a Leg Splint Shaped the Iconic Eames Chair," *Hyperallergic*, October 17, 2016, https://hyperallergic.com/328930/leg-splint-shaped-iconic-eames-chair/. See also "Charles and Ray Eames," timeline, Vitra Design Museum, accessed January 7, 2022, https://collection.design-museum.de/#/en/person/2967?_k=zn4hkm.
11 The patent for the splint is Charles Eames, "Laminated Splint," U.S. Patent No. 2,548,470, April 10, 1951. See also

Charles Eames, "Method of Making Laminated Articles," U.S. Patent No. 2,395,468, February 26, 1946. Neither patent uses the term "Plyformed," however. See https://eames.com/en/war-time-leg-splint, accessed March 7, 2022.
12 The Evans Products Company had been founded by Edward Steptoe Evans Sr. (1879–1945), a lumberman from Virginia. His invention of the "Evans Block," a wooden wedge that secured automobiles during transportation via rail, was the start of the Detroit-based multi-million-dollar company. The company became one of America's "largest suppliers of plywood and railroad loading equipment." In the mid-20th century, the company formed smaller entities and was renamed Evans Industries, Inc.
13 "The Work of Charles and Ray Eames: A Legacy of Invention," exhibition website, Library of Congress, 1999, accessed September 4, 2015, https://www.loc.gov/exhibits/eames/furniture.html. See also Cherie Fehrman and Kenneth Fehrman, *Interior Design Innovators 1910–1960* (San Francisco: Fehrman Books, 2009), 46.
14 "The Pilot Seat," Eames Office, accessed December 9, 2021, https://www.eamesoffice.com/the-work/the-pilot-seat/.
15 "LCW," Eames Office, accessed September 4, 2015, http://www.eamesoffice.com/the-work/lcw/.
16 "New Furniture Designs and Techniques Have Initial Showing at Museum of Modern Art," press release, Museum of Modern Art, March 11, 1946, https://assets.moma.org/documents/moma_press-release_325508.pdf. It is worth noting that Ray Eames was not fully recognized for her contributions until more recently. Therefore, many historical quotes and references mention Charles only.
17 "Eames Furniture to Be Exhibited," *New York Times*, March 13, 1946.
18 David Helm, "Famous Furniture: Eames Molded Plywood Chairs," *Woodcraft Magazine*, February/March 2020, 56.
19 Herman Miller began as Star Furniture Company in 1906. The company changed names to the Michigan Star

Company under the guidance of Dirk Jan (D.J.) De Pree and was renamed Herman Miller Furniture in 1923, in honor of De Pree's father-in-law, the majority shareholder. Gilbert Rohde (1894–1944), a New York designer, was influential in steering the company toward new American styles in an effort to successfully transition the traditional wood furniture company out of the Depression. Rohde's 1942 Executive Office Group designs marked the beginning of the company's office furniture line.
20 "To Distribute Furniture," *New York Times*, December 1, 1946.
21 Charles Eames, "Design for a Chair," U.S. Design Patent No. 150,683, filed March 27, 1947, issued August 24, 1948, U.S. Patent Office; Charles Eames, "Furniture Construction," U.S. Patent No. 2,554,490, filed March 1, 1947, issued May 29, 1951, U.S. Patent Office.
22 Eames, "Furniture Construction."
23 Eames.
24 Miller, *Chairs*, 201.
25 Florence de Dampierre, *Chairs: A History* (New York: Abrams, 2006), 377.
26 Haskell, *American Century*, 292.
27 Betty Pepis, "Eames Has a New Chair in Three Sections," *New York Times*, March 14, 1956.
28 "Eames Lounge Chair Debut in 1956 on NBC," part 1 of 2, video, https://www.youtube.com/watch?v=zfzLzOI795E.
29 "Eames Lounge Chair Debut."
30 "Eames Lounge Chair Debut." Special thanks to David Kammerman for his research on this topic, which helped to shape this essay.
31 "Eames Lounge Chair Debut."
32 "Eames Lounge Chair Debut."
33 National Historic Landmark Nomination for Eames House, United States Department of the Interior, National Park Service, prepared May 2005, approved September 20, 2006, https://www.getty.edu/conservation/our_projects/field_projects/eameshouse/EamesHouseNHL.pdf.
34 "The Work of Charles and Ray Eames."

'Grasshopper' Chair (Model 61U)

32

designed 1946; produced 1946–1965;
this example executed c. 1955

Designed by Eero Saarinen (1910–1961)

Manufactured by Knoll, Inc. (active 1938–present, East Greenville, Pennsylvania, and New York, New York)

Laminated birch, upholstery (replaced)

35 ½ x 26 ½ x 34 in.

WHAT DOES THIS chair, the Gateway Arch in St. Louis, and an insect that leaps have in common? In 1946, Knoll Associates, Inc.,[1] commissioned architect Eero Saarinen, future designer of the Arch, to also design their first lounge chair (Fig. 32.1). Though officially named the *Model 61U*, it became commonly known as the *"Grasshopper" Chair* because the shape of the continuous, bent laminated birchwood arms and legs resembles that of the insect's rear legs (Figs. 32.3 and 32.4). Illustrating the biomorphic modernist style, the chair also reflects Saarinen's understanding of the postwar psyche and lifestyle.[2]

While an early model—perhaps a prototype[3]—featured upholstery made from surplus woven military parachute webbing, the production model possessed button-tufted upholstery designed and manufactured by Knoll Textiles.[4] The innovative base system allows the padded and upholstered one-piece molded plywood seat, back, and headrest to provide maximum comfort.[5] Connected to the wooden elements by joints hidden under the upholstery, the body appears to float above hairpin curves, which foreshadow Saarinen's design for the Gateway Arch (Fig. 32.2).[6]

Instilled in this design is Saarinen's proficiency as a sculptor and architect as well as his experiences at Cranbrook Academy of Art with his colleagues Charles Eames, with whom he collaborated on molded plywood furniture for the Crow Island School (Cat. No. 29), and Ray Kaiser Eames (Cat. No. 31). During World War II, until 1944, Saarinen worked for the Office of Strategic Services illustrating bomb disassembly manuals and creating designs for the White House War Room.[7] Throughout this time, he continued to experiment with seating designs and models.[8] Saarinen was also involved in the Case Study House project promoted by *Arts & Architecture* magazine, and thus was familiar with the aspiration to promote modernism in aesthetically pleasing, affordable, functional, and comfortable domestic architecture. In 1946 he joined Knoll Associates, Inc., to help design its first line of domestic seating furniture.

Hans Knoll (1914–1955) incorporated the Hans G. Knoll Furniture Company in New York City in 1938. Knoll, a German immigrant, originally planned to build a company that retailed European imports. However, due to the war and its impact on ensuring a stable inventory of imports, Knoll turned to manufacturing furniture domestically; he opened a factory in East Greenville, Pennsylvania, in 1941. Two years later, Florence Schust (1917–2019) joined Knoll and made a lasting and profound impact on the company.[9] A student of both the Cranbrook Academy of Art and the Illinois Institute of Technology under Mies van der Rohe, Schust injected vitality into the company through her interior design experience and rapport with architects. In 1946, Schust and Hans Knoll married, and she became a full business partner. Consequently, Hans G. Knoll Furniture Company officially became Knoll Associates, Inc. Ever since, the firm has produced acclaimed furniture by such designers as Saarinen, Harry Bertoia (1915–1978, Cat. No. 35), Isamu Noguchi (1904–1988, Cat. No. 36), and Robert Venturi (1925–2018, Cat. No. 43), whose influential designs are also represented in the DeMell Jacobsen Collection.

Postwar Americans enjoyed prosperity due to the economic stimulation provided by the G.I. Bill of Rights through low-cost mortgages and tuition toward education. As the suburbs developed, the general lifestyle promoted relaxation and enjoyment. Prior to the end of World War II, Knoll's production line consisted of small side or pull-up chairs and a few larger upholstered chairs, though no lounge chairs.[10] At the invitation of Florence Schust Knoll, Saarinen designed a lounge chair whose back angled for a more relaxed position yet remained true to his idea of comfort as a function of form, as seen in his earlier chairs for the Organic Design in Home Furnishings competition. As he acknowledged in his design for the *"Grasshopper" Chair*, "People sit differently today … They want to sit lower and they like to slouch. I [have] attempted to shape the slouch in an organized way, giving support for the back as well as the seat, shoulders and head."[11]

Like his organic furniture designs for the Museum of Modern Art in 1941, Saarinen focused on comfort by creating three angles for contact points to support the human form. In contrast to Frank Lloyd Wright's three-legged chair for the Johnson Wax administration offices (Cat. No. 28), whose design dictated a theoretically idealistic posture, Saarinen's chair responded to how people actually preferred to sit. The

"Grasshopper" Chair embodied Saarinen's approach to the art of seating, ergonomic design, and his concern for "human anatomy and its relationship to furniture."[12] Florence Schust Knoll praised Saarinen's understanding of the human body in his design: "If you look at the side elevation of the chair, there's a seat and then a back that angles up from it and then another angle that goes for the head. Eero worked on that form to make it generally accessible and comfortable for different types of people. He did the seat in the form of the body—for comfort—and then also for that form to connect to the base."[13]

While purely unique, Saarinen's *"Grasshopper" Chair* design is undoubtedly informed and influenced by a number of chairs produced in the preceding decade. Its overall aesthetic recalls Marcel Breuer's *Lounge Chair* (1935) as well as designs by several Scandinavian designers, including Axel Larsson's *Armchair* (1937) and Gustav Axel Berg's *Torparen (The Farmer)* lounge chair (1942). The cantilevered arms of the *"Grasshopper" Chair* suggest those found on the *Barwa* outdoor lounge chair (1946) by Edgar Bartolucci and Jack Waldheim,

or Ralph Rapson's *Model No. 657 ("Rapid Rocker")* rocking chair (c. 1945), which Knoll also manufactured.[14] But in its overall philosophical approach, it is perhaps most closely aligned to the *Pernilla Lounge Chair and Ottoman* (c. 1935) by Bruno Mathsson (1907–1988), who acknowledged "comfortable sitting is an 'art'—it ought not to be. Instead, the making of chairs has to be done with such an 'art' that the sitting will not be any 'art.'"[15]

It is interesting to compare this lounge chair with Warren McArthur's *Lounge Chair* (Cat. No. 27). Both designs provide a reclined seat that appears to float between side rails, as well as an overall simplicity and streamlining. However, there are significant differences. Saarinen's form firmly supports the back, head, and knees, while McArthur's seat acts as a soft hammock. McArthur's chair is a masterful combination of the metallic and linear forms of the Bauhaus, International Style, and Art Deco, whereas Saarinen's organic modernism favors lines and curves fashioned in birchwood and a more traditional woven fabric. The chair came in both cloth upholstery, with and without button tufting (*Model 61U*),[16] and

webbed upholstery (*Model 61W*). Knoll also offered a complementary ottoman, but both chair and ottoman were discontinued in 1965 due to flagging sales as well as the introduction of other Saarinen designs, such as his *"Womb" Chair and Ottoman (Model No. 70).*[17]

While developing the *"Grasshopper" Chair*, Saarinen was most likely beginning to conceptualize his submission for a competition that had been announced the year before to design a memorial to Thomas Jefferson and the Westward expansion in St. Louis, Missouri. Standing 590 feet tall, Saarinen's arch-shaped "Gateway to the West" was pronounced the winning design in 1948 and was hailed as a "work of architectural genius."[18] For the arch design, the laminated birchwood hairpin legs were reimagined in stainless steel. Saarinen leapt forward to innovative designs with modern materials, culminating in the famous molded fiberglass and plastic-bonded *Tulip Chair*, which is supported by a single pedestal base. Despite his premature death in 1961 during an operation for a brain tumor, Saarinen's legacy lives on through his iconic designs for buildings and furniture.[19]

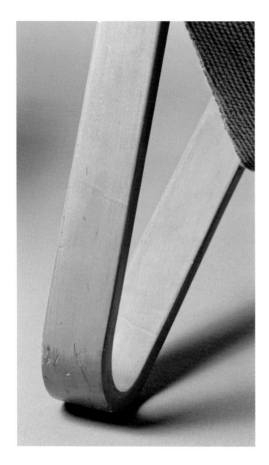

Figs. 32.3 and 32.4
Detail of chair leg and arms.

1 The Knoll corporate name has changed several times over the last 75 years: Hans G. Knoll Furniture Company (1938–43); H. G. Knoll Associates (1943–46); Knoll Associates, Inc. (1946–69); Knoll International (1969–90); Knoll Group (1990–95); and Knoll, Inc. (1995–2021). See Earl Martin, ed., *Knoll Textiles, 1945–2010* (New York: Bard Graduate Center and Yale University Press, 2011), 25. In 2021, Herman Miller acquired Knoll, Inc., and announced the combined companies will operate under the name MillerKnoll. Both Herman Miller and Knoll remain distinct brands. See "Herman Miller and Knoll Announce New Name: MillerKnoll," press release, Knoll, July 20, 2021, https://www.knoll.com/knollnewsdetail/herman-miller-knoll-announce-new-name.

2 Special thanks to David Kammerman. His research on this chair helped to shape this essay.

3 See "1946 Product: The Grasshopper Chair," Timeline, Archive, Knoll, accessed January 7, 2022, https://www.knoll.com/the-archive/?detail=b16&mode=timeline.

4 Jens Risom, an early designer for Knoll, recalled that the company first acquired webbing from prewar supplies until the government requisitioned them. As the supplies dried up, Risom discovered quantities of cotton parachute belting that had not met government specifications, and Knoll was able to purchase the defective materials. "We didn't care if it was strong enough to swing a man in the air in a parachute," he recalled. Initially, Knoll's standard webbing was "olive drab," dictated by its military origins, or could be dyed green or brown at a slightly higher price. See Paul Makovsky, "Knoll Before Knoll Textiles, 1940–1946," in Martin, *Knoll Textiles*, 82–83.

5 Charlotte Fiell and Peter Fiell, *1,000 Chairs* (Cologne, Germany: Taschen, 1997), 228.

6 Special thanks to Andrew VanStyn for his research and expertise. His contributions helped shape this essay.

7 Wendy Gilmartin, "The Secret Life of Eero Saarinen, Architect of the St. Louis Arch and ... the White House War Room?," *LA Weekly*, October 9, 2012, https://www.laweekly.com/the-secret-life-of-eero-saarinen-architect-of-the-st-louis-arch-and-the-white-house-war-room/.

8 Eeva-Liisa Pelkonen, Donald Albrecht, et al., *Eero Saarinen: Shaping the Future* (New Haven, CT: Yale University Press, 2006), 250–52.

9 See Amy L. Arnold and Jessica L. Puff, "The Knoll Look: Florence Schust Knoll Bassett and the Reinvention of the Modern Interior," in *Michigan Modern: Design That Shaped America*, ed. Amy L. Arnold and Brian D. Conway (Layton, UT: Gibbs Smith, 2016), 189–97.

10 Pelkonen, Albrecht, et al., *Eero Saarinen*, 251.

11 Pelkonen, Albrecht, et al., 251.

12 Charlotte Fiell and Peter Fiell, *Modern Chairs* (Cologne, Germany: Taschen, 1993), 65.

13 Pelkonen, Albrecht, et al., *Eero Saarinen*, 251.

14 Ralph Rapson was a fellow designer at Knoll and studied at Cranbrook with Saarinen, Charles and Ray Eames, and Florence Schust. For a thorough analysis of Rapson and his designs, see Jane King Hession et al., *Ralph Rapson: Sixty Years of Modern Design* (Afton: MN: Afton Historical Society Press, 1999). See also Rip Rapson, "Ralph Rapson: Design and the Mercy of Inspiration," in Arnold and Conway, *Michigan Modern*, 275–83.

15 Quoted in Charlotte Fiell and Peter Fiell, *Chairs: 1,000 Masterpieces of Modern Design, 1800 to the Present Day* (London: Goodman Fiell, 2012), 175.

16 The upholstery of early *"Grasshopper" Chairs* may have been designed by Antoinette Lackner Webster (1909–1998). An award-winning designer and teacher, Webster had a brief career as a professional weaver and created an iconic Knoll fabric—*Prestini*. The fabric, made by Louisville Textiles, was released in 1948, just as the upholsterer dropped Prestini, her first husband's surname, from her name, when she remarried. The identity of "Toni Prestini" (as she was credited in Knoll press releases and price lists at the time) thus became obscured in subsequent decades, while the fabric she designed remained a key component of Knoll's textile collections for over 30 years. See Martin, *Knoll Textiles*, 350–51. This *"Grasshopper" Chair* features a *Cato* fabric, an 86 percent wool and 14 percent rayon blend that was introduced in 1961. Like *Prestini*, *Cato* recalls the long tradition of handwoven fabrics at Knoll Textiles.

17 Florence Knoll acknowledged, "it was a perfectly nice chair but it wasn't one of the great successes." Quoted in Fiell and Fiell, *1,000 Chairs*, 286.

18 William M. Blair, "St. Louis Chooses Arch as Memorial," *New York Times*, February 19, 1948, 30.

19 The DeMell Jacobsen Collection also features the matching ottoman for the *"Grasshopper" Chair (Model 61U)*.

Spring Chair or Recliner (Experimental)

33

c. 1946/1947

Designed by Herbert von Thaden (1898–1969)

Manufactured by Thaden-Jordan Furniture Corporation (active 1946–1952, Roanoke, Virginia)

Laminated birch plywood, solid birch, brass

37 ⅛ x 20 x 35 ½ in.

WHEN VIEWED FROM its side, this adjustable recliner is a poetic flow of line and sinuous curves, extending from the top of its rounded crest through its sloping knee to its foot.[1] Designed by Herbert von Thaden, the recliner is an innovative design and blends its inventor's interests in both aeronautical engineering and furniture production. Like other postwar modern designers, notably Charles and Ray Eames (Cat. Nos. 29 and 31) and Eero Saarinen (Cat. Nos. 29 and 32), Thaden's use of plywood resulted in a chair that was lightweight, flexible, and durable. Equally important, Thaden was mindful of modernist trends, exploring the intersections of ergonomics and the economic efficiency of mass production.[2]

In his 1946 patent application for a "Spring Chair" (Fig. 33.2), a modified version of the present example, Thaden outlined three guiding objectives regarding its design and construction. First, it should consist "of simple and relatively inexpensive construction," while conforming "to the sitting or reclining position of the body." Second, the chair should be "highly flexible, but ... put together in such a way that the flexing does not result in breaking stresses." And third, it should be made of parts "which may be readily assembled and disassembled and which, when disassembled, may be packed in a relatively small space."[3]

Although Thaden allowed for metal or other materials to be used in the chair's manufacture, he insisted that plywood "is preferred because of its light weight, the facility with which it can be shaped or molded, its low heat conductivity compared to that of metal and its durability when exposed to out of door weather conditions."[4] Thaden specified plywood of ³⁄₁₆-inch thickness, which he found "to be amply strong and at the same time to have the desired high flexibility." A continuous, or "unitary resilient sheet," of laminated birch plywood constitutes the body of the chair, forming the back, seat, and front leg. A second birch plywood panel reinforces the rear and can be secured at two different heights, which allows for either inclined or reclined pitch positions. A third, thinner piece of plywood serves as a seat support. The front and back sheets are secured by brass "button type" automobile fasteners, all of which rest atop solid birch feet that provide a stable base and lateral support (Fig. 33.1).[5] The front leg turns back slightly under the seat, which Thaden advised would "avoid a tendency for the front legs and seat to flatten out if the front legs are too far forward or to fold under if the front

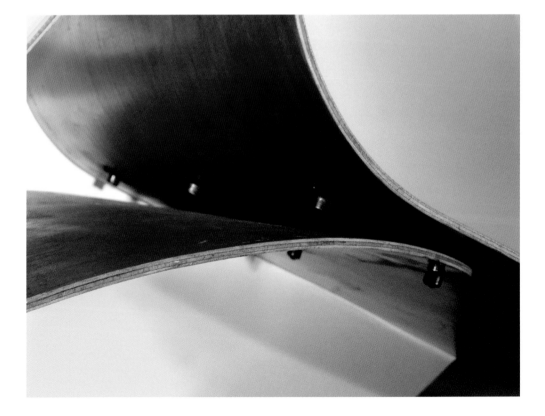

Fig. 33.1 Detail of brass "button type" automobile fasteners.

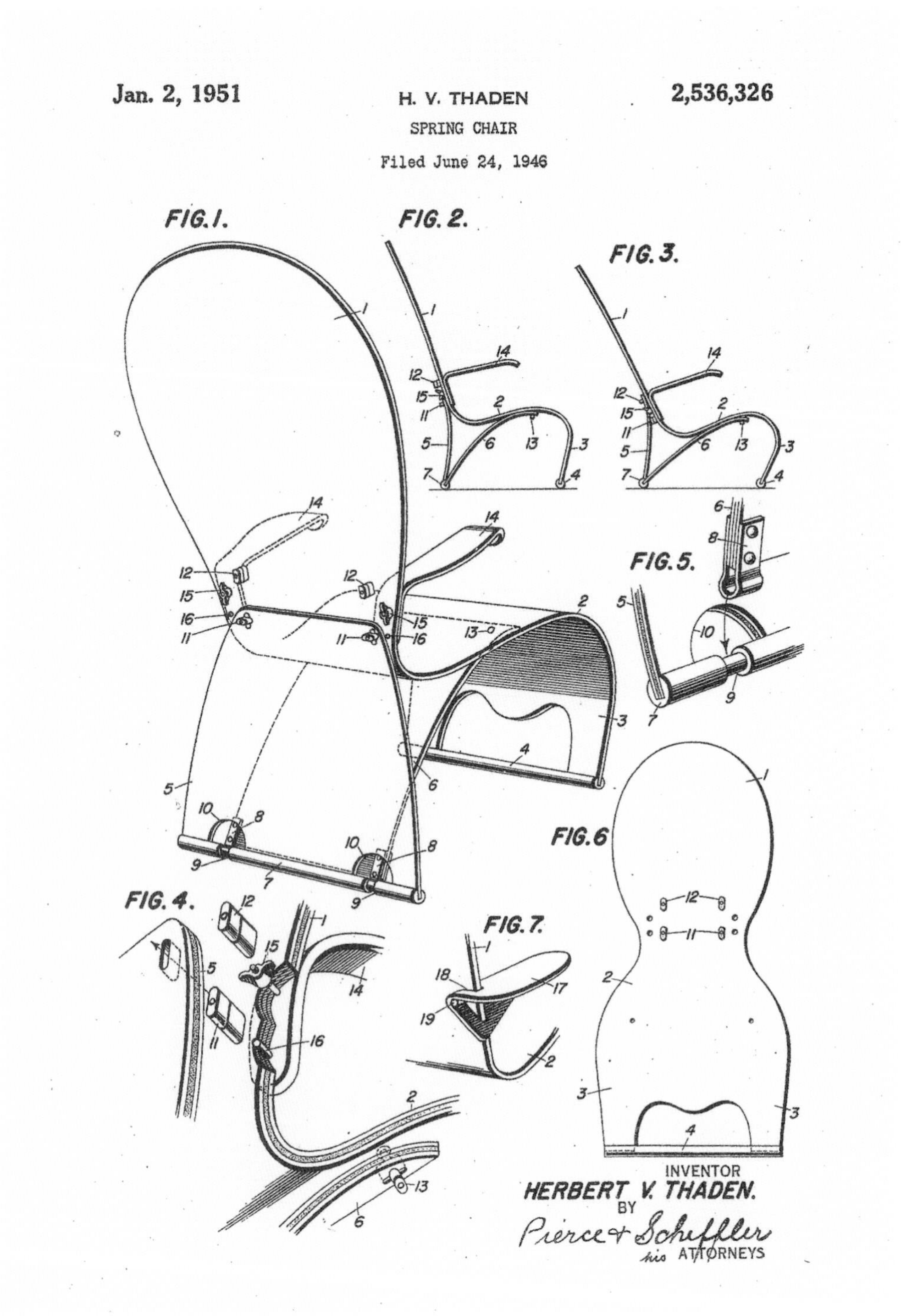

Jan. 2, 1951   H. V. THADEN   2,536,326

SPRING CHAIR

Filed June 24, 1946

FIG. 1.   FIG. 2.   FIG. 3.

FIG. 5.

FIG. 4.   FIG. 6.

FIG. 7.

INVENTOR

HERBERT V. THADEN.

BY

Pierce & Scheffler

his ATTORNEYS

Fig. 33.2 Herbert V. Thaden, "Spring Chair," U.S. Patent No. 2,536,326, filed June 24, 1946, issued January 2, 1951, U.S. Patent Office.

legs are too far back."[6] While Thaden's use of a continuous curve recalls the graceful aesthetics of both Samuel Gragg's patented *"Elastic" Side Chair* (Cat. No. 2) or Isaac Cole's 1874 design for a chair, his *Spring Chair* is a wholly updated design for a 20th-century consumer.[7]

With its rounded crest rail, Thaden's design for the *Spring Chair* undoubtedly shows the influence of the more than a

quarter of a decade he spent as an aircraft designer and pilot. Thaden served as an Army Signal Corps pilot and in 1920 founded the Thaden Aeromobile Manufacturing Company in Atlanta, Georgia, which manufactured aircraft and parts.[8] He later established the Thaden Metal Aircraft Company in San Francisco in 1928, the year he married Iris Louise Marcellus McPhetridge (1905–1979), herself an

accomplished pilot. The Thaden Metal Aircraft Company built the Thaden T-1 Argonaut, an eight-seat all-metal cabin monoplane, the first such plane of its kind to be manufactured in the United States.[9] In 1929, the company was renamed the Pittsburgh Metal Airplane Company when it was bought by the Pittsburgh Aviation Industries Corporation (PAIC) for $100,000. When the newly named company failed to

Fig. 33.3 The Thaden-Jordan Furniture Corporation, Roanoke, Virginia, c. 1950.

break into the commercial market, PAIC sold it in 1930 to the General Aviation Corporation, which renamed it the Metalair Corporation. Two years later, Thaden was in Baltimore, Maryland, where he oversaw the manufacture of a single-engine low-wing all-metal airplane that was intended to hold 10 passengers.

Like her husband, Louise Thaden was a highly skilled aviatrix and achieved considerable fame of her own. In 1928 she set the world record for women's altitude by reaching 20,260 feet, smashing the previous record of 14,000 feet set by her good friend and arch-rival, Amelia Earhart, in 1922.[10] In 1929, she won the first Women's National Air Derby, commonly called the "Powder Puff Derby." In 1934, Louise and Herbert participated in the Melbourne Free-for-All, a long-distance race that stretched 11,000 miles from London to Melbourne, Australia.[11] In 1936, Louise Thaden won the Bendix Transcontinental Trophy Race, the first year women were allowed to enter the contest. In it, Louise and her co-pilot, Blanche Noyes, flew a Beechcraft Model C17R Staggerwing from New York to Los Angeles in under 15 hours, setting a new coast-to-coast record. That same year she also won the prestigious Harmon National Trophy from the Ligue Internationale des Aviateurs, which was awarded annually to an outstanding aviator from each of the 21 member countries. The Bentonville Municipal Airport in Louise Thaden's Arkansas hometown was renamed Louise M. Thaden Field in her honor.

In the mid-1940s, the Thadens moved to Roanoke, Virginia, where they formed the Thaden Engineering Company, a supplier of various aviation products for the Navy and Army. Shortly after relocating, Herbert also partnered with Donald Lewis Jordan (1896–1979),[12] a Virginia native with experience in banking and manufacturing, to establish the Thaden-Jordan Furniture Corporation (Fig. 33.3). Located at 312 Kessler Mill Road, the company principally made molded and laminated birch plywood furniture for living and dining rooms, including side tables, dining tables and chairs, and sideboards. The corporation closed in 1952, after only six years in operation. Thaden and his wife relocated to High Point, North Carolina, where they established the Thaden Molding Corporation, which made molded furniture and other components made of plastic. Louise continued to lead the furniture business after Herbert's death in 1969.

1   Special thanks to Andrew VanStyn for his research and expertise. His contributions helped shape this essay. Additional thanks to David Kammerman for his research.
2   Despite being intended for mass production, it is estimated that fewer than two dozen examples of this chair were produced. Several museums possess examples in their collections, including the Los Angeles County Museum of Art (M.2011.186); the Vitra Design Museum, Weil am Rhein, Germany (acc. no. MUS-1012); and the Minneapolis Institute of Art (88.4).
3   Herbert V. Thaden, "Spring Chair," U.S. Patent No. 2,536,326, filed June 24, 1946, issued January 2, 1951, U.S. Patent Office.
4   Thaden.
5   Thaden.
6   Thaden.

7   Isaac I. Cole, "Chairs," U.S. Patent No. 148,350, filed December 29, 1873, issued March 10, 1874, U.S. Patent Office.
8   *Iron Age* 105, no. 15 (April 8, 1920): 1078.
9   "Thaden T-1/Argonaut," All-Aero, accessed December 21, 2021, http://all-aero.com/index.php/55-planes-t-u/19002-thaden-t-1-thaden-argonaut.
10   William S. Powell, *Dictionary of North Carolina Biography, Vol. 6* (Chapel Hill: University of North Carolina Press, 1996).
11   "Greatest Test of the World's Wings," *New York Times*, October 14, 1934.
12   "Donald Lewis Jordan," Prabook, accessed May 13, 2018, https://prabook.com/web/donald_lewis.jordan/89843. Jordan had a long and distinguished career in the furniture industry, locally and nationally. He worked at

the Johnson-Carper Furniture Company in Roanoke in a variety of senior-level administrative capacities between 1927 and 1964. He was vice president and director from 1946 to 1952, and he served as chairman of the board of directors from 1964 to 1992. He was a member of the board of governors for the American Furniture Mart Building in Chicago from 1949 to 1992 and its national chairman from 1952 to 1953. He also was a member of the board of governors for the Atlanta Furniture Mart from 1961 to 1992. For a detailed account of his career, see Edward W. Rushton, *Donald Lewis Jordan: An Industrial Odyssey* (Columbia, SC: R. L. Bryan Company, 1975).

4

A Nation Matures
From Space Age
to Space Saver
(1950–Present)

The second half of the 20th century continued to be a dramatic time in the history of the United States, one marked by significant political, social, cultural, and technological events and advances. Returning World War II veterans caused a population increase between the years 1946 and 1964—the "Baby Boom"—as they established families and fueled suburban growth through their purchase of homes and automobiles. The American furniture industry responded accordingly, designing and manufacturing inexpensive yet stylish home furnishings to satisfy the new demand.

Meanwhile, continued political unrest in Southeast Asia—specifically in Korea and Vietnam— once again saw the country drawn into military engagements for much of the 1950s and 1960s. Domestic protests of the Vietnamese conflict in particular resulted in the establishment of a counterculture, giving rise to "peaceniks," "flower children," and a new generation of American consumer—one influenced by Hollywood, motorcycles and automobiles, rock and roll, Woodstock, and other forms of popular culture.

However, it was the continued nuclear threat posed by Russia and the resultant Cold War between the United States and that country that had the most profound— yet unintentional—impact on American popular culture as well as furniture design. The pledge by President Kennedy in 1961 to send a man to the moon and successfully bring him back to Earth by the end of the decade fueled Americans' interest in outer space and inspired the American furniture industry to design "Space Age" furniture.

By the last quarter of the 20th century, the center of the design world moved from the United States to Europe—specifically Switzerland and Italy—a shift caused by a general decline in American manufacturing due to increased global competition. To help fill the void created by this shift, a second generation of studio artists gradually emerged and today remain an integral and important component in the world of contemporary furniture design.

Hairpin Lounge Chair

c. 1950

Designed by Hobart Wells (dates not known)

Manufactured and distributed by the Lensol-Wells Company (active Los Angeles, California, dates not known)

Textile manufactured by Glenn of California (active 1948–1992, Arcadia, California) and possibly designed by Greta Magnusson Grossman (1906–1999)

Rubber manufactured by the Chemold Company (active Glendale, California, dates not known)

Injection-molded plastic embedded with textile, iron, rubber

30 ¾ x 22 ¼ x 21 ¾ in.

IN THE YEARS immediately following World War II, Southern California was one of the largest markets for home furnishings due to suburban growth propelled by postwar industry. The International Competition for Low-Cost Furniture Design, organized in 1948 by the Museum of Modern Art, challenged both designers and manufacturers to propose innovative uses for materials—tubular metal, plywood, and molded plastics—that could be mass produced and offered at affordable prices for a rising, and often mobile, middle class. This chair is but one of many examples that illustrate the continued evolution of the International Style's preference for industrial materials—metal and glass—and embraces the use of a still emerging material—molded plastics and fiberglass—infused with a California-inspired love of nature.

Fiberglass is technically an injection-molded plastic reinforced with glass fibers. Games Slayter (1896–1964) recognized its potential for use in mass production when he developed and patented glass wool for the Owens-Corning Fiberglass Corporation. Advances in product development during World War II found fiberglass to be an ideal replacement for molded plywood in aircraft radomes, which housed radar antenna. The most important property of fiberglass was its ability to transmit microwaves, but it was also lightweight, durable, and inexpensive to both produce and mold. After the war, fiberglass was quickly adapted by commercial enterprises in the manufacture of boats, cars, and furniture. A 1952 article in the *San Bernardino County Sun-Telegram* reported that "plastic materials in the manufacture of furniture have been widely received by home-makers in recent years. Their durability, resistance to weather, burns and scratches, ease in cleaning and maintenance, and their adaptability to practical design are features that have made plastics very much in favor in modern homes."[1]

However, one of the biggest challenges both designers and manufacturers had to overcome in using plastic in furniture was its stark, often bland, appearance. They remedied this by introducing color, pattern, and texture. One such manufacturer was the Lensol-Wells Company of Los Angeles, which developed "a series of molded chairs with fabric, Fiberglas [*sic*], or Philippine grass cloth impregnated into the basic plastic material to gain decorative and textural relief."[2] Designed by Hobart Wells, the chairs came in both dining and lounge models with black iron "Parkerized" frames, which made them completely rustproof. The molded plastic seats and backs—made separately—were "extremely comfortable due to their resilience" and the use of rubber shock mounts to affix them to the iron frame.[3] In his 1953 publication, *Chairs*, designer George Nelson (Cat. No. 38) discussed a different chair designed by Wells, which possessed "a plastic shell with a glued-on plastic connector for the metal supporting frame." Offered in six colors, the piece was "light-weight" and "resistant to flame, water and stains."[4]

To complement the chairs, the Lensol-Wells Company also offered circular, wedge-shaped, and rectangular dining tables in five standard sizes, all with "Formica plastic tops that [were] equally resistant to burns, water, acids, scratches, and scuffs."[5] The Formica came in three patterns—primavera, walnut, and dawn gray—which could also be placed on coordinating cocktail and end tables. Their widespread acceptance within a matter of months "has resulted in a reduction in price based on volume."[6] Perhaps also propelling their awareness was their appearance in a photograph of the Koenig House No. 1 (1950), designed by Pierre Koenig (1925–2004), a Southern California modernist architect who later participated in the Case Study House program. The photograph of the dining room shows a Formica-topped table atop coordinating hairpin iron legs, surrounded by Wells-designed chairs with molded plastic seats and backs embedded with Philippine grass cloth (Fig. 34.1).

Poetically suited to organic modernism, the leafy tendrils in the printed fabric seem to emanate from the bent hairpin metal legs below. Although the finished product is a hard plastic, it nonetheless allows a 20th-century comparison to the floral-patterned upholstery found on several 19th-century chairs in the DeMell Jacobsen Collection, including the *Gothic Revival Side Chair* (Cat. No. 6), the *Centripetal Spring Arm Chair* (Cat. No. 7), the Belter-designed chairs (Cat. No. 9), and the Herter-designed *Side Chair* (Cat. No. 13), to name but a few. The chair seats and backs were made by the Chemold Company of nearby Glendale, California.[7] Embedded in the plastic was a floral-print

textile made by Glenn of California. While the designer of the textile itself is unknown, it was possibly Greta Magnusson Grossman.[8]

One of the few female designers and architects in a male-dominated field, Grossman was an internationally influential mid-20th-century artist. Together with Milo Ray Baughman Jr., Grossman designed a "California Modern" collection for Glenn of California in 1948.[9] Grossman had studied woodworking and earned a scholarship to attend the Konstfack, the prominent art institute in Stockholm. Mastering draftsmanship, she concentrated on designing furniture, textiles, and ceramics.[10] In 1933, 27-year-old Grossman was the first woman to receive an award for furniture design from Svensk Form, the Swedish Society of Craft and Industrial Design.[11] Following her retail and workshop debut in central Stockholm, Grossman's commissions and fame spread. Her designs for Swedish Princess Birgitta's crib in 1937 and exhibitions at the Galerie Moderne brought further acclaim.

The German occupation of Denmark and Norway in April 1940 precipitated Grossman's departure in July together with her British-born band-leader husband, Billy Grossman, "The Benny Goodman of Sweden." The couple immigrated to California, arriving in San Francisco in 1941.[12] Their arrival was serendipitous as the annual furniture exhibition was in progress. Grossman had brought sketches of her furniture designs with her, and she quickly found work with a Los Angeles–based company.

The duo immediately relocated to Los Angeles, where Grossman opened a home furnishings store on Rodeo Drive, which was regularly frequented by Greta Garbo, Ingrid Bergman, Joan Fontaine, and Gracie Allen.[13] For the nearly two decades that followed, Grossman worked with California manufacturers to develop a uniquely "California Modern" style. Her designs blended her unique understanding of form and materials, often utilizing native materials like California walnut contrasted with functionally sophisticated materials, such as black plastic laminate, fiberglass, or wrought iron. During the 1940s she designed furniture exclusively for Barker Brothers. In the years that followed she designed tables, consoles, and chairs for Glenn of California and innovative lamps for the Ralph O. Smith Company, one of which

Fig. 34.1 Koenig House No. 1, Glendale, California, c. 1950.

was exhibited in the *Good Design* exhibition at the Museum of Modern Art.[14]

Grossman-designed homes were showcased in *Arts & Architecture* and she competed against Richard Neutra for commissions. As her works were exhibited and published both nationally and internationally, the U.S. Department of State promoted Grossman as "a true picture ... of the American way of life."[15] Greta Grossman nurtured the next generation of designers through her teaching at both the University of California and the Art Center School in Los Angeles. Although she retired to care for her ailing husband in the 1960s, her work continues to be exhibited and reissued for production. Her philosophy on design remains current to this day: "modern furniture is a growth, progressing out of the needs of contemporary living. It is not a superimposed style, but an answer to our present conditions ... It has developed out of our own preference for living in a modern way. It expresses our habits and our tastes."[16]

1   "Plastics Gain Wide Use in Home Articles," *San Bernardino County Sun-Telegram*, September 21, 1952, 20.
2   "Plastics Gain Wide Use," 20.
3   "Plastics Gain Wide Use," 20.
4   George Nelson, *Chairs* (1953; repr. New York: Acanthus Press, 1994), 57.
5   "Plastics Gain Wide Use," 20.
6   "Plastics Gain Wide Use," 20.
7   The Chemold Company, which advertised itself as "Chemold Means Chemistry Molded," was a division of Western Plastics, Inc., located in Glendale, California. Established circa 1942 as a division of Western Plastics, Chemold secured several government contracts, manufacturing droppable containers for the military, experimental landing watercraft, and scientific instrument cases. They later manufactured personal watercraft, components for furniture, and the "Fireball," the "world's first perfect gold ball." See especially Daniel Spurr, *Heart of Glass: Plastic Boats and the Men Who Made Them* (Camden, ME: International Marine, 2000): 9–11, and *Motor Boating* (November 1944): 9.
8   "Mid-Century Hobart Wells Hairpin Lounge Chair for Lensol-Wells," 1st Dibs, accessed April 11, 2022, https://www.1stdibs.com/furniture/seating/chairs/mid-century-hobart-wells-hairpin-lounge-chair-lensol-wells/id-f_23891902/.
9   DC Hillier, "Glenn of California," *MCM Daily*, June 16, 2015, https://www.mcmdaily.com/glenn-of-california/.
10 For a thorough examination of Grossman and her designs, see *Greta Magnusson Grossman: Designer* (New York: 20th Century Design, 2000), and *Greta Magnusson Grossman: Furniture and Lighting* (New York: Drawing Center, 2008).
11 *Greta Magnusson Grossman: Designer*, 12.
12 Christopher Turner, "Greta Grossman Reissue," *Icon*, May 23, 2011, https://www.iconeye.com/design/news/greta-grossman-reissue-3.
13 Caroline Rou, "Interiors from the Archive: Swedish-Born Designer Greta Grossman's Work Is Undergoing a Revival," *Independent*, February 4, 2011, http://www.independent.co.uk/property/interiors/interiors-from-the-archive-swedishborn-designer-greta-grossmans-work-is-undergoing-a-revival-2203860.html.
14 "Greta Magnusson Grossman," R & Company, accessed December 22, 2021, https://www.r-and-company.com/designers/greta-magnusson-grossman/.
15 "Greta Magnusson Grossman."
16 Rose Henderson, "A Swedish Furniture Designer in America: An Interview with Greta Magnusson Grossman," *American Artist* 15, no. 10, issue 150 (December 1951): 56.

Bertoia Chairs

c. 1952

Designed by Arri ("Arieto" or "Harry") Bertoia
(1915–1978)

Manufactured by Knoll Associates, Inc. (active
1938–present, East Greenville, Pennsylvania, and
New York, New York)

Large Diamond Chair (No. 422), c. 1952
Chrome-plated and welded steel wire, green wool
upholstery (original); Knoll Harrison wool and nylon
Campbell Blue upholstery (replacement)[1]
28 ¼ x 45 x 31 ½ in.

Bird Lounge Chair (No. 423), c. 1952
Chrome-plated and welded steel wire, green wool
upholstery (original)
40 ¼ x 38 ½ x 33 in.

IN 1949, CAROL Channing performed the
song "Diamonds Are a Girl's Best Friend"
in the hit Broadway production *Gentlemen
Prefer Blondes*. The film version starring
Marilyn Monroe was released in 1953. In the
time between those debuts, Harry Bertoia
designed the now iconic *Large Diamond
Chair (No. 422)* for Knoll.[2]

Like a real diamond with its array
of facets, the main body of the *Large
Diamond Chair* is composed of smaller
diamond shapes formed by a network of
crisscrossed, chrome-plated, welded steel
wires (Fig. 35.1). Harry Bertoia intended this
sculptural chair to be viewed in the round,
befitting the modernist mid-century design
of streamlined, sparse furnishings that could
endure indoor and outdoor environments.
For additional comfort, the manufacturer
added a removable upholstered cover.
Relying on his various experiences, Bertoia
shaped industrial materials into an organic
nested form that acts like a cradle with a
slight rocking motion. Introduced by Knoll
in 1952, the Bertoia Diamond Collection
included the *Large Diamond Chair* and the
Bird Lounge Chair (No. 423) (Fig. 35.2).

Arri (called Arieto or "Little Arri") Bertoia
was born in 1915 in San Lorenzo, Italy.
Already a budding artist by the age of 15,
Bertoia visited his brother Oreste, who
was then living in Detroit, and decided to
stay. He assumed an Americanized name,
Harry, and enrolled first at the Davison
Americanization School, where he learned
English and history, and then attended

the Cleveland Elementary School. Next,
he enrolled in the Cass Technical High
School, where he studied art, design, and
metal jewelry between 1930 and 1936. He
then attended the Art School of the Detroit
Society of Arts and Crafts, and later applied
to the Cranbrook Academy of Art. On his
application, the 21-year-old wrote: "I am
rather silent, resolute and industrious. I can
use any tool or machinery with dexterity."[3]
Awarded a scholarship for painting and
drawing, Bertoia entered the Cranbrook
Academy of Art in 1937. Two years later,
Eliel Saarinen, president of the academy,
reopened the metalwork department and
asked Bertoia to lead it. However, due to
restrictions on the use of metals during
World War II, Bertoia concentrated on making
jewelry, including pendants, brooches,
bracelets, and necklaces. He also made
rings, including, most significantly, the
wedding rings for his friends Charles Eames
and Ray Kaiser Eames (Cat. Nos. 29 and 31).[4]
While at Cranbrook, Bertoia also forged
friendships with Eero Saarinen (Cat. No. 32)
and Florence Schust, a textile designer who
would later marry Hans G. Knoll, founder of
the eponymous furniture company.

At Cranbrook, Bertoia was involved in the
designs for the complex contoured plywood
chairs submitted by Eames and Saarinen to
the Organic Designs in Home Furnishings
competition organized by the Museum of
Modern Art (1940–41), which grew out of
their earlier designs for the Crow Island
School (Cat. No. 29). In 1943, Bertoia moved
to California with his bride, Brigitta Valentiner
(1920–2007), a fiber artist and daughter
of the director of the Detroit Institute of
Arts. There, Bertoia continued to work
with the Eameses on their experimental
plywood designs for mass production as
well as wartime airplane components
produced by the Molded Plywood Division
of Evans Products Company under Charles
Eames's directorship.

Around the time the Eameses' iconic
LCW (Lounge Chair Wood or *Low Chair
Wood)* (Cat. No. 31) gained national
recognition, however, frustrated by a lack
of credit for his role in a number of their
designs, Bertoia departed Los Angeles for
San Diego to work at the Point Loma Naval
Electronics Laboratory.[5] Bertoia focused
on studying the human body with respect
to the design of comfortable equipment.
These studies, which today incorporate the

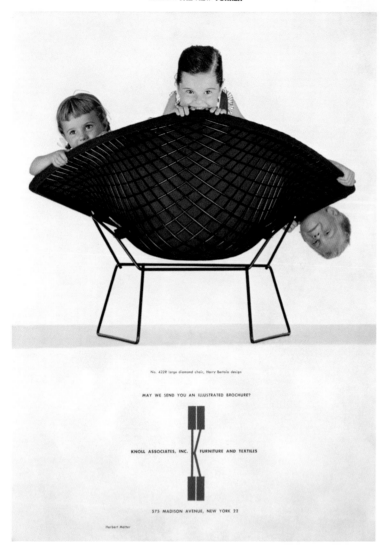

No. 422R large diamond chair, Harry Bertoia design

MAY WE SEND YOU AN ILLUSTRATED BROCHURE?

KNOLL ASSOCIATES, INC. FURNITURE AND TEXTILES

575 MADISON AVENUE, NEW YORK 22

Herbert Matter

Fig. 35.1 (left)
Advertisement for
Harry Bertoia's *Large
Diamond Chair (No.
422)*.

Fig. 35.2 (above) Harry
Bertoia seated in his
*Bird Lounge Chair
(No. 423)* with *Large
Diamond Chair (No.
422)* in background,
date unknown.

field of ergonomics, would later inform his chair designs. Meanwhile, in his spare time, Bertoia made monotypes and other prints, as well as creating sculptures in metal.[6]

An enticing opportunity arrived in 1950 when Florence Schust Knoll and her husband Hans encouraged Bertoia to join them at their factory in East Greenville, Pennsylvania. He accepted their invitation to "work at what you will, and if a design for furniture comes out of your work, Knoll would produce the design."[7] The Bertoia family moved east, and Harry established a metal studio in the manufacturing building. The Hans G. Knoll Furniture Company had opened the East Greenville factory in 1941. Hans and Florence had married in 1946 and the company changed its name to Knoll Associates, Inc. Under Florence's leadership, a group of talented designers,

including Eero Saarinen, collaborated with the firm. In 1951, as Europe was recovering from World War II with programs that encouraged local productions, Knoll opened branches in France and Germany, and the company was renamed Knoll International.

Bertoia's two years of experiments with metal wire ultimately resulted in a seating collection for Knoll Associates, Inc. The metal designer developed the various chair forms as well as the machinery needed for production by the firm. Representing the machine aesthetic both in appearance and manufacturing, the chairs required intensive welding and hammering; consequently, early productions were handmade.[8] Of his designs, Bertoia stated, "In sculpture, I am concerned primarily with space, form and the characteristics of metal. In the chairs, many functional problems have to be satisfied first

... but when you get right down to it, the chairs are studies in space, form, and metal too. If you will look at them, you will find they are mostly made of air, just like sculpture. Space passes right through them."[9]

Bertoia illustrated and described his "Flexible Contour Chair" in a patent filed on July 5, 1952 (Fig. 35.3). He discussed the "article of repose" with its "continuous wire frame extending around the periphery of the unit," a wire mesh "shell-like body," and wire legs.[10] Resilient and supportive of the human body, the chair was also intended to be flexible so that "a person sitting on the article may perform rocking movements to some extent."[11] Eighteen days later, Bertoia filed a design patent for a chair similar in shape to his *Bird Lounge Chair* (Fig. 35.4). A patent filed in March 1955 re-examined his "Article of Repose for Supporting the Body of a Person,"

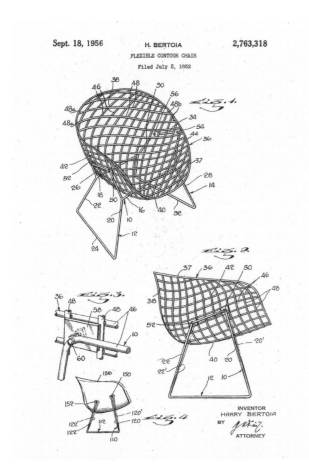

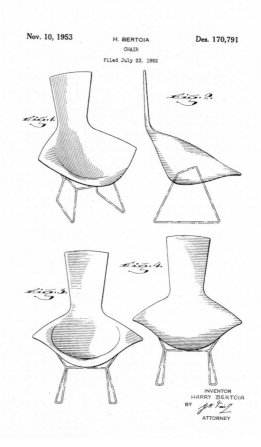

Sept. 18, 1956   H. BERTOIA   2,763,318
FLEXIBLE CONTOUR CHAIR
Filed July 5, 1952

Nov. 10, 1953   H. BERTOIA   Des. 170,791
CHAIR
Filed July 23, 1952

Fig. 35.3 (far left) Harry Bertoia, "Flexible Contour Chair," U.S. Patent No. 2,763,318, filed July 5, 1952, issued September 18, 1956, U.S. Patent Office.

Fig. 35.4 (left) Harry Bertoia, "Chair," U.S. Design Patent No. 170,791, filed July 23, 1952, issued November 10, 1953, U.S. Patent Office.

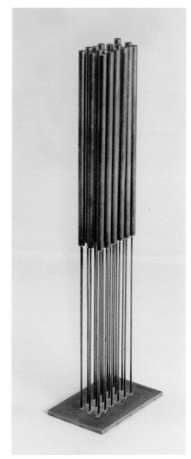

Fig. 35.5 (far left) The Bertoia Diamond Collection featured two versions of the *Diamond Lounge Chair*, an ottoman, and the *Bird Lounge Chair*.

Fig. 35.6 (left) Harry Bertoia (1915–1978), *Small Sonambient Sculpture*, (c. 1960–1978), beryllium copper and brass, 20 ½ x 6 x 4 in., DeMell Jacobsen Collection.

with illustrations of the supportive rubber cushioning elements as seen in these two examples in the DeMell Jacobsen Collection.[12]

In December 1952, Knoll debuted the new Bertoia designs in a dramatic exhibition at their corporate showroom. The *New York Times* described the installation: "All the usual furnishings in the Knoll showrooms at 575 Madison Avenue have been removed to increase the impact of the display and the entire floor given over to wire and metal structures, some meant simply to be looked at, others to be sat upon."[13] All the chairs in the exhibition were "variations on a theme"[14] and had a wire shell into which was "fitted a foam rubber cushion upholstered with a brilliant color."[15] The shell was supported on a cradle of steel, which could either be shiny chrome or plastic-coated in "black, white, or bright red."[16] The collection included both a small and large version of the *Diamond Chair*, the *Bird Lounge Chair* with an extended back, a foot stool, two other chairs, and a bar stool; a child-sized chair debuted in 1955 (Fig. 35.5).[17]

In 1955, Bertoia was awarded "Designer of the Year" for his innovative *Diamond Chair*. His thought process for producing the collection is best explained by Bertoia himself:

Once more, I went through the procedure of positioning, considering the possibility of shapes, then relating, of course, what the wire itself could be, what shapes it might take, whether there were any tools to do it with. There are many aspects of the same things coming into one's mind, but the very first thing was whether a shape would come up that would begin to serve as a chair, sitting on it, etc. One was taking the shape of a side chair; another was beginning to extend to care of the head. This developed to the point where something could be held on to ... You know, when you have something in front of you that can really physically be held, it becomes easier to make changes.[18]

Following the release of the wire furniture collection for Knoll, Bertoia changed direction and focused on designing sculpture. He received many notable sculpture commissions, including a screen panel for the General Motors Technical Center (1953) and an altar screen for the Massachusetts Institute of Technology Chapel (1955). Bertoia's many design awards included the craftsmanship medal from the American Institute of Architects and AIA's Gold Medal. Following his separation from Knoll, Bertoia devoted the remainder of his career to fabricating his *Sonambient* sculptures, which combined his love of metal and music with a unique blend of visual and acoustic splendor (Fig. 35.6). Reflecting on his furniture designs, Bertoia wrote, "I was never satisfied with my own designs, no matter whether they were flops or masterpieces."[19] Perhaps with posterity in mind, Bertoia also remarked, "Furniture is nothing to me—it was a means of eating."[20]

1   While on exhibition in 2016, the chair's original fabric cover suffered staining due to an overhead ceiling leak. The green wool upholstery (pictured) was replaced with Knoll Harrison wool and nylon Campbell Blue upholstery.
2   Special thanks to David Kammerman for his research on the *Diamond Chair*.
3   "About Harry," Harry Bertoia Foundation, accessed January 13, 2022, https://harrybertoia.org/harry/.
4   For a detailed examination of Bertoia's jewelry, see Shelley Selim, ed., *Bent, Cast, and Forged: The Jewelry Harry Bertoia* (Bloomfield Hills, MI: Cranbrook Art Museum, 2015).
5   See Pat Kirkham, *Charles and Ray Eames: Designers of the Twentieth Century* (Cambridge, MA: MIT Press, 1995), 92–93.

6   In 1946 Bertoia became an American citizen.
7   Steven Rouland and Linda Rouland, *Knoll Furniture* (Atglen, PA: Schiffer Publishing, 1999), 17.
8   Rouland and Rouland, 18.
9   Charlotte Fiell and Peter Fiell, *Modern Chairs* (Cologne, Germany: Taschen, 1993), 70.
10 Harry Bertoia, "Flexible Contour Chair," U.S. Patent No. 2,763,318, filed July 5, 1952, issued September 18, 1956, U.S. Patent Office.
11 Bertoia.
12 Harry Bertoia, "Article of Repose for Supporting the Body of a Person," U.S. Patent No. 2,804,915, filed March 1, 1955, issued September 3, 1957, U.S. Patent Office.
13 Betty Pepis, "Sculptor Designs Wire-Shell Chairs," *New York Times*, December 10, 1952, 46.

14 Pepis, 46.
15 Pepis, 46.
16 Pepis, 46.
17 The pieces remain in production today. In 2015 Knoll released a gold-plated edition of the *Diamond Lounge Chair*.
18 "Bertoia Diamond Chair," Knoll, accessed January 13, 2022, https://www.knoll.com/product/bertoia-diamond-chair.
19 Bertoia quoted in Karl Mang, *Geschichte des Modernen Mobels* (Stuttgart, Germany: Hatje, 1978), 143.
20 Bertoia quoted in David A. Hanks, *Design, 1935–1965: What Modern Was: Selections from the Liliane and David M. Stewart Collection* (Montreal: Musée des Arts Décoratifs de Montreal, 1991), 215.

Rocking Stool (Model 86T)

36

designed 1953; this example executed c. 1955

Designed by Isamu Noguchi (1904–1988)

Manufactured by Knoll Associates, Inc. (active 1938–present, East Greenville, Pennsylvania, and New York, New York)

Walnut, chromium-plated steel wire

16 ¾ x 14 x 14 in.

LIFE MAGAZINE featured this modernist-style design as a "Teeter Stool" in 1956.[1] The stool was described as a playful structure on which the sitter could "tilt, rock back and forth and even spin around with a fair chance of not tipping over."[2] Two hand-turned, polished walnut disks are connected by hairpin-bent chromium-plated steel wires sculpturally intertwined to suggest a twist. The top disk provides a concave seat, while the bottom disk is a convex shape capable of rolling. Isamu Noguchi (Fig. 36.1), one of the leading 20th-century sculptors, developed the design in 1953, and Knoll began manufacturing the *Rocking Stool* in 1954. The stool was produced in two sizes, a 10½-inch model for children (*Model 85T*) and a 16¾-inch model for adults (*Model 86T*); this example is one of the rarer, larger-size models.[3] When Noguchi filed his patent in January 1956, the examiner requested the application be divided, since two designs— for a stool and a table—were submitted and the patent office would accept only one design per patent. The stool was redrawn in an application filed in June 1957, but not redesigned (Fig. 36.2).[4]

Born in 1904 in Los Angeles to a Japanese poet, Yone Noguchi (1875–1947), and an American writer, Léonie Gilmour (1873–1933), Isamu Noguchi spent his formative years in Japan.[5] In 1918 he returned to America and settled in La Porte, Indiana, where he briefly studied. He moved to New York City in 1922 to study pre-medicine at Columbia University. At night, the aspiring sculptor took classes under Onorio Ruotolo (1888–1966), an Italian sculptor who founded the Leonardo da Vinci Art School in the Lower East Side. With his mother's encouragement, Noguchi abandoned his studies in medicine and turned his full attention to sculpture.

By 1927 Noguchi had moved to Paris on a John Simon Guggenheim Fellowship, where he served as a studio assistant to sculptor Constantin Brâncuși (1876–1957). There, Noguchi was influenced by other contemporary artists and sculptors, such as Pablo Picasso (1881–1973), Alexander Calder (1898–1976), and Alberto Giacometti (1901–1966), as well as the avant-garde Constructivist style. During the Depression, Noguchi returned to America, but he continued to travel regularly to Europe and Mexico. He practiced abstract art and created portrait sculptures. By the end of

the 1930s, he achieved recognition for his public commissions, the most notable of which was *News* (1938–1940), a nine-ton stainless-steel bas-relief above the entrance to the former Associated Press building at 50 Rockefeller Plaza.

In the summer of 1941, Noguchi traveled across the country to California with his friend the artist Arshile Gorky (1904–1948) and Gorky's fiancée. Despite Noguchi's success as an artist, his connections, and his Los Angeles origins, he experienced negative sentiments against Japanese (and Japanese Americans) following the bombing of Pearl Harbor. During World War II, Noguchi founded the Nisei Writers and Artists Mobilization for Democracy and took affirmative measures to combat prejudice against Japanese Americans. In 1942 he voluntarily entered the War Relocation Authority camp in Poston, Arizona, to improve conditions by designing community areas.[6] When released from the camp, he was later charged with espionage but was cleared with the aid of the American Civil Liberties Union.

Noguchi's prolific work in sculptures, theater set designs, and public works continued throughout the war and postwar eras. In 1944, his stage set was featured in *Appalachian Spring*, performed by Martha Graham with music composed by Aaron Copland. The performance included an updated interpretation of the Shaker song "Simple Gifts" (see Cat. No. 5). In 1948, he combined biomorphic forms in a glass-topped table for Herman Miller. Many of his sculptures were included in exhibitions, and in 1949 he had a solo show at the Charles Egan Gallery in New York.

Perhaps due to a disillusionment with art, World War II and its nuclear outcome, and his friend Gorky's suicide, Noguchi applied for a fellowship from the Bollingen Foundation "to study the environment of leisure, its meaning, its use, and its relationship to society."[7] Noguchi found that the "ultimate character" of leisure "was one of play and it was intimately bound to art."[8] In 1951, sponsored by the fellowship, he traveled to Japan, returning to America two years later.

An inveterate world traveler, Noguchi's sculpture and furniture designs reflect many international influences. Two versions of the story of Noguchi's design inspiration for the *Rocking Stool* have been recounted over

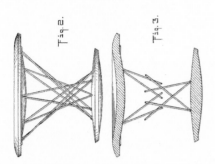

United States Patent Office

Des. 182,038
Patented Feb. 4, 1958

182,038
STOOL
Isamu Noguchi, Carmel, N. Y.

Original application January 3, 1956, Serial No. 39,549.
Divided and this application June 13, 1957, Serial No.
46,676

Term of patent 14 years

(Cl. D15—8)

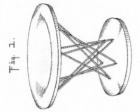

Fig. 1 is a perspective view of a stool embodying my new design;
Fig. 2 is an elevational view of the stool of Fig. 1; and
Fig. 3 is a vertical central cross-sectional view of the stool shown in Figs. 1 and 2.
This application is a division of my copending application Serial No. 39,549, filed January 3, 1956, for a table or the like.
I claim:
The ornamental design for a stool, substantially as shown and described.

References Cited in the file of this patent

UNITED STATES PATENTS

D. 159,561   Tanier _____ Aug. 1, 1950
2,049,539   Greenwood _____ Aug. 4, 1936

OTHER REFERENCES

Howell Modern Chromsteel Furniture Catalog No. 20, © 1939, page 26, No. 350, at top right of page (description on page 27).
Lloyd Chromium Furniture Catalog No. 41-A, 1949, page 44, item T–59–C.
House Beautiful, March 1955, page 83, Brancusi adv., at top right of page.

Fig. 36.1 (opposite) Isamu Noguchi pictured with *Rocking Stool* and *Cyclone Table*, c. 1960s.

Fig. 36.2 (left) Isamu Noguchi, "Stool," U.S. Design Patent No. 182,038, filed June 13, 1957, issued February 4, 1958, U.S. Patent Office.

time. The first contends it was a modern interpretation of a mahogany Belgian Congo stool the artist had seen in the collection of his friend Eliot Elisofon (1911–1973), a photographer for *Life* magazine. Noguchi was reportedly inspired by its form but "found the stool ungainly when he tipped back on its rim. Fascinated but frustrated, he brooded about stools for a year [and] finally designed a similarly shaped one with a rounded bottom."[9]

The second account, provided by the sculptor later in his life, credits manufacturer Hans Knoll with the idea of a stool made of wood and steel wire. According to Noguchi, Knoll had seen a plastic stool the artist had designed following his trip to Japan in 1951, said to have been hourglass in shape and resilient to the sitter. The manufacturer had just released the wire chairs designed by

Harry Bertoia (Cat. No. 35) and may well have wanted other products to complement the line.[10] The firm later released a child-sized table of similar design and promoted it with child-sized wire chairs designed by Bertoia. In 1957, Knoll (without Noguchi's participation) introduced a full-sized dining table named *Cyclone Table*, which featured a laminate top and a chrome-plated wire substructure set into a round, cast iron base.

The works of Isamu Noguchi, and especially his *Rocking Stool*, represent a hybrid of modernism and traditional international influences. Noguchi created sensual yet structural works utilizing a multitude of materials, including stone, wood, metals, plastic, string, clay, and more. Before his death in 1988, he established the Noguchi Museum in Long Island City, located across from his studio.

1   "The New Seat with a Neater Teeter," *Life* 40, no. 6 (February 6, 1956): 122, 125.
2   "The New Seat."
3   The stool was manufactured for only five years, between 1954 and 1958.
4   Special thanks to Andrew VanStyn for his research and expertise. His contributions helped shape this essay.
5   For a full biography of Noguchi see Hayden Herrera, *Listening to Stone: The Art and Life of Isamu Noguchi* (New York: Farrar, Straus & Giroux, 2015).
6   See Kathleen Massara, "The Japanese-American Artist Who Went to the Camps to Help," *New Yorker*, January 31, 2017, https://www.newyorker.com/culture/culture-desk/the-japanese-american-artist-who-went-to-the-camps-to-help.
7   "Noguchi: The Bollingen Journey 1949–1956," *Art IT*, September 7, 2004, https://www.art-it.asia/u/maisonhermes/TjElKrcN12BaXd4tb5k7/?lang=en.
8   "Noguchi."
9   "The New Seat," 122, 125.
10 Martin P. Eidelberg, Paul Johnson, and Kate Carmel, *Design 1935–1965: What Modern Was; Selections from the Liliane and David M. Stewart Collection* (Montreal: Musée des Arts Décoratifs de Montréal, 1991), 216.

'Lily' Chair (95-LI) (Invisible Group)

37

1959

Designed by Erwine Laverne (1909–2003) and Estelle Laverne (1915–1997)

Manufactured by Laverne International, Limited (active 1957–c. 1972, New York, New York)

Molded acrylic, polyester upholstery (modern)

36 ½ x 29 ½ x 34 in.

IMAGINE YOURSELF entering a room and seeing people who are seemingly floating on air while seated. Such would be the case with the chairs in the *Invisible Group*, which were designed by another husband-and-wife team, Erwine Laverne and Estelle Lester Laverne.[1] The couples' approach to chair design was rooted in their firm foundation in the arts. While painting students at the Art Students League in 1932, the pair undoubtedly would have been exposed to artist Hans Hofmann's philosophy that "space is filled with movement."[2] Marrying in 1934, the couple survived the Depression by producing hand-printed wallpaper. In 1938 they established Laverne Originals, which also manufactured textiles, collaborating with such artists as Alvin Lustig (1915–1955), Ray Komai (1918–2010), and Alexander Calder (1898–1976). In 1942, a serendipitous meeting with a vice president at Macy's increased their brand recognition and buoyed their commercial success.

In 1948 the Lavernes resided in Laurel Hollow, New York, in the carriage house of Louis Comfort Tiffany's Laurelton Hall. Although the former estate had been preserved in Tiffany's will as an artists' center, the property was divided due to the high cost of postwar taxes. The presence of Tiffany's artistic glass and the natural beauty of the environment were inspiring, but mass production in a residential area produced litigious challenges. The Lavernes were a multifaceted operation involved in design, production, promotion, and retail. As artists, they approached their designs by starting with a form and then working out the technical mechanics.[3] In addition to creating visually arresting and dramatic patterns, Estelle added her lyrical talents to the titles of their designs.[4] By 1952, their showroom at 160 East 57th Street in New York City garnered recognition for its unique, uncluttered presentation of decorative art amidst exhibitions of fine art. That same year, Laverne International collaborated with William Katavolos (1924–2020), Ross Littell (1924–2000), and Douglas Kelley (b. 1928), all graduates of Pratt Institute, to design the "New Furniture" line, which included the award-winning *"T" Chair (3/LC)*.[5] Perhaps presaging the design of the chairs in the *Invisible Group*, the *"T" Chair* featured a leather sling seat that seemed to float effortlessly atop three chrome-plated steel legs supported by a T-shaped stretcher.

During the 1950s, architects and designers, particularly George Nelson (Cat. No. 38), became ever more mindful of the "subscape" of room interiors. Nelson coined the word to refer to the area in a room "ordinarily viewed only by crawling babies, dogs and cats."[6] On bending down to retrieve a fallen magazine, Nelson observed the abundant use of hairpin metal legs on the furniture within the room, similar to those on a chair designed by Hobart Wells (Cat. No. 34). To Nelson, the hairpin legs seemed a dramatic improvement over the robust heavy legs found on furniture from only the decade prior, such as Eero Saarinen's *"Grasshopper" Chair* (Cat. No. 32). By the mid-1950s, Nelson and others were pursuing chair designs that featured only a single support. In 1957 Knoll Associates, Inc. released Saarinen's futuristic *Tulip Chair* (1955), which possessed a molded fiberglass seat "floating" atop a fluted, enamel-coated aluminum pedestal. That same year, Erwine introduced a pedestal table with a four-pronged base, and in June 1958 released a pedestal chair "that not only swivels but may also be raised and lowered."[7] Its development was "an outgrowth of increased use of plastics and aluminum. The pedestal, says Mr. Laverne, gives a chair a quality of being suspended in air."[8]

In 1959, the Lavernes debuted their most revolutionary furniture designs at the semiannual wholesale furniture fair held at the Merchandise Mart in Chicago. Called "the chair that isn't there," the *Invisible* chairs were a group of seating furniture made from clear molded plastic; there were four models: *Lily*, *Buttercup*, *Jonquil*, and *Daffodil*.[9] Named for their floriform shapes, the chairs became the first examples of modern furniture constructed with translucent molded acrylic resin, commonly known as Plexiglas or Lucite. The *"Lily"* Chair was the largest in the group, and the most expensive at $280; by comparison, the *Buttercup* cost $140.[10] Though completely transparent, they could be fitted with a "foam cushion upholstered in Lemon Yellow, Gold, Orange, Crimson, Beige, White, Black, Bright Green, Royal Blue orlon fleece or c.o.m."[11] Alternately, a water-filled iridescent plastic pillow could be procured by special order. The thick plastic hide was inflated with water because, according to Erwine, "water is more comfortable than air to sit on."[12]

Fig. 37.1 Tiger Morse seated in a *"Lily"*
Chair in the film *Four Stars* (****) by
Andy Warhol, reel 14, c. 1967.

Estelle acknowledged Saarinen's
influence on the couples' chair designs
for the *Invisible Group*. "He cleared up the
clutter of the legs in rooms, but we wanted
to go one step further," she said.[13] Similarly,
the Lavernes' unobtrusive see-through
chairs are spatially akin to Harry Bertoia's
concept of an open-space network of
chrome wires in the *Large Diamond Chair
(No. 422)* (Cat. No. 35). Convinced that "the
most important element in rooms is people,
not furniture,"[14] Erwine sought a clear
plastic, strong and durable enough to be
used in furniture design. With the assistance
of his chemist brother, Dr. Albert Laverne,

Erwine embraced the use of Plexiglas, a type
of clear acrylic first made in Germany and at
the time just beginning to be manufactured
in the United States.[15] Preproduction models
in the *Invisible Group* had a thickness of one-
quarter inch and weighed approximately
five and a half pounds. The final production
pieces were made from one-half-inch thick
acrylic and weighed between 11 and 14
pounds. The chairs were molded in two
separate parts—base and seat—before they
were joined.

So popular and progressive were
the chairs in the *Invisible Group* that
the *"Lily"* was used as a prop in a 1959
advertising campaign promoting fashion
designs and appeared on the cover of the
January 1960 issue of *Harper's Bazaar*;
it also featured in advertisements for
Chemstrand nylon (1962) and Syl-Mer.[16]

With its futuristic design, the chair also
appealed to celebrities and pop culture
personalities. One such person was Joan
"Tiger" Morse (1932–1972, Fig. 37.1), a New
York fashion designer and member of Andy
Warhol's Factory Group, who previously
owned the *"Lily"* Chair in the DeMell
Jacobsen Collection.[17] Morse specialized
in minidresses, vibrant colors, and
synthetic materials. In her loft apartment,
she held "happenings" staged with a
fluorescent drip-painted floor reminiscent
of Jackson Pollock's (1912–1956) Abstract
Expressionist art, colorful silk drapes, black
lights, mirrored disco balls, music, and
dance. Warhol (1928–1987) recalled that
"Almost every group event in the sixties
eventually got called a 'happening'—to the
point where the Supremes even did a song
by that name. Happenings were started by

the artists, but the fashion designer Tiger Morse made them more pop and less art—by having fashion shows in swimming pools and just generally staging big crazy parties and calling them 'happenings.'"[18] In August 1966, Morse opened Teenie Weenie, a boutique on 53rd Street at Broadway. Warhol said, "I've heard people say, 'Tiger Morse was a fraud.' Well of course she was, but she was a *real* fraud. She'd make up more stories about herself for the newspapers than I did. Nobody knew where she came from, really, but who cared? She was an original, and she showed a lot of people how to have fun."[19]

Laverne International went on to create a number of other revolutionary designs using clear acrylic and fiberglass. These include the *Lotus* and *Tulip* (1959), the *Light* (1960), the *Champagne* (1962), and the *Luminor* (1967). The latter was a Plexiglas screen on which ever-changing abstract color pictures appeared when the screen was plugged into a hi-fi sound system. "Vibrations of music create the cloud-like shapes," said Erwine. "Any intensification in the sound intensifies the color patterns. A pianissimo gives a soft play of color."[20]

Despite these and other commercial successes, however, Laverne International struggled financially due to ongoing litigation it faced from neighbors in the residential area surrounding Laurel Hollow and the Tiffany estate. Their case ultimately advanced to the Supreme Court of the United States in the late 1960s, but it was not processed. Financially destitute and living in a nursing home, Estelle died in 1997 followed by Erwine in 2003.

1 For a thorough examination of the designs of Estelle and Erwine Laverne, see Michael Krzyzanowski, *Laverne: Furniture, Textiles and Wallcovering* (Atglen, PA: Schiffer Publishing, 2007). Additionally, special thanks to Andrew VanStyn for his research and expertise. His contributions helped shape this essay.
2 "The Invisibles," The New York Times, Elaine Mayers Salkaln, April 18, 2004.
3 Salkaln.
4 Salkaln.
5 Cherie Fehrman and Kenneth R. Fehrman, *Interior Design Innovators, 1910–1960* (San Francisco: Fehrman Books, 2009), 109.
6 Rita Reif, "Pedestal Chair Appears in New Interpretations," *New York Times*, June 10, 1958, 37.
7 Reif.
8 Reif.
9 Past scholarship has perpetuated a design date of 1957 for the chairs in the *Invisible Group*; however, Krzyzanowski states the chairs were designed and introduced in 1959. See Krzyzanowski, *Laverne*, 109.
10 Krzyzanowski, 109.
11 Krzyzanowski, 188. C.o.m.. stands for "customer's own material."
12 Rita Reif, "Invisible Chairs Among New Whimsical Pieces," *New York Times*, June 13, 1959, 18.
13 Reif.
14 Reif.
15 Poly (methyl methacrylate) clear plastic is derived from an acrylic acid first isolated in 1843. A polymerization process in 1877 led to the patent for "Plexiglas" in 1933 by Otto Rohm, trademarked by the Rohm & Haas Company. By 1936, the company now known as Lucite International had begun to commercially produce the material. The lightweight, shatter-resistant transparent acrylic glass was installed in World War II aircrafts and submarines. General Motors debuted a Pontiac Deluxe Six Plexiglas car at the New York World's Fair in 1939. As Krzyzanowski states, the "Invisible chairs originally appeared with the notion invented by the Lavernes that they were made from 'Enreval' glass, a wild and new, space-age, highly technical, secretly formulated plastic known only to Laverne. The Laverne sense of humor and irreverence was once again mischievously evident. The Invisible chairs were in fact molded acrylic, and 'Enreval' was 'Laverne' spelled backward." See Krzyzanowski, *Laverne*, 111.
16 See Patricia Peterson, "Pet Pelt for Fall," *New York Times Magazine*, August 2, 1959, 32–33, and Michael Krzyzanowski, *Laverne*, 109, 110, 139, 140.
17 Walter Kelly, personal communication to the Thomas H. and Diane DeMell Jacobsen Ph.D. Foundation, August 2010.
18 Andy Warhol and Pat Hackett, *POPism: The Warhol Sixties* (New York: Harcourt Brace Jovanovich, 1980), 65.
19 Warhol and Hackett, 223.
20 Rita Reif, "Furniture Shows Its Colors for Fall," *New York Times*, June 19, 1967, 38.

MAF (Medium Arm Fiberglass) Swaged Leg Chair

designed in 1958, produced 1958–1964

Designed by George Nelson (1908–1986)
and Charles R. Pollock (1930–2013)

Manufactured by the Herman Miller
Furniture Company (active 1923–present,
Zeeland, Michigan)

Fiberglass, enameled tubular steel

27 ¾ x 29 x 23 in.

FOLLOWING THE International Competition for Low-Cost Furniture Design (1948), organized by the Museum of Modern Art, New York, molded plastic and fiberglass chairs became ubiquitous in the furniture industry throughout the subsequent two decades. California designers like Charles and Ray Eames (Cat. No. 31) and Hobart Wells (Cat. No. 34), as well as those on the East Coast, developed low-cost chairs using a variety of interchangeable components and materials, which made them affordable to middle-class consumers.[1]

This chair is a rare example of the now-iconic *MAF (Medium Arm Fiberglass) Swaged Leg Chair*, designed by George Nelson and Charles R. Pollock. The two-toned fiberglass is unusual and heightens the visual contrast of the separate pieces that form the back and seat. However, it is the process of swaging, the application of pressure to taper and bend metal tubes, that distinguishes the *Swaged Leg Group* as a unique mid-century modern design that is both sculptural and functional. Herman Miller produced the chairs from 1958 to 1964, then reissued the design in 2006 made from recyclable polypropylene.

Born in Hartford, Connecticut, George Nelson later studied at Yale University.[2] After earning his bachelor of arts degree in 1928, he attended the Yale School of Fine Arts, from which he graduated with honors in 1931. In 1933 he was an associate editor of *Architectural Forum*; by 1943 he was its co-manager together with Henry Wright (1878–1936). As an author, Nelson influenced both industrial and urban design. His article "Your Children Could Romp Here While You Shop" in the *Saturday Evening Post* conceptualized a revitalization of city centers with a pedestrian shopping area free of vehicles, which led to the advent of the urban shopping mall.[3]

In 1945, Nelson and Wright co-authored *Tomorrow's House: A Complete Guide for the Home-Builder*, subtitled *How to Plan Your Post-War Home Now*. Offering novel approaches to and solutions for the modern domestic space—such as the Storagewall, an organizational wall-storage system—they defined what would become the modern family room. Their innovative Storagewall system attracted the attention of Dirk Jan "D. J." DePree (1891–1990), founder of Herman Miller, who had been looking for a designer to lead the firm after

the unexpected death of his advisor and designer, Gilbert Rohde (1894–1944).[4] Hired by DePree in 1946 as Herman Miller's first director of design, Nelson would later engage the talents of Charles and Ray Eames and Isamu Noguchi (Cat. No. 36). Additionally, and while still affiliated with the furniture company, Nelson would form his own architectural firm and design studio in 1947, George Nelson Associates, Inc.

Charles Randolph "Chuck" Pollock was born in Philadelphia in 1930. Moving to Detroit, he attended Cass Technical High School. While still a student, he worked at the Chrysler Corporation and earned a full scholarship to the Pratt Institute in Brooklyn, New York. Pollock's studies at Pratt focused on the disciplines of sketching and model-making. After sketching his ideas, Pollock would make wire models that he would alter numerous times until he was satisfied with the design.

During his time at Pratt in the early 1950s, Pollock met Nelson. Visiting the school for a lecture and tour, Nelson admired one of Pollock's sculptural furniture designs made from wire.[5] Pollock later visited Nelson at his studio, gifting him the sculpture with the hope of working with the prominent industrial designer. In 1953 Pollock graduated from Pratt's first industrial design class and then entered the Army. Following his return to New York City after his military commitment, Pollock secured employment in Nelson's studio. Together, they perfected the swaging technique that Pollock had begun to utilize as a student.[6] Pollock, like Nelson, felt a chair was "like a sculpture" and that all his designs start "as a thought, and then become an idea, something I might think about for years. When the time is right, I express it on paper, usually as a simple line in space. Finally, it takes shape."[7]

Nowhere is this philosophy more evident than in their collaborative design for the *MAF (Medium Arm Fiberglass) Swaged Leg Chair*. Starting with a base pedestal, they developed a structurally stable set of four identical sinuous, sculpted-metal legs—physical manifestations of Pollock's "simple line in space" (Fig. 38.1). Clustered together and secured by tension fasteners to provide a "positive lock," the swaged legs were also simple to assemble and disassemble for shipping purposes.[8] The only tool a customer needed to assemble

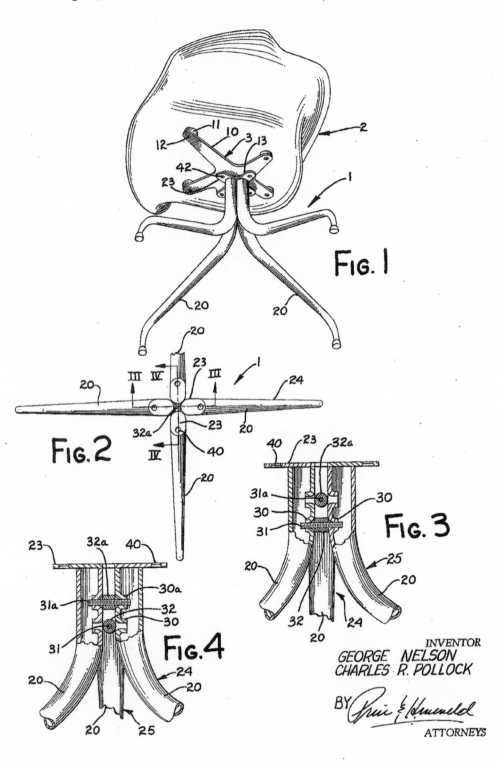

May 1, 1962   G. NELSON ET AL   3,032,307

LEG STRUCTURE FOR FURNITURE

Filed Aug. 3, 1959   2 Sheets—Sheet 1

FIG. 1

FIG. 2

FIG. 3

FIG. 4

INVENTOR
GEORGE NELSON
CHARLES R. POLLOCK

BY

ATTORNEYS

Fig. 38.1 (left) George Nelson and Charles R. Pollock, "Leg Structure for Furniture," U.S. Patent No. 3,032,307, filed August 3, 1959, issued May 1, 1962, U.S. Patent Office.

Fig. 38.2 (opposite) George Nelson and Charles R. Pollock, "Multi-Piece Formed Furniture Construction," U.S. Patent No. 3,027,195, filed December 1, 1958, issued March 27, 1962, U.S. Patent Office.

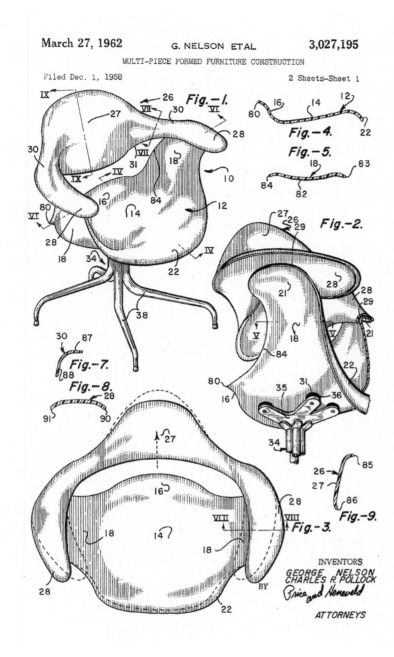

March 27, 1962   G. NELSON ET AL   3,027,195

MULTI-PIECE FORMED FURNITURE CONSTRUCTION

Filed Dec. 1, 1958   2 Sheets-Sheet 1

Fig.-1.

Fig.-4.

Fig.-5.

Fig.-2.

Fig.-7.

Fig.-8.

Fig.-9.

Fig.-3.

INVENTORS
GEORGE NELSON
CHARLES R. POLLOCK
BY Price and Heneveld
ATTORNEYS

the pedestal was "the common screw driver."[9] Machine-shaped and finished, the swaged legs were inexpensive to produce and were interchangeable with other designs in the *Swaged Leg Group*, such as the more common *DAF (Desk Armchair Fiberglass)* seat, which is two inches higher than the *MAF*.[10] In time, the *Swaged Leg Group* contained approximately 10 different designs, including a table, desk, and a variety of chairs.

As with the many other designers who experimented with molded-plastic or fiberglass seats, Nelson and Pollock sought to design a piece of furniture that was comfortable. In their "Multi-piece Formed Furniture Construction" patent (Fig. 38.2), the designers stressed that the popularity of "molded resin, shell type chairs" was due to the "ease and cost of manufacture."[11] After seeking permission from colleagues Charles and Ray Eames for their patented molded fiberglass process, Nelson and Pollock adhered two sections for comfort with flexibility, airflow, and wide armrests. The *MAF* embodies Nelson's philosophy that "Design is an activity which expresses the style, the living rhythm, of a society."[12] With growing families, lucrative jobs, and the prevalence of single-family homes,

Americans sought comfort through efficient designs.

After designing the *Swaged Leg Group*, Nelson and Pollock parted ways to pursue separate careers. Nelson's furniture, clocks, and lamps were among several successful lines manufactured by Herman Miller. He died in 1986 leaving a legacy of publications and iconic modernist designs. Pollock subsequently collaborated with Florence Knoll, who produced both the *657* chair in 1960 and the *Pollock Executive Chair* in 1965. The Italian firm of Giulio Castelli produced his *Penelope* chair in 1982. Thirty years later, Pollock re-entered the design field with Bernhardt Design, for whom he designed a variety of seating furniture, most notable being *CP Lounge* in 2012. Tragically, Pollock perished in a fire in his studio in Queens, New York, in 2013.

1   Special thanks to Andrew VanStyn for his research and expertise. His contributions helped shape this essay.
2   For a thorough examination of George Nelson and his career, see Stanley Abercrombie, *George Nelson: The Design of Modern Design* (Cambridge, MA: MIT Press, 1995), and Stanley Abercrombie et al., *George Nelson: Architect, Writer, Designer, Teacher* (Weil am Rhein, Germany: Vitra Design Museum, 2013). See also *Nelson, Eames, Girard, Propst: The Design Process at Herman Miller, Design Quarterly 98/99* (Minneapolis, MN: Walker Art Center, 1975).
3   George Nelson, "Your Children Could Romp Here While You Shop," *Saturday Evening Post*, February 13, 1943, 58.
4   Rohde brought an innovative industrial approach to furniture design and was responsible for introducing modernism to American consumers during the interwar years. Rohde's designs for furniture stressed comfort, multifunctionality, and informality. A champion of modular components, Rohde experimented with emerging industrial materials such as Plexiglas and produced furniture with organic, biomorphic forms. For a thorough examination of Rohde, see Phyllis Ross, *Gilbert Rohde: Modern Design for Modern Living* (New Haven, CT: Yale University Press, 2009).
5   "Charles Pollock," Bernhardt Design, accessed September 24, 2015, https://bernhardtdesign.com/designers/charles-pollock/; Douglas Martin, "Charles Pollock, Designer of Popular Office Chair, Dies at 83," *New York Times*, August 26, 2013, B7.
6   "Charles Pollock," Bernhardt Design.
7   Martin, "Charles Pollock."
8   George Nelson and Charles R. Pollock, "Leg Structure for Furniture," U.S. Patent No. 3,032,307, filed August 3, 1959, issued May 1, 1962, U.S. Patent Office.
9   Nelson and Pollock.
10 Andrew VanStyn discovered the difference in height, resulting in the identification of this chair as an *MAF*.
11 George Nelson and Charles R. Pollock, "Multi-Piece Formed Furniture Construction," U.S. Patent No. 3,027,195, filed December 1, 1958, issued March 27, 1962, U.S. Patent Office.
12 George Nelson, "Design and Values" (commencement address, Philadelphia Museum College of Art, 1962), https://archive.org/stream/philadelphiamuse00nels/philadelphiamuse00nels.

Conoid Chair

39

1966

Designed by George Nakashima (1905–1990)

Manufactured by Nakashima Studios
(active 1945–present, New Hope, Pennsylvania)

Walnut and hickory

35 ½ x 20 x 21 ½ in.

"INSTEAD OF A LONG running and bloody battle with nature, to dominate her, we can walk in step with a tree to release a joy in her grains, to join with her to realize her potential, to enhance the environment of man."[1] Such was the philosophy of George Nakashima, a first-generation leader of the Studio Furniture Movement and designer of the *Conoid Chair*.[2] Named after his Conoid Studio, Nakashima's iconic chair is a synthesis of historic artistic styles, incorporating such elements as the spindle backs of 18th-century Windsor chairs, the unadorned simplicity of Shaker furniture, and the flat planes of the International Style.

Born to Japanese immigrants Katsuharu and Suzu Thoma Nakashima and raised in Spokane, Washington, George Nakashima was influenced by his familial samurai antecedents. An interest in the Northwestern woods and hiking first led to a study in forestry, but he subsequently pursued a degree in architecture at the University of Washington and the non-theoretical curriculum at the Massachusetts Institute of Technology. In the years following the Great Depression, he traveled to Paris, Tokyo, and India. In 1934, Nakashima worked in the Tokyo office of architect Antonin Raymond (1888–1976), who had worked with Frank Lloyd Wright (1867–1959, Cat. No. 28) on the Imperial Hotel (1923) in Tokyo, and who was later instrumental in synthesizing modernist and Japanese-style architecture. Through his employment with the firm, in 1937 Nakashima traveled to Pondicherry (now Puducherry), India, where he designed and supervised construction of Golconde, the principal dormitory at the Sri Aurobindo Ashram. The structure was one of the first high-strength reinforced concrete buildings in India and contained furniture designed by Nakashima. "Furniture making at Pondicherry was an elemental baptism in the craft of woodworking," Nakashima later recalled.[3]

In 1939, Nakashima returned to Tokyo, where he remained for six months and met Marion Okajima (1912–2004), who would become his wife, mother of his two children, and business partner. He permanently returned to the United States and settled in Seattle, Washington; Marion later joined him, and the couple married in 1941. During this time, Nakashima thought he should take a road trip from Seattle to California "to see firsthand what was considered the best of modern American architecture."[4]

Nakashima found the work of Richard Neutra (1892–1970) and Frank Lloyd Wright to be "especially disappointing ... although the forms used were interesting and the results were causing a certain excitement in the architectural world. I found the structure and the bones of the building somehow inadequate, however, and the workmanship shoddy."[5] He felt he needed to pursue a new vocation, "something that I could coordinate from beginning to end,"[6] and decided to pursue woodworking as his life's work. Nakashima, like many architects, found structural craftsmanship on a smaller scale more rewarding. "The woodworker has a special intensity," Nakashima believed, "a striving for perfection, a conviction that any task must be executed with all his skill ... to create the best object he is capable of creating."[7]

America's entry into World War II after the Japanese attack on Pearl Harbor hindered Nakashima's emerging career, with his family subjected to anti-Japanese sentiments. Like nearly 120,000 other Japanese Americans viewed as potential enemy sympathizers or enemy combatants, Nakashima was forcibly relocated with his wife and one-year-old daughter from Washington to the Minidoka internment camp in Idaho. Under the tutelage of Gentaro Hikogawa (1902–1963), an internee who had emigrated from Shikoku, Japan, to Tacoma, Washington, Nakashima learned traditional Japanese methods of joinery and the proper use of hand tools from the *daiku,* or master carpenter.[8] His time in the camp was not entirely unproductive. "There was wood, and a very fine Japanese carpenter, so I became his designer and his apprentice at the same time."[9] To enliven the rather spartan interiors of the crude shelters, Nakashima designed a model apartment out of scrap lumber and covered the walls with wallpaper fashioned out of recycled blueprints.[10] "I learned a great deal from this man [Gentaro Hikogawa], through his hundreds of small acts of perfection. He helped me with many of the basic woodworking skills, for instance the correct sharpening of a chisel ... He also taught me to sharpen a Japanese handsaw with its very deep gullet ... Working with him was a rewarding experience and one that I greatly appreciated."[11]

Through the sponsorship of Antonin Raymond and his wife, Naomi, Nakashima

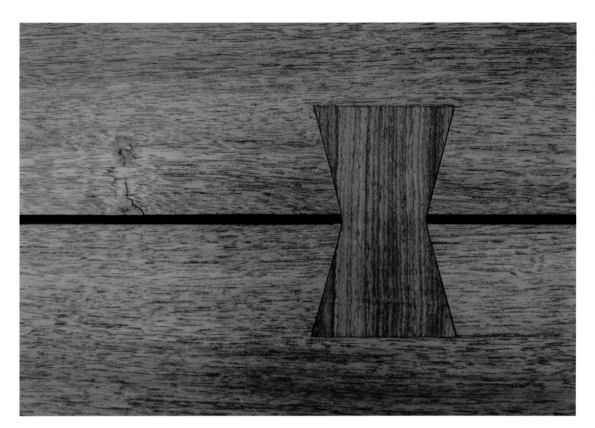

Fig. 39.1 Detail of Nakashima's famous butterfly joint on *"Frenchman's Cove" Dining Table* (1970), DeMell Jacobsen Collection.

was able to leave the internment camp and move to Pennsylvania, where he secured employment on Raymond's farm. After a year of working on the farm, Nakashima realized that "chickens and I were not compatible,"[12] and left with his family to establish his first woodworking shop, in which he "at first worked only with hand tools, building chairs, tables and benches. Gradually I added machines."[13] In 1944, Nakashima introduced his *Straight Chair* and authorized Knoll to mass-produce it. Knoll manufactured the chair under the name *N19* from 1946 to 1954.[14] To complement the chairs, Nakashima also designed three tables for Knoll, including the *Splay-Leg Table*, which was also produced between 1946 and 1954.

Through his work with Knoll, Nakashima sought "to pioneer a craft concept in a world that was growing accustomed to mass-produced goods."[15] His "simple, pleasantly handcrafted wooden stool"[16] appeared in *Design for Use, USA* (1951), an international traveling exhibition organized by the Museum of Modern Art. The following year, the Metropolitan Museum of Art opened the exhibition *Handicrafts in the United States*, which subsequently departed on a similar international tour. Organized by the American Craftsmen's Educational

Council under the auspices of the U.S. Department of State, the exhibition sought to "indicate to citizens of other lands that there is a healthy and flourishing handcraft movement in this country" that would "correct an erroneous belief sometimes held abroad that Americans are solely concerned with developing the machine and its products."[17] Though the exhibition did not contain actual pieces of furniture, it did feature photographs of furniture made by George Nakashima, Isamu Noguchi (Cat. No. 36), and a group of designers associated with the School for American Craftsmen in Rochester, New York, which furnished "proof that the handcraft movement in the United States is not restricted to small objects."[18]

At the "Good Design Could Be Better" symposium held at the Museum of Modern Art in 1952, Nakashima expressed the opinion that while the modern design movement had rejected an old set of prejudices, it was suffering from new ones. This, he believed, "had led to a false emphasis on 'design for design's sake,' which occurs when design is superimposed on material rather than naturally growing from it."[19] In spite of his increasing disillusion toward the designer market, combined with his prior experience with

Knoll, in 1958 Nakashima became design director for Widdicomb-Mueller. Unveiled at the wholesale furniture market in Grand Rapids, Michigan, Nakashima's designs were praised "as if they had been precisely designed by an architect and then hand-hewn out of tree trunks. Despite its traditional inspiration, the result is a boldly modern approach ... His success with a factory-made collection may indicate a new source of design talent for an industry in which creative designers are at such a premium that the work of a handful of men is copied or, in one manufacturer's word, 'rehashed' over and over."[20] Immediately following their debut, Nakashima's spindle-backed side chairs, chests with fronts resembling burled wood, and butterfly-shaped side tables were heralded as "the new American look," or "the handcrafted look," all of which greatly amused Nakashima as he "could not accept the thesis that spindles are strictly an American heritage."[21]

Royalties from the sale of his designs through both Knoll and Widdicomb-Mueller provided Nakashima with much-needed capital to make continued improvements to his workshop. In 1960, he finished construction of his Conoid Studio, with a 40-foot-long arching roof shaped in a double-reverse conoid made of concrete poured to a thickness of two and a half inches. The span had no supporting beams or poles, with the entire weight resting on the arch on the south side of the building and the eight-foot-high wall on the north side. Nakashima's completion of the Conoid Studio coincided with the debut of perhaps his most celebrated design: the *Conoid Chair*. A harmony of color is created by the contrast of dark walnut stiles and light hickory spindles. A walnut saddle seat cantilevers above two oblong walnut feet, which were specially designed for sliding along carpets.[22] Nakashima once recalled, "I started this chair because I felt you needed only two legs, then I put the base on it because it had to be supported and it seemed to work out because so many homes are carpeted. Legs on a carpet floor are a bad solution, you can't move the chair, whereas this one will slide on the carpet."[23] Betty Pepis, a noted *New York Times* reporter, observed, "designer Nakashima has the utmost regard for the potential of wood as a decorative medium as well as a respectful interest in the importance of each detail (Fig. 39.1). For example, the striking natural grain of some streaked walnut sapwood is used to make a patterned headboard in the bedroom. Similarly, dowels and pegs which show on several of the tables and stools are placed to create a design."[24]

Nakashima believed that "each flitch, each board, each plank, can have only one ideal use. The woodworker, applying a thousand skills, must find that ideal use and then shape the wood to realize its true potential. The result is our ultimate object, plain and simple."[25] Though Nakashima died in 1990, his daughter, Mira (b. 1942), continues his legacy of producing handcrafted furniture. As a first-generation member of the Studio Furniture Movement, Nakashima is often mentioned along with fellow Pennsylvanian Wharton Esherick (1887–1970), as well as Californians Arthur Espenet Carpenter (1920–2006) and Sam Maloof (1916–2009). His devotion to his craft helped to pave the way for subsequent generations of artists, including Jon Brooks (Cat. No. 41), Vivian Beer (Cat. No. 46), and Laura Kishimoto (Cat. No. 49). Perhaps presaging recognition of these and other artists of the Studio Furniture Movement, Pepis wrote in her 1951 review of a Philadelphia exhibition that contained Nakashima-designed furniture, "Another indication that the designing of contemporary furniture has achieved the stature of an art was seen here today in the inclusion of chairs, chests and tables with the oils and drawings that made up the opening exhibition of the season at the Art Alliance."[26]

1 George Nakashima, "Philosophy," George Nakashima Woodworkers, accessed November 25, 2018, https://nakashimawoodworkers.com/philosophy/.

2 For a thorough examination of Nakashima's artistic philosophy, see George Nakashima, *The Soul of a Tree: A Woodworker's Reflections* (Tokyo and New York: Kodansha International, 1981). For his biography, see especially Derek E. Ostergard, *George Nakashima: Full Circle* (London: Weidenfeld & Nicolson, 1989); Steven Beyer, *George Nakashima and the Modernist Moment* (New York: D.A.P., 2002); and Mira Nakashima, *Nature, Form and Spirit: The Life and Legacy of George Nakashima* (New York: Harry N. Abrams, 2003).

3 Nakashima, *Soul of a Tree*, 64.

4 Nakashima, 69.

5 Nakashima, 69. See also George Nakashima, "Craftsmanship in Architecture," *Craft Horizons* 16, no. 3 (May/June 1956): 26–31.

6 Nakashima, *Soul of a Tree*, 69.

7 Nakashima, "Philosophy."

8 David Lane, "Gentaro Kenneth Hikogawa," *Densho Encyclopedia*, last updated May 26, 2017, https://encyclopedia.densho.org/Gentaro_Kenneth_Hikogawa/.

9 John Kelsey, "George Nakashima: For Each Plant There's One Perfect Use," *Fine Woodworking*, no. 14 (January/February 1979): 40–46.

10 See Alexandra Lange, "The Forgotten History of Japanese-American Designers' World War II Internment," *Curbed*, January 31, 2017, https://www.curbed.com/2017/1/31/14445484/japanese-designers-wwii-internment.

11 Nakashima, *Soul of a Tree*, 70.

12 Nakashima, 70.

13 Nakashima, 70.

14 "Celebrating the Straight Chair: A conversation with Mira Nakashima," *The Magazine ANTIQUES*, May 26, 2009. https://www.themagazineantiques.com/article/celebrating-the-straight-chair-a-conversation-with-mira-nakashima/.

15 "Celebrating the Straight Chair."

16 Betty Pepis, "Exhibit of Current U.S. Home Furnishings Is Being Sent to Europe by Modern Museum," *New York Times*, January 8, 1951, 18.

17 Betty Pepis, "Handcrafts of U.S. in Museum Exhibit," *New York Times*, October 10, 1952, 22.

18 Pepis, 22.

19 Betty Pepis, "Design's Progress Found Hampered," *New York Times*, November 14, 1952, 17.

20 Cynthia Kellogg, "A New 'American Look' in Furniture Is Unveiled," *New York Times*, June 14, 1958, 25.

21 Rita Reif, "Craftsman's Feeling for Wood Lends Greatness to His Furniture," *New York Times*, August 25, 1958, 25.

22 "Conoid Chair," Smithsonian American Art Museum and the Renwick Gallery, accessed January 22, 2022, https://americanart.si.edu/artwork/conoid-chair-32469.

23 John Kelsey, "George Nakashima," 46.

24 Betty Pepis, "The Handicraft Theme," *New York Times Magazine*, August 19, 1951, 38–39.

25 Nakashima, *Soul of a Tree*, xxi.

26 Betty Pepis, "Furniture Display Flavors Art Show," *New York Times*, October 6, 1951, 9.

40

Butterfly Love Seat

1967

Designed and manufactured by Wendell Keith Castle (1932–2018) (active 1961–2018, Scottsville, New York)

Stack-laminated oak

18 ¼ x 49 x 19 in.

Signed on base: WC 67

IN A CAREER THAT spanned more than 50 years, Wendell Castle fostered an ongoing dialogue between furniture and sculpture, which he often viewed as interchangeable. In the process, he challenged the public perceptions of furniture, which he viewed as a metaphor for everyday life and the paradoxical relationship of form versus function. Whether carved, laminated, manufactured, fabricated, or assembled, his designs reveal an incisive command of form and content, combined with a highly sophisticated use of diverse materials and processes.

Castle grew up on his family's farm in Emporia, Kansas, a rural area of the state. He recalled he "had a natural ability to be facile. I was around the farm where they built things and my dad built some things."[1] Throughout his childhood, he struggled with dyslexia and found a creative outlet through art. Castle once recalled, "I was not good at anything … But I was very good at daydreaming. I think that was a good thing because what daydreaming does—and I think it is important in any field—is you picture yourself achieving certain things … I actually imagined myself being good at something and then I was good at it … that was art."[2]

A second-generation studio furniture maker, Castle earned his undergraduate degree in industrial design and sculpture at the University of Kansas and then pursued his graduate degree in sculpture at the same institution. He preferred sculpture because it allowed him to work with "real things."[3] Upon graduating, Castle moved first to New York City and then upstate to Rochester, where in 1965 he became an instructor in furniture design at the School for American Craftsmen, part of the Rochester Institute

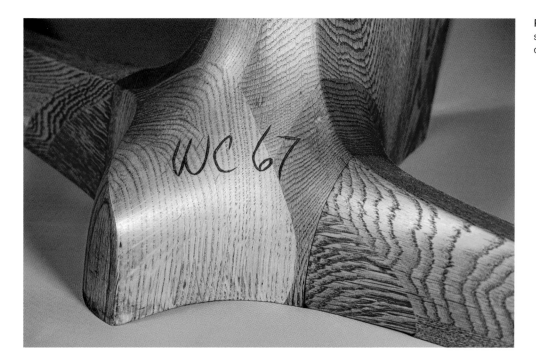

Fig. 40.1 Detail of signature on base of love seat.

of Technology. While there, he began to explore the use of stack lamination, a process in which multiple pieces of wood are glued together and then carved into a form, much like an artist carves a work from marble. As Castle observed, "You do two things when you are sculpting: you either add or subtract ... That's the good thing about lamination. Basically, you add first, then subtract; if you subtract too much, you can always add some more back on. It's perfect. It's forgiving. You get to do exactly what sculptors have always done, but with a little more freedom because you don't have the restrictions of working with a block of any particular size."[4] Ongoing experimentation with the process resulted in his definitive publication on the subject, *The Wendell Castle Book of Wood Lamination* (1980).

Though his early designs suggest a familiarity with other American furniture makers, such as Wharton Esherick (1887–1970) and George Nakashima (Cat. No. 39), Castle professed to have had no knowledge of their work during his school years. "As a woodworker, I am self-taught," Castle later recalled, "which explains why it has taken so long for my advanced ideas to become reality."[5] By 1965, Castle's work and influence positioned him at the forefront of the growing Studio Furniture Movement, which was then sweeping the nation. He was a standout among a group of artists

who became known for their skillfully handmade furniture that emphasized individual design and beauty, propelling their craft into a new category: art. For this, Castle is widely acknowledged as the father of the Art Furniture Movement.

Castle sought to make furniture that was inventive and playful, and "makes life an adventure."[6] His journey began when he received a solo exhibition in late 1965 at the Memorial Art Gallery in Rochester, New York, following his winning entry in the *Rochester Finger Lakes Exhibition* the preceding year. The exhibition contained 11 recent pieces of furniture, which were enhanced by a "frieze-like display of thirty of his visionary sketches."[7] In his review of the exhibition for *Craft Horizons*, Donald McKinley praised Castle's drawings for "their economy of line and shadow ... reminiscent of Erich Mendelsohn's tantalizing architectural studies, although the forms are more often linked with art nouveau. These preliminary drawings documented Castle's continuing form development, yet merely sampled his prolific search for the natural line."[8] McKinley continued by praising Castle's prowess with wood, and declaring that he "earns unanimous respect for his flawless joinery and immaculate contouring. Particularly successful is the recurring use of the accent edge or sharp change-of-plane: a cross section of leg or mast will

be an inflated triangle rather than circular ... The transitions catch the eye and then evaporate—topological phenomena that enrich the form and entrance the viewer."[9]

It was Castle's inclusion in the seminal exhibition *Fantasy Furniture* at the Museum of Contemporary Crafts in 1966 that catapulted him to the forefront of the Studio Furniture Movement. There, his work appeared alongside that of four other artists from around the world: the collaborative duo of Fabio de Sanctis and Ugo Sterpini (Rome, Italy); Pedro Friedeberg (Mexico City); and Thomas Simpson (Elgin, Illinois). Collectively, the furniture in the exhibition challenged "the modern concept of furniture as functional form—pure material and line devoted to the ultimates of service for storage or support ... made primarily to occupy space rather than to save it, to offer flamboyant presence and rollicking pleasure rather than merely good taste and efficiency."[10] Among Castle's entries in the exhibition were a chest of drawers with many legs and a cherrywood chest whose bulbous, organic shape suggested a marriage between a double gourd and a pomegranate. In his artist's statement for the exhibition, Castle said,

My furniture goes against the mainstream of twentieth-century designs. I have no special interest in form following function. I try in my work to fulfill both the aesthetic and the practical purpose, but if one were to become dominant I would choose the aesthetic. To be inventive and playful and produce furniture which is a complement to nature rather than in contrast to it, is my philosophy. My idea is not to reconstruct or stylize natural forms, but to produce a synthesis or metamorphosis of natural forms. A philosophy like this may not produce work in the accepted taste of the day, but this has little to do with its essential and final value.[11]

Castle's adventurous furniture caught the eye of Lee Nordness (1922–1995), a New York gallery dealer who purchased Castle's chest of drawers from the *Fantasy Furniture* exhibition. In a letter sent to the sculptor, Nordness wrote, "I am just mad about your furniture, feeling that your handsome pieces are as much sculpture as furniture."[12] Nordness requested photographs of existing pieces that remained available for purchase and was willing to commission a suite of furniture for the living room in his new apartment. "I am now living on apple crates in the living room, but I am willing to wait so that I can have the pleasure of living with your beautiful furniture."[13] Castle typed a hand-annotated draft response in which he related he was working hard on the furniture plan. "Well I finally have it," Castle wrote. "I wanted to make absolutely [*sic*] sure of every thing, as the placement of the furniture has to do with the shape of the furniture."[14] After much deliberation over at "least 50 different floor plans," he mentioned a bench and a sofa, which centered the room and had a "bow swing around the back of the sofa forming a bar

and a counter balance for the sofa."[15]

In 1967 Castle completed the stack-laminated oak *Butterfly Love Seat*, which Nordness had commissioned.[16] It and nine other pieces of furniture—a desk, a serpent-form table, a bone-like column, a music stand, a bookcase, and a few other works—debuted the following year in his solo exhibition *Handcrafted Furniture by Wendell Castle* at Nordness's eponymous gallery. "The free-form shapes employed, and the highly imaginative design, tend to give each piece a very personal and individualistic presence," wrote a reviewer for *Arts Magazine*, the first national arts journal to cover a Castle exhibition.[17]

Butterfly Love Seat is a visual *tour de force* and a superlative example of Castle's ability to create dynamism and a sense of motion using the weighty medium of wood. Its crescent-shaped or ellipsoid foot, a common form in the artist's vocabulary, provides stability and gives rise to a columnar leg (Fig. 40.1). Perhaps paying homage to Eero Saarinen (Cat. Nos. 29 and 32), who explored the concept of a legless chair, Castle similarly professed a desire that "one leg for a chair pleases me. I have been trying to get furniture off its legs for some time."[18] The leg then seemingly sprouts "wings," which echo the shape of the base below, and suggests a butterfly about to take flight. The double seats are finely carved and envelop the sitter as they perch atop the chair.

An advertisement for the Lee Nordness Galleries that appeared in a contemporary issue of *Art in America* pictured a three-seat sofa by Castle. The narrative that accompanied the image posed the question

"Dare a sculpture endorse a sofa?" The answer that followed was "Yes, when the sofa is created by one of the new breed of craftsmen-cum-artists."[19] Following the debut exhibition, Nordness further propelled Castle's career by including him in the exhibition *Objects: USA*. The show traveled to 22 domestic and 11 international venues over a four-year period following its initial presentation at the Smithsonian Institution. Funded by the S. C. Johnson Company of Racine, Wisconsin, whose headquarters were designed by Frank Lloyd Wright (Cat. No. 28), the exhibition laid a firm foundation for the promotion and appreciation of American craft. A brochure produced by the Lee Nordness Galleries described Castle: "Considered the most innovative woodworker in the U.S., he altered traditional furniture making concepts by introducing the large laminated block, which is then carved as a sculptor attacks a block of marble. Castle extends his furniture forms as far toward sculpture as possible without forfeiting function."[20]

Wendell Castle's contributions to and advancement of the Studio Furniture Movement are legendary, as demonstrated by his works in numerous museum collections such as the Arkansas Museum of Fine Arts, the Museum of Modern Art, the Metropolitan Museum of Art, the Renwick Gallery of the Smithsonian American Art Museum, the Art Institute of Chicago, and others. The Brooklyn Museum honored him with the 2007 *Modernism* Lifetime Achievement Award. Most importantly to the DeMell Jacobsen Collection, he mentored Jon Brooks (Cat. No. 41) at the School for American Craftsmen.

1   Bebe Pritam Johnson and Warren Eames Johnson, *Speaking of Furniture: Conversations with Fourteen American Craftsmen* (New York: Artist Book Foundation, 2013), 49.
2   Johnson and Johnson, 49.
3   Burchfield Penney Art Center, "Living Legacy Interview: Wendell Castle," video, 12 mins., August 13, 2015, https://vimeo.com/136210902.
4   Johnson and Johnson, *Speaking of Furniture*, 55.
5   Rita Reif, "Furniture That Seems to Be Growing," *New York Times*, April 9, 1968, 50.
6   Castle quoted in Friedman Benda, "Wendell Castle: A New Vocabulary, September 5–October 12, 2019," Artsy, https://www.artsy.net/show/friedman-benda-wendell-castle-a-new-vocabulary/info. See also Friedman Benda, "Wendell Castle," accessed December 22, 2021, https://www.friedmanbenda.com/artists/wendell-castle/.
7   Donald McKinley, "Wendell Castle," *Craft Horizons* 26, no. 2 (March/April 1966): 41.

8   McKinley, 41.
9   McKinley, 41.
10 "Fantasy Furniture," *Craft Horizons* 26, no. 1 (January/February 1966): 11.
11 "Fantasy Furniture," 15.
12 "Fantasy Furniture," 15.
13 "Fantasy Furniture," 15.
14 Wendell Castle to Lee Nordness, 1966, Archives of American Art, Smithsonian Institution, Washington, D.C., https://www.aaa.si.edu/collections/items/detail/wendell-castle-rochester-ny-letter-to-lee-nordness-new-york-ny-208.
15 Castle to Nordness.
16 The *Butterfly Love Seat* is documented by the Wendell Castle Studio as inventory number 114. See also Emily Evans Eerdmans et al., *Wendell Castle: A Catalogue Raisonné: 1958–2012* (New York: Artist Book Foundation, 2014), 137.

17 Quoted in Alastair Gordon, *Wendell Castle: Wandering Forms—Works from 1959–1979* (New York: Gregory R. Miller & Co. / Aldrich Contemporary Art Museum, 2012), 119–120. While the author indicates that the review appeared in *Art in America*, it could not be located. Two reviews did appear in other national arts publications. See Rita Simon, "Galleries: Wendell Castle," *Arts Magazine* 42, Issue 7, May 1968, 64 and M. L., "Wendell Castle," *ARTnews* 67, Issue 4, Summer 1968, 13.
18 Rita Reif, "Furniture That Seems to be Growing," *The New York Times*, April 9, 1968, 50.
19 *Art in America* 56, no. 5 (September/October 1968).
20 Lee Nordness Galleries, *Arts/Objects: USA; Capsule Information about the Artists* (New York: Lee Nordness Galleries, 1972), 2, https://digital.craftcouncil.org/digital/collection/p15785coll7/id/5847.

Ball Chair

41

1970

Designed and manufactured by Jon Brooks
(b. 1944) (active San Francisco, California,
and New Boston, New Hampshire)

Solid elm, chain-sawn and hand-carved

24 x 22 x 28 in.

Signed on underside: Jon Brooks / 1970

IN STARK CONTRAST to all the other chairs in the DeMell Jacobsen Collection, which were assembled from various component parts, this example by Jon Brooks was made using a subtractive process.[1] In general, furniture design is a process in which the maker-designer envisions a form, either on paper or in their mind, and then procures the materials necessary to realize that form. When using a subtractive method, however, the maker-designer permits the material—be it a section of log, branch, burl, or natural-edge plank—to serve as the inspiration from which the final form emerges. This approach changes the artist's role from that of a "form giver to a form selector."[2]

To execute his subtractive furniture designs, Brooks slowly and methodically shapes his pieces with a chainsaw from massive, unprocessed found logs and tree trunks.[3] He removes only the necessary elements, exposing the rich natural grain to artistically heighten the visual effect (Fig. 41.1). The artist explains:

> My artwork is about collaboration with nature, using naturally formed hardwood, which is found and harvested in the local forests that surround my home and studio in southern New Hampshire. This wood presents itself in an array of shapes and forms suggesting possibilities for furniture and sculpture. I am attracted to the architecture of nature as a compelling dance of control and chaos.[4]

A self-proclaimed obsession with the spherical shape led Brooks to carve a variety of stools and chairs exploring the form. *Ball Chair* is one of only two examples made in this scale; sadly, the second perished in a house fire in Oakland, California.[5] The handles on either side of the chair and its high back support, which is shaped for added comfort, are unique characteristics. A natural fissure, which formed as the wood dried, enlivens the chair. "I feel that the cracks enhance a piece when they have been rounded on the edges," Brooks said of the present example.[6] Other inherent properties of the wood—knots, grain patterns, and medullary rays—are similarly celebrated in the composition. "My art is about cooperating with the tree shapes I find to create a balance of form, function, and craftsmanship. Color and surface design play an important part of my expression."[7]

Born in Manchester, New Hampshire, Brooks attended art classes at the Currier Museum of Art in his hometown. As a boy, Brooks knew early on he wanted to pursue a career in making art. He studied books about abstract sculptors Constantin Brâncuși (1876–1957) and Henry Moore (1898–1986), which provided inspiration and sparked his early interest in carving wood. Brooks recalled his "primary desire was to do wood sculpture ... I had an absolute obsession with wood ... an obsession with three-dimensional objects and life-sized forms."[8] Although accepted to the Rhode Island School of Design, Brooks earned his bachelor of fine arts (1966) and master of fine arts (1967) degrees from the School for American Craftsmen (now the School for American Crafts) at the Rochester Institute of Technology in Rochester, New York. He began studying there in 1962, taking courses in painting and drawing, as well as woodworking and cabinetmaking with William Keyser (b. 1936) and Wendell Castle (1932–2018, Cat. No. 40). Brooks recalled that Keyser was "a wizard with joinery."[9] From him, Brooks received a strong foundation in technical proficiency and a design philosophy that sought to unite a sculptural aesthetic with functionality. These approaches were further reinforced by Castle, then newly hired by the School for American Craftsmen. Brooks would apprentice with Castle, who became his mentor. To Brooks, Castle "was someone who really opened my eyes to the potential of the combination of art and craft, the idea of fusion of utility with aesthetic."[10]

Following graduation, Brooks moved to San Francisco, where he visited galleries and museums. There, he was exposed to the Funk Art Movement and the work of William T. Wiley (1937–2021) and Robert Hudson (b. 1938), both of whom made humorous drawings, paintings, and three-dimensional sculptures from scavenged materials. In 1969, Brooks had his first two important solo exhibitions, the first at Shop One Galleries in Rochester, and the second at the Taylor and Ng Gallery in San Francisco. Both were critical and financial successes. Wendell Castle's review of the Rochester exhibition stated that Brooks's work "represents an exciting and individual approach ... The strong organic forms do not always imply their functions at first glance. Two chairs which Brooks made from

Fig. 41.1 (left) Detail of natural wood grain and cracks on underside of *Ball Chair* with signature and date.

Fig. 41.2 (above) Jon Brooks's fire-damaged studio with several destroyed *Ball Chairs*, 2010.

stumps are most successful and come on particularly strong as sculpture. As furniture they are also quite comfortable."[11]

As a counterpoint to the superficial use of materials in Pop Art and the space-age designs of the 1960s, there was a resurgence of self-reliance and "back to the land" living by artists of the contemporaneous Studio Craft Movement. Brooks embraced this philosophy and returned to his native New Hampshire in March 1970, immediately following the approval of his application for conscientious-objector status during the Vietnam War. Brooks purchased 15 acres in New Boston from his parents and began construction of a home and studio (Fig. 41.3).[12] In October 2010, Dr. Jacobsen visited Brooks's home

and enjoyed seeing the artist's fabulous creations (Fig. 41.4). During her visit, she was able to see his studio, where several smaller *Ball Chairs* in the process of production had been tragically burned in a fire in January (Fig. 41.2). Despite his earlier exhibition successes, Brooks did not find ready acceptance into either the League of New Hampshire Craftsmen nor the New Hampshire Art Association because of his nontraditional furniture style and his abstract approach to sculpture. Undaunted, Brooks found encouragement from local artists Gerry Williams (1926–2014), a ceramicist, and Blanche Dombeck (1914–1987), an abstract sculptor in wood. He also traveled to Pennsylvania to meet with George Nakashima (Cat. No. 39) and

to visit the home and studio of Wharton Esherick (1887–1970), both well-established artisans in the Studio Furniture Movement. In addition, Brooks consulted Sam Maloof (1916–2009), another woodworker active in California while Brooks lived there.

Through additional exhibitions and publications, Brooks gained national and international recognition as an emerging artist, one who was actively pushing the boundaries of art and craft, furniture, and sculpture. Just as Castle had done for him, Brooks became a mentor to others and regularly taught and lectured at important studio programs, including the Penland School of Craft (Penland, North Carolina); his alma mater, the School of American Crafts; and the Haystack Mountain School

of Crafts (Deer Isle, Maine). During a year-long residency at the University of Tasmania in Australia (1983–1984), Brooks became intrigued by the construction and decoration of Indigenous Australian art and began to incorporate those elements into his own work. The award-winning craftsman's work has been exhibited worldwide and is included in the collections of the Philadelphia Museum of Art; the Museum of Fine Arts, Boston; the Renwick Gallery of the Smithsonian American Art Museum;

and the Currier Museum of Art. In 2011, Brooks received the Lotte Jacobi Living Treasure Award, given by the New Hampshire State Council on the Arts to a New Hampshire artist working in any discipline "who has made a significant contribution to his or her art form and to the arts community of New Hampshire, reflecting a lifetime of achievement."[13] Today, Brooks is recognized as a prominent leader of the second generation of Studio Furniture Movement practitioners.

Fig. 41.3 (above left) Jon Brooks outside his home in New Boston, New Hampshire, 2010.

Fig. 41.4 (above right) Interior of Jon Brooks's home, featuring his creations, 2010.

1   See David Holzapfel, "Subtractive Woodworking: Furniture from Logs and Limbs," *Fine Woodworking*, no. 54 (September/October 1985): 88–93. Additional thanks to Andrew VanStyn for his research and expertise. His contributions helped shape this essay.

2   Wendell Castle, "Jonathan Brooks," *Craft Horizons* 29, no. 2 (March/April 1969): 42.

3   Many examples of Brooks's furniture are executed from salvaged elm trees, which he gathered personally from his own property and from surrounding lands. Many towns and cities along the East Coast were shaded by the tall leafy trees until the 1970s, when a fungus named Dutch Elm Disease devastated the species.

4   "Jon's Vision," Jon Brooks, accessed October 7, 2018, https://www.jonbrooks.org/vision.html.

5   Jon Brooks to Diane DeMell Jacobsen Ph.D., email, April 21, 2010, Foundation curatorial files.

6   Jon Brooks to Marshall Reisman, personal correspondence, August 4, 1971.

7   "Jon's Vision."

8   Brooks quoted in P. Andrew Spahr, "A Passion for Art and Nature," *Jon Brooks: A Collaboration with Nature* (Manchester, NH: Currier Museum of Art, 2011), 14.

9   Brooks quoted in Spahr, 14.

10   Brooks quoted in D. Quincy Whitney, "Nature, Carver Collaborate to Create Unique Works in Wood," *Boston Globe*, May 24, 1987, NH22, cited in Spahr, 17.

11   Castle, "Jonathan Brooks," 42.

12   See Jane Holtz Kay, "Three Furniture Craftsmen at Home," *New York Times*, February 16, 1984, C8.

13   "2011 Governors Arts Awards: Lotte Jacobi Living Treasure," New Hampshire State Council on the Arts, accessed November 4, 2018, https://www.nh.gov/nharts/artsandartists/gaa/2011%20GAA/Bios/brooks.html.

Contour Bar Stool (No. 10-415)

42

1972

Designed by Frank Owen Gehry (b. 1929)

Manufactured by Easy Edges, Incorporated (active 1969–1972, New York, New York, and Venice, California)

Edge Board (laminated corrugated cardboard, fiberboard)

28 ¾ x 12 ¼ x 17 in.

FRANK GEHRY HAS been known to blur "the conventional lines between the fine and applied arts," as well as those between art and architecture.[1] His choice of corrugated cardboard in *Contour Bar Stool (No. 10-415)* recalls the innovative use of discarded materials by both Cyrus Wakefield (Cat. No. 15) and Wenzel Friedrich (Cat. No. 19) nearly a century earlier. Visually captivating, with zigzag folds visible along the structure's width, the body-contoured cardboard elements of Gehry's stool belie its functional strength.[2]

Corrugated cardboard had its origins in pleated paper, which was first patented in England in 1856 for use as a hat liner. Pleated paper with a liner sheet was later patented by New Yorker Albert Jones in 1871 as a packing material to protect glass. Oliver Long added a second liner in his 1874 patent, which led to development of the material as it is known today; a machine to mass-produce the product was invented the same year. In 1890 Robert Gair, a Brooklyn merchant, created the corrugated fiberboard box involving cuts and creases for folding preparation.[3]

Folded materials have fascinated artists for centuries. Gehry experimented with a method to strengthen the conventional material, much like John Henry Belter's (Cat. No. 9) laminated veneers in the mid-1850s. Corrugated cardboard sheets were layered in alternating directions and adhered to form blocks from which individual elements could be die-cut, a product that became known in the trade as Edge Board. The sculpted elements could then be fastened with "stringers" inserted into slots. Gehry's patent explained the construction of his cardboard furniture, including the *Contour Bar Stool*, which began with "unitary cardboard pieces" (Fig. 42.3).[4] These pieces were die-cut, coated with glue, and "placed in a jig under compression," with three stringers included for additional adhesive protection.[5] The ends were faced with a stronger Masonite or fiberboard, and the stool was finished with wax and a fire-resistant coating. The form of the *Contour Bar Stool* seems fluid, with gentle folds creating an integrated seat and footrest. So sturdy was the design, a contemporary advertisement showed three stools supporting a Volkswagen Beetle (Fig. 42.1)!

Born in Toronto, Canada, Frank Owen Goldberg moved to Los Angeles in 1947 with his parents, Irwin and Thelma.[6] Of Polish descent, the Goldbergs had immigrated to Canada prior to the onset of World War II and later changed their name to Gehry after moving to California. Inspired by the small cities he had constructed out of materials in his grandparents' store and influenced by the works of Frank Lloyd Wright (Cat. No. 28), Gehry studied architecture at the University of Southern California, from which he graduated in 1954. After gaining experience in the architecture field, Gehry enrolled in the Harvard Graduate School of Design but was disappointed in their architecture program, so he relocated to Paris to work. He returned to Los Angeles in 1962 and formed his own firm.

In 1969, Los Angeles artist Robert Irwin (b. 1928) asked Gehry to refashion his studio, which was to host a NASA-sponsored symposium about art and technology. Working within a modest budget, Gehry conceived and made some simple furniture out of cardboard, which "seemed like a way to transform the space that would be both cheap enough to fit within the budget and unconventional enough to allow it to seem, if a bit funky, at least vaguely futuristic at the same time."[7] Inspired by the potential of the material, especially the exposed ends of the corrugated sheets, Gehry recalled he "started to make shapes with it, which were very fuzzy, with a nice texture. I loved it because it was like corduroy. You get a texture that's pleasant, and I could make a tabletop that wasn't very heavy, which seemed promising."[8] What John Henry Belter and Charles and Ray Eames (Cat. Nos. 29 and 31) had done with thin sheets of wood, Gehry did with cardboard, layering sheets in alternating directions, which resulted in a material as strong as laminated wood but far more flexible. Gehry later recalled, "the surprising strength of the cardboard chairs ... demonstrates how even the most banal things can become a part of the domain from which architecture can select its raw materials."[9]

Gehry went on to design and fabricate several prototype furnishings for his office made from laminated cardboard. These included a desk, a file cabinet, partitions, shelves, chairs, and side tables. Irwin helped Gehry design an armchair, which ultimately gave rise to what would become one of his best-known pieces: the *Wiggle Chair*. Named for its squiggly shape, the chair

©Easy Edge Inc. 1972

Easy Edges

Easy Edges Incorporated
~~162 East 62nd Street~~ — moved to:
~~New York, N. Y. 10021~~   160 East 56th Street
~~Telephone (212) 832-1653~~   New York, N. Y. 10022
                                  Telephone (212) 832-1653

CARE AND MAINTENANCE

1   Before using your furniture, lightly spray with
    Easy Edges wax on it to seal the surface against
    penetration of spilled liquids and food stains.
    A damp sponge will remove all spills from
    the waxed surface. Vigorous rubbing or
    brushing will not harm the texture because
    of its rich density. On the contrary, it will
    make it more velvety.

2   Soiled or stained areas — even char marks from
    a cigarette — can be removed by using a wire
    suede brush or rough sandpaper.

3   To remove excess dust or food particles vacuum
    your Easy Edges surfaces periodically. Follow
    with light application of protective Easy Edges
    wax.

Easy Edges

EASY EDGES furniture is a revolutionary concept and a major breakthrough in home furnishings. It combines a brand new use of a material with excellent design at true budget prices. The material, EDGE-BOARD section, created by a special process of laminating layers of corrugated fiberboard, has the appearance of suede, the tactile quality of velvet and the strength of hard wood. It lends itself to a variety of curving furniture shapes, which rock, contract or spring back. Whimsical, intricate sculptured forms, which would be prohibitive in any other material, can be produced out of Edge-board sections at minimal cost.

Designed by award winning California architect, Frank O. Gehry. EASY EDGES furniture is a successful blending of classic simplicity with graceful sculptured lines. The furniture is as much at home in a sophisticated city apartment as it is in a country house, an office or mobile home. It compliments traditional interiors and fits naturally any modern decor.

Its appeal is truly universal. Wherever the line is shown it creates excitement translated into sales on the part of the buyers of all ages, divergent tastes and socio-economic backgrounds.

The present collection includes body contoured chairs, bar stools, rockers, dining, cocktail, conference, console and lamp tables. Desks, etageres, nesting cubes, nesting chairs, lounges and bed frames. Many of the designs serve multiple uses as seating units, tables, table bases or pillars.

EASY EDGES furniture is not only beautiful, practical and inexpensive, but it is easy to live with and easy to care for. In a test of strength three bar stools supported a Volkswagen easily. It can withstand rough treatment without marring, denting, scratching or scuffing.

Even char marks from a cigarette can be easily removed with a suede steel brush or a coarse sandpaper. The texture of the furniture is intrinsic therefore it requires no paints or varnishes. An occasional spray waxing to help seal the surfaces, vacuuming to remove dust accumulation is all that is needed. Spilled liquids can be mopped up with a damp cloth or sponge.

The material has remarkable acoustical properties. Rooms furnished with EASY EDGES have shown a reduction of noise volume at the source as high as fifty percent. This makes the furniture particularly suitable for active living in family rooms, schools and offices. Available now in its natural woodlike color, like wood, it can be easily stained with regular wood stain.

SIDE CHAIR

No. 10-351. This graceful spring-back chair is ideal for dining and fits into any living room setting.

CONTOUR BAR STOOL

No. 10-415. The sculptured lines provide a visual delight combined with comfort. Useful as breakfast-counter stool as well as bar.

WIGGLE SIDE CHAIR

No. 10-361. One of the Wiggle family, spring design provides comfort for dining, working or relaxing.

WIGGLE STOOL

No. 10-401. This multi-purpose spring design serves as an accessory seating unit side table or upended becomes a sculptured table base.

CHAISE LOUNGE

No. 10-420. Cantilevered construction of this chaise gives it remarkable resilience. Forms reclining unit with ottoman.

OTTOMAN

No. 10-402. Fits snugly into the chaise lounge creating a perfect recliner.

ARM TABLE

No. 10-122. This sculptured design makes ideal arm rest and/or occasional table.

CONTOUR ROCKER

No. 10-421. This ample rocker has extraordinary bounce in its body curving line.

Fig. 42.1 *Easy Edges*
brochure (1972),
showing a Volkswagen
Beetle supported by
three Easy Edges
stools.

Fig. 42.2 *Easy Edges*
brochure (1972),
showing various Easy
Edges models.

featured a long, narrow slab of corrugated cardboard that was upright at the top to form the back of a chair, bent forward into a seat, and then bent back and forth in an S-shape to provide support in place of any legs. Lightweight, low-cost, and easily mass-produced and maintained, the cardboard furniture would be seen by Gehry as a counter to the "ponderous, overpriced and tyrannical"[10] furniture found in stores and a viable alternative to the plethora of plastic seating that had emerged in the 1960s.

At the invitation of yet another artist friend, fashion designer Rudi Gernreich, Gehry participated in a program about fashion and design at the Hotel Bel-Air. In the audience was Richard Salomon, a New Yorker who was the head of Lanvin-Charles of the Ritz. Salomon promoted himself as

a businessman who could help creative people build a brand around their names. Salomon had had success in the past with fashion designer Yves Saint Laurent and hair stylist Vidal Sassoon and felt he could do the same for Gehry and his cardboard furniture. The aspiring partners settled on Easy Edges as a simple and memorable brand name. Richard Salomon made an initial investment to get production started in exchange for 40 percent of the company.[11]

The Easy Edges line was designed by Gehry in collaboration with Irwin and Jack Brogan (b. 1930) and manufactured between 1969 and 1972. While Easy Edges Inc. was headquartered in New York City, the actual fabrication of the pieces took place in a warehouse in Venice, California. In an April 1972 review of the line's debut at

Bloomingdale's, a reviewer for the *New York Times* observed, "The laminated corrugated carboard designs by Frank Gehry, a Santa Monica, Calif., architect, may not look new in shape (there's more than a touch of Alvar Aalto and John Mascheroni) but the velvety texture of the multi-layered material and the way the furniture feels in use, is innovative."[12] A brochure promoting the line touted the furniture as a "revolutionary concept and a major breakthrough in home furnishings ... blending of classic simplicity with graceful sculptured lines" (Fig. 42.2).[13] Edge Board was hailed as a new material with "the appearance of suede, the tactile quality of velvet and the strength of hard wood."[14] The soft texture was complemented by comfortable resilience, as the corrugated cardboard would "rock, contract or spring back."[15] The furniture line was promoted for its universal appeal, both stylistically and economically, as well as for the acoustic and environmental benefits the material provided.

Although the Easy Edges furniture gave him instant design fame and offered a faster, small-scale, cost-effective opportunity, Gehry chose to focus on architecture and halted production shortly after the line was introduced. "I started to feel threatened," Gehry recalled. "I closed myself off for weeks at a time in a room to rethink my life. I decided that I was an architect, not a furniture designer … and I simply stopped doing it."[16] In the years following, Gehry's architectural designs have become iconic structures. His continued exploration of the contoured fold resulted in his designs for the Guggenheim Museum in Bilbao (1993–1997), the Walt Disney Concert Hall in Los Angeles (2002), and 8 Spruce Street, a residential tower in Manhattan. Gehry returned to furniture design with the cardboard Experimental Edges (1979–1982) and the bent-wood Cross Check Furniture Collection manufactured by Knoll (designed 1989–1992). A portion of the Easy Edges line was reissued for manufacture by Vitra Design in 1986. Gehry later teamed with the Electric Machine and Equipment Company (Emeco) to produce the aluminum *SUPERLIGHT Chair* (designed in 2004), which is also represented in the DeMell Jacobsen Collection (Cat. No. 47).

Fig. 42.3 Frank O. Gehry, "Article of Furniture or the Like," U.S. Patent No. 4,067,615, filed May 15, 1972, issued January 10, 1978, U.S. Patent Office.

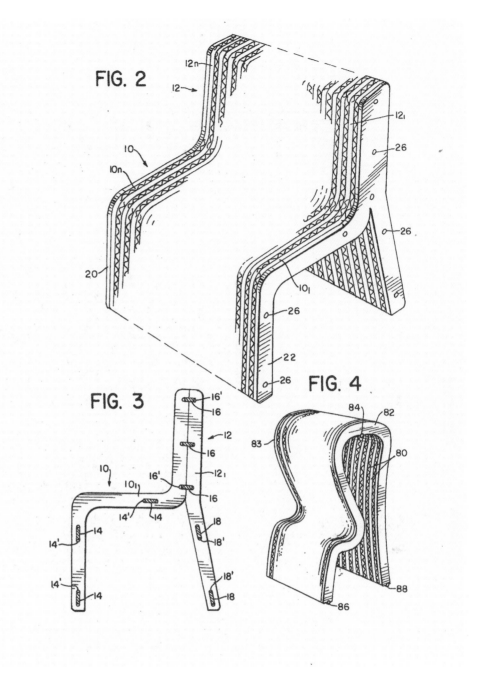

1   Karla Klein Albertson, "Frank Gehry: A Household Name in Architecture," Live Auctioneers, accessed October 1, 2015, https://www.liveauctioneers.com/news/style-century-magazine/frank-gehry-exceptional-furniture-enhanced/; "Frank O. Gehry," Academy of Achievement, last modified January 31, 2022, https://achievement.org/achiever/frank-gehry/.

2   Special thanks to Andrew VanStyn for his research and expertise. His contributions helped shape this essay.

3   "The History of the Cardboard Box," Attic Self Storage blog, May 29, 2017, https://www.atticstorage.co.uk/blog/the-history-of-the-cardboard-box.

4   Frank O. Gehry, "Article of Furniture or the Like," U.S. Patent No. 4,067,615, filed May 15, 1972, issued January 10, 1978, U.S. Patent Office.

5   Gehry.

6   For a thorough biography of Gehry, see Paul Goldberger, *Building Art: The Life and Work of Frank Gehry* (New York: Alfred A. Knopf, 1972); for a discussion of Gehry's cardboard furniture designs, see especially 170–76.

7   Gehry quoted in Goldberger, 170.

8   Gehry quoted in Goldberger, 171.

9   Gehry quoted in Francesco Dal Co and Kurt Walter Forster, *Frank O. Gehry: The Complete Works* (New York: Monacelli Press, 1998), 47.

10 Susan Grant Lewin, "Insight," *House Beautiful* 114, no. 5 (May 1972): 10.

11 Goldberger, 171–72.

12 Rita Reif, "Shop Talk: Mediterranean Style Upstaged," *New York Times*, April 12, 1972, 38. See also Norma Skurka, "Paper Furniture for Penny Pinchers," *New York Times Magazine*, April 9, 1972, 90–91.

13 *Easy Edges* brochure (New York: Easy Edges, Inc., 1972), Foundation curatorial files.

14 *Easy Edges* brochure.

15 *Easy Edges* brochure.

16 Gehry quoted in Rosemarie Haag Bletter, *The Architecture of Frank Gehry* (New York: Rizzoli, 1986), 64.

Sheraton Chair (No. 664)

43

designed 1978–1984; this example dated 1986

Designed by Robert Charles Venturi (1925–2018)

Manufactured by Knoll International
(active 1938–present, East Greenville, Pennsylvania,
and New York, New York)

Screen-printed plastic laminate over molded
plywood, leather upholstery

33 ½ x 23 ½ x 24 in.

AS THE ARC OF American styles continued its curve, new designs emerged in the 1980s and 1990s that were inspired by historical antecedents yet maintained the look and construction of modern materials and techniques. With whimsical and witty stylistic references, the *Sheraton Chair (No. 664)*—designed by Robert Venturi and a design team that included his wife Denise Scott Brown (b. 1931)—presents a sculptural and ornamental design that remains an iconic example of the Postmodern aesthetic.[1] Like the Sankofa bird that flies forward while looking back, the *Sheraton Chair* merged the use of modern materials, techniques, art, and architecture with a multicolored abstract version of Thomas Sheraton's late-18th-century designs for parlor chairs and chair backs (Fig. 43.1).

The *Sheraton Chair* was one in a collection that featured two tables, one sofa, and eight other seating examples, all of which were based on historic precedents and designed between 1978 and 1984. In addition to the *Sheraton Chair*, other seating examples included the *Chippendale Chair*, *Queen Anne Chair*, *Hepplewhite Chair*, *Empire Chair*, *Biedermeier Chair*, *Gothic Revival Chair*, *Art Nouveau Chair*, and *Art Deco Chair*. Following the modern process for designs with minimal materials, cost-effective mass production, and plywood molded for maximum comfort, Knoll produced an abundance of styles and surface patterns between 1984 and 1988.[2] While Robert Venturi was in charge of the design project, credit should also be given to project manager Maurice Weintraub and the design team of Denise Scott Brown, Erica Gees, Paul Muller, and John Rauch.[3] Venturi filed a design patent as an assignor to Knoll International, in 1983, in which he illustrated various viewpoints of the *Chippendale Chair* (Fig. 43.2).

Denise Scott Brown (née Lakofski) was born in Nkana, Northern Rhodesia (now Zambia), and always dreamed of becoming an architect. She first studied architecture in London and, following the death of her first husband in 1959, she continued her studies at the University of Pennsylvania, joining the faculty after her graduation in 1960. There she met fellow professor Robert Venturi; the couple married in 1967. Scott Brown joined the firm of Venturi and Rauch and became a full partner in 1969. Since then, she has continued to advance the field and advocate for the recognition of females in architecture and the workplace.

A native Philadelphian, Robert Venturi attended Princeton University, earning a bachelor of arts in 1947 and a master of fine arts in 1950. Further studies in Rome exposed Venturi to classical architecture. Upon his return, he gained practical experience with Eero Saarinen (Cat. Nos. 29 and 32), established his own firm, and became a professor of architecture. In 1966 he published his seminal work, *Complexity and Contradiction in Architecture*. Challenging the modernist mantra that "form follows function," Venturi believed "blatant simplification means bland architecture. Less is a bore."[4]

As a three-dimensional sculptural form, the *Sheraton Chair*—as with the others in the DeMell Jacobsen Collection—was intended to be viewed in the round.[5] The side view pays homage to the Eameses' (Cat. Nos. 29 and 31) and Alvar Aalto's plywood chairs. The *Sheraton Chair* is constructed of two sheets of molded, laminated, plywood "cut, shaped, and joined."[6] The edges are finished to retain the original state of the laminated wood, while a plastic laminate coats the back, seat, and legs. The lamination process was refined, resulting in a varied number of layers to accommodate structural and decorative needs. Inside the square seat back, the vase-shaped back splat is festooned with a draped swag, gadroon ornamentation, and plumed feathers. Allusions to carved elements, which suggest depth and dimension, are achieved through shaded tones and cutouts. As the designer explained, "our historical references are intended to be used symbolically and representationally, not accurately. The historic representation is a picture of a style. It is not intended to fool you. The profile is abstracted and generalized to stress silhouette. Our aim is exemplification and representation, not reproduction."[7] A black leather cushion softens the seating experience.

In 1972, Robert Venturi, Denise Scott Brown, and Stephen Izenour (1940–2001) co-authored another important publication, *Learning from Las Vegas: The Forgotten Symbolism of Architectural Form*, in which the authors "call[ed] for architects to be more receptive to the tastes and values of 'common' people and less immodest in

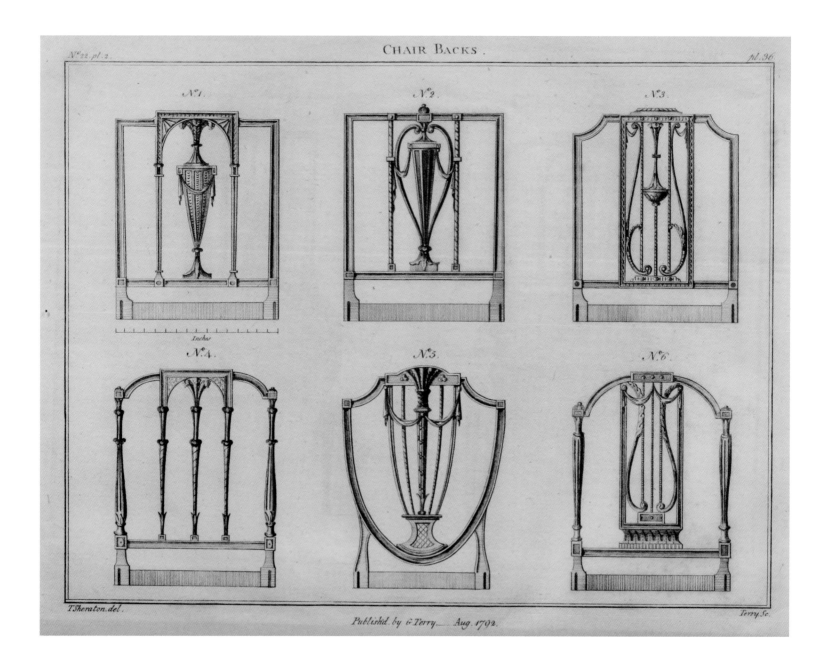

N.1.   N.2.   N.3.

Inches

N.4.   N.5.   N.6.

T.Sheraton.del.

Publish'd by G Terry __ Aug. 1792.

Terry Sc.

their erections of 'heroic,' self-aggrandizing monuments."[8] The design for the *Sheraton Chair* embodies the concepts from the Las Vegas studies with a colorful façade. The screen-printing process recalls the works of Andy Warhol (1928–1987). The chair is a lesson in intellectually analyzing past cultures and designs while incorporating them into modern styles and methods.

Awarded the Pritzker Prize in 1991, Robert Venturi credited his wife, Denise Scott Brown, and together they advanced Postmodern designs by incorporating traditional and vernacular styles. In 2009, Venturi stated, "We were revolutionary in being evolutionary."[9] Their award-winning

Philadelphia firm VSBA, LLC (Venturi Scott Brown Associates) focuses on academic, cultural, civic, and institutional architectural and design projects. Architectural masterpieces include the Vanna Venturi home in Philadelphia, the Sainsbury Wing of the National Gallery in London, the Denver Public Library, and the Seattle Art Museum, among others.

1   Special thanks to Andrew VanStyn for sharing his research and expertise on the history and design of this chair, which has helped to shape this essay.

2   David Bruce Brownlee, Robert Venturi, and Denise Scott Brown, *Out of the Ordinary: Robert Venturi, Denise Scott Brown and Associates: Architecture, Urbanism, Design* (Philadelphia: Philadelphia Museum of Art in association with Yale University Press, 2001), 215.

3   Sue Scanlon (personal assistant to Denise Scott Brown, VSBA) to Foundation staff, email, May 1, 2013.

4   Karissa Rosenfield, "History for Sale: Postmodern Vanna Venturi House on the Market," *Arch Daily*, July 15, 2015, https://www.archdaily.com/770423/history-for-sale-postmodern-vanna-venturi-house-on-the-market.

5   See Robert Venturi, "Chair," U.S. Design Patent No. 287,438, filed November 1, 1983, issued December 30, 1986, U.S. Patent Office.

6   Robert Venturi and Denise Scott Brown, "Process and Symbol in the Design of Furniture for Knoll," *Space Design*, no. 241 (October 1984).

7   Venturi and Brown.

8   See https://sicm.mitpress.mit.edu/books/learning-las-vegas-revised-edition, accessed May 11, 2022.

9   Andrea Tamas, "Interview: Robert Venturi & Denise Scott Brown," *Arch Daily*, April 25, 2011, https://www.archdaily.com/130389/interview-robert-venturi-denise-scott-brown-by-andrea-tamas.

Fig. 43.1 (opposite) Late-18th-century designs for chair backs, from Thomas Sheraton, *The Cabinet-Maker and Upholsterer's Drawing Book* (1802).

Fig. 43.2 (right) Robert Venturi, "Chair", U.S. Design Patent No. 287,438, filed November 1, 1983, issued December 30, 1986, U.S. Patent Office.

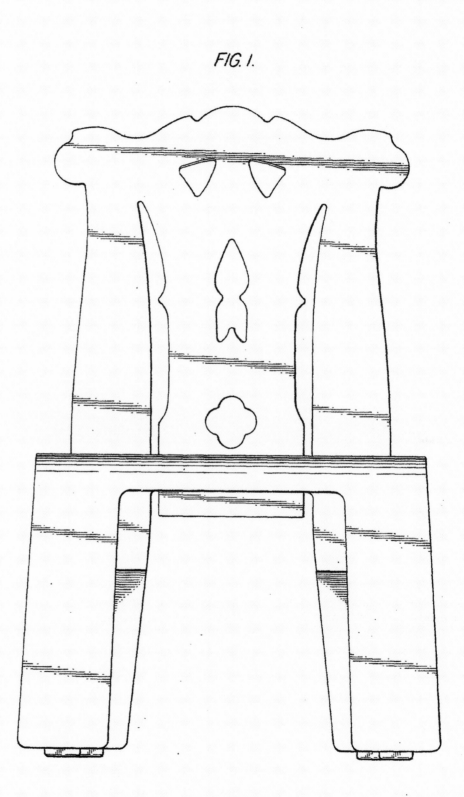

FIG. 1.

Brushstroke Chair, Wood and Brushstroke Ottoman, Wood

44

1986–1988

Designed by Roy Fox Lichtenstein
(1923–1997) in collaboration with
Graphicstudio, University of South Florida
(active 1968–present, Tampa, Florida)

Manufactured by Beeken Parsons
(active 1983–present, Shelburne, Vermont)

Laminated white birch veneer, paint,
and clear varnish

Chair: 70 11/16 x 18 x 27 1/4 in.
Ottoman: 20 3/4 x 17 3/4 x 24 in.

Signed (on underside of chair and
ottoman) R. Lichtenstein / B.A.T.

WHAT IF THE elemental essence of a painting—the brushstroke—existed in a three-dimensional functional form? American Pop artist Roy Lichtenstein envisioned just such a creation and collaborated with Graphicstudio, an atelier at the University of South Florida in Tampa, to realize limited editions of the *Brushstroke Chair, Wood* and *Brushstroke Ottoman, Wood* in which the sitter—even the artist himself—becomes part of the narrative of the creative act of painting (Fig. 44.1). The DeMell Jacobsen Collection example is a *bon à tirer*—the final proof approved by the artist prior to execution of the editioned multiples—annotated "B.A.T." by Lichtenstein (Fig. 44.2). The edition contained a total of 12 chairs, four of which were paired with ottomans.[1]

Artists contemplate and explore the painterly hand through brushstrokes. A smooth, glossy application of oil paint to canvas erases all evidence of human intervention, while the quick daubs made famous by the Impressionists emphasize it. Thick layers of paint were dripped and splattered by Abstract Expressionists, or slathered on with palette knives and other tools by contemporary artists. Lichtenstein, an important 20th-century artist and a leader of the Pop Art movement, conducted his

own investigation of the brushstroke after viewing a comic by Dick Giordano (1932–2010) that appeared in the October 1964 issue (#72) of *Strange Suspense Stories*.[2] Lichtenstein recalled, "Although I had played with the idea before, it started with a comic book image of a mad cartoonist crossing out, with a large brushstroke 'X,' the face of a fiend that was haunting him ... I did a painting of this ... The very nature of a brushstroke is anathema to outlining and filling in as used in cartoons. So I developed a form for it, which is what I am trying to do in the explosions, airplanes, and people— that is, to get a standardized thing—a stamp or image ... The brushstrokes obviously refer to Abstract Expressionism."[3]

Born and raised in New York City, Lichtenstein's passion for art began at a young age when his mother, Beatrice Werner Lichtenstein, took her son to museums. He often visited the Museum of Modern Art, where his favorite painting, *Guernica* (1937) by Pablo Picasso (1881–1973), was on long-term loan.[4] After graduating from high school in 1940, Lichtenstein enrolled at the Art Students League, where he took classes with Reginald Marsh (1898–1954). Next, he studied art under Hoyt Lee Sherman (1903–1981) at the Ohio State University in Columbus, Ohio. Sherman's tutelage greatly influenced Lichtenstein's lifelong quest to reconsider and question the "accepted canons of taste" and to explore a "perception-based approach to art."[5] Lichtenstein's active service in the U.S. Army both during and after World War II placed his education on hold. Although he planned to continue his studies at the Sorbonne in 1945, he returned to New York City to be near his father, Milton Lichtenstein, who was in declining health. Following the death of his father in 1946, Lichtenstein returned to Columbus, finished his bachelor of fine arts degree, and became an instructor in the School of Fine and Applied Arts at Ohio State.

By 1957 Lichtenstein, his wife, and their two sons had moved to Oswego, New York, where he became an industrial design instructor at the State University of New York. There, Lichtenstein experimented with gestural abstraction by "applying broad swaths of pigment to the canvas by dragging the paint across its surface with a rag wrapped around his arm."[6] Simultaneously, he began to feature figures inspired by comic books in his works. In 1960 Lichtenstein

accepted a position at Douglass College in New Brunswick, New Jersey. There, he revisited his use of cartoon characters and began to incorporate his trademark Ben-Day dots.[7] His February 1962 solo exhibition at the Leo Castelli Gallery in New York, combined with his subsequent inclusion in the *International Exhibition of the New Realists*— the first important Pop Art show, held at the Sidney Janis Gallery, New York—catapulted Lichtenstein onto the Pop Art scene.

During his career, Lichtenstein analyzed the brushstroke in a variety of media and dimensions. In 1965 and 1966 he created the *Brushstroke* series of paintings as a response to Abstract Expressionism through a parody of brushstrokes and splatters executed in a cartoon-like application (Fig. 44.3). "By rendering these spontaneous, autographic marks in a clichéd commercial art style, Lichtenstein questioned the authority of these purportedly inimitable gestures."[8] The artist explained, "Brushstrokes in a painting convey a sense of grand gesture; but in my hands, the brushstroke becomes a depiction of a grand gesture."[9]

Fig. 44.1 Roy Lichtenstein holding a paintbrush while seated in his *Brushstroke Chair, Bronze* with *Brushstroke Ottoman, Bronze*, July 1987.

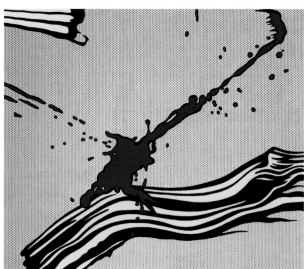

Fig. 44.2 (above) Detail of signature and "B.A.T." (*bon à tirer*) annotation on underside of chair.

Fig. 44.3 (left) Roy Lichtenstein (1923–1997), *Brushstroke with Spatter*, 1966, oil and magna on canvas, 68 x 80 in., Art Institute of Chicago.

Nearly 30 years later, Lichtenstein's three-dimensional sculpture *Brushstrokes in Flight* (1984) debuted at the Columbus International Airport in Ohio, followed by his *Salute to Painting* (1986) at the Walker Art Center in Minneapolis, Minnesota. Of their inspiration Lichtenstein said: "It [the *Brushstroke*] was the way of portraying this romantic and bravura symbol in its opposite style, classicism. The *Brushstroke* plays a big part in the history of art. Brushstroke almost means painting or art. I did isolated *Brushstroke*s in 1965 and used cartoon brushstrokes to depict subject matters in the 80s. I also did *Brushstroke* sculptures in bronze and wood to make them more palpable ... the *Brushstroke*, it is just an idea to start with, and painting it makes it more concrete, but when

you do it in bronze sculpture, it becomes real and has weight and is absurd, contradictory and funny."[10] Four years later, Lichtenstein further pushed the boundaries of his iconic brushstroke and human interaction with his functional sculptures *Brushstroke Chair, Wood* and *Brushstroke Ottoman, Wood* (Figs. 44.4 and 44.5).

In the mid-1980s Lichtenstein also collaborated with Graphicstudio to create a number of prints and decorative art objects featuring his signature brushstrokes. Founded by Donald J. Saff (b. 1937) in 1968, Graphicstudio combines art, education, and the production of fine art publications. From its inception, the atelier collaborated with artists of the Pop Art movement, beginning with Robert Rauschenberg (1925–2008),

to produce innovative and affordable art. Today, Graphicstudio continues to work with emerging and established international artists in a variety of printmaking techniques to produce sculptural multiples in a variety of media.[11]

Brushstroke Chair, Wood and *Brushstroke Ottoman, Wood* were a serendipitous outcome of initial research and fabrication experiments at Graphicstudio leading up to Lichtenstein's *Brushstroke Figures* series of eight prints (1987–1989). Saff recounted: "our experiments at Graphicstudio with the Brushstroke form from Mr. Lichtenstein's studio floor included rendering the sample shape in virtually every sculpture medium but bronze. These forms, along with the other experiments in waxtype and various other print media, were presented to Mr. Lichtenstein for this review. He would later relate to me that, upon seeing the samples, his mind immediately grasped the idea for a sculpture project and that the concept of a furniture motif would not leave his thoughts."[12]

Following nine months of exhaustive research into the structural requirements as well as the visual aesthetics of various wood veneers, the furniture-making shop of Beeken Parsons in Shelburne, Vermont, created a wood prototype. Using a cardboard mock-up made by Lichtenstein, the duo made drawings on Mylar, including side elevations, which next helped guide them with the design and fabrication of a mold into which the veneers would be pressed. Jeff Parsons (b. 1956) recalled, "We made patterns from those [drawings]. From the patterns we made the parts of the forms, then bolted all the parts of the forms together, and *then* we made the prototype."[13]

The process of creating a sinuous three-dimensional brushstroke form that was structurally sturdy and stable enough to hold a seated person presented a challenge to the woodworkers: "There was more involved than we thought there probably would be at the onset. Fairly quickly we realized that the amount of pressure that was going to be required to meet the glue specifications was going to be significant. With some primitive calculations we realized the best thing we could do was get some engineering help. A couple of engineers [from] the University of Vermont sat down with us and in about

two hours of calculations came up with a shopping list of the steel that we needed to distribute the pressure evenly and deliver the amount of pressure that was going to be required."[14] To ultimately close the form, Beeken and Parsons discovered that more pressure was needed to shape and adhere the veneers.

Each of the finished wood chairs in the edition were assembled from two key components: the front leg, seat, and back of the chair were one component, and the back leg and underside were another. The ottoman was constructed in similar manner. Each component consisted of 27 sheets of white birch veneer, glued together in three individual layers: seven veneer sheets were pressed and glued to form the top layer, seven additional sheets were pressed and glued to form the bottom

layer, and 13 sheets formed the inner core. Once the exterior layers were fabricated, a jigsaw was used to fashion the cut-out areas, guided by a template made from the full-scale drawing. Before being placed in a mold for a final gluing, the central core was hand-painted in blue. Lastly, the jigsaw was again used to shape the outer edges, and the chairs were sanded and then sealed using a clear varnish.

The *Brushstroke Chair, Wood* and *Brushstroke Ottoman, Wood* straddle the boundaries of contemporary art, sculpture, and functional decorative art. The elemental basis of a chair is literally a work of art for the aesthetic quality, comfort, and support of a human form. Its performance in the theater of decorative art and design set the stage for future designers, such as Vivian Beer (Cat. No. 46).

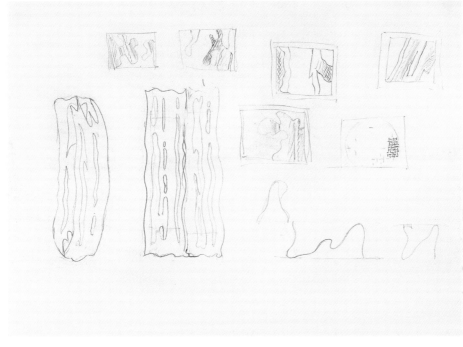

Figs. 44.4 and 44.5
Roy Lichtenstein (1923–1997), workshop drawings for *Brushstroke Chair, Wood*, c. 1986.

1   In addition to the *bon à tirer* proof in the DeMell Jacobsen Collection, the edition included one proof for the National Gallery of Art, one proof for the University of South Florida, and three artist's proofs. Another series cast in bronze and with a blue-and-black color scheme, in an edition of five, was titled *Brushstroke Chair, Bronze* and *Brushstroke Ottoman, Bronze* (1986–1988). For a thorough description of the editions and their fabrication, see Ruth E. Fine and Mary Lee Corlett, *Graphicstudio: Contemporary Art from the Collaborative Workshop at the University of South Florida* (Washington, DC: National Gallery of Art, 1991), 265–69. See also Jade Dellinger, *Graphicstudio: Uncommon Practice at USF* (London: Giles, 2014).

2   "Roy Lichtenstein, Brushstroke Chair and Ottoman," *Masterworks*, Wright, Chicago, November 21, 2017,

lot 10, https://www.wright20.com/auctions/2017/11/masterworks/10.

3   John Coplans, "Talking with Roy Lichtenstein," *Artforum* 5, no. 9 (May 1967): 34–39.

4   Avis Berman, "Biography," Roy Lichtenstein Foundation, accessed August 4, 2018, https://lichtensteinfoundation.org/biography/.

5   Berman.

6   Berman.

7   Dating from 1879 and named for Benjamin Hardy Day Jr., this printing process uses small dots to create the effect, color, and shading desired. Comic books printed in the 1950s and 1960s used the process to great effect, which Lichtenstein appropriated.

8   "Brushstrokes, 1965 by Roy Lichtenstein," Roy Lichtenstein, accessed August 11, 2018, https://www.roylichtenstein.com/brushstrokes.jsp.

9   "Brushstrokes, 1965."

10   Gianni Mercurio, *Roy Lichtenstein: Meditations on Art* (Milan: Skira, 2010). 211.

11   "Graphicstudio," University of South Florida, accessed August 4, 2018, http://www.graphicstudio.usf.edu/GS/gs_about.html.

12   Donald J. Saff quoted in Fine and Corlett, Graphicstudio, 266.

13   Jeff Parsons quoted in Fine and Corlett, 267.

14   Fine and Corlett, 267.

Synergistic Synthesis XVII_{B1} (or sub B1) [Informed Intuition] Chair

45

2003

Designed and manufactured by Kenneth Smythe
(b. 1937) (active 1968–present, Berkeley, California)

Finnish birch laminate, Formica ColorCore,
latigo leather, Sunbrella acrylic, top-grain leather,
foam rubber, steel, maple dowels

32 x 32 x 32 in.

DYNAMIC, COLORFUL, and a truly unique design, the *Synergistic Synthesis XVII_{B1} (or sub B1) [Informed Intuition] Chair* is a contemporary piece that has yet to be classified or associated with any modern art movement or style. Its design evolved through numerous drawings and was handcrafted by Kenneth Smythe.[1] His process involves creating scaled graph-paper drawings, continuing through multiple iterations until he arrives at a final design. Smythe conceives of his designs as continuations within a series, like the Fibonacci sequence, rather than as singular works, and he fabricates his unique creations by hand in his studio and workshop in Berkeley, California (Fig. 45.1).

Kenneth Smythe was reared in New Britain, Connecticut, and relocated to Berkeley in 1968 to study architecture. Settling on the West Coast, he is accomplished in science, art, design, and furniture making. Throughout his career, his designs demonstrate a specific evolution. While the design focus is consistent with a defined seat height and line, the qualities change according to Smythe's preferences over time. It is the journey of the design that intrigues him. Each series is a permutation of complex theories, as seen in the evolutionary models of nature. Numerous influences inform Smythe's designs, including the theories of mathematician and philosopher Bertrand Russell (1872–1970) and composer Frederick A. T. Delius (1862–1934).

The drawing for *Synergistic Synthesis XVII_{B1}* (or *sub B1*) *[Informed Intuition] Chair*, presented at 1/5 scale, indicates the side profile was conceived and designed in July–August 1998 (Fig. 45.2). This chair's lateral stacking of plywood components, or "front view spacing," dates back to his design for *Synergistic Synthesis III_{B1}*, subtitled "A Catholic Vocabulary." That chair was initially conceived in July 1982, with 11 subsequent refinements through 1998 (Fig. 45.3). The example in the DeMell Jacobsen Collection was executed in 2003.

As with many of his early designs, Smythe's chairs are often comprised of Finnish birch laminate, layered and faced with Formica ColorCore plastic. The materials are bound with a threaded rod whose ends are covered with decorative and functional large disk bosses. While the chair may appear able to rock on a curule-shaped undercarriage, the seat is static. The Sunbrella and latigo-leather sling seat and back are secured by maple rods tethered in an alternating pattern. These dowel-shaped rods create the perception of flexibility; if the viewer were able to remove a rod, the many individual parts that comprise the chair would be seen.[2] Colorful accents decorate the side surfaces to highlight individual elements of the composition and represent mathematical calculations. The composition is balanced for an even distribution of weight—functionally and visually—resulting in a symbiotic relationship.

Although contemporary laser-cutting technology might industrialize the production, Smythe prefers to hand-cut and hand-finish the edges, which seems counter to his stated goal of creating mass-produced unique designs. Smythe, through his draftsmanship and craftsmanship, gives both a theoretical and practical presentation of a contemporary chair within the continuum of artistry and design. Rather than biomorphism, the aesthetic suggests construction by a futuristic computer or artificial intelligence—a quantum leap in furniture design.

1   Andrew VanStyn spoke with the artist in 2010. Special thanks to him for sharing his extensive research, which has greatly helped to shape this essay.
2   Information about the rods and structure of the chair was provided to Aaron Garvey directly by the artist. Foundation curatorial files, January 2011.

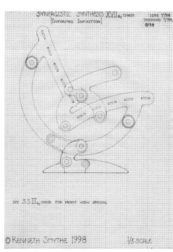

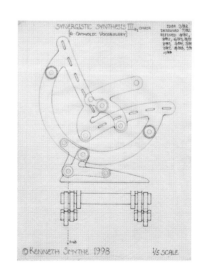

Fig. 45.1 Kenneth Smythe in his studio, Berkeley, California, date unknown.

Fig. 45.2 Kenneth Smythe (b. 1937), Design drawing for *Synergistic Synthesis XVII_{B1}*, 1998.

Fig 45.3 Kenneth Smythe (b. 1937), Design drawing for *Synergistic Synthesis III_{B1}*, 1998.

Current, No. 2

designed 2004; this example executed in 2007

Designed and manufactured by Vivian Beer (b. 1977) (active Penland, North Carolina, and Manchester, New Hampshire)

Bent and welded steel, auto-body paint

36 x 16 x 24 in.

Signed on underside: Vivian Beer 2007 / 'current' no. 2 (Fig. 46.1)

JUST AS SAMUEL GRAGG (Cat. No. 2) gave elasticity to steam-bent wood in his revolutionary chair designs of the early 19th century, so Vivian Beer challenges our perceptions through her use of heat-bent and welded steel to create *Current, No. 2*, an organically flowing and ergonomically pleasing chair. Beginning with a self-described "sophisticated daydreaming" process, she selects a variety of items that "embody beauty and power: flags, fenders, clouds, tides, tail feathers, rodeos and corporate logos all come into the mix."[1] To these she adds "a sense of architecture and furniture design to create objects that are steel calligrapher's lines in three-dimensions."[2] She combines traditional decorative motifs, modern aesthetics, and classic abstraction to create unique or small-editioned pieces of furniture that "reference the long arc of history" but "are a simple thing to touch and sit on and a pleasure to live with."[3] In her design for this chair, Beer conceptualized a form "that is strong like a bridge and light like a breeze ... a thing that we are caught in like the running tide."[4]

Current visually appears to be constructed from a single sheet of steel sliced into strips that separate and bend in oblique and acute curves to form the back, seat, and legs of a chair. In actuality, the form consists of steel strips that were heated and bent over a jig and "carefully fabricated to seem as if it was cut apart rather than assembled," which creates a *trompe l'oeil* (fool the eye) effect (Figs. 46.2 and 46.3).[5] For Beer, the process of formation is essential

"because it creates a slight modulation in the stock, which punctuates each bend," giving "the overall form a visceral 'truth' to reinforce the 'trick' of its fabrication."[6] Beer explains, "I wanted this chair to seem as if it had been cut and crushed out of a single sheet of metal. At the same time, I wanted it to feel as fast and clean as water in its silhouette with the power of an implied brutal forming in the background. The balance and trickery is important."[7] Welded, ground, and sanded smooth to complete the subtle trick of the eye, the chair was coated with vivid blue auto-body paint. Chosen for their durability, industrial auto paints also resonate with a cultural knowledge. *Current* represents the artist's introduction of counterbalancing color with "the strong and raw nature of steel and form."[8] She states, "It gives the chair a cultural access point, as the form gives it a visceral one."[9]

Born in rural Bar Harbor, Maine, Beer was reared with an ethos of fine craftsmanship and has worked with tools since childhood. At the Maine College of Art, she received a "very formal, Bauhaus-style art education,"[10] which continued to influence her designs and her embrace of abstraction. *Current* is a culmination of her "Permutations," which she began in 2004 when she was studying metalworking toward her master of fine arts degree at the Cranbrook Academy of Art. Steeped in the historical development of architecture and industrial furniture design, Cranbrook gave Beer an introduction to the decorative arts and the complex challenges of designing furniture.[11] Beer's design

Fig. 46.1 Detail of signature on underside of chair.

of *Current*—which she initially executed during her residency at the Penland School of Craft—offers an interesting comparison with another Cranbrook alumnus: metalwork department head Harry Bertoia and his *Large Diamond Chair* (Cat. No. 35), in which space and air were part of the design.

As a furniture designer and maker, Beer continues the rich tradition of other American artists of the Studio Furniture Movement, such as Wharton Esherick (1887–1970), George Nakashima (Cat. No. 39), Sam Maloof (1916–2009), Wendell Castle (Cat. No. 40), and Jon Brooks (Cat. No. 41). For Beer, a piece of furniture is not only a form of sculpture, but also part of a conversation and performance for the sitter. She believes that "form follows imagination, and function is a script for where and how we interact with these creatures we live with."[12]

From her studio in Manchester, New Hampshire, Beer "deftly counterbalances a strong knowledge of contemporary furniture design with the history of industry and architecture to create furniture that intends to transform our expectations of and relationships to the domestic landscape."[13] Whether she wields a blowtorch, an English wheel, or an electric buffer, she approaches the material with power and manipulates it into unique aesthetic forms. Her furniture pushes the boundaries between art and craft, utilitarian object and sculpture, while initiating imaginative dialogues. The artist contends that "when you sit on a chair, you enter the story of that chair ... They have arms and backs and legs just like us. They have a personality and a story just like us."[14] When a sitter on a chair is viewed by others, Beer continues, "it becomes in a subtle sense, a performance."[15]

Examples of Beer's furniture may be found in the collections of the Brooklyn Museum; the Fuller Craft Museum, Brockton, Massachusetts; the Currier Museum of Art; the Museum of Fine Arts, Boston; and the Renwick Gallery, Smithsonian American Art Museum, Washington, D.C. In addition, the artist has received a number of public commissions, including those in Winslow Park in Portland, Maine; the National Ornamental Metal Museum in Memphis, Tennessee; and Old Morse Park in Cambridge, Massachusetts. She served as an artist in residence at the Penland School of Craft in 2005–2008, at Purchase College in New York in 2011, and at San Diego State University in California in 2012. That same year, her work was included in the seminal exhibition *40 Under 40: Craft Futures* organized by the Renwick Gallery. Pursuing her fascination with metalworking and the design of automobiles and aircraft, in 2015 Beer took a position as a research fellow at the National Air and Space Museum, Smithsonian Institution. Most recently, Beer bested seven other designers and emerged victorious in season two of *Ellen's Design Challenge*, hosted by design collector and television personality Ellen DeGeneres.

1   Vivian Beer, "Artist Statement," Foundation curatorial files.
2   Beer.
3   Tina Coplan, "Young Visionaries," *Home & Design Magazine*, July/August 2012, 188–94.
4   Vivian Beer, "Designing Current," personal communication to the Foundation, December 2010.
5   Beer, "Designing Current."
6   Beer.
7   Beer.
8   Beer.
9   Beer.
10 Julie K. Hanus, "Curves Ahead," *American Craft* 71, no. 3 (June/July 2011): 36.
11 Hanus, 36.
12 Beer, "Artist Statement."
13 Vivian Beer, "Bio," Foundation curatorial files.
14 Beer quoted in Jennifer Osborn, "The Sculptor's Hand," *Ellsworth American* (Hancock County, ME), September 11, 2008.
15 Beer quoted in Osborn.

SUPERLIGHT Chair

designed 2004; this example (SUPERX model) designed 2005, executed 2010–2011[1]

Designed by Frank Owen Gehry (b. 1929). Manufactured by the Electric Machine and Equipment Company (Emeco; active 1944–present, Hanover, Pennsylvania)

Anodized and hand-brushed recycled aluminum

31 ¾ x 16 ½ x 20 ½ in.

FRANK GEHRY'S design for the *SUPERLIGHT Chair* illustrates his most recent and successful effort to create a lightweight chair that requires minimal construction, echoing his architectural designs in a technical and material sense. "I wanted three things in this chair: comfort, light weight, and strength. Aluminum was the obvious choice and Emeco was the only company that could make it."[2]

Intrigued by Emeco's *1006 Navy Chair* (Cat. No. 30) and Philippe Starck–designed *Hudson* chairs, which had been purchased for his architectural office, Gehry approached Gregg Buchbinder, Emeco's chairman, about designing his own chair for the firm (Fig. 47.3). The result was a chair made from anodized and hand-brushed recycled aluminum that weighs an incredibly light nine pounds.[3] Despite its minimal weight, the chair's frame and body-conforming "skin" can support 750 pounds. The single-panel seat and back wrap around a tubular aluminum frame that, owing to its delicacy and hinge mount, allows the chair to respond to the sitter's weight with a gentle swaying motion. *SUPERLIGHT* "moves to accommodate all body types—the sitter activates the chair," said Gehry.[4]

Emeco chairman Gregg Buchbinder described the collaboration:

Emeco spent sixty years perfecting strong, rigid chairs. Frank asked us to keep the strength but add flex and movement. It was a challenge that our production experts ate up. Our proprietary heat treatment creates a structure that is three times the strength of steel. We found an old machine on site that turns the aluminum like hemming fabric, and at the same time creates a structural tube along the edge of the chair's shell. This enabled us to perfect the single sheet skin. This is an honest example of a dialogue between a manufacturer with a unique production method, and a designer with a unique vision. Our relationship is based on respect and freedom, enjoyment and intensity.[5]

Following an 11-month design period, the chair debuted in April 2004 at the Salone

U.S. Patent Jul. 18, 2006 Sheet 1 of 5 US D525,041 S

FIG. 1

Fig. 47.1 Frank O. Gehry, "Chair," U.S. Design Patent No. 525,041, filed September 12, 2005, issued July 18, 2006.

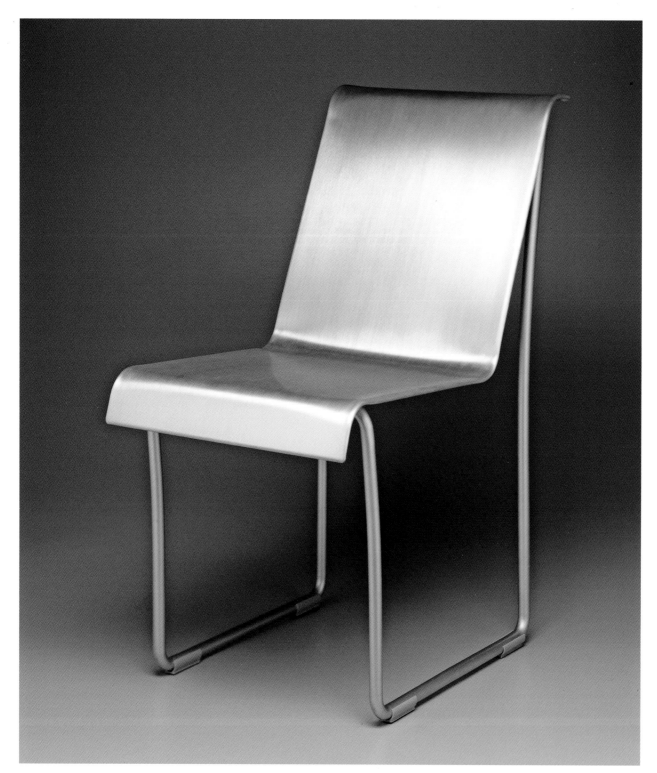

Fig. 47.2 Early version of the *SUPERLIGHT Chair* with parallel leg design.

del Mobile in Milan. Gehry acknowledged Gio Ponti's 1957 *Superleggera* (Italian for "superlight") as the inspiration for the *SUPERLIGHT*'s design: "I've always wanted to design a super lightweight chair. I tried to extract the essence—structure and skin, where engineering and design are one thing."[6]

Unlike Ponti's chair, however, which was largely made from wood, the tubular construction of Gehry's design more appropriately references another innovative mid-century "superlight": the tube-frame or superleggera construction of the Aston Martin sports car.[7] Like the automobile, the chair's frame (structure)

and skin (surface) neatly unite to meet the functional and aesthetic requirements of the whole. Similarly, Gehry's chair may draw parallels to the *Lounge Chair* designed by Warren McArthur Jr. (Cat. No. 27), also made of tubular anodized aluminum, as well as the *"Elastic" Side Chair* (Cat. No. 2) designed and made by

Samuel Gragg from steam-bent wood nearly two centuries before.

Early versions of the *SUPERLIGHT Chair* possessed legs that were aligned in parallel (Fig. 47.2). However, in 2005 Gehry filed a subsequent patent for the chair with an X-shaped base (Fig 47.1), which became known as the *SUPERX* model. The year it was introduced, the *SUPERLIGHT Chair* received the Good Design Award and was featured as one of *Architectural Record* magazine's top products. The design

is found in many museum collections, including Cooper Hewitt, Smithsonian Design Museum in New York, the Dallas Museum of Art, the San Francisco Museum of Modern Art, and the Pinakothek der Moderne in Munich, Germany.

1   Special thanks to the Electric Machine and Equipment Company (Emeco) for the generous donation of the *SUPERLIGHT Chair* to the Thomas H. and Diane DeMell Jacobsen Ph.D. Foundation.
2   "Frank Gehry," Emeco, accessed January 10, 2022, https://www.emeco.net/about/designers/frank-gehry.
3   Earlier versions of the *SUPERLIGHT Chair* weighed 6.5 pounds. Frank Gehry describes his "nutty passion" for making a lightweight chair in Eames Demetrios's 2004 short film *Ping Pong* (video, 23 mins.), https://vimeo.com/42639732. Eames Demetrios is the grandson of Charles and Ray Eames (Cat. Nos. 29 and 31).
4   *SUPERLIGHT by Gehry*, product brochure, Emeco, accessed January 13, 2019, https://emeco.centracdn.net/client/dynamic/articles/emeco-superlight-by-gehry_1258.pdf.
5   Paul Petrunia, "Newest Chair Design by Frank Gehry," *Archinect*, June 2, 2004, https://archinect.com/news/article/1666/newest-chair-design-by-frank-gehry.
6   Gehry quoted in "Frank Gehry."
7   Aston Martin DBS was referred to as DBS Superleggera in models built prior to 2022.

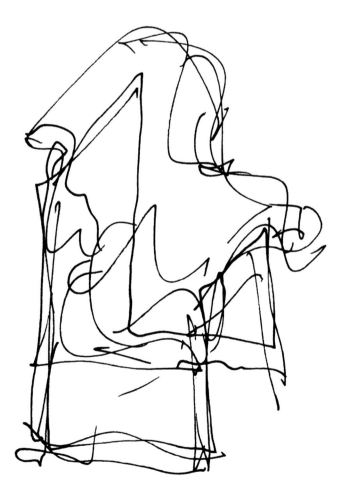

Fig. 47.3 Frank Gehry (b. 1929), Initial design sketch for the *SUPERLIGHT Chair*, May 2003.

Ionic Bench

48

2010

Designed by Laurie Beckerman (b. 1953)

Manufactured by Wellstone NYC Custom Woodworking, formerly Heritage Woodshop, Inc. (active 1995–present, Brooklyn, New York)

Laminated Baltic birch plywood, clear Italian acrylic varnish

21 x 49 x 18 in.

SPANNING TWO centuries of American seating furniture, this chair collection represents a full circle of design with the classical yet thoroughly contemporary *Ionic Bench*. In form and function, the *Ionic Bench* is a perfect synthesis of balance, order, and harmony. While its design references historic antecedents, it is purely contemporary in both method and material. This example is the first *Ionic Bench* produced by Laurie Beckerman; other iterations of the design include a steel version.

Born in Brooklyn, Beckerman graduated from New York University with a bachelor of arts in anthropology and earned a second bachelor of arts degree in architecture from Pratt Institute. Upon graduation, she designed low-income housing in Brooklyn and Harlem for the Pratt Architectural Collaborative and later worked for architect Steven Holl (b. 1947). While a student, Beckerman developed an interest in the material, form, function, process, and scale of furniture design. Working at the Cathedral of St. John the Divine in New York City as a liaison between the architecture office and the stone yard, she gained invaluable hands-on experience and a deeper appreciation of working with stone. Her first furniture design, a table, was made from stone. She has experimented with designing other forms, including chairs and lamps.

In her brainstorming process for the *Ionic Bench*, Beckerman didn't initially set out to reinvent the ancient Grecian column capital. As her sketches emerged, however, she contemplated its universal and timeless appeal:

It wasn't until I looked at the sketch that it reminded me of the capital of an Ionic Column—it must have been some shape

that I liked, unconsciously. This is the first time that I've referred to a classical form to inspire me, but as I researched it I learned that it is considered a feminine form, pleasing, sensual, symmetrical/balanced, it could be a woman's body, cinched at the waist -----. which may explain it's [*sic*] universal appeal, then and in modern times.[1]

A key development in Beckerman's design of the scrolls was her understanding and use of the golden ratio. Mathematically and geometrically, the golden ratio is an equation that compares the proportional balance and harmony of individual parts to the whole in a ratio of 1:1.618. Found in nature and music, the golden ratio has been applied to art and architecture for millennia, dating back to the Egyptian pyramids and the Greek sculptures of Phidias. Known as the Divine Proportion during the Renaissance, the formula was employed in the design of both Romanesque- and Gothic-style buildings. The ratio also appeared in artwork, ranging from that of Leonardo da Vinci and Michelangelo to later artists including Georges Seurat,

Salvador Dalí, and Piet Mondrian. Le Corbusier combined the golden ratio with the studies of Leonardo's *Vitruvian Man* and the Fibonacci sequence in his International Style designs. Beckerman considered the harmony of the *Ionic Bench*: "Because of the simplicity of the bench, this is especially critical—it's all about a beautiful proportion ... Not only do I strive to achieve proportion between the physical components of the form but of the space in between."[2]

After numerous hand-drawings and refinements to hone the profile of the shape (Figs. 48.1 and 48.2), Beckerman fabricated a small three-dimensional maquette and executed full-scale drawings. Having resolved the form, she next sought a suitable material and fabricator. Rather than replicating the classical design in traditional stone, however, the artist envisioned a "light, resilient and elegant" example. "Sometimes a material is the inspiration and then I would ask myself what form will show it off best," explained Beckerman. "In this case, the form came first so I ask, what material would best express it. A strong form like this could be made in many materials—Corian, which would be smooth, sensual and pristine, or

acrylic—light and ethereal, or metal—sleek and modern. Each material would give it something else. I try to imagine it in each."[3]

Initially rejecting the use of acrylic and metal due to the high cost of the materials, Beckerman ultimately settled on Baltic birch plywood for its "warm, earthy, sensual" qualities. "I never worked in wood before, so this in itself was interesting. And then I thought how great it's going to look revealing the plies. Turns out it was so logical using plywood in this way—to make a form that appears so light, yet be strong enough to carry 400 pounds (2 men) and give this unusual illusion. What is going on here—to see the plies on the seat surface as opposed to the usual place along the side edges. A trick to the eye—I liked that twist. The plies also add life and movement."[4] In her effort to create illusion, Beckerman's design for the *Ionic Bench* inspires parallels with *Current, No. 2* by Vivian Beer (Cat. No. 46), while her use of exposed plies recalls Frank Gehry's use of laminated die-cut cardboard in his design for the *Contour Bar Stool (No. 10-415)* (Cat. No. 42).

Beckerman fashioned a full-scale mock-up of the bench, which she lived with

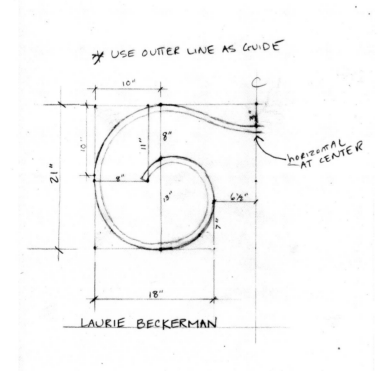

※ USE OUTTER LINE AS GUIDE

LAURIE BECKERMAN

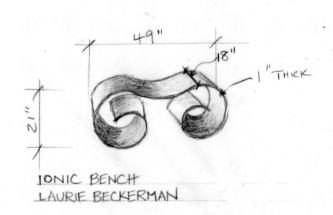

IONIC BENCH
LAURIE BECKERMAN

Figs. 48.1 and 48.2 (opposite)
Laurie Beckerman (b. 1953),
Design drawings for the *Ionic
Bench*, undated.

Fig. 48.3 (left) Laurie
Beckerman (b. 1953), Cutting
plan for plywood scrolls for the
Ionic Bench.

to consider its ergonomic, aesthetic, and functional presence within a domestic or public environment. Beckerman carefully considered each part of the whole, including the lines, dimensions, proportions, and function: "Is it beautiful—where would it look good in a room—silhouetted against a window? On a bare floor? How will it function?"[5] In particular, she contemplated the scrolls. She envisioned the inner curves to serve functionally as storage and limited their lowest contact point with the floor surface to evoke buoyancy. She reasoned that, as the sinuous bench accommodated a sitter, "the scrolls luxuriously frame the human form" and the topmost surfaces of the upper curves provide a gentle and natural resting place for the hands.[6]

Working from the final full-scale sketch, Beckerman engaged the Brooklyn firm of Heritage Woodshop (now Wellstone NYC Custom Woodworking) to convert the initial drawing into a computer drawing using a grid with key points. After further refinements, the design was finalized and a thin, three-dimensional test profile was cut using a computer numerical control (CNC) machine (Fig. 48.3). An advantage to the automated process was that the design could be precisely replicated multiple times. Eighteen slices of one-inch-thick Baltic birch plywood were cut and then laminated together. The profiles of the outer sides were cut in single sections, while the centers were cost-effectively formed by separate pieces seamed at the top.

The *Ionic Bench* illustrates the essence of Beckerman's design philosophy, expressing "simplicity, strength, beauty, elegance, lightness, spaciousness and playfulness."[7]

In 2010, Dr. Jacobsen had the opportunity to meet the artist, who described visualizing the bench in an entry foyer, allowing the sitter to change shoes and store them in the bench's voids. In every furniture design, Beckerman strives to balance the aesthetics of comfort and tactile properties, to create "furniture that invites, and makes people feel good."[8] Her embrace of technology and understanding of today's lifestyles further advances contemporary American design.

1   Laurie Beckerman, "Ionic Bench Package," unpublished document, 2010, 4, Foundation curatorial files.
2   Beckerman, 2.
3   Beckerman, 4.
4   Beckerman, 5.
5   Beckerman, 6.
6   Beckerman, 2.
7   Beckerman, 2.
8   Beckerman, 2.

Yumi Chair II

49

2014

Designed and manufactured by Laura Kishimoto
(b. 1991) (active 2014–present, Denver, Colorado)

Ash veneer, mild steel

47 x 48 x 42 in.

YUMI CHAIR II by Laura Kishimoto represents the continuum of furniture design rooted in traditional education, training, and hand production. Though she uses contemporary methods, Kishimoto references historic antecedents in her designs. Her innovative use of freeform bent lamination is a contemporary interpretation of the centuries-long Japanese technique used to fabricate asymmetrical bows called *yumi* wielded by samurai. Similarly, it pays homage to mid-century Japanese-American and Japanese designs, such as the *Side Chair* (1949) by Ray Komai (1918–2010) and the *Butterfly Stool* (1956) by Sori Yanagi (1915–2011), both of which employ laminated and bentwood technologies.[1] Like these, Kishimoto's design perfectly illustrates the *raison d'être* of the DeMell Jacobsen Collection—to assemble a collection of chairs that showcase significant advances and styles of American furniture design as well as an innovative use of materials.

Yumi Chair II is constructed with flexible grained ash strips poised on arched steel legs, each piece forming complex curves as they overlap and sweep upwards (Fig. 49.1). As the strips terminate in alignment at the back, they create symmetrical shoulders that envelop the sitter. Spaces between the strips give the appearance of a ribcage (Fig. 49.2) and recall other slatted chairs in this collection, such as Samuel Gragg's *"Elastic" Side Chair* (Cat. No. 2) and Vivian Beer's *Current, No. 2* (Cat. No. 46). Kishimoto's *Yumi Chair II* enters the collection as the newest design to further challenge the boundaries between furniture and sculpture.

The initial design for the chair was modeled using paper strips adhered with tape and then translated into wood and metal (Fig. 49.3). In researching the methods needed to execute her first *Yumi Chair*, Kishimoto was inspired by those used to fabricate Japanese asymmetrical bows, which regularly exceed six feet in length and date back to the third century. Japanese artisans fashioned the bows from a small sapling or tree limb and achieved the freeform curvature by using binding cords and bamboo wedges. Kishimoto uses 1/16-inch slices of ash veneer cut into strips. Her freeform, experimental technique of bending and twisting the flexible strips is a dance between the designer and the inherent properties of the material.[2] She manipulates the strips through a variety of methods—molds, armatures, and vacuum pressure. The result is a chair possessing complex, three-dimensional curves with an overall sweeping and sinuous form. "You could sit in it," Kishimoto says, "but you probably wouldn't want to ... the main reason why I don't focus on functionality is that the world is filled with people who can make more comfortable chairs than I can."[3] Dr. Jacobsen met the artist in 2015 and had the rare opportunity to test these words by sitting in her spectacular sculptural creation (Fig. 49.4). Kishimoto continues, "My strength and passion lies in creating beautiful and uninhibited forms. Furniture is just the medium I work in."[4]

A four-week trip taken by Kishimoto in 2010 to the Dark Canyon in Utah would later prove prophetic to the designer. The towering canyon walls awakened an emotional response, which compelled her to create a chair that enveloped the user.[5] Determined to fully realize her inspiration, she credits her professor Lothar Windels (b. 1967) for guiding her through the process of fabricating a prototype, which she completed in 2012. With a year of experience working in Ireland under the mentorship of Joseph Walsh (b. 1979), who likewise pushes the boundaries of his materials in his inventive furniture,[6] Kishimoto refined her initial design, resolved a number of technical challenges, honed her craftsmanship, and in the process established her identity as an up-and-coming contemporary American designer.

Fascinated by the relationship between fine art and design in creating furniture, Kishimoto says, "With careful balance I can create a cohesive object that compels the viewers to respond to it and appears to have formed organically, without intervention."[7] Kishimoto acknowledges the function and meaning of furniture is only fully realized by the participation of the sitter and viewer. "With my furniture design, I hope to draw the viewer/user's attention back to the division of space furniture creates, its intimate interaction with the human body, and the three-dimensional composition created with and without a user."[8] In addition, Kishimoto hopes people will "speculate on the designer's intentions and process, and then ultimately begin to project their own interpretations and personal narratives onto the piece."[9]

Figs. 49.1 and 49.2 Detail views of *Yumi Chair II.*

Made nearly two hundred years prior, the *Ladder-Back Doll's Chair* (Cat. No. 4), one of the earliest examples in the DeMell Jacobsen Collection, embodied the social and cultural training of a youth in early 19th-century Massachusetts. Similarly, in the early 21st century in Lexington, Laura's father, Dr. Takashi Kei Kishimoto (b. 1960), gave her "roots and wings" to pursue her dream of being a furniture designer, nurturing those pursuits by enrolling her in art lessons. Later, after Laura was accepted to the prestigious Rhode Island School of Design (RISD), her father cautioned that her fear of failure should not be a deciding factor and that she should pursue her dream. She graduated from RISD with a bachelor of fine arts in furniture design in 2013.

Kishimoto acknowledges that her father has always shown considerable support for her and her work, and credits him with her successful fabrication of *Yumi Chair II.* Despite pouring all the time and energy she could spare into its development, the artist fell behind schedule and went over budget due to a number of unforeseen complications. As the deadline for its debut in a gallery exhibition approached, Kishimoto stated, "I called my dad and told him in order to finish *Yumi II* and get it to the gallery in Philadelphia on time I would have to cancel the scheduled freight delivery and drive it across the country myself. Rather than berating me for my poor time management, he responded with a counter-offer: he would fly to Colorado on Thanksgiving Day and drive with me."[10]

In giving his daughter the freedom and confidence to pursue a career of innovation and creativity, Takashi Kishimoto may have channeled inspiration from one of the nation's Founding Fathers, John Adams. In 1780, Adams wrote from Paris to his wife:

It is not indeed the fine Arts, which our Country requires. The Usefull, the mechanic Arts, are those which We have occasion for in a young Country, as yet simple and not far advanced in Luxury, altho perhaps much too far for her Age and Character ... I must study Politicks and War, that our sons may have liberty to study ... Mathematicks and Philosophy—

Fig. 49.3 (far left)
Laura Kishimoto
(b. 1991), Paper model
for *Yumi Chair II*, 2012.

Fig. 49.4 (left)
Dr. Jacobsen in
Yumi Chair II, 2015.

my sons ought to study Mathematicks and Philosophy, Geography, natural History and Naval Architecture, navigation, Commerce and Agriculture, in order to give their Children a right to study Painting, Poetry, Musick, Architecture, Statuary, Tapestry and Porcelaine.[11]

Wisely—and thankfully—Takashi Kishimoto knew this philosophy similarly applied to the future of young women and to the study of design. Currently working in Denver, Kishimoto disseminates her knowledge of craft to the next generation as an instructor in fine woodworking at Red Rocks Community College. Following the acquisition of *Yumi Chair II* by the DeMell Jacobsen Collection, Kishimoto made another *yumi*-inspired design; however, she intentionally made only three in this style in order for the chairs to maintain their unique qualities. This variant, made of ash veneer tinted with white oil on a wood base, appeared in the exhibition *Sit by Me* (2016–2017) at the Riverside Art Museum in California. The exhibition featured designs by leading American artists paired with examples by studio furniture icon Sam Maloof. "One thing that really excites me about furniture," Kishimoto says, "is that while nearly everyone has a preconception of what it should be, no one can seem to agree on a definition. I feel a strong need to make a lasting contribution to my field. As such a wide spectrum of artists and designers celebrate furniture as their medium, I am confident I can make that happen."[12]

1   The Museum of Modern Art contains examples of both Komai's *Side Chair* (467.1951) and Yanagi's *Butterfly Stool* (153.1958.1).

2   While the use of bent strips of thin wood might visually draw comparisons between Frank Gehry's *Cross Check Chair* and Kishimoto's *Yumi Chair II*, there are notable differences. Gehry's chairs were mass-produced by Knoll, while Kishimoto handmade her chair in her studio. Gehry used maple and Kishimoto used ash. Gehry's chairs are described in the tradition of bentwood furniture, while Kishimoto's method is freeform bent lamination using a modern application of historic Japanese techniques. As explained by Kishimoto, "Bent lamination is a woodworking technique that involved cutting wood into thin slices (I use ¹⁄₁₆-inch). The slices are so thin that it lends the wood tremendous flexibility to bend and twist. I shape the wood into the curve I want and then glue it back together into a solid piece. The freeform aspect means that rather than using molds to create an extruded, two-dimensional curve, I use experimental techniques to make a geometrically complex, three-dimensional curve." Laura Kishimoto, personal communication to the Foundation, October 11, 2015.

3   Batya Stepelman, "Laura Kishimoto's Fine-Art Furniture," *Colorado Homes and Lifestyles*, July 11, 2016, https://www.coloradohomesmag.com/Life/Laura-Kishimotos-Fine-Art-Furniture/.

4   Stepelman.

5   Laura Kishimoto, personal communication to the Foundation, October 24, 2015.

6   Joseph Walsh's 2010 piece *Enignum Motion* was commissioned by the Mint Museum in Charlotte, North Carolina, for Project Ten Ten Ten (2010.85). While in the city to give a lecture at Duke University, noted immunologist and father of the artist Dr. Takashi Kishimoto visited the museum to see *Yumi II*, which appeared in a gallery near her teacher's work.

7   "Design after Dark: Artist Spotlight—Laura Kishimoto," *Modern in Denver*, January 28, 2015, https://www.modernindenver.com/2015/01/design-after-dark-artist-spotlight/.

8   "Design after Dark."

9   "Design after Dark."

10 Sigal Burvitz Hin, "Laura Kishimoto," Formative Designs, accessed November 25, 2018, https://formative.squarespace.com/laura-kishimoto/.

11 John Adams to Abigail Adams, post May 12, 1780, *Adams Family Papers: An Electronic Archive*, Massachusetts Historical Society, https://www.masshist.org/digitaladams/archive/doc?id=L17800512jasecond.

12 Yelena Moroz Alpert, "The Furniture Maker: Laura Kishimoto," Luxe Interiors and Design, accessed October 12, 2015, https://www.luxesource.com/luxedaily/article/the-furniture-maker-laura-kishimoto.

Further reading

While the entry notes contain the most relevant sources for each object, additional important sources are available for some objects; these are listed below.

1. *Klismos Side Chair*, 1810–1815; *Grecian Settee*, c. 1823–1827

Baltimore Museum of Art. *Baltimore Furniture: The Work of Baltimore and Annapolis Cabinetmakers from 1760 to 1810*. Baltimore: Baltimore Museum of Art, 1947.

Cooper, Wendy A. *Classical Taste in America, 1800–1840*. Baltimore: Baltimore Museum of Art, 1993.

Cooper, Wendy A. "Classical Taste in America, 1800–1840." *The Magazine ANTIQUES*, May 1993, 764–775.

D'Ambrosio, Anna Tobin. *Masterpieces of American Furniture from the Munson-Williams-Proctor Institute*. Utica, NY: Munson-Williams-Proctor Arts Institute, 1999.

Deurenberg, Rian M. H. "Examination and Treatment of a Set of Klismos Chairs, Attr. to John and Hugh Finlay." *Journal of the American Institute for Conservation* 47, no 2 (Summer 2008): 97–117.

Elder, William Voss, III, and Jayne E. Stokes. *American Furniture, 1680–1880, from the Collection of the Baltimore Museum of Art*. Baltimore: Baltimore Museum of Art, 1987.

Feld, Elizabeth P., and Stuart Feld. *Of the Newest Fashion: Masterpieces of American Neo-Classical Decorative Arts*. New York: Hirschl & Adler Galleries, 2001.

Feld, Elizabeth P., and Stuart Feld. *Very Rich & Handsome: American Neo-Classical Decorative Arts*. New York: Hirschl & Adler Galleries, 2014.

Feld, Elizabeth P., and Stuart Feld. *Augmenting the Canon: Recent Acquisitions of American Neo-Classical Decorative Arts*. New York: Hirschl & Adler Galleries, 2018.

Garrett, Elisabeth Donaghy. "Living with Antiques, Old Richmond, the Houston guest cottage of Mr. and Mrs. Fred T. Couper Jr." *The Magazine ANTIQUES*, September 1977.

Hope, Thomas. *Household Furniture and Interior Decoration*. London: T. Bensley, 1807. https://archive.org/details/Householdfurnit00Hope.

Hurst, Ronald L., and Jonathan Prown. *Southern Furniture, 1680–1830: The Colonial Williamsburg Collection*. Williamsburg: Colonial Williamsburg Foundation; New York: Abrams, 1997.

Kirtley, Alexandra Alevizatos. "'Superfluity & Excess': Quaker Philadelphia Falls for Classical Splendor." *The Magazine ANTIQUES*, March/April 2016, 88–97.

Kirtley, Alexandra Alevizatos, and Peggy A. Olley. *Classical Splendor: Painted Furniture for a Grand Philadelphia House*. Philadelphia: Philadelphia Museum of Art, 2017.

Sheraton, Thomas. "Ornament for a Frieze or Tablet." *The Cabinet-Maker and Upholsterer's Drawing Book*. London, 1802 (first published 1792), plate 56 (opposite p. 430). https://archive.org/stream/cabinetmakerupho00sher#page/n717/mode/2up.

Watkin, David, and Philip Hewat-Jabor, eds. *Thomas Hope: Regency Designer*. New Haven: Yale University Press in association with Bard Graduate Center for Studies in the Decorative Arts, Design, and Culture, New York, 2008.

Weidman, Gregory R. "The Furniture of Classical Maryland, 1815–1845." In *Classical Maryland, 1815–1845: Fine and Decorative Arts from the Golden Age*, by Gregory R. Weidman et al. Baltimore: Maryland Historical Society, 1993.

Weidman, Gregory R. "The Painted Furniture of John and Hugh Finlay." *The Magazine ANTIQUES*, May 1993, 744–755.

2. *"Elastic" Side Chair*, c. 1815

Harwood, Barry Robert. *The Furniture of George Hunzinger: Invention and Innovation in Nineteenth Century America*. Brooklyn, NY: Brooklyn Museum of Art, 1997.

Kirtley, Alexandra Alevizatos. "Benjamin Henry Latrobe and the Furniture of John and Hugh Finlay." *The Magazine ANTIQUES,* December 9, 2009. https://www.themagazineantiques.com/article/benjamin-henry-latrobe-and-the-furniture-of-john-and-hugh-finlay/.

Klein, Susan, and Cynthia V. A. Schaffner. *American Painted Furniture 1790–1880*. New York: Clarkson Potter Publishers, 1997.

Mésangère, Pierre de la. *Collection de meubles et objets de goût*. Paris: Au Bureau du Journal des Dames et des Modes, 1802.

Percier, Charles, and Pierre-Francois-Leonard Fontaine. *Recueil de decorations intérieures, comprenant tout ce qui a rapport a l'ameublement ...* Paris, 1801.

5. *#6 Rocking Arm Chair*, c. 1840

Burks, Jean M., ed. *Shaker Design: Out of This World*. New Haven: Yale University Press, 2008.

Editors of Fine Woodworking. *In the Shaker Style: Building Furniture Inspired by the Shaker Tradition*. Newtown, CT: Taunton Press, 2001.

Esplund, Lance. "The First American Modernists." *Wall Street Journal*, August 7, 2014.

Miller, M. Stephen. *Inspired Innovations: A Celebration of Shaker Ingenuity*. Lebanon, NH: University Press of New England, 2010.

Muller, Charles R., and Timothy D. Rieman. *The Shaker Chair*. Winchester, OH: Canal Press, 1984.

6. *Gothic Revival Side Chair*, c. 1845–1855

Trent, Robert F., and Harry Mack Truax II. *Vaulting Ambition: Philadelphia Gothic Revival; Furniture and Other Decorative Arts, 1830–1860*. Philadelphia: Philadelphia Antiques Show Committee, 2005.

Warren, David B. "The Gothic Revival Style in America: Domestic Architecture and Decorative Arts." In *Pointed Style: The Gothic Revival in America, 1800–1860*. New York: Hirschl & Adler Galleries, 2009.

7. *Centripetal Spring Arm Chair*, c. 1850

Munson-Williams-Proctor Institute and Anna Tobin D'Ambrosio. *Masterpieces of American Furniture from the Munson-Williams-Proctor Institute*. Utica, NY: Munson-Williams-Proctor Institute, 1999.

8. *Rustic Settee*, c. 1855

Architect of the Capitol. "Capitol Dome." Accessed April 9, 2015. https://www.aoc.gov/explore-capitol-campus/buildings-grounds/capitol-building/capitol-dome.

Architect of the Capitol. "Dome Restoration Project Overview." Accessed January 4, 2022. https://www.aoc.gov/what-we-do/projects/dome-restoration-project

Janes, Beebe & Company. *Illustrated Catalogue of Ornamental Iron Work*. New York: Janes, Beebe & Co., 1855.

Janes, Kirtland & Company. *Illustrated Catalogue of Ornamental Iron Work*. New York: Janes, Kirtland & Co., 1870.

Piper, John E. "The Janes and Kirtland Ironworks." *Bronx County Historical Society Journal* 11, no. 2 (Fall 1974).

Wheeler, Jesse M. "Ramble." CentralPark.com. Accessed January 4, 2022. https://www.centralpark.com/things-to-do/attractions/ramble/.

9. *Slipper Chair ("Grape Vine and Oak Leaf")*, c. 1860; *Side Chair ("Fountain Elms" with Foliate Foot)*, c. 1855; *Side Chair ("Fountain Elms" with Scroll Foot)*, c. 1855

Bishop, Robert. *Centuries and Styles of the American Chair, 1640–1970*. New York: E. P. Dutton & Co., Inc., 1972.

D'Ambrosio, Anna Tobin. *Masterpieces of American Furniture from the Munson- Williams-Proctor Arts Institute*. Utica, NY: Munson-Williams-Proctor Arts Institute, 1999.

The Henry Ford. "Armchair, Owned by Mary Todd Lincoln, 1845–1865." Accessed March 1, 2020. https://www.thehenryford.org/collections-and-research/digital-collections/artifact/63337.

Peirce, Donald C. *Art & Enterprise: American Decorative Art, 1825–1917, The Virginia Carroll Crawford Collection*. Atlanta: High Museum of Art, 1999.

10. *House of Representatives Chamber Arm Chair*, 1857

History, Art & Archives, United States House of Representatives. "Congressional Row, in the U.S. House of Representatives, Midnight of Friday, February 5th, 1858." Accessed April 20, 2015. https://history.house.gov/Collection/Listing/2009/2009-129-007/.

History, Art & Archives, United States House of Representatives. "Furniture & Decorative Arts." Accessed January 4, 2022. https://history.house.gov/Collection/Search?Classification=Furniture+%26+Decorative+Arts.

McElroy & Co.'s Philadelphia City Business Directory. Philadelphia: McElroy & Co., 1851, 1854, 1856, 1857, 1858, and 1861.

Neal Auction Company. "A Rare American Carved Oak U.S. House of Representatives Chair." Sale, October 6 and 7, 2007, lot 92. Accessed January 4, 2022. https://www.nealauction.com/auction-lot/a-rare-american-carved-oak-u-s-house-of_F1NZJO0XL2/.

Smithsonian Libraries. "Collection Highlight: Kimbel & Cabus Firm Trade Catalog." Accessed January 4, 2022. https://library.si.edu/libraries/cooper-hewitt/highlights.

Sotheby's. "Renaissance Revival Carved Oak 'United States House of Representatives' Armchair, Attributed to John Hammitt's Desk Manufacturing Company, Philadelphia circa 1857." Important Americana, January 23, 2015, lot 958. https://www.sothebys.com/en/auctions/ecatalogue/2015/americana-n09300/lot.958.html.

11. *Side Chair with Curule Base*, c. 1870;

Side Chair, c. 1870; *Side Chair with Wire Seat*, c. 1876

Brooklyn Museum. *The Furniture of George Hunzinger: Invention & Innovation in 19th-Century America*. Exhibition, November 20, 1997–February 15, 1998. Accessed January 4, 2022. https://www.brooklynmuseum.org/opencollection/exhibitions/1056/The_Furniture_of_George_Hunzinger%3A_Invention_and_Innovation_in_19th-Century_America.

Munson-Williams-Proctor Institute and Anna Tobin D'Ambrosio. *Masterpieces of American Furniture from the Munson-Williams-Proctor Institute*. Utica, NY: Munson-Williams-Proctor Institute, 1999.

Naeve, Milo M. Review of the publication and exhibition *The Furniture of George Hunzinger: Invention and Innovation in Nineteenth-Century America*. Chipstone. Accessed May 4, 2015. http://www.chipstone.org/html/publications/1998AF/TableofCont/harwood.html.

United States Patent and Trademark Office. "U.S. Patent Activity, Calendar Years 1790 to the Present." Accessed January 4, 2022. https://www.uspto.gov/web/offices/ac/ido/oeip/taf/h_counts.htm.

12. *Egyptian Revival Side Chair*, c. 1875

D'Ambrosio, Anna Tobin. "High-Style Mass-Produced American Furniture." in *The Magazine ANTIQUES*, May 1999.

Eckels, Claire Witter. "The Egyptian Revival in America." *Archaeology* 3, no. 3 (September 1950).

Hope, Thomas. *Household Furniture and Interior Decoration*. London: T. Bensley, 1807. https://archive.org/details/Householdfurnit00Hope.

Howe, Katherine S., Alice Cooney Frelinghuysen, and Catherine Hoover Voorsanger. *Herter Brothers: Furniture and Interiors for a Gilded Age*. New York: Harry N. Abrams, 1994.

Humbert, Jean-Marcel, et al. *Egyptomania: Egypt in Western Art, 1730–1930*. Ottawa: National Gallery of Canada, 1994.

Peirce, Donald C. *Art & Enterprise: American Decorative Art, 1825–1917, The Virginia Carroll Crawford Collection*. Atlanta: High Museum of Art, 1999.

Sigler, Bernadette M. *The Sphinx and the Lotus: The Egyptian Movement in American Decorative Arts, 1865–1935*. Yonkers, NY: Hudson River Museum, 1990.

The Temple of Dendur, completed by 10 B.C., Egyptian, Roman period. Metropolitan Museum of Art. Accessed May 17, 2015. https://www.metmuseum.org/art/collection/search/547802.

Tracy, Berry B., et al. *19th Century America: Furniture and Other Decorative Arts*. New York: Metropolitan Museum of Art, 1970.

Watkin, David, and Philip Hewat-Jaboor, eds. *Thomas Hope: Regency Designer*. New Haven: Yale University Press in association with Bard Graduate Center for Studies in the Decorative Arts, Design, and Culture, New York, 2008.

13. *Side Chair*, c. 1880

Burke, Doreen Bolger, et al. *In Pursuit of Beauty: Americans and the Aesthetic Movement*. New York: Metropolitan Museum of Art, 1986.

Cooper Hewitt. "Herter Brothers." Accessed May 27, 2015. https://collection.cooperhewitt.org/people/18062991/bio.

Harwood, Barry R. "A Herter Brothers Library Rediscovered." *The Magazine ANTIQUES*, May 2002.

Munson-Williams-Proctor Institute and Anna Tobin D'Ambrosio. *Masterpieces of American furniture from the Munson-Williams-Proctor Institute*. Utica, NY: Munson-Williams-Proctor Institute, 1999.

Ross, Nancy L. "Furnishings: Herter Brothers Crafted Pieces for a Gilded Age." *Los Angeles Times*, August 27, 1994.

14. *Side Chair*, c. 1880

F. Krutina advertisement. *New York Daily*, December 9, 1879.

James R. Osgood & Company. *American Architect and Building News* 13 (January–June 1883).

Oshinsky, Sara J. "Christopher Dresser (1834–1904)." *Heilbrunn Timeline of Art History*. Metropolitan Museum of Art. Accessed January 4, 2022. https://www.metmuseum.org/toah/hd/cdrs/hd_cdrs.htm.

15. *Lady's Reception Chair*, c. 1885; *Child's Reclining Arm Chair*, c. 1880–1895

Burke, Doreen Bolger, et al. *In Pursuit of Beauty: Americans and the Aesthetic Movement*. New York: Metropolitan Museum of Art, 1986.

De Dampierre, Florence. *Chairs: A History*. New York: Harry N. Abrams, 2006.

Massachusetts Cultural Resource Information System. "Wakefield Rattan Company." Accessed January 4, 2022. https://mhc-macris.net/.

Scherer, Barrymore Laurence. "Children, Be Seated." *The Magazine ANTIQUES*, November/December 2014.

Banks, Tom. "Christopher Dresser: Britain's First Independent Industrial Designer." *Design Week*, August 22, 2014. https://www.designweek.co.uk/issues/august-2014/christopher-dresser-britains-first-independent-industrial-designer/.

16. *Faux Bamboo Chair*, c. 1885

Abe, Namiko. "Bamboo and Japanese Culture." ThoughtCo. Last modified February 13, 2019. https://www.thoughtco.com/bamboo-in-japanese-culture-2028043.

Miller, Tom. "The 1886 Robert J. Horner Building—61–65 West 23rd Street." *Daytonian in Manhattan*, December 9, 2010. https://daytoninmanhattan.blogspot.com/2010/12/1886-robert-j-horner-building-61-65.html.

Miller, Tom. "The George C. Flint Furniture Co. Building—No. 43 West 23rd Street." *Daytonian in Manhattan*, February 21, 2011. https://daytoninmanhattan.blogspot.com/2011/02/george-c-flint-furniture-co-building-no.html.

17. *Slipper Chair*, c. 1880–1895

Edwards, Owen. "The Story Behind the Peacock Room's Princess." *Smithsonian Magazine*, June 2011. https://www.smithsonianmag.com/arts-culture/the-story-behind-the-peacock-rooms-princess-159271229/.

Glessner House. "The Collection." Accessed February 15, 2022. https://www.glessnerhouse.org/the-collection.

MacCarthy, Fiona. "The Aesthetic Movement." *Guardian*, March 26, 2011. https://www.theguardian.com/artanddesign/2011/mar/26/aestheticism-exhibition-victoria-albert-museum.

19. *Texas Longhorn Arm Chair*, c. 1885

Rogers, Alan W. "The Horn Palace and the Buckhorn." National Texas Longhorn Museum. Accessed June 23, 2014. http://www.longhornmuseum.com/BuckhornHornPalace.htm.

20. *Appalachian Bent Willow Arm Chair*, 1890–1910

Jones, Whitney. "Master, Apprentice Make Bentwood Willow Chairs." WKMS, Murray State's NPR Station. December 9, 2012. https://www.wkms.org/arts-culture/2012-12-09/master-apprentice-make-bentwood-willow-chairs.

21. *'McKinley' Arm Chair*, c. 1894–1896

Barter, Judith A. "The Prairie School and Decorative Arts at the Art Institute of Chicago." *Art Institute of Chicago Museum Studies* 21, no. 2 (1995).

Chung, Jen. "What the 1900 Auto Show Looked Like at Madison Square Garden." *Gothamist*, Arts & Entertainment, April 9, 2012. https://gothamist.com/arts-entertainment/what-the-1900-auto-show-looked-like-at-madison-square-garden.

Fisher, Ernest B. *Grand Rapids and Kent County, Michigan: History and Account of Their Progress from First Settlement to the Present Time*. Vol. 1. Chicago: R. O. Law Company, 1918.

Furniture City History. "Phoenix Furniture Co." Accessed May 7, 2012. http://www.furniturecityhistory.org/company/3773/phoenix-furniture-co.

Kaplan, Wendy, et al. *"The Art That Is Life": The Arts & Crafts Movement in America, 1875–1920*. Boston: Little, Brown, 1987.

22. *Hall Chair*, 1900

Brandt, Beverly K. "The Artistic Furniture of Charles Rohlfs." In *American Furniture: 2010*, edited by Luke Beckerdite. Milwaukee, WI: Chipstone Foundation, 2010.

Clark, Robert Judson, ed. *The Arts and Crafts Movement in America, 1876–1916*. Princeton, NJ: Princeton University Press, 1972.

Kaplan, Wendy, et al. *"The Art That Is Life": The Arts & Crafts Movement in America, 1875–1920*. Boston: Little, Brown, 1987.

Milwaukee Art Museum. "The Artistic Furniture of Charles Rohlfs." Accessed February 15, 2022. https://mam.org/exhibitions/details/american/charles_rohlfs.php.

Peirce, Donald C. *Art and Enterprise: American Decorative Art, 1825–1917, The Virginia Carroll Crawford Collection*. Atlanta: High Museum of Art, 1999.

23. *Oxbow Arm Chair*, c. 1903

Charles P. Limbert Co. *Limbert Arts and Crafts Furniture: The Complete 1903 Catalog*. New York: Dover Publications, 1992.

Furniture City History. "Stickley Brothers Furniture Co." Accessed July 7, 2015. http://www.furniturecityhistory.org/company/3847/stickley-brothers-furniture-co.

Lang, Brian J. "The Art of Seating: 200 Years of American Design." *Antiques and Fine Art*, Spring 2012.

Marek, Don. *Arts and Crafts Furniture Design: The Grand Rapids Contribution 1895–1915*. Grand Rapids, MI: Grand Rapids Art Museum, 1987.

McInnis, Raymond. "Spindles/Slats, in the Arts and Crafts Style." *An Online Dictionary of Woodworking*. Accessed January 4, 2022. http://www.woodworkinghistory.com/glossary_spindles_in_A&C_style.htm.

Stern, Robert A. M., Gregory Gilmarin, and John Massengale. *New York 1900: Metropolitan Architecture and Urbanism 1890–1915*. New York: Rizzoli, 1995.

Stickley Museum. Accessed July 7, 2015. https://www.stickleymuseum.org/.

24. *Plank-Back Hall Chair*, 1905

Artsncrafts.com. "Stickley Era Information: The Work of Charles Limbert." Accessed January 4, 2022. http://www.artsncrafts.com/charleslimbertfurniture/index.htm.

Charles P. Limbert Company. *Limberts Holland Dutch Arts and Crafts Furniture*. Booklet no. 114. Grand Rapids, MI: Charles P. Limbert Company, c. 1900. https://archive.org/details/limbertsholla00char. Note: This booklet was most likely produced between no. 112 (c. 1910) and no. 117 (c. 1914).

Reif, Rita. "Arts/Artifacts: If Stickley Was Hertz, Then Limbert Was Avis." *New York Times*, October 29, 1995. https://www.nytimes.com/1995/10/29/arts/arts-artifacts-if-stickley-was-hertz-then-limbert-was-avis.html (subscription required).

WOKA. "Wiener Werkstaette, 1903–1932." Accessed January 4, 2022. https://www.woka.com/en/lexicon/wiener-werkstaette.html.

25. *Side Chair*, c. 1910

Arnason, H. H. *History of Modern Art: Painting, Sculpture, Architecture, Photography*. 3rd ed. New York: Harry N. Abrams, 1986.

Campbell, Gordon, ed. *The Grove Encyclopedia of Decorative Arts: Volume Two, Labhardt–Zwischengoldglas*. New York: Oxford University Press, 2006.

"George C. Flint & Company's Furniture Storehouse Burned." *New York Times*, April 25, 1882.

"Goods for Summer Homes." *New York Times*, June 3, 1885.

Grutchfield, Walter. "Flint & Horner, 66 W. 47th St., New York, 2012." WalterGrutchfield.net. Accessed June 17, 2015. https://www.waltergrutchfield.net/flint&horner.htm.

National Gallery of Art. "Anatomy of an Exhibition: Art Nouveau, 1890–1914; The Paris World's Fair, 1900." Accessed January 4, 2022. https://www.nga.gov/exhibitions/2000/nouveau.html.

Ulmer, Renate, and Alphonse Mucha. *Alfons Mucha*. Cologne: Taschen, 1994.

West, Rebecca. *1900*. New York: Viking Press, 1982.

26. *Colonial Revival Comb-Back Windsor Arm Chair*, c. 1930

Liberty Chair Works. "Comb-Back Arm Chairs." Accessed February 15, 2022. http://www.libertychairworks.com/arm-chairs/comb-back-arm-chairs/.

Nutting, Wallace. *Checklist of Early American Reproductions. With an Introductory Essay on the Art-Crafts Ideology; Or, Wallace Nutting's Colonial Revival, by John Freeman*. Watkins Glen, NY: American Life Foundation, 1969.

Watt, Peter. "A Guide to the Virginia Craftsmen Ledgers, 1938–1955." James Madison University Libraries. July 2013. https://ead.lib.virginia.edu/vivaxtf/view?docId=jmu/vihart00164.xml.

27. *Lounge Chair*, c. 1935

Design2Share. "Warren McArthur." December 26, 2007. http://design2share.squarespace.com/designers-we-love/2007/12/26/warren-mcarthur.html.

Dirks, Tim. "The History of Film: The 1930s." Filmsite. Accessed January 4, 2022. https://www.

filmsite.org/30sintro3.html.

Duncan, Alastair. *Art Deco*. New York: Thames & Hudson, 1988.

Frank Lloyd Wright Stained Glass. "McArthur House." Accessed August 20, 2015. http://franklloydwright.tercenim.com/stained_glass.htm.

Lang, Brian J. "The Art of Seating: 200 Years of American Design." *Antiques and Fine Art*, Spring 2012.

Lefebvre's Upholstery & Refinishing. "My Furniture Is Stuffed with WHAT?" June 29, 2014. https://lefebvreupholstery.blogspot.com/2014/06/my-furniture-is-stuffed-with-what.html.

McArthur, W., Jr. "Furniture." U.S. Patent No. 2,035,489. Filed March 5, 1934, issued March 31, 1936. U.S. Patent Office.

Museum of Modern Art. Philip Johnson Papers. Accessed January 4, 2022. https://www.moma.org/research-and-learning/archives/finding-aids/PJohnsonPapersf.

Winton, Alexandra Griffith. "The Bauhaus, 1919–1933." *Heilbrunn Timeline of Art History*. Metropolitan Museum of Art. August 2007, revised October 2016. https://www.metmuseum.org/toah/hd/bauh/hd_bauh.htm.

Wright Library. "SC Johnson Administration Building." Accessed August 21, 2015. http://www.steinerag.com/flw/Artifact%20Pages/PhotoJW.htm.

28. *S. C. Johnson & Son Administration Building Chair*, 1936–1939

Arnason, H. H. *History of Modern Art: Painting, Sculpture, Architecture, Photography*. 3rd ed. New York: Harry N. Abrams, 1986.

Gill, Brendan. *Many Masks: A Life of Frank Lloyd Wright*. New York: Putnam, 1987.

National Park Service. "Listing of National Historic Landmarks By State." Accessed January 4, 2022. https://www.nps.gov/subjects/nationalhistoriclandmarks/list-of-nhls-by-state.htm.

Planetclaire.org. "List of Frank Lloyd Wright Works (chronological)." Accessed January 4, 2022. https://www.planetclaire.tv/fllw/works.html.

29. *Crow Island School Chair*, 1939

Arnason, H. H. *History of Modern Art: Painting, Sculpture, Architecture, Photograph*, 3rd ed. New York: Harry N. Abrams, 1986.

PBS. "Only A Teacher: Schoolhouse Pioneers, John Dewey (1859–1952)." Accessed September 1, 2014. https://www.pbs.org/onlyateacher/john.html.

Winnetka Public Schools District 36. "History of Crow Island School." Accessed November

17, 2021. https://www.winnetka36.org/domain/35.

Wright. "Charles Eames and Eero Saarinen, Rare and Early Chair for the Crow Island School, Winnetka IL." Design Masterworks, May 19, 2015, lot 6. https://www.wright20.com/auctions/2015/05/design-masterworks/6.

30. *1006 Navy Chair*, designed 1944

Lasky, Julie. "French Twist." *Interiors Magazine*, May 2000.

31. *LCW (Lounge Chair Wood or Low Chair Wood)*, designed 1945; this example executed 1946–1948

Evans Industries, Inc. "About Evans Industries, Inc." Accessed April 8, 2018. http://eiihq.com/wp/#about.

Fiell, Charlotte, Peter Fiell, Simone Philippi, and Susanne Uppenbrock. *1000 Chairs*. Cologne: Taschen, 1997.

Greif, Steve. "Evans Products Company." *Oregon Encyclopedia*. Last modified March 17, 2018. https://www.oregonencyclopedia.org/articles/evans_products_company/#.YdSajhNKhMN.

33. *Spring Chair or Recliner (Experimental)*, c. 1946/1947

Museum of Modern Art. "Plywood: Material, Process, Form." Exhibition, February 2, 2011–February 27, 2012. https://www.moma.org/calendar/exhibitions/1119.

Thaden, Louise McPhetridge. *High, Wide, and Frightened*. Fayetteville: University of Arkansas Press, 2004.

U-Haul. "Our History." Accessed September 11, 2015. https://www.uhaul.com/About/History/.

34. *Hairpin Lounge Chair*, c. 1950

Collectors Weekly. "Fiberglass Chairs." Accessed October 12, 2015. https://www.collectorsweekly.com/stories/12126-fiberglass-chairs.

Eames, Charles, and Ray Eames. *Prototype for Chaise Longue (La Chaise)*, 1948. Museum of Modern Art. Accessed February 15, 2022. https://www.moma.org/collection/works/2133.

Leagle. "Smith v. Commissioner." Filed June 25, 1965, accessed September 15, 2015. https://www.leagle.com/decision/196592324fntcm8991754.

Nelson, George. *Chairs*. New York: Whitney Publications, 1953.

University of Southern California. Pierre Koenig Collection, Architectural Teaching Slide Collection. Accessed February 15, 2022. https://digitallibrary.usc.edu/archive/Architectural-Teaching-Slide-Collection-2A3BF1JINP.html. See especially images of Koenig residence, Glendale, Calif., 1950(?).

35. *Large Diamond Chair (No. 422)*, c. 1952; *Bird Lounge Chair (No. 423)*, c. 1952

Remmele, Mathias. "422 Large Diamond Chair, 1950–1952, Harry Bertoia." Vitra Design Museum. Accessed February 15, 2022. https://collection.design-museum.de/#/en/object/42032?_k=wzijzg.

36. *Rocking Stool, Model 86T*, designed 1953; this example executed c. 1955

Johnson, Ken. "A Stillness in the City: The Raw Grace of Noguchi's Nimble Constructions." *New York Times*, September 1, 2009.

38. *MAF (Medium Arm Fiberglass) Swaged Leg Chair*, designed 1958, produced 1958–1964

George Nelson Foundation. "Key Dates from George Nelson's Life and Career." Accessed September 24, 2015. http://www.georgenelsonfoundation.org/george-nelson/index.html#milestones.

Keith, Kelsey. "Charles Pollock (1930–2013)." *Artforum*, February 21, 2014. https://www.artforum.com/passages/kelsey-keith-on-charles-pollock-1930-2013-45383.

Museum of Modern Art. "Awards Given in International Low-Cost Furniture Competition." Press release, January 19, 1949. https://www.moma.org/momaorg/shared/pdfs/docs/press_archives/1291/releases/MOMA_1949_0005_1949-01-13_490113-5.pdf?2010.

Priest, Tyler. *The Offshore Imperative Shell Oil's Search for Petroleum in Postwar America*. College Station: Texas A&M University Press, 2007.

39. *Conoid Chair*, 1966

Binzen, Jonathan. "The Soul of Nakashima." *Fine Woodworking*, no. 231 (January/February 2013): 51–55.

George Nakashima Woodworkers. Accessed December 14, 2021. https://nakashimawoodworkers.com.

Kelsey, John. "George Nakashima: For Each Plank There's One Perfect Use." *Fine Woodworking*, no. 14 (January/February 1979): 40–46.

Kimmerly, David (Historic Preservation Specialist, Heritage Conservancy). National Historic Landmark Nomination: George Nakashima Woodworker Complex. United States Department of the Interior, National Park Service, Form 10-900. November 2007, October 2012. https://npgallery.nps.gov/GetAsset/cb995759-75e4-425c-9b39-17bb6de164a4.

Laurence, Vincent. "The Nakashimas." *Fine Woodworking*, no. 116 (January/February 1996): 92–95.

Lyon, Mary. "Nakashima." *Craft Horizons* 9, no. 3

(Autumn 1949): 16–19.

Moderne Gallery. "Wharton Esherick." Accessed September 28, 2015. https://modernegallery.com/collections/wharton-esherick.

Renwick Gallery. *Woodenworks: Furniture Objects by Five Contemporary Craftsmen*. Washington, DC: Renwick Gallery, 1972.

40. *Butterfly Love Seat*, 1967

Adamson, Glenn, et al. *Wendell Castle Remastered*. New York: Museum of Arts and Design / Artist Book Foundation, 2015.

Barry Friedman Ltd. *Wendell Castle*. Exh. cat. New York: Barry Friedman Ltd., 2008.

Blankemeyer, Dennis. *Craft Furniture: The Legacy of the Human Hand*. Atglen, PA: Schiffer Publishing, 2003.

Cooke, Edward S., Jr. *New American Furniture: The Second Generation of Studio Furnituremakers*. Boston: Museum of Fine Arts, Boston, 1989.

Danto, Arthur C., et al. *Angel Chairs: New Work by Wendell Castle*. New York: Peter Joseph Gallery, 1991.

Diamonstein, Barbaralee. *Handmade in America: Conversations with Fourteen Craftmasters*. New York: Harry N. Abrams, 1983.

Giambruni, Helen. "Wendell Castle." *Craft Horizons* 28, no. 3 (May/June 1968).

Giambruni, Helen. "Wendell Castle." *Craft Horizons* 28, no. 5 (September/October 1968).

Jacobson, Sebby Wilson. "Wendell Castle: A Portrait of the Artist as a Very Young Octogenarian." *American Craft* 72, no. 6 (December/January 2013).

Joseph, Peter T., and Emma C. Cobb. "Itty Bitty Tables and Apocalyptic Chairs." In *Angel Chairs: New Work by Wendell Castle*, by Arthur C. Danto et al. New York: Peter Joseph Gallery, 1991.

Nordness, Lee. Floorplan sketch for Wendell Castle. November 4, 1966. Wendell Castle papers, 1965–1975. Archives of American Art, Smithsonian Institution. Accessed February 15, 2022.

https://www.aaa.si.edu/collections/items/detail/lee-nordness-floorplan-sketch-wendell-castle-12747.

Nordness, Lee, Letter to Wendell Castle, Rochester, N.Y. November 4, 1966. Wendell Castle papers, 1965–1975. Archives of American Art, Smithsonian Institution. Accessed February 15, 2022. https://www.aaa.si.edu/collections/items/detail/lee-nordness-new-york-ny-letter-to-wendell-castle-rochester-ny-207.

Phillips. "Wendell Castle, Unique 'Butterfly Love Seat.'" Design, New York Auction, June 6, 2019, lot 85. Accessed January 4, 2022. https://www.phillips.com/detail/wendell-castle/NY050119/85.

Taragin, Davira S., et al. *Furniture by Wendell Castle*. New York: Hudson Hills Press; Detroit: Founders Society Detroit Institute of Arts, 1989.

42. *Contour Bar Stool (No. 10-415)*, 1972

Andersen, Kurt. "Design: Building Beauty the Hard Way." *Time*, October 13, 1986. http://content.time.com/time/subscriber/article/0,33009,962504,00.html.

Cooperman, Jackie. "Gehry's World." *Wall Street Journal*, April 2–3, 2011.

Eggert, Barbara M. "Wiggle Side Chair, 1969–1972, Frank Gehry." Vitra Design Museum. Accessed December 20, 2021. https://collection.design-museum.de/#/en/object/38955?_k=ql71a4.

Guggenheim Museum. "Frank Gehry, Architect, Furniture Designs 1969–92." Accessed October 1, 2015. http://pastexhibitions.guggenheim.org/gehry/furniture_01.html.

43. *Sheraton Chair (No. 664)*, designed 1978–1984; this example dated 1986.

Knoll. "Knoll Designer Bios: Robert Venturi." Accessed October 3, 2015. https://www.knoll.com/designer/Robert-Venturi.

Sheraton, Thomas. "Chair Backs." *The Cabinet-Maker and Upholsterer's Drawing Book*. London, 1802 (first published 1792), plate 36 (opposite p. 387). https://archive.org/stream/cabinetmakerupho00sher#page/n441/mode/2up.

VSBA Architects and Planners. "Who We Are." Accessed October 3, 2015. https://www.vsba.com/who-we-are/.

44. *Brushstroke Chair, Wood* and *Brushstroke Ottoman, Wood*, 1986–1988

Alloway, Lawrence. *Roy Lichtenstein*. New York: Abbeville Press, 1983.

Art Institute of Chicago. "Brushstrokes 1965–71, Explosions 1963–68." *Roy Lichtenstein: A Retrospective*. Accessed January 4, 2022. https://archive.artic.edu/lichtenstein/themes/Brushstrokes.

Art Institute of Chicago. "Brushstroke with Spatter." *Roy Lichtenstein: A Retrospective*. Accessed August 4, 2018. https://archive.artic.edu/lichtenstein/24836.

Bianchini, Paul. *Roy Lichtenstein: Drawings and Prints*. Introduction by Diane Waldman. New York: Chelsea House Publishers, 1973.

Christie's. "Roy Lichtenstein (1923–1997), Brushstroke Chair and Ottoman." Post-War, Live Auction 9576, New York, November 15, 2000, lot 25. Accessed August 4, 2018. https://www.christies.com/lotfinder/Lot/roy-lichtenstein-1923-1977-brushstroke-chair-and-1931612-details.aspx.

Corlett, Mary Lee. *The Prints of Roy Lichtenstein: A Catalogue Raisonné, 1948–1993*. New York: Hudson Hills Press in association with the National Gallery of Art, Washington, DC, 1994.

Cowart, Jack. *Roy Lichtenstein, 1970–1980*. New York: Hudson Hills Press; St. Louis, MO: St. Louis Art Museum, 1981.

Mercurio, Gianni. *Roy Lichtenstein: Meditations on Art*. Milan: Skira; New York: Rizzoli, 2010.

Lichtenstein, Roy. *Brushstroke*, 1965. Tate. Accessed August 11, 2018. https://www.tate.org.uk/art/artworks/lichtenstein-brushstroke-p07354.

Lichtenstein, Roy. *Brushstroke with Spatter*, 1966. Art Institute of Chicago. Accessed August 5, 2018. https://www.artic.edu/artworks/24836/brushstroke-with-spatter.

Tuten, Frederic. *Roy Lichtenstein's Last Still Life*. Ithaca, NY: Herbert F. Johnson Museum of Art, 1998.

45. Synergistic Synthesis XVIIB1 (or sub B1) [Informed Intuition] Chair, 2003

Smythe, Kenneth. "Modular Chairs Around a Standard Seat," *Fine Woodworking*, no. 44 (January/February 1984): 68–69.

46. *Current, No. 2*, designed 2004; this example executed in 2007

Bell, Nicholas R. *40 Under 40: Craft Futures*. Washington, DC: Renwick Gallery/Yale University Press, 2012.

Pascucci, Marisa J. "Vivian Beer: Artist to Watch." *Art Economist* 1, no. 4, 2011.

47. *SUPERLIGHT Chair*, designed 2004; this example (*SUPERX* model) designed 2005, executed 2010–2011

Hales, Linda. "Seating That's Worth a Standing Ovation." *Washington Post*, September 18, 2004.

48. *Ionic Bench*, 2010

Brown, Phaedra. "Seating: Ahead of the Curve? Try Resting on It." *New York Times*, May 27, 2010.

Image credits

Catalogue Plates

1a, 2, and 29 Bryan Whitney.

1b Drew Baron, Columbia Museum of Art.

3, 4, 5, 6, 7, 9d, 9e, 9f, 9g, 10, 11a, 11b, 11c, 12, 13, 14, 15a, 16, 17, 18, 19, 20, 21, 23, 24, 26, 27, 28, 31, 33, 34, 36, 38, 41, 42, 43, and 45 Photography by Michael Koryta with Andrew VanStyn.

8, 9a, 9b, 9c, 15b, 32, 35a, 35b, 37, 39, 46, and 48 Photography by Douglas J. Eng.

22 Photography by Brion McCarthy.

25 Heidi Cleaves Smith.

30 and 47 Courtesy of Emeco.

40 Image courtesy of The Mint Museum, Charlotte, NC. Photo: Brandon Scott.

44 Artwork © Estate of Roy Lichtenstein; photography courtesy of The Nelson-Atkins Museum of Art, Kansas City, Missouri. Photo: Dana Anderson.

49 Courtesy of Wexler Gallery, Philadelphia.

Figure Illustrations

Fig. 3 Image in the public domain, courtesy of the Metropolitan Museum of Art, Rogers Fund, 1947, 47.100.1.

Fig. 4 © Fine Art Images/Fine Art Images/agefotostock.

Fig. 1.1 Art Institute of Chicago, Simeon B. Williams Fund, 1939.533.

Figs. 1.2 and 1.3 Courtesy of Maryland Historical Society.

Fig. 1.4 Metropolitan Museum of Art, Rogers Fund, 1925, 25.190.

Figs. 2.2 and 2.3 Madison Memorabilia Collection, Special Collections, Carrier Library, James Madison University Library, Harrisonburg, Virginia.

Fig. 3.1 Image reproduced from *Ackermann's Repository of Arts* 1, no. 3 (March 1809).

Figs. 3.2 and 3.3 Camera Work, Inc., Little Rock, AR.

Fig. 5.1 Shaker Museum | Mount Lebanon, Old Chatham and New Lebanon, New York.

Fig. 5.2 Courtesy, the Winterthur Library: The Edward Deming Andrews Memorial Shaker Collection.

Fig. 7.1 U.S. Patent Office.

Fig. 7.2 Camera Work, Inc., Little Rock, AR.

Fig. 7.3 Image reproduced from *The Art Journal Illustrated Catalogue: The Industry of All Nations* (London: Published for the proprietors of the Crystal Palace Exhibition by George Virtue, 1851), p. 152.

Fig. 8.1 Image reproduced from Calvert Vaux, *Villas and Cottages: A Series of Designs Prepared for Execution in the United States* (1857; repr. New York: Dover Publications, 1970), p. 288.

Fig. 8.2 Image reproduced from Janes, Beebe & Co., *Illustrated Catalogue of Ornamental Iron Work* (New York: Janes, Beebe & Co., 1855), pp. 140–44. The Athenaeum of Philadelphia.

Fig. 8.3 Image courtesy of The Mint Museum, Charlotte, NC. Photo: Brandon Scott.

Figs. 9.1 and 9.2 U.S. Patent Office.

Fig. 9.3 Photography by Michael Koryta with Andrew VanStyn.

Fig. 10.1 Photography by Michael Koryta with Andrew VanStyn.

Fig. 10.2 Published by Casimir Bohn, Washington, D.C. Prints and Photographs Division, Library of Congress, Washington, D.C., LC-DIGpga-04078, https://www.loc.gov/item/98507527/.

Fig. 10.3 Courtesy of the Architect of the Capitol.

Fig. 10.4 Photo by Alexander Gardner. Prints and Photographs Division, Library of Congress, Washington, D.C., LC-USZ62-2280, https://www.loc.gov/item/2009630691/.

Fig. 10.5 Brady-Handy photograph collection, Prints and Photographs Division, Library of Congress, Washington, D.C., LC-BH83-1823, https://www.loc.gov/item/90705922/.

Fig. 11.1 Courtesy of The Strong, Rochester, New York.

Figs. 11.2, 11.4, 11.7, and 11.8 Camera Work, Inc., Little Rock, AR.

Fig. 11.3 Photo courtesy of Crystal Bridges Museum of American Art.

Figs. 11.5 and 11.6 U.S. Patent Office.

Fig. 12.1 Image reproduced from James D. McCabe, *The Illustrated History of the Centennial Exhibition* (Philadelphia: National Publishing Company, 1876).

Fig. 12.2 Image reproduced from Thomas Hope, *Household Furniture and Interior Decoration* (London: T. Bensley, 1807). Courtesy of the Smithsonian Libraries, Washington, D.C.

Fig. 12.3 Image reproduced from *Description de L'Égypte* (Paris: Imprimerie Impériale, 1809–22), vol. 3, plate 8. Courtesy, the Winterthur Library: Printed Book and Periodical Collection.

Fig. 12.4 Camera Work, Inc., Little Rock, AR.

Fig. 12.5 Flagler Museum Archives.

Fig. 13.1 Marian S. Carson Collection, Prints and Photographs Division, Library of Congress, Washington, D.C., LC-DIG-stereo-1s08635, https://www.loc.gov/pictures/item/2017651233/.

Fig. 13.2 Camera Work, Inc., Little Rock, AR.

Fig. 14.1 Image reproduced from *Insurance Maps of the City of New York*, vol. 2 (New York: Perris Browne, 1877). New-York Historical Society, image #93914d.

Fig. 14.2 David Davis Mansion, Monroe and Davis Streets, Bloomington, Illinois. Architect, Alfred H.

Piquenard. Historic American Buildings Survey, Prints and Photographs Division, Library of Congress, Washington, D.C., HABS ILL,57-BLOOM,2-, https://www.loc.gov/item/il0078.

Fig. 14.3 Minnesota Historical Society Collection, MR2.9 SP3.2gr, p. 47.

Fig. 15.1 Image reproduced from *Heywood Brothers and Wakefield Company: Makers of Reed and Rattan Furniture* (Chicago, 1898), p. 60. Courtesy of Hagley Museum and Library.

Fig. 16.1 Museum purchase, Munson-Williams-Proctor Arts Institute, Museum of Art, Utica, NY, 94.13.1-2.

Fig. 17.1 © Victoria and Albert Museum, London.

Fig. 18.1 Image reproduced from Herts Brothers, *Artistic Furniture, Interior Decorations* (New York: Herts Brothers, 1893), front and back cover. Courtesy, the Winterthur Library: Joseph Downs Collection of Manuscripts and Printed Ephemera.

Fig. 18.2 Photo by Centennial Photographic Co. (fl. 1876). Free Library of Philadelphia / Bridgeman Images.

Fig. 19.1 Image reproduced from Wenzel Friedrich, *Manufacturer of Horn Furniture* (San Antonio: John Routledge, 1890). Courtesy, the Winterthur Library: Printed Book and Periodical Collection.

Fig. 19.2 Sackett, Wilhelms & Betzig (active late 19th century). Trade card for the firm Lang & Nau, after 1882. Polychromed lithograph, 4 3/8 x 5 3/8 in. Brooklyn Museum, Gift of Paul Jeromack, 1989.63.

Fig. 20.1 Courtesy of the Library of Congress, Washington, D.C. (Copyright by Canton O. Courtory, 1900).

Fig. 20.2 Photo courtesy of Cowan's Auctions Inc., Cincinnati, OH. Twig Table by Rev. Ben Davis of North Carolina, Sale 4/12/2014, Lot 883.

Fig. 21.1 Detroit Publishing Company photograph collection, Prints and Photographs Division, Library of Congress, Washington, D.C., LC-DIG-det-4a18681, https://www.loc.gov/pictures/item/2016811744/.

Fig. 21.2 Owned and used with permission of the Library and Archive of Kendall College of Art and Design of Ferris State University.

Fig. 21.3 Tom Wagner and Kendall College of Art and Design, Collections of the Grand Rapids Public Museum, Purchase, 1991.64.1.

Fig. 21.4 U.S. Patent Office.

Fig. 21.5 Camera Work, Inc., Little Rock, AR.

Figs. 22.1, 22.2, and 22.3 Photography by Brion McCarthy.

Fig. 23.1 Keystone-Mast Collection, UCR/California Museum of Photography, University of California at Riverside, 1996.0009.WX8563.

Fig. 23.2 Fine Arts Museums of San Francisco, museum purchase, gift of Martha and William Steen, 2002.5.

Index